Chinese Religion

CHINESE
RELIGION

AN
ANTHOLOGY
OF SOURCES

EDITED BY

Deborah Sommer

New York   Oxford
OXFORD UNIVERSITY PRESS
1995

Oxford University Press

Oxford   New York
Athens   Auckland   Bangkok   Bombay
Calcutta   Capetown   Dar es Salaam   Delhi
Florence   Hong Kong   Istanbul   Karachi
Kuala Lumpur   Madras   Madrid   Melbourne
Mexico City   Nairobi   Paris   Singapore
Taipei   Tokyo   Toronto

and associated companies in
Berlin   Ibadan

Copyright © 1995 by Oxford University Press, Inc.

Published by Oxford University Press, Inc.
200 Madison Avenue, New York, New York 10016

Library of Congress Cataloging-in-Publication Data
Chinese religion : an anthology of sources /
edited by Deborah Sommer.
p. cm.   Translated from Chinese.
ISBN 0-19-508894-8.—ISBN 0-19-508895-6 (pbk.)
1. China—Religion—History—Sources.
2. Philosophy, Chinese—History—Sources.
BL1802.C5477   1995
299'.51—dc20   94-7557
Pages xix–xxv are an extension of the copyright page.

2 4 6 8 9 7 5 3 1

Printed in the United States of America
on acid-free paper

To Wing-tsit Chan

Preface

Chinese Religion is a textbook anthology of source readings for college courses in Chinese religion. Compiled primarily from previously published sources, the reader brings together selections from many different types of literature that reflect Chinese ways of spirituality. In the West, these ways or teachings are usually called religions, a term that might be borrowed to create the somewhat artificial expression "Chinese religion," which could be very broadly defined as the culture of beliefs and practices that guide the interactions between the spiritual realm, the natural world, and human beings. In China, these beliefs and practices are manifested in diverse cultural expressions in ritual performances, literature, and drama. The texts selected here have been chosen to suggest the great variety and richness of this tradition of expression. Confucius is represented, but so are female shamans, exorcists, hermits, goddesses, and Ch'an masters.

This collection of readings includes many of the most important works of the Chinese tradition from antiquity to the modern era. The selections are arranged chronologically rather than thematically, as they do not lend themselves well to the latter kind of categorization. Such expressions as "Confucianism," "Taoism," and "Neo-Confucianism" are in many ways the artificial constructs of Western sinology that have no corresponding terms in Chinese or that have Chinese counterparts with considerably different connotations. Whenever possible, these categories have been avoided unless the texts themselves suggest it, and I have looked instead at such comparative themes as ritual or cosmology.

In the short introductions to the selections, I have focused primarily on pointing out the main ideas students might consider in their readings. Some of these points may seem all too obvious to those for whom reading texts is a profession, but I believe that students benefit when provided with clues for interpreting and analyzing primary sources from a tradition that is probably entirely foreign to their acquaintance. Some historical background is provided, but I have concentrated on ideas rather than history, for such historical materials are available elsewhere. Occasionally themes are suggested for comparison with other traditions: in classroom discussion, the opening passages of the *Tao-te ching,* for example, can usefully be compared with the opening passages of Genesis.

Possible comparisons between different selections are also indicated, and many of the entries have been chosen because they lend themselves well to this kind of pedagogy. One might contrast Pan Chao's real woman perfected by ritual, for example, with the imaginary goddess of the Lo River, the Buddhist goddess of the *Vimalakīrti* scripture, the Taoist adept Sun Pu-erh, or the Moon Lady who is confronted by the astronauts of Apollo X. A large percentage of the selections are either by or about women, and even ancient bronze inscriptions to female ancestral spirits attest to women's long-standing position in the Chinese spiritual tradition.

The anthology includes as many genres of literature as possible—poetry, drama, invocations, philosophical texts, religious treatises, and modern fiction—and illustrates many different approaches to spirituality rather than providing comprehensive coverage within each dynastic period. In addition to including the more philosophical writings of Chu Hsi and Wang Yang-ming, it also includes prayers and correspondence that illustrate their views on such religious matters as sacrifices for rain and invocations of spirits. Selected readings from the philosophers of antiquity focus on their views of the spirit world, heaven, spirits, and ritual but also include their most important writings on more general topics.

Some selections may be supplemented with videos, and these resources are listed at the end of the book. Many readings are from texts that may be adopted in their entirety for classroom use, and whenever possible they have been chosen from works that are currently available in paperback editions. The bibliographic section is intended to help students locate basic sources for writing papers. In addition, it lists very recent scholarly works that may be of assistance to scholars of Asian studies who do not specialize in China, and it also includes titles from related fields that might not otherwise be mentioned in bibliographies specific to Chinese religion. Chinese sources listed in the credits do not appear in the bibliography. A glossary describes terms not explained in the introductions; some figures from popular lore, however, are not identifiable.

In the selections I have translated anew, I have tried to translate a particular Chinese term consistently throughout; places where my translations of terms differ from those of others are noted. Parenthetical expressions have sometimes been added to make otherwise unintelligible passages understandable; when persons are known by different names, I have chosen only one. I have refrained from using many Chinese terms, for they tend to alienate the general student and are unnecessary for scholars of Chinese. Scholarly annotations have also been kept to a minimum. In editing new translations submitted for this volume by others, I have kept these same principles in mind.

In an anthology of this nature, the romanization of terms presents special difficulties, as the selections employ the Wade-Giles, the pinyin, and the post office systems of romanization. Whenever possible, I have followed the Wade-Giles system, but in the introductions to selections employing pinyin I have used pinyin. Alternate romanizations for important persons are provided in parentheses after the first appearance of their names.

This work is dedicated to Wing-tsit Chan, who for more years than I know commuted weekly from Pittsburgh to teach a Friday afternoon seminar at Columbia on translations from the Chinese classics. Even in his late eighties, he came up from Newark Airport via the Port Authority bus terminal; his trips on the New York subway system must have been watched over by the spirit of the banyan tree that adopted him in his youth. Some of his translations are included here. I am grateful to other professors of Asian studies at Columbia: Wm. Theodore de Bary, Philip Yampolsky, Irene Bloom, and many others, for without their instruction I could not have compiled this anthology.

This book would never have come about without the encouragement of Claude Conyers at Oxford University Press, or without the guidance of Cynthia A. Read, Paul Schlotthauer, and Peter Ohlin, also at Oxford. I am grateful to Constance A. Cook, Kenneth Dean, R. Randle Edwards, and Anne Behnke Kinney, who submitted new translations for this volume. Any inaccuracies introduced in the process of turning their scholarly translations into readings for a general anthology are my own responsibility. The compilation of anthologies and commentaries is a long-standing Chinese tradition, and I hope that this one will promote a greater appreciation of the efforts of the authors and translators represented here and make their work available to a larger audience.

Wing-tsit Chan passed away at the age of ninety-two just as this book was going to press, but he left behind to younger scholars a voluminous body of research and translation. In his later years, he was very conscious that he was writing for future generations: typical of his inimitable style, in his comically matter-of-fact yet totally self-effacing way, he once modestly remarked of one of his later works on Chu Hsi that people five hundred years hence would still be reading it. And some of us students secretly suspected that, in some mysterious way, Professor Chan *was* Chu Hsi. Wang Yang-ming, in his reply to questions about immortals, said that Yen Hui passed away at the age of thirty-two and yet still lives today—the same could be said of Wing-tsit Chan.

Indianapolis   D. S.
January 1994

Contents

Han (202 B.C.E.–220 C.E.) *and Wei* (220–264) *Dynasties*

Six Dynasties Period (220–589)

Sui (581–618) and T'ang (618–907) Dynasties

Sung (960–1279) and Yüan (1279–1368) Dynasties

Ming Dynasty (1368–1644)

Ch'ing Dynasty (1644–1911)

Modern Era (1911–   )

Credits

The *Book of Changes*

All selections from Patricia Buckley Ebrey, *Chinese Civilization and Society: A Sourcebook*. Copyright © 1981 by The Free Press, a division of Macmillan, Inc. Reprinted with permission of the publisher.

The *Book of History*

"The Great Norm"

Wing-tsit Chan, tr., *A Source Book in Chinese Philosophy*. Copyright © 1963 by Princeton University Press. Reprinted with permission of the publisher.

"The Announcement on Alcohol"

Translated by Deborah Sommer, from Tsai Shen, ed., *Shu-ching chi-chuan* (Collected commentaries on the *Book of History*) (Shanghai: Shang-hai ku-chi ch'u-pan-she, 1987).

Inscriptions from Ritual Bronzes

All selections translated by Constance A. Cook, from Ma Ch'eng-yüan, ed., *Shang-Chou ch'ing-t'ung-ch'i ming-wen-hsüan* (Beijing: Wen-wu, 1986–90), 3.34, 3.46–48, 3.56–58, 3.273–74, and 3.274–75, respectively.

The *Book of Odes*

Burton Watson, *The Columbia Book of Chinese Poetry from Early Times to the Thirteenth Century*. Copyright © 1984 by Columbia University Press. Reprinted with permission of the publisher.

The *Tso Chuan*

All selections translated by Deborah Sommer, from James Legge, *The Chinese Classics*, vol. 5, *The Ch'un Ts'ew with The Tso Chuen* (Taipei: Southern Materials Center, 1985).

The *Rites of Chou*

All selections translated by Deborah Sommer, from Sun I-jang, ed., *Chou-li cheng-i* (Verifying the meanings in the *Rites of Chou*) (Beijing: Chung-hua shu-chü, 1987). Numbers in brackets refer to page numbers from this edition.

The *Book of Rites*

"The Principles of Sacrifice"

Translated by Deborah Sommer, from Ch'en Hao, ed., *Li-chi chi-shuo* (Collected sayings on the *Book of Rites*) (Shanghai: Shanghai ku-chi ch'u-pan-she, 1987).

"Centrality and Equilibrium"; "The Great Learning"
Translated by Deborah Sommer, from Chu Hsi, ed., *Ssu-shu chi-chu* (Collected commentaries on the Four Books) (Hong Kong: Ch'en Hsiang-chi shu-chü, n.d.). Chapter numbers follow Legge 1985a.

The *Analects* of Confucius
All selections translated by Deborah Sommer, from Chu Hsi, ed., *Ssu-shu chi-chu* (Collected commentaries on the Four Books) (Hong Kong: Ch'en Hsiang-chi shu-chü, n.d.). Chapter numbers follow Legge 1985a.

Mo Tzu
All selections from Burton Watson, *Mo Tzu: Basic Writings*. Copyright © 1963 by Columbia University Press. Reprinted with permission of the publisher.

Mencius
All selections translated by Deborah Sommer, from Chu Hsi, ed., *Ssu-shu chi-chu* (Collected commentaries on the Four Books) (Hong Kong: Ch'en Hsiang-chi shu-chü, n.d.). Chapter numbers follow Legge 1985a.

Hsün Tzu
All selections translated by Deborah Sommer, from Yang Liang, ed., *Hsün Tzu* (Shanghai: Shang-hai ku-chi ch'u-pan she, 1989). Paragraph indentations follow Liang Shu-jen, ed., *Hsün Tzu yüeh-chu* (Taipei: Shih-chieh shu-chü, 1982).

The *Tao-te ching* of Lao Tzu
Wing-tsit Chan, tr., *The Way of Lao Tzu (Tao-te ching)*. Copyright © 1963 by Macmillan College Publishing Company, Inc. Reprinted with permission of the publisher.

Chuang Tzu
All selections from Burton Watson, *Chuang Tzu: Basic Writings*. Copyright © 1964 by Columbia University Press. Reprinted with permission of the publisher.

The *Songs of the South*
All selections translated by Deborah Sommer, from the *Ch'u Tz'u* (Songs of the south), *Ssu-pu pei-yao* edition, in consultation with Hawkes 1985. Titles of poems are modeled after Hawkes.

Wang Fu's *Discourses of a Recluse*
Translated by Anne Behnke Kinney, from P'eng To, ed., *Ch'ien-fu-lun chien chiao-cheng* (Beijing: Chung-hua shu-chü, 1985). For complete references see Kinney 1990 and 1991. The translation from the *Odes* is by Deborah Sommer and follows Legge 1985c.

Pan Chao's Perfected Woman
Lessons for Women
Nancy Lee Swann, *Pan Chao: Foremost Woman Scholar of China*. Copyright © 1968 by Russell & Russell. Reprinted with permission of the publisher.

The Unattainable Goddess

"Rhyme-Prose on the Goddess of the Lo"
Burton Watson, *The Columbia Book of Chinese Poetry from Early Times to the Thirteenth Century.* Copyright © 1984 by Columbia University Press. Reprinted with permission of the publisher.

The Buddhist Pure Land

The *Scripture of the Pure Land*
Edward Conze, tr., *Buddhist Scriptures.* Copyright © 1959 by Edward Conze. Reprinted with permission of Penguin Books Ltd.

The *Lotus Sutra*

Bunnō Katō, Yoshirō Tamura, and Kōjirō Miyasaka, *The Threefold Lotus Sutra.* Copyright © 1975 by Kosei Publishing Company. Reprinted with permission of the publisher.

Emptiness Is Form

The *Heart Sutra*
Edward Conze, tr., *Buddhist Scriptures.* Copyright © 1959 by Edward Conze. Reprinted with permission of Penguin Books Ltd.

The Holy Teaching of Vimalakīrti

All selections from Robert A. F. Thurman, *The Holy Teaching of Vimalakīrti.* Copyright © 1976 by The Pennsylvania State University. Reprinted with permission of the publisher.

Meditations on the Body

The *Secret Instructions of the Holy Lord on the Scripture of Great Peace*
Livia Kohn, *The Taoist Experience: An Anthology.* Copyright © 1993 by the State University of New York. Reprinted with permission of the publisher.

Alchemical Recipes for Immortality

The *Book of the Master Who Embraces Simplicity*
Translated by Deborah Sommer, from the *Pao P'u-tzu nei-p'ien, Ssu-pu pei-yao* edition, *chüan* 4, "Chin tan," pp. 3b–5a, in consultation with Kohn 1993, pp. 308–10.

The Mind-to-Mind Transmission of the Dharma

The *Platform Sutra of the Sixth Patriarch*
Philip B. Yampolsky, *The Platform Sutra of the Sixth Patriarch.* Copyright © 1967 by Columbia University Press. Reprinted with permission of the publisher.

Nailing a Stick into Empty Space: Ch'an Master I-hsüan

The *Recorded Conversations of Ch'an Master I-hsüan*
Wing-tsit Chan, tr., *A Source Book in Chinese Philosophy.* Copyright © 1963 by Princeton University Press. Reprinted with permission of the publisher.

The Poetry of Cold Mountain

Poems of Han-shan
Translated by Deborah Sommer, from the *Han-shan Tzu shih-chi* (Collected poems of Master Han-shan), *Ssu-pu ts'ung-k'an* edition. Numbering of the poems follows Henricks 1990.

The Writings of Han Yü

"Memorial on the Bone of Buddha"; "Against the God of the Wind"; "Proclamation to the Crocodile"
Cyril Birch, ed., *Anthology of Chinese Literature*. Copyright © 1965 by Grove Press, Inc. Reprinted with permission of Grove/Atlantic, Inc.

"The Girl of Mt. Hua"
Burton Watson, *The Columbia Book of Chinese Poetry from Early Times to the Thirteenth Century*. Copyright © 1984 by Columbia University Press. Reprinted with permission of the publisher.

In Search of a Woman's Spirit: The Poetry of Po Chü-i

Cyril Birch, ed., *Anthology of Chinese Literature*. Copyright © 1965 by Grove Press, Inc. Reprinted with permission of Grove/Atlantic, Inc.

The Great Ultimate of Chou Tun-i

"An Explanation of the Diagram of the Great Ultimate"
Wing-tsit Chan, tr., *A Source Book in Chinese Philosophy*. Copyright © 1963 by Princeton University Press. Reprinted with permission of the publisher.

All People Are Brothers and Sisters: Chang Tsai's *Western Inscription*

Wing-tsit Chan, tr., *A Source Book in Chinese Philosophy*. Copyright © 1963 by Princeton University Press. Reprinted with permission of the publisher.

The Writings of Chu Hsi

The Mind, the Nature, and the Feelings; Principle *(Li)* and Material Force *(Ch'i);* Heaven and Earth
Wing-tsit Chan, tr., *A Source Book in Chinese Philosophy*. Copyright © 1963 by Princeton University Press. Reprinted with permission of the publisher.

"Sacrificial Report to Confucius on the Completion of the Restorations at the White Deer Hollow Academy"
Translated by Deborah Sommer, from the *Chu Tzu wen-chi* (Collected writings of Master Chu), *Ssu-pu pei-yao* edition, titled *Chu Tzu ta-ch'üan* (Complete collection of Master Chu), 86.3b–4a.

Draft Memorial of 1189
Translated by Deborah Sommer, from the *Chu Tzu wen-chi* (Collected writings of Master Chu), *Ssu-pu pei-yao* edition, titled *Chu Tzu ta-ch'üan* (Complete collection of Master Chu), 12.5a, the draft *chi-yu* memorial. See also Chan 1987, p. 148, and Sommer 1993, pp. 339–42. I am grateful to Wing-tsit Chan for assistance in this translation.

Confessions of a Ghost

"Ch'ang-ko Complains of a Grievance"
Translated by R. Randle Edwards, from Yüan Mei, *Tzu pu yü (What the Master Did Not Discuss)*, vol. 70 of the *Ch'ing-tai pi-chi ts'ung k'an*.

The Story of the Stone

The Invocation of the Hibiscus Fairy
Cao Xueqin, *The Story of the Stone*, vol. 3. Translated by David Hawkes. Copyright © 1980 by David Hawkes. Reprinted with permission of Penguin Books Ltd.

The Exorcism of the Garden
Cao Xueqin, *The Story of the Stone*, vol. 5. Translated by John Minford. Copyright © 1986 by John Minford. Reprinted with permission of Penguin Books Ltd.

Lu Hsün's Critique of Tradition

"The New-Year Sacrifice"
Lu Xun, *Lu Xun: Selected Works*. Translated by Yang Xianyi and Gladys Yang, vol. 1, 2d ed. (Foreign Languages Press, 1980). Reprinted with permission of China Books & Periodicals, Inc.

The Hypocrisy of Modern Confucianism

Chang T'ien-i's "The Bulwark"
Joseph S. M. Lau, C. T. Hsia, and Leo Ou-fan Lee, *Modern Chinese Stories and Novellas: 1919–1949*. Copyright © 1981 by Columbia University Press. Reprinted with permission of the publisher.

Mao Tse-tung Overthrows Religious Authority

"Overthrowing the Clan Authority of the Ancestral Temples and Clan Elders, the Religious Authority of Town and Village Gods, and the Masculine Authority of Husbands"
Mao Tse-tung, *Selected Works of Mao Tse-tung*, vol. 1 (Foreign Languages Press, 1965). Reprinted with permission of China Books & Periodicals, Inc.

The Cult of Mao

" 'Father Is Close, Mother Is Close, but Neither Is as Close as Chairman Mao'—The Cult of Mao (1964–1965)"
Jung Chang, *Wild Swans: Three Daughters of China*. Copyright © 1991 by Globalfair Ltd. Reprinted by permission of Simon & Schuster, Inc.

The Revival of the Spiritual Tradition: The God of Theater

The Legend of the God
Translated by Kenneth Dean from accounts collected from marionettists in Ch'üan-chou, Fukien Province.

The Great Showing of Su
Translated by Kenneth Dean, from a translation of the text of *The Great Showing of Su* transcribed by Ch'en T'ian-pao and Yang Tu and collated by Tsai Chun (Ch'üan-chou: Ch'üan-chou Marionette Theater, 1986).

The Fall of the Goddess

Contemporary Ch'an Practice: Ch'an Master Sheng-yen's *Faith in Mind*

Buddhism Comes to America

SHANG

(ca. 1200-1059 B.C.E.*)*

AND CHOU

(1059-ca. 249 B.C.E.*)*

DYNASTIES

The *Book of Changes*

Many cultures trace their origins to a single primordial genesis, but accounts of the creation of the universe are relatively insignificant in the literature of ancient China. The *Book of Changes,* a divinatory handbook that is perhaps the earliest text of Chinese antiquity, is relatively silent on this issue. The ancients were less concerned with cosmogony, or the origins of the cosmos, than with the comportment of human life within a universe that was not created just once but was continually generating and regenerating itself. That universe was the constant, ultimate source of life, and if one could interpret the visible traces of its movements, one could act in harmony with the transformations of heaven and earth and prosper in the midst of change.

To interpret those movements, one could consult the *Book of Changes,* a directory of sixty-four abstract symbols made of solid and broken lines whose configurations suggested the structure and operations of the cosmos. Its basic symbols are eight trigrams (images of three lines, or "places"), which, when paired in all possible combinations, yield a total of sixty-four hexagrams (images of six lines). Each hexagram is associated with a particular concept, such as The Creative, The Receptive, Retreat, Progress, Limitation, and Recovery. To each hexagram are appended several layers of commentaries that magnify its nuances and subtleties, without, however, providing a direct explanation. The commentaries are cryptic by nature and cannot be read as conventional narratives: as observations of the natural world, they too, must be observed and interpreted. In the process of divination, the diviner poses a question and creates a hexagram by randomly throwing longer and shorter stalks of grain (analogous to solid and broken lines); the diviner then consults the relevant entry from the *Changes* and interprets and reflects upon the textual commentary before deciding on an appropriate plan of action. A general deciding military strategy who divines the hexagram "Retreat," for example, would have to plan his maneuvers accordingly.

Expressions such as "Nine in the second place" or "Six in the seventh place" refer to certain numerical extremes that may appear in the individual lines, or places.

Like all the texts of ancient China, the *Book of Changes* is a composite work assembled over a period of centuries. The hexagrams themselves date perhaps to the Shang dynasty (ca. 1200–1059 B.C.E.), but the commentaries date to the Chou dynasty (1059–ca. 249 B.C.E.). Originally a book of divination, over the centuries the *Changes* became the subject of voluminous philosophical commentaries by China's most eminent thinkers.

The first two hexagrams of the *Changes,* along with their commentaries, are presented here: *Ch'ien,* The Creative, or Heaven; and *K'un,* The Receptive, or Earth. The cosmology, or structure of the universe, suggested by these terms includes no anthropomorphic deities but instead describes a cosmos that operates through forces of its own. Even without divinities to establish covenants with the human realm or to dispense moral judgments, this universe is not an amoral one, for humans are enjoined to admire such qualities as virtue, harmony, perseverance, caution, and effort. Human action is not circumscribed by dualities of good and evil but is guided by the principles of appropriateness and timeliness, qualities that mirror the seasonal periodicity of the natural world.

Ch'ien (The Creative, Heaven)

Ch'ien above ═══

Ch'ien below ═══

The Judgment: Ch'ien is the ultimate source. There is great success. There is benefit in perseverance.

Nine at the beginning: There is a hidden dragon. Do not use.

Nine in the second place: See the dragon in the field. It is beneficial to see a great man.

Nine in the third place: The gentleman strives to be creative all day. At night he acts with caution and restraint. There is no fault.

Nine in the fourth place: There is an uncertain leap at the abyss. There is no fault.

Nine in the fifth place: There is a flying dragon in Heaven. It is beneficial to see a great man.

Nine in the sixth place: The overbearing dragon is cause for regret.

Nine in all the lines: There appears a myriad of dragons without heads. This is good fortune.

Commentary: Great indeed is *ch'ien* the ultimate source. The ten thousand things receive their beginnings from it. It governs Heaven. The clouds drift by and the rain falls. All things flow into their forms. The ends and the beginnings are greatly illuminated. The six lines of the hexagram take shape at their own times.

In timely fashion they ride the six dragons and so rule over the heavens. The way of *ch'ien* is change and transformation. Each thing thereby achieves its true nature and destiny and assures that it is in accord with great harmony. There is great benefit and constancy. It stands out from all the things of the world, and the nations of the earth enjoy peace.

The Image: The movements of Heaven have great force. The gentleman invigorates himself and does not become jaded. There is a hidden dragon. Do not use it. The Yang still is buried below. See the dragon in the field. Virtue is everywhere. The gentleman strives to be creative all day. He always follows the correct way. There is an uncertain leap at the abyss. There is no fault in going forward. There is a flying dragon in the heavens. The great man is creative. The overbearing dragon is cause for regret. That which overflows cannot last for long. Nine in all the lines. The virtue of Heaven is not to act as head.

K'un (The Receptive, Earth)

K'un above ═ ═

K'un below ═ ═

The Judgment: K'un is the ultimate of receptivity. There is great success. There is benefit in the perseverance of a mare. If the gentleman has a particular goal and attempts to attain it, at first he may lose his way, but ultimately he will achieve it. It is beneficial to make friends in the west and the south, but avoid friends in the east and north. Peaceful perseverance will yield good fortune.

Commentary: Great indeed is that originating in *k'un*. The ten thousand things all receive life from it when it is in harmonious union with Heaven. *K'un* contains everything in abundance. Its virtue is in harmony with the infinite. It encompasses all things and illuminates the universe. Each individual thing achieves perfect success. The mare is an animal of the land. It wanders freely over the land. It is gentle and obedient and symbolizes great benefit through perseverance. The gentleman should conduct himself in a like manner. At first he may lose his way, but later by being humbly obedient he will achieve it forever. In the west and south there are friends. One may associate with people of a sympathetic nature. In the east and north there are no friends, but in the end one may gain benefit from this. The good fortune of peaceful perseverance will result from being in harmony with the forces of the Earth.

The Image: The power of the Earth lies in receptivity. The gentleman with great virtue encompasses all things.

Six at the beginning: When one steps on hoarfrost, one knows that solid ice will soon appear.

Comment: When one steps on hoarfrost, one

knows that solid ice will appear soon. When the forces of Yin begin to congeal and follow this way, the time of solid ice is about to arrive.

Six in the second place: It is straight, square, and great. Without hustle and bustle there is nothing that does not prosper.

Comment: The movement of six in the second place is straight by means of being square. Without hustle and bustle there is nothing that does not prosper. There is brilliance in the Way of the Earth.

Six in the third place: One's badges are hidden. One can persevere. If in the service of a king, do not try to force affairs but rather bring them to completion.

Comment: One's badges are hidden. One can persevere. At the proper time come forth. If you are in the service of a king, you should have the wisdom to spread greatness.

Six in the fourth place: To be closemouthed like a tied-up sack is neither blameworthy nor praiseworthy.

Comment: To be closemouthed like a tied-up sack is neither blameworthy nor praiseworthy. If one is careful there will be no trouble.

Six in the fifth place: There is great fortune in yellow clothing.

Comment: There is great fortune in yellow clothing. Brilliance lies within.

Six at the top: Dragons do battle in the fields. Their blood is black and yellow.

Comment: Dragons do battle in the fields. Their Way has run its course.

Six in all the lines: There is benefit in steadfast perseverance.

Comment: When all six lines yield six, it shows steadfast perseverance. In this way one can achieve great ends.

The *Book of History*

Some traditions attribute the beginnings of culture and civilization to divine assistance, but some ancient Chinese texts focus not on deities but on revered legendary sage rulers, men of extraordinary diligence and virtue who devoted their energies to the ministration of the human realm. Their achievements are related in the *Book of History* (or *Book of Documents*), which purports to record historical events from the third millennium to roughly the seventh century B.C.E. Events before the eighth century B.C.E. cannot be dated with any accuracy, and the work is thus a combination of history and traditional legend. Regardless of their historicity, documents from the *History* such as the "Great Norm" and "The Announcement on Alcohol" are important in that they articulate ideals that greatly influenced later thought.

The culture heroes of ancient China relied not on divine revelation to create formulations of governance but instead surveyed the movements of the heavens, observed the constant cyclicality of the seasons, and then transferred the ordered motion of the universe into a measured harmony of human relations. The *History* opens with a description of the first official acts of the legendary ruler Shun (floruit third millennium B.C.E.), who performed a ceremonial circumambulation of the realm throughout the four directions, marking each juncture of time and space with ritual offerings to communicate his movements to spiritual beings and to establish a new cosmic order. His carefully calibrated ritual choreography captured the periodicity of the celestial and earthly realms and infused it into the regulation of human affairs.

The cosmological worldview revealed in the *History,* which lauds the efficacy of human effort, nevertheless acknowledges the existence of spiritual beings. The Shang people revered the Lord on High *(Shang-ti),* a divinity associated with the highest ancestral spirit of their ruling house, and revered other ancestral spirits as well. When the succeeding Chou dynasty (subdivided into the Western Chou and Eastern Chou, 1059–770 B.C.E. and 771–ca. 249 B.C.E., respectively) super-seded the Shang and incorporated Shang culture and religious beliefs into its own, however, the earlier notion of the Lord on High merged with the Chou concept of heaven *(t'ien)*, a vaguely defined yet morally upright and beneficent source that intervened in human affairs. The exact relationship of the Lord on High to heaven is not clearly articulated in the *History* and was not fully under-stood by later Chinese scholars. Although the idea of the Lord on High did not disappear, the Chou people primarily revered heaven; prayers and sacrifices were also offered to lesser celestial and terrestrial natural forces. The *History* asserts that human beings, if possessed of profound inner virtue *(te)* and sincere integ-rity *(ch'eng)*, could communicate with spirits and could invoke their assistance in worldly matters.

A general overview of the interdependent cosmology of heaven, earth, and human beings is outlined in the "Great Norm" (or "Great Plan"), which is offered as a dialogue of 1121 B.C.E. between Viscount Chi and King Wu (reign 1122–1116 B.C.E., according to traditional dates), one of the virtuous founding rulers of the Chou dynasty. The Shang dynasty has just been eclipsed, and in this early Chou document, heaven is still described in somewhat anthropomor-phic terms as a Lord who exhibits the human emotion of anger. The nine categories of the norm describe the interrelatedness of all things: the human body, governmental measures, and the celestial firmament. The individual is figuratively conjoined to the larger cosmos, for even the human sense faculties are associated with the Five Agents (Five Elements or Five Phases) of water, fire, wood, metal, and earth, which must be understood figuratively as the essen-tial substances or forces of the universe. The role of the human sovereign, who adheres to the Supreme Standard of royal perfection, is to facilitate the harmoni-ous development of the relationships between the nine categories.

Rulers who shirk these responsibilities lose the mandate of heaven, the man-date to rule that is bestowed by heaven on morally upright sovereigns but is revoked from the corrupt. The Shang dynasty, according to Chou accounts, was once governed by sage rulers but eventually decayed and lost power due to the moral turpitude of its later sovereigns, and it was eventually overthrown by the virtuous Chou founders, kings Wen (traditional dates 1169–1116 B.C.E.) and Wu. "The Announcement on Alcohol" relates how the last Shang rulers lost the mandate when they dissipated themselves in drunkenness and profligate behav-ior, and the Shang officials are consequently incorporated into the Chou bureaucracy. The narrator of the "Announcement" is not clearly named, but it is thought to be narrated by the Duke of Chou (Duke of Zhou; regent from 1115–1108 B.C.E., according to traditional dates). The Duke of Chou is the brother of King Wu and regent to Wu's young successor, King Ch'eng. Here the duke speaks on behalf of King Ch'eng to the people of Mei and to his own brother, Feng. The duke warns that while libations of alcohol customarily accompany the sacrificial offerings to ancestral spirits, addiction to liquor prevents government officials from carrying out their duties and ultimately leads to the loss of the mandate of heaven. Heaven is not an arbitrary judge, and human beings are not its pawns, for its intervention in the earthly realm is the result of human behavior. The people of Shang (also known as the Yin) caused their own demise: it is not that heaven was cruel in revoking the mandate of heaven from the Shang, the Duke of Chou states, for they committed offenses of their own accord. Their history is a mirror from which moral lessons can be learned.

The "Announcement" also describes the role of the ruler in educating the people and in exhorting them to comply with social mores, and it reveals the close connection between the ruler's personal conduct and the fate of the nation. The people, for their part, are enjoined to present sacrificial offerings to ancestral spirits, but they are encouraged first to develop a sense of filial piety, or love for their parents, and care for the needs of the living before attending to libations to the dead.

The "Great Norm"

In the thirteenth year (1121 B.C.) the King [Wu] visited Viscount Chi. The King said, "Oh! Viscount Chi. Heaven, working unseen, has decisively made men with certain hidden springs of character, aiding also the harmonious development of it in their various conditions. I do not know how the various virtues and their relations should be regulated."

Viscount Chi thereupon replied, "I have heard that of old (Great Yü's father) Kun dammed up the flood and thereby created a chaos among the Five Agents. The Lord (of Heaven) was aroused to anger and did not give him the Great Norm with its Nine Categories. The various virtues and their relations declined in due course, and Kun was executed. Yü thereupon rose to continue the heritage. Heaven gave him the Great Norm with its Nine Categories. And the various virtues and their relations were regulated. . . .

"The first category is the Five Agents (Five Elements); namely, Water, Fire, Wood, Metal, and Earth [which correspond to various human activities]. . . . The second category is the Five Activities; namely, appearance, speech, seeing, hearing, and thinking. The virtue of appearance is respectfulness; that of speech is accordance [with reason]; that of seeing is clearness; that of hearing is distinctness; and that of thinking is penetration and profundity. Respectfulness leads to gravity; accordance with reason, to orderliness; clearness, to wisdom; distinctness, to deliberation; and penetration and profundity, to sageness [all of which should be cultivated by the ruler]. The third category is the Eight Governmental Offices; namely, those of food, commodities, sacrifices, public works, education, and justice, the reception of guests, and the army. [All these functions should be fulfilled in harmony with the next category.] The fourth category is the Five Arrangements of Time, namely, the year, the month, the day, the stars, planets, zodiacal signs, and the calendaric calculations. The fifth category is the Supreme Standard. The sovereign, having established the highest standard, gathers in him the Five Blessings and spreads over his people. Then the people, following your standard, preserve it with you. . . .

"The sixth category is the Three Virtues; namely, correctness and uprightness, strong government, and weak government. In times of peace and tranquillity, apply correctness and uprightness; in times of violence and disorder, apply strong government; and in times of harmony and order, apply weak government. Apply strong government to the reserved and retiring, and apply weak government to the lofty and intelligent. . . . The seventh category is the Examination of Doubts. Select and appoint officers for divination by tortoise shells and by stalks, and command them thus to divine. . . . The calculation of the passage of events is the function of experts whose duty it is to perform the divination. When three of them divine, follow the words of two of them. If you have any doubt about important matters, consult with your own conscience, consult with your ministers and officers, consult with the common people, and consult the tortoise shells and stalks. If you, the tortoise shells, the stalks, the ministers and officers, and the common people all agree, this is called a great concord. There will be welfare to your own person and prosperity to your descendants. The result will be auspicious. If you, the tortoise shells, and the stalks agree but the ministers and officers and the common people oppose, the result will be auspicious. If the ministers and officers, the tortoise shells, and the stalks agree but you and the common people oppose, the result will be auspicious. If the common people, the tortoise shells, and the stalks agree but you and the ministers and the officers oppose, the result will be auspicious. If you and the tortoise shells agree but the stalks, ministers and officers, and the common people oppose, internal operations will be auspicious but external operations will be unlucky. If both the tortoise shells and stalks oppose the views of men, inactivity will be auspicious but active operations will be unlucky.

"The eighth category is the General Verifications [that is, checking governmental measures against natural phenomena], namely, rain, sunshine, heat, cold, wind, and seasonableness [corresponding to the Five Agents]. When the five all come and are complete, and each in its proper order, even the common grain will be luxuriant. . . . The ninth category is the Five Blessings, namely, longevity, wealth, physical and mental health, cultivation of excellent virtue, and an end crowning a good life.

"Negatively, these are the Six Extremities [a punishment for evil conduct]; namely, premature death, sickness, sorrow, poverty, wickedness, and weakness."

"The Announcement on Alcohol"

"Promulgate this throughout the land of Mei," said the king. "When your pious father, King Wen, secured our kingdom in the west, in his announcements he continually cautioned the princes, officers, and even lesser administrators, saying, 'Alcohol should be employed for sacrificial offerings.' When heaven sent down the mandate and established our people, it was used at the great sacrifices. But when heaven sent down its awesome majesty as the people lapsed into chaos and virtue perished, it was because they abused liquor. Even greater and lesser states perished because they misused it. King Wen taught the young and those in office to refrain from alcohol. In every state, people should drink only if they are sacrificing. Virtue lies in sobriety."

He continued, "Our people should teach the young to respect the fruits of the earth, and the young should bear this in mind and follow the admonitions of their forebears concerning libations to the ancestors. They should consider lesser and greater virtues with the same consistency.

"People of the land of Mei, exert yourselves and diligently cultivate your millet, and assiduously attend to the affairs of your parents and elders. If you diligently go about attending to your business, you can take care of your parents in a filial way; when your parents are happy, you may clarify and fortify your liquors, and set them forth.

"Functionaries, officers, and nobles, listen to my injunctions. Once you have cared for your elderly and served your ruler, you may then satiate yourselves with food and drink. Likewise, if you are circumspect, reflective, and possessed of virtue, you may participate in sacrificial offerings and then enjoy yourselves. Thus you will truly serve your king, heaven will countenance your virtue, and you will never be forgotten in the royal house."

The king said, "In our western lands those princes, ministers, and officials who kept to King Wen's teachings did not become sotted with alcohol. And now I have received the mandate from Yin."

The king said, "Feng, I have heard it said that in times past the first Yin kings, discerning men who held heaven in awe and who were brilliant to their people, were possessed of virtue and held fast to wisdom. From T'ang the Successful to Emperor Yi, they realized their duties as kings and respected their ministers; their officers dutifully assisted them without rest or ease, much less insobriety. None overindulged in drink, neither the princes and chieftains of the outer domains in Hou, Tien, Nan, and Wei, nor the officials, directors, sundry officers, heads of noble houses, and retired officers of the inner domains. Not only did they not get drunk, but they did not have the leisure for such things, so engaged were they in promoting the kingship in all its virtue and brilliancy, and in encouraging the people to support its measures.

"I have also heard it said that when the last scion of those kings became overly fond of drink, his mandate no longer manifested itself to the people. He incurred the people's wrath but did not correct himself; abandoned to drunkenness, he overindulged in food and drink and lost all sense of propriety. The people were greatly anguished. Wasted and inebriated, unwilling to stop and becoming ever more excessive, he took leave of his senses, and not even death frightened him. His offenses persisted in the city of Shang, and as the country of Yin neared oblivion, he remained unmoved. He offered no fragrant sacrifices whose scent of virtue might ascend to heaven, and the people were angered. But many others indulged in alcohol, and their stench was smelled on high. Thus heaven sent ruination upon the Yin and lost its solicitude for them because of their excesses. It is not that heaven was cruel: the people themselves perpetrated these offenses."

The king said, "Feng, I have little more to say. Of old there was this saying: 'People see not their own reflections in water, but see them in other people.' Now the Yin has lost the mandate: should we not seriously reflect on this?"

I say that you should sternly admonish the worthy ministers of Yin; the chiefs of the Hou, Tien, Nan, and Wei domains; the grand scribes and the inner scribes; the worthy ministers and heads of noble houses; those who serve you; as well as your colleagues the minister of war, the minister of agriculture, and the minister of works; to monitor strictly their intake of alcohol. If you are told of groups gathering to drink, spare no leniency. Apprehend them and send them to the Chou court, and I will execute them. The Yin ministers and officials who are alcoholics need not be put to death but may be given counsel. If they heed it, they may yet earn distinction, but if they disregard it, I will show them no pity. If they cannot rid themselves of their addiction and serve well, then they will also be executed.

The king said, "Feng, follow my injunctions. If you do not manage your officials, the people will become addicted to alcohol."

Inscriptions from Ritual Bronzes

While the *Book of Changes* outlines the basic structure of Chinese cosmology, inscriptions carved on bronze vessels document the details of the complex ritual interactions of the Shang and Chou periods, where the political and religious realms, as well as the realms of the living and the dead, were but different aspects of a contiguous whole bound together by reciprocal obligations. As containers for the votive offerings presented to spirits, ritual bronzes were the focal point at which all these realms met, and they thus constituted important symbols of religious and political power and status. Translations of the archaic language of the inscriptions can only be somewhat tentative in places, but they nevertheless clearly outline themes that were to be of key importance in the following centuries: filial piety, or reverence toward one's parents; a quest for long life and prosperity; and respect for spirits, expressed through memorial offerings. Ancestral spirits could influence the fortunes of descendants, who sought their favor by supplicating them with food offerings presented in specially commissioned bronze vessels.

Although reverence for ancestors in China is often considered to be a patriarchal tradition, the inscription on the bucket of Hsiao-tzu Feng documents the veneration accorded female ancestors in antiquity. Feng had the bucket made in honor of an ancestral spirit, Mother Hsin, after he is rewarded for his efforts in administering to the people of Jen. Similarly, the tureen of Liang Ch'i records how Liang had the vessel made to honor his late mother, Hui Yi.

The inscription on the tureen of Shen-tzu T'a, however, is a supplication to T'a's paternal ancestral spirits, from whom he petitioned auspiciousness and long life. In exchange for memorial food offerings, Shen-tzu T'a expected the spirit of his late father, as well as the spirits of the Chou lords, to help him provide for his line of paternal descendants. Bronze musical instruments, as well as ritual vessels, also invoked ancestral spirits, and hence Liang Ch'i, the Chief Ritualist of Food, commissioned a bell whose sounds reached the spirit world.

Shang and Chou dynasty cultures were hierarchical societies, and political power was publicly conferred by rulers on lesser lords and ministers in rites of gift giving accompanied by sacrifices and libations to ancestral spirits, who acted as witnesses to the transaction. Material benefits bestowed on individuals by earthly rulers were converted into bronzes, which would then attract the beneficent attentions of ancestral spirits, who could in turn help ensure that earthly material benefits would continue for succeeding generations. The square beaker of Mai, for example, relates the descending order of ritual relationships between rulers and ministers and details the religious context in which transferrals of economic and political power were effected. The king, or Son of Heaven, conducted rites to his royal ancestors before conferring gifts upon the Archer Lord of Ching, who then reported his new acquisitions to his own ancestors before apportioning a measure of bronze to Scribe Mai, who has a sacrificial beaker made for the Archer Lord. The custom of reporting to the spirit world any events of great importance in the human realm continued well into late imperial times.

The great age of bronze manufacture ended before the second century B.C.E., but plainer vessels of bronze were employed in sacrificial offerings in the imperial court well into the fourteenth century of the common era, when they were replaced with porcelain look-alikes. The practice of presenting offerings to ancestral spirits and other spiritual beings, however, continues to modern times.

The following inscriptions are from bronzes that date from the late Shang to the Western Chou periods.

Bucket of Hsiao-tzu Feng

(LATE SHANG PERIOD)

On the day *yi-ssu* [day forty-two], the Tzu official commanded Hsiao-tzu Feng first to take the Jen people to the Chin region. Tzu gloriously presented Feng with two strings of cowrie shells and said, "The cowries are to recognize your accumulated merit." Feng used them to make a sacrificial vessel for Mother Hsin. This was in the twelfth month, when Tzu said, "I command you to go to the Jen region." [Clan sign.]

Square Beaker of Mai

(EARLY WESTERN CHOU PERIOD)

The king commanded our leader, the Archer Lord of Ching, to leave P'ei. The Archer Lord went to Ching. In the second month, the Archer Lord went to visit the court at Ancestral Chou without incident. He met with the king, who performed the wine libation and ritual sacrifice to the royal ancestors at Hao capital. On the next day, while residing at Pi-yung pool, the king boarded a boat to perform the Grand Rite. The king shot at a Great P'eng bird and caught it. The Archer Lord boarded a boat with red flags and followed. The Grand Rite was completed. On this day, the king had the Archer Lord enter the Inner Chamber. The Archer Lord was presented with a dark-colored engraved dagger-ax. When the king was residing at An, on the bank of the Pi-yung pool, on the evening of the day *ssu* the Archer Lord was presented with two hundred households of barefoot slaves, with chariots and horses that the king used, and with a bronze chariot piece, a cloak, an apron, and some shoes. Upon returning to Ching, the Archer Lord presented the Son of Heaven's gifts and reported to his ancestors without incident. With respectful demeanor, I quiet the Archer Lord's spirit and display filial offerings to the Archer Lord of Ching. I, Scribe Mai, was presented with bronze from leader Archer Lord. I, Mai, in extolling the Archer Lord of Ching's merit, use it to make a treasured sacrificial beaker vessel in order to make offer-ings to those who give and receive at the Archer Lord's temple and in order to display the luminous mandate. This was in the year that the Son of Heaven gave gifts to Mai's leader, the Archer Lord. May his progeny have eternal life without end and use this vessel to receive virtuous power, to pacify the many associates, and to present memorial feasts to those mandated ones who flit back and forth.

Tureen of Shen-tzu T'a

(EARLY WESTERN CHOU PERIOD)

T'a said: "Bowing and bumping my head, I dare to summon and report to our Deceased Father. You, Deceased Father, command your troubled Shen-Tzu T'a to make a libation at the Chou lords' temple. I step up to the two lords and do not dare but perform the libation. Praise to all the lords whose achievements pacify the spirit of my Deceased Father and thereby make him manifest. He illustriously received the mandate. Oh! It was my Deceased Father who longed for the former kings and former lords, who had conquered the Yin and reported to their ancestors the stunning success. Thus, my Deceased Father was able to go even farther! Now I, Shen-tzu, may tranquilly embrace the protective good fortune of the many lords. Oh! Your Shen-tzu gains merit and satisfaction in the Lord's grace. I, Shen-tzu, from beginning to end have accumulated stores of goods to make this sacrificial tureen to feast Lord Yi and to make the many lords descend. May you take up and pity your Shen-tzu T'a and make me fortunate. I use the tureen to make my life auspicious; I use the tureen to pacify the lords so that I may live long. I, T'a, use the tureen to embrace and aid our many younger brothers and grandsons to enable them to emulate and learn from their father, this son of yours."

Bell of Liang Ch'i

(LATE WESTERN CHOU PERIOD)

Liang Ch'i said: "Oh greatly manifested Brilliant Ancestors and Deceased Father, stately and solemn, orderly and protective, who were able to make their powers wise and who strenuously served the former kings, gaining accumulated merit without loss! I, Liang Ch'i, having from the start followed and modeled myself on the luminous virtuous power grasped by my Brilliant Ancestors and Deceased Father, respectfully serve the leader, the Son of Heaven, from dawn to dusk. The Son of Heaven entrusted me, Liang Ch'i, into his service as a Country Lord Grand Governor. Taking this opportunity, the Son of Heaven has fondly awarded Liang Ch'i's merit. I, Liang Ch'i, daring to respond to the Son of Heaven's greatly manifest gift, extol his grace and avail myself of it to make a harmonious bell for my Brilliant Ancestors and Deceased Father. Clang! Clang! Clong! Clong! Ding! Ding! Dong! Dong! I use it to summon down and give pleasure to the Former Accomplished Ones. I use it to pray for peace, pleasure, riches, spiritual aid, and extensive benefits. May the Brilliant Ancestors and Deceased Father, majestically re-siding above, never cease to send down to me great and plentiful good fortune in abundance, such abundance! I use it to protect and glorify myself and to inherit from them the eternal mandate. I, Liang Ch'i, will ably serve the Brilliant Kings for ten thousand years without limit, and with extended long life I shall eternally treasure this bell."

Tureen of Liang Ch'i

(LATE WESTERN CHOU PERIOD)

The Chief Ritualist of Food, Liang Ch'i, made an honored sacrificial tureen for his Brilliant Deceased Father, Hui Chung, and his Brilliant Deceased Mother, Hui Yi. I use it to follow after them and to present memorial feasts and filial offerings. I use it to pray for extended long life, extended long life without limit, for a hundred sons and a thousand grandsons. May my progeny eternally treasure it and use it to present memorial offerings.

The *Book of Odes*

Along with the *Book of History* and *Book of Changes,* the *Book of Odes* is among the oldest documents of ancient China and contains materials from roughly 1000 to 600 B.C.E. Also known as the *Book of Poetry* or *Book of Songs,* the *Odes* is a collection of over three hundred sacrificial hymns, praise songs, and love poems, most of which date to the Chou period, although about five are thought to date from the Shang era. Many are love poems, sometimes written in the female voice, that describe everyday life in a rural agricultural society. Some, however, are praise songs in honor of culture heroes such as Hou Chi, who eventually became revered as one of the tutelary deities of agriculture. "She Who First Bore Our People" recounts his miraculous conception and birth. The legendary Hou Chi was born of Lady Yüan, a barren woman who was able to rid herself of childlessness by performing *yin* sacrifices, rites that were expressions of the pure intentions of the sacrificer. Hou Chi's parentage was half divine, for his mother conceived by treading in the toe print of the Lord, or Lord on High (sometimes translated as "God"). Later Chinese philosophers did not interpret this passage literally, and none noted any possible sexual imagery in the reference to the toe print of the Lord on High; most doubted the actual possibility of conceiving in such a manner, but some readily conceded that the poem figuratively represented the idea that heaven would respond favorably to the supplications of the pious petitioner.

Why the infant Hou Chi was cast out into the wilds is unclear, and whether he was placed there by his mother or by a third party is unknown, but his ability to survive by evoking the assistance of animals suggests his special association with the forces of nature. Instead of seeking revenge on the human beings who rejected him, however, he provides them with new kinds of husbandry and crops. Hou Chi is an inventor or discoverer rather than a warriorlike culture hero. His special gifts with plants stem more from human effort than from supranormal abilities: he accelerates plant growth with weeding and planting, not with magic, and he has characteristics that are both human and divine. The kinds of millet he introduces to humanity become the votive gifts of sacrifices he also initiates, and his genesis from the Lord on High comes full circle as the fragrances of the sacrificial millet ascend back to Hou Chi's progenitor.

No formal written covenant existed between human beings and figures such as Hou Chi and the Lord on High, but this verse reveals that people generally understood that boons when granted had to be repaid with thanksgiving offerings. Offerings were conducted as communal meals where the divine guest, present in spirit, consumed not the actual foods themselves but their aromas. From a certain perspective this is a verse less about divinities than about food itself, for much of its imagery is devoted to describing its cultivation and preparation. This song, composed perhaps in the seventh century B.C.E., ends by noting that Hou Chi's sacrifices are still continued; in the twentieth century, presenting sacrificial food offerings to spirits is still very much a part of contemporary Chinese religious practice.

She Who First Bore Our People

She who first bore our people
was Lady Yüan of Chiang.
How did she bear them?
She knew how to make *yin* and *ssu*
     sacrifices
so she would not be childless.
She stepped in the footprint of God's big
     toe and was quickened,
she was magnified, she was blessed,
she was stirred to pregnancy, quickly it
     came.
She bore him, she nurtured him:
this was Hou Chi.

She fulfilled her months
and her first-born came forth.
There was no rending, no tearing,
no injury, no harm,
showing that it was divine.
Did the Lord on High not give her ease?
Did he not receive her sacrifices?
Effortlessly she bore her child.

They laid him in the narrow lane,
but the oxen and sheep stood about to
     shelter him.
They laid him in the forest of the plain,
but he was found by woodcutters of the
     forest.
They laid him on the cold ice,
but the birds covered him with their
     wings.
When the birds had departed,
Hou Chi began to wail.

Long he cried, loud he cried,
that voice of his was huge.
Then he began to crawl,
he could straddle, he could stand firm
to seek food for his mouth.
And he planted big beans,
big beans that grew like banners,
rich rich the rows of grain,

luxuriant the hemp and wheat,
plump plump the young melons.

Hou Chi's husbandry
had ways to help the growing.
He cleared the rank grasses,
planted his yellow treasure,
it filled the field, abundant.
Once planted, it grew,
it flowered, it formed ears,
it was firm, of fine quality,
drooping and full-kerneled.
And then he made his home in T'ai.

He bestowed on us good grain,
black millet, double-kerneled black
     millet,
red millet, white millet.
The black millet he planted far and
     wide,
reaped it, took it by the fieldful.
The red and white he planted far and
     wide,
shouldered it, bore it on his back,
took it home to commence the sacrifices.

What are our sacrifices like?
Some pound the grain, some scoop it,
some winnow it, some trample it.
We soak it, slosh slosh,
we steam it, hiss hiss.
We plan carefully, we ponder,
we gather sagebrush, offer up fat,
choose a ram for the spirits of the road.
We roast, we broil
in order to begin the coming year.

We heap high the platters,
the platters and earthen vessels.
When the fragrance begins to rise,
the Lord on High rests contented—
how timely is the sweet aroma!
Hou Chi commenced the sacrifices
and without error or reproach
they've been carried on till today.

The *Tso Chuan*

The *Tso chuan,* or *Master Tso's Commentary,* is a commentary by Tso Ch'iu-ming (fifth century B.C.E.) on the *Spring and Autumn Annals,* so called because it relates the historical events of all seasons of the year. This latter work is but a terse list of incidents that occurred in the states of northern China from 722 to 481 B.C.E., and it contains virtually no narrative. The *Tso chuan,* however, is a compilation of historical tales, anecdotes, and legends from the same time period that were correlated with the *Spring and Autumn Annals* to serve as a kind of commentary to its calendrical register. According to tradition, the *Tso* was edited by Confucius (551–479 B.C.E.), and hence some entries close with his comments. Many of the *Tso's* dialogues record the moral dilemmas confronted by rulers and ministers in the day-to-day conduct of government.

The religious culture of the *Tso* describes an underlying continuity between the numinous powers of spirits, the celestial and terrestrial powers of heaven and earth, and the power of the inner values of human beings. The latter is the pivot on which relationships with spirits and the natural world are balanced; a lack of inner virtue on the part of human beings will eventually become manifest as anomalies in nature, and unvirtuous people will not gain the favor of spiritual beings. The minister Kung Chih-chi, for example, admonishes Duke Yü that the mechanical presentation of generous votive gifts does not in and of itself assure the cooperation of spirits, for what actually attracts them is not the aromas of the food offerings but the fragrance of the inner quality of virtue.

One's relationships with the spirit world were circumscribed by one's status in the human hierarchy: the Son of Heaven, who possessed domain over all under heaven, sacrificed to heaven and to all lesser powers, but the dukes enfeoffed in subordinate states might sacrifice only to the numinous powers within their own domains and perform such rites as the Distant *(wang)* sacrifices to mountains and rivers, so called, some commentators suggest, because they were performed at a distance from their recipients. When divination reveals to King Chao of Ch'u that the Ho River (the Yellow River), a river outside his domain, is a baneful influence, he refuses to sacrifice to it because such rites are the prerogative only of the person controlling the lands around the Ho. He cites as authority the historical precedent of the sacrificial canon mandated by the earlier rulers of the Three Dynasties (the protohistorical Hsia dynasty of the third millennium B.C.E., the Shang dynasty, and the Chou dynasty). Whether this passage actually represents a turning away from earlier kinds of divination is unclear, but it does suggest that a ruler must consider the parameters set by historical precedent as well as the results divined by prognostication.

King Chao's officers were in effect improperly encouraging Chao to bribe the Ho River. Duke Kuo likewise attempts to sacrifice to a spirit in Hsin to benefit himself but is chastised by the recorder of the ritual proceedings, the scribe Yin, for not understanding that spirits are intelligent, morally upright, and uniformly consistent; they respond favorably only to virtuous human behavior. The notion that spirits possess these three qualities pervades Chinese beliefs toward the spirit world over the centuries, and even today when the outcome of sacrificial supplications is not what the sacrificer had originally hoped for, the blame in most cases is placed not on the spirits but on the sacrificer's lack of moral rectitude. To say that spirits are intelligent, upright, and consistent is not to say that they invariably grant the boons asked of them, for in their wisdom they might perceive the disadvantages of so doing.

Spirits *(shen)*, however, should not be confused with other beings called wraiths *(li)*, whose malevolent powers are related in the story of the wraith of Po-yu, an otherwise talented man whose drunken behavior resulted in his own violent death. In antiquity it was believed that when people died they became ghosts *(kuei)*, which were not necessarily malevolent but could become so if they had nowhere to rest, and hence special places were set aside for them in sacrificial offerings. The appearance of these places in antiquity is unknown, but in later centuries they took the form of spirit tablets, ruler-shaped plaques carved with the name of the deceased. Nevertheless, human beings were particularly liable to cause harm after death if they died violently or died the victims of injustice. If their descendants did not present offerings or were unable to do so, ghosts became malicious wraiths capable of causing destruction and death in the human world. But when Tzu-ch'an makes it possible for Po-yu's son to continue his sacrifices, Po-yu's terrorizing ceases. Belief in such wraiths continued well into late imperial times, and in a more modern era the once neutral term "ghost" has taken on the malevolent connotations once reserved for wraiths. Contemporary folk belief, for example, holds that victims of fatal car accidents will linger about the site of the wreck and cause yet more casualties, and that ghosts of people wrongly executed by the judicial system will cause the judges' secretaries to suffer miscarriages.

But just as not all people currently subscribe to such beliefs, some people of Chou times were also somewhat skeptical, for Chao Ching-tzu asked Tzu-ch'an whether it was actually possible that Po-yu really had become a wraith. Tzu-ch'an relates the process, describing the interaction of various essences, energies, and souls within the human body. While his explanation of the physical, corporeal soul, or *p'o,* and the ethereal anima soul, or *hun,* is only one of many notions of the soul current in Chou times, generally it was believed that the corporeal *p'o* soul dissipated into the ground after death, while the incorporeal *hun* soul ascended into the sky.

The people were benefited by Tzu-ch'an's handling of the wraith of Po-yu, and the minister Chi Liang advises his ruler to benefit his own people and give them priority over spirits, without, however, neglecting the latter. Only when the ruler focuses first on good governance and human relationships, Chi Liang admonishes, will spirits grant blessings. Viscount Ning-wu also offers advice on the spirit world to his ruler, Duke Ch'eng, who had been encouraged in a dream to give offerings to the spirit of Hsiang, a ruler from the ancient Hsia dynasty. The viscount warns the duke that people are limited to offering sacrifices only to those spirits with whom they have a true relationship as prescribed by social rank or family ties. As Duke Ch'eng had neither connection with Hsiang, the viscount concluded, he had no right to sacrifice to the spirit.

The connections between human inner qualities and the natural world are reflected in the accounts of the comet in Ch'i and the landslide on Mount Liang. Uncanny manifestations in the sky or on the earth typically prompted exorcisms and other deprecatory rites, but when a comet, or "broom star," appears in Ch'i, Ang-tzu encourages the marquis to purify his inner virtue rather than rely on external exorcism. Similarly, when a landslide occurs on Mount Liang, the cart puller states that a ruler should respond first with austere living and only then conduct rituals. From a certain perspective the advice of these two men might seem like a "rational" development away from exorcistic practices, yet they do not entirely reject the effectiveness of ritual itself but only question the validity of outer form devoid of inner sentiment. And neither Ang-tzu nor the cart puller questions the notion that events in the natural world are closely associated with the personal behavior of the ruler. This idea, too, has persisted well into modern times. The expression still used for the death of a political leader is *peng,* which literally means "landslide," and in the popular imagination the death of Chairman Mao Tse-tung (1893–1976) in 1976 was associated with the earthquakes in T'ang-shan in northern China.

The entries from the *Tso* translated here concern the proper stance leaders should take regarding their obligations to the people on the one hand and numinous forces on the other. Their headings have been provided by the translator and are not part of the original text. Names and numbers in parentheses at the end of each entry refer to the duke and to the year of his reign in which the event occurred.

The Fragrance of Virtue

Duke Yü said, "My sacrificial offerings are bountiful and pure. The spirits will maintain me."

Kung Chih-chi remonstrated with the duke, saying, "It is not simply that ghosts and spirits are attracted to human beings: it is virtue that attracts them. Hence the 'Book of Chou' in the *Book of History* says, 'August heaven has no partial affections; it supports only the virtuous.' It also says, 'It is not the millet that is fragrant; it is bright virtue that is fragrant.' And it also says, 'The people did not trifle with their offerings, for virtue alone was what they offered.' So unless one is virtuous, the people will not be in harmony and spirits will not partake of one's offerings. What the spirits are attracted to is one's virtue. Now if Chin invades Yü and then displays its 'virtue' with fragrant offerings, won't the spirits just vomit them out?" The duke did not listen to him.

[DUKE HSI 5]

Divination of the River Ho

Earlier, when King Chao of Ch'u had been ill, the divination said, "The Ho River is a baneful influence." But the king nevertheless did not offer sacrifices to placate it. Even though his great officers pleaded with him to sacrifice in the area outside the city, the king said, "According to the sacrifices mandated by the Three Dynasties, the sacrifices I should perform do not go beyond performing the Distant sacrifices to mountains and rivers within my domain. Now the Chiang, the Han, the Chü, and the Chang rivers are the effluents to which I might properly offer Distant sacrifices here in Ch'u. Whatever misfortunes or blessings I might incur will not stem from my not offering a sacrifice to the Ho. Even though I am not virtuous, I have not transgressed against the Ho." Consequently he did not sacrifice to it.

Confucius said, "King Chao of Ch'u understood the great Way. It was fitting that he did not lose his state."

[DUKE AI 6]

The Spirit of Hsin

A spirit came and stayed in Hsin for six months. Duke Kuo had invocator Ying, temple steward Ch'ü, and scribe Yin offer the spirit sacrifices so that it might grant him lands and fields. Scribe Yin said, "Kuo has perished! I have heard that when a state is about to flourish, it harkens to the people, and when it is about to perish, it harkens to the spirits. The spirits are intelligent and upright and are always consistent. Their movements depend on human beings. Kuo makes a travesty of virtue. How could he hope to acquire more land?"

[DUKE CHUANG 32]

The Wraith of Po-yu

The people of Cheng were all frightened of Po-yu, and if someone said, "Po-yu is here!" they would all run away heedless of where they went. In the second month, when the punishments were being decided, someone dreamed that Po-yu appeared in armor and walked around, saying, "On the day *jen-tzu* I will kill Ti, and next year, on the day *jen-yin,* I will kill Tuan." When the day *jen-tzu* arrived and Ti did actually die, the people became even more frightened; when Kung-sun Tuan died on the day *jen-yin* in the month when the states Ch'i and Yen made peace, they became absolutely terrified. In the next month, Tzu-ch'an gave appointments to Kung-sun Hsieh and to Liang Chih, the son of Po-yu, to placate the wraith. The incidents stopped. When Tzu-t'ai Shu asked Tzu-ch'an why he did this, he replied, "When ghosts have a place to return to, they do not become wraiths, and now I have given them a place to return to. . . ."

When Tzu-ch'an went to Chin, Chao Ching-tzu asked him whether it was possible that Po-yu really had become a ghost. Tzu-ch'an replied, "It is possible. When humans are born, they first develop what is called the corporeal soul. When the yang force develops, then there is the anima soul. By interacting with things their subtle energies increase, and the corporeal and anima souls strengthen. Eventually their energies intensify until they become numinous and bright. If average men or women should die violently, they are able to linger near people as malevolent wraiths. . . . Po-yu was from a family that held political power for three generations. He had access to many things, and his subtle energies were strong. He came from a great and distinguished clan. Doesn't it stand to reason that it was possible for him to become a wraith when he suffered a violent death?"

[DUKE CHAO 7]

The Advice of Chi Liang

Chi Liang spoke to the Duke of Sui, saying, "The people are the hosts of the spirits, and therefore the sage kings first took care of the people and only then attended to the spirits. . . . They attended to their administrative duties throughout the year and cultivated the five human relationships; they were close to their kin and performed their Pure sacrifices. Hence the people were harmonious, spirits sent down blessings, and they were successful in everything they did. But now, in your case, the people are not of one mind, and the ghosts and spirits have no hosts. Although you alone may have plenty, what kind of blessing is that?"

[DUKE HUAN 6]

The Dream of Duke Ch'eng

Wei moved its capital to Ti-ch'iu. . . . Duke Ch'eng of Wei dreamed that K'ang-shu, the first Duke of Wei, told him that Hsiang, a former ruler of the Hsia dynasty who once lived in Ti-ch'iu, had snatched away the offerings presented to him. So the duke ordered that sacrifices also be given to Hsiang. Viscount Ning-wu, however, would not allow it, and said, "Unless ghosts and spirits are of one's class and kind, they will not partake of one's sacrificial offerings. What business have we to do with what is the prerogative of Ch'i and Tseng, the descendants of the Hsia? Hsiang has not partaken of sacrificial offerings here for a long time, but that is not Wei's fault. One cannot diverge from the sacrifices mandated by King Ch'eng and the Duke of Chou."

[DUKE HSI 31]

Exorcism of the Comet

A comet appeared in Ch'i. The Marquis of Ch'i ordered a Jang exorcism to be performed, but Ang-tzu said, "It is useless. You are making a mistake. Heaven's way leaves no room for doubt, and its mandate does not waver. Why this exorcism? Moreover, heaven's 'broom-star' sweeps away unclean things. If your virtue is not unclean, then why this exorcism? And if your virtue is unclean, then there is nothing to be gained by exorcism. . . . Do not transgress against virtue, and people from all quarters will come to you. Why trouble yourself over a comet? . . . If your virtue is disheveled, then the people will be lost, and there is nothing that invocators and scribes can do to redress the situation." The duke said, "Stop the exorcism."

[DUKE CHAO 26]

The Landslide on Mount Liang

There was a landslide on Mount Liang. The Marquis of Chin sent for Po-tsung. On his way to court, Po-tsung ran into a cart puller and asked him to make way, to which the cart puller replied, "Instead of waiting for me, you'd best find a shortcut." Po-tsung asked where the man was from, and he said "I'm from Chiang." When asked about the news from Chiang, the cart puller answered, "There's been a landslide on Mount Liang, and Po-tsung has been summoned to help decide what to do." "And what would you do?" asked Po-tsung. "When a mountain becomes unstable and landslides happen, what can be done? A state is responsible for its mountains and rivers, and when there is a landslide or when a river dries up, the ruler should live austerely and dress accordingly. Riding only in a simple carriage, let him silence the music of the court and leave the city. Invocators then prepare offerings and scribes compose invocations for their rituals. This is what has to be done. What more could even Po-tsung do?" Po-tsung invited the cart puller to appear at court, but he declined; Po-tsung reported the man's advice, and it was followed.

[DUKE CH'ENG 5]

The *Rites of Chou*

While the *Rites of Chou* is stylistically a graceless catalogue of the administrative duties of the officials of the Chou bureaucracy, even the titles of the personnel described therein suggest a culture of interesting religious imagination, for here are diviners of dreams, exorcists, invocators, and male and female shamans. The *Rites of Chou* has been relatively neglected in modern sinology, and it has not been translated into English. Noting its descriptions of blood sacrifices and deprecations, however, is a useful antidote to the notion that the Chinese tradition is primarily a kind of ethical humanism of only faint ritual expression.

The very fact that a ritual text is also an outline of bureaucratic responsibilities indicates the absence of a distinction between the political and religious realms. The text cannot be accurately dated, although it may have been compiled in late Chou or even early Han dynasties (202 B.C.E.–220 C.E.); modern scholars question whether it provides an actual or only idealized account of the structure of the Chou government. In terms of language, the vocabulary of the *Rites of Chou* was so archaic as to have confounded even commentators of the late Han; the numerous rites and ceremonies mentioned in the text are in many cases known only by name, and their actual content is a matter of conjecture.

Nearly four hundred officials and their duties are registered in the *Rites of Chou,* and most entries are merely a few lines long. Selections from the entries for the Grand Minister of Rites, Master of Sacrifices, and Grand Invocator are translated here, but the other items are translated in full. Because of the nature of the text, some areas of the translation are only tentative interpretations that rely on Han and later commentaries. The *Rites of Chou* does not offer the interpretive essays on ritual included in the *Book of Rites* (another ritual text of the late Chou and early Han eras), and many of its entries are primarily enumerations of terms; it nevertheless reveals a great richness of ceremonial culture and ritual usage, and it describes in some detail the performative rites that expressed the desire of the people of an agricultural society to interact harmoniously with the forces of nature. Balance was diagnosed with divination and maintained by votive offerings; imbalance could be redressed or prevented by shamans and exorcists.

Regardless of the historicity of the text, the *Rites of Chou* was for centuries consulted as a model of governmental structure. At least as late as the fifteenth century, officials at court called for the revival of some of its ritual usages, and in modern Taiwan people in rural areas continue the mourning practices it describes. Seasonal deprecatory ceremonies similar to the Nuo rite performed by the Exorcist are still performed in southern China.

Grand Minister of Rites

The Grand Minister of Rites supervises the rituals of the vassal states, overseeing the rites offered to heavenly spirits, human ghosts, and terrestrial divinities. He helps the king establish and protect the various states. He serves ghosts and spirits of the state with auspicious rituals, and with pure Yin sacrifices he conducts rites to August Heaven, the Lord on High. He presents burnt offerings to the sun, moon, stars, and planets; he makes similar burnt offerings to the greater and lesser Lords of Fate and to the Lords of Wind and Rain. He offers blood sacrifices to the altars of the land and grain, to the five tutelary deities of the house, and to the five sacred mountains. By drowning sacrificial animals he sacrifices to the mountains, forests, rivers, and lakes, and offers the split carcasses of sacrificial animals to the four directions and the myriad things.

[TA TSUNG-PO, 1296]

Master of Sacrifices

The responsibility of the Master of Sacrifices is to supervise the rituals of sacrifices of the vassal states and to assist the Grand Minister of Rites. In conducting the greater sacrifices he employs jade, silk, and solid-colored sacrificial animals; for the secondary sacrifices, he uses only sacrificial animals and silk; for the minor sacrifices, he uses only sacrificial animals. He arranges the sacrificial offerings according to the calendar and the seasons.

[SSU-SHIH, 1465]

Chief Shaman

The Chief Shaman supervises the administration of all the shamans. When the state experiences a serious drought, he leads all the shamans in dancing the rain sacrifice. When the state experiences some great calamity, he leads all the other shamans in consulting the records of ancient shamans. When a sacrificial offering is conducted, the Chief Shaman presents the boxed case, the spirit cloth, and the wicker basket. Whenever there are sacrifices, he oversees the burial of the votive gifts, and for mourning services, he supervises the rites of spirit possession.

[SSU WU, 2062]

Male Shaman

The Male Shaman supervises the Distant sacrifices to mountains and rivers and also oversees the Distant exorcisms. He transmits the special names of the ritual implements, and with whips of sedge he summons spirits from all quarters. In winter he dispels baneful influences from houses near and far; in spring, he summons auspiciousness and wards off inauspiciousness, and he dispels epidemics. When the king is in mourning, the Male Shaman comes forward with the invocator.

[NAN WU, 2072]

Female Shaman

The Female Shaman supervises the expiations and herbal lustrations of the calendrical year. In the event of droughts, she dances the rain sacrifice. If the queen is in mourning, the Female Shaman comes forward with the invocator. If a great calamity should befall the state, she chants and cries in supplication.

[NÜ WU, 2075]

Grand Invocator

The Grand Invocator manages the liturgies of the six invocations to serve ghosts, spirits, and terrestrial divinities. He prays for blessings and auspiciousness and beseeches longevity and uprightness. These are the six invocations: the invocation of concordance, the annual invocation, the auspicious invocation, the transformative invocation, the propitious invocation, and the milfoil invocation. The six prayers he uses to commune with ghosts, spirits, and terrestrial divinities are the Especial prayer, the Tsao prayer, the Kuei exorcistic prayer, the prayer of the Minor Yung exorcism, the Kung exorcistic prayer, and the Yüeh prayer. He performs the six liturgies to communicate with high and low, near and far. . . . He distinguishes the six kinds of special appellations, which are the names of the spirits, ghosts, terrestrial divinities, sacrificial animals, grains, and silks.

[TA CHU, 1985]

Female Invocator

The Female Invocator supervises the inner sacrificial offerings of the queen, as well as her supplications and thanksgiving offerings for blessings. She is in charge of the seasonal invocations, expiations, exorcisms, and deprecations. She also dispels pestilence.

[NÜ CHU, 562]

Exorcist

The Exorcist wears a headdress of bear fur ornamented with four-eyed yellow gold decorations, and he is attired in a black cloak and vermilion robe. Clutching halberd and shield, he leads the hundred minor officials in the seasonal Nuo exorcism as they drive out pestilence from the chambers. At mourning processions he walks at the head of the file, and at the grave site he enters the tomb and waves his halberd in all directions to dispel baneful terrestrial influences.

[FANG-HSIANG SHIH, 2493]

Diviner of Dreams

The Diviner of Dreams supervises the calendrical observations of the concourse of heaven and earth and discerns the vital forces of yin and yang. Observing the sun, moon, stars, and celestial bodies, he divines the auspiciousness and inauspiciousness of the six dreams. The first of these are called even dreams; the second, terrifying dreams; the third, thought dreams; the fourth, dreams of realization; the fifth, joyful dreams; and the sixth, frightening dreams. In the last month of winter, he does inquiries concerning the king's dreams and does a rendering of the auspicious ones. The king respectfully accepts this rendering. The diviner presents herbal offerings to the four directions to dispel terrifying dreams, and it is he who sends the orders for the beginning of the Nuo exorcism to dispel pestilence.

[CHAN-MENG, 1968]

The *Book of Rites*

The *Rites of Chou* describes the vocabulary, regalia, and staffing of ritual proceedings, but it relates nothing of their purpose or import. Such themes, however, are discussed at length in the *Book of Rites,* a collection of miscellaneous discourses compiled in the Former Han dynasty (206 B.C.E.–8 C.E.) of materials from the late Chou, Ch'in (221–206 B.C.E.), and early Han periods. While the *Rites of Chou* lists particulars, the *Book of Rites* elaborates values and principles. The Chinese word for ritual, *li,* encompasses all kinds of ritualized behavior, both public and private, from table manners to rites of passage, seasonal festivals, and government functions. Ritual is both an inner sense of personal decorum and the external performance of public ceremonies. Selections from three important chapters from the *Rites* are translated here: "Principles of Sacrifice," "The Great Learning," and "Centrality and Equilibrium."

The selection from the beginning of the chapter "Principles of Sacrifice" *(Chi t'ung)* sets forth the underlying themes of sacrificial offerings, which are one subcategory of ritual. It relates that sacrifice stems from an internal sense of awe produced by a resonance with the outside world; it is not a mechanical means for manipulating spirits but a means of developing the self within the context of the family and the larger public social network. It is an expression of inner qualities of sincerity and reverence articulated with no selfish boon in mind. Ritual spaces where the food offerings are placed become microcosms of the entire world; ritual gestures performed by ruler and minister, husband and wife, are norms for the whole world to emulate.

The presacrificial vigils described here are observed before presenting sacrifices to the spirits of the ancestors. They serve to focus the sacrificer's concentration of the will and clarification of inner virtue, which is accomplished by a gradual sense deprivation that directs the attention of the sacrificer inward. Those sacrificing are encouraged to think continually of the ancestor until they seem to see that person before them in a kind of eidetic vision, a moving vision of virtual reality that makes the hidden world of spiritual beings visible. When human beings die they are considered ghosts *(kuei)*, but they might also be considered spirits *(shen)*, a term that encompasses not only the numinous powers of natural forces but also the numinous essences of human beings. The two terms occur together as the compound *kuei-shen*, or spiritual beings. The precise nature of ghosts and spirits is very ambiguous and was systematically deliberated for centuries by scholars, but no one view was accepted by all philosophers.

After the vigils are performed and the sacrifice is in progress, the actual presence of the ancestor is suggested physically by someone, usually a male descendant, who plays the role of the personator of the dead and accepts the sacrifice on the deceased's behalf. The ancestral spirits are both fed and entertained as living guests might be feted at a festive banquet, and the motions of the dance both amuse the personator and figuratively suggest a larger joy that pervades the entire realm. Spirits symbolically partake of the aromas of the votive gifts, but the actual food offerings themselves are consumed by the guests invited to participate; the public communal meal following the ceremony reinforces and displays the hierarchical norms and reciprocal obligations that govern the social order. Public display of paradigmatic values and social mores in ritual performances serves as a kind of instruction expounded by the ruler and emulated by the people.

"Centrality and Equilibrium" is a more literal translation of the title of a chapter often translated as the "Doctrine of the Mean"; it describes the subtle underlying principles not of ritual but of the entire cosmos. Selected passages that focus on cosmology, spirits, and human perfection are translated here. The "Centrality" includes sayings attributed to Confucius, "the master," as for example his account of the ineffable qualities of spiritual beings. Here also is an articulation of the important "five relationships" between ruler and minister, parent and child, husband and wife, elder and younger brother, and friend and friend, relationships of reciprocal obligations and duties that have structured the social order up to modern times.

The term "centrality" in the title suggests an inner quiescence, but the term "equilibrium" is not explained in the body of the text. Aphoristic and evocative in style, but scarcely systematic in the elucidation of concepts, the chapter "Centrality and Equilibrium" articulates an appreciation of the invisible transformative potentialities within the universe both in stillness and in motion. One can enter into these powers and engage in a tripartite harmony with heaven and earth not by ritual but by the inner quality of sincerity, the way of heaven that humans must fully embody before participating in the transformations of the cosmos. Change and transformation are perceived as positive qualities. One may embody sincerity not through prayer or mystical contemplation but through painfully vigorous study, inquiry, deliberation, and earnest action, activities that must be performed personally without the intermediary of any professional religious practitioners. Heaven is in a sense already part of each person, for the idea of the mandate of heaven *(ming)* has shifted from a more political concept to an inner quality infused into each human being (sometimes translated as "destiny" or "fate"), which here is called the nature.

In this chapter, heaven and earth are directly observed with an expanded vision that draws the mind's eye from a spoonful of water to the depths of the ocean. This is not a vision of an otherworldly paradise, or of a land that can only be reached after death, or of a lost Garden of Eden, and shamans make no celestial journeys here; it is a realm accessible to all in this very life.

Transformation and subtlety are replaced by distinct priorities and careful ordering in the opening passage selected from the beginning of the chapter "The Great Learning." A ladderlike series of steps, or perhaps concentric series of spheres, connects the individual to the larger world, and a discretely ordered cosmos is constructed by organizing what is nearer and then extending that structure outward to wider circles of activity. First three main principles are delineated: clarifying virtue, loving the people, and abiding in the highest good. These are followed by eight particular steps: investigating things, extending knowledge, making thoughts sincere, rectifying the mind, developing the self, managing the family, governing the state, and establishing peace throughout the world. These steps provide a structural framework and a direction for personal development, but they specify no particular content. That content must come from one's own personal investigation of "things," which are primarily understood as physical objects, and the process of world building begins not with any kind of revelation but with the observation of the natural world.

Later interpreters, however, each supplied their own content in innumerable commentaries on the "Great Learning," and in the twelfth century the scholar Chu Hsi (1130–1200) excerpted both the "Centrality and Equilibrium" and the "Great Learning" from the *Book of Rites* and elevated them to the status of independent texts. Chu Hsi rearranged the eight steps of the text to begin with the investigation of things, although it originally began with making thoughts sincere. Since his version is the one most influential today, his arrangement has been followed here. Along with the *Analects* of Confucius and the *Mencius,* described later, the "Centrality" and "Great Learning" came to be called the "Four Books." In the fourteenth century they were placed on the list of readings required for the civil service examinations requisite to government service and remained there until the imperial examination system was abolished in the early twentieth century.

"The Principles of Sacrifice"

Of all the ways of governing human beings well, none is more compelling than ritual; of the five categories of rites, none is more important than sacrificial offerings. Sacrifice does not enter from without: it issues from within, in the mind. When the mind is in awe, it is expressed through ritual. Only worthies are able to plumb the meaning of sacrifice.

The sacrifices of worthy persons receive their blessings, but these are not what the world ordinarily calls blessings. The term "blessings" here means "completion," an expression that means complete accord. When everything is in accord, there is completion. This is to say that internally, there is full completion of the self; externally, there is complete accord with the Way. When loyal ministers serve their sovereigns and filial children serve their parents, they act from this same fundamental basis. When this happens, then on high there is complete accord with ghosts and spiritual beings; outside the family sphere, there is accord with sovereigns and seniors; inside the family sphere, there is filiality toward parents. This then is completion. Only worthy people can attain to this completion, and when they do they may then sacrifice. The sacrifices of worthy people may be described thus: the sacrificers perfect their sincerity and good faith with loyalty and reverence and then offer their votive gifts following the way of ritual, accompanying the rites with music and performing them at the appropriate time. They offer them openly, without seeking anything. This then is the attitude of the filial child.

By sacrificing, one continues to care for one's parents and act with filiality. Filiality means "to care for," and caring means according with the Way and not transgressing proper conventions of behavior. Filial people serve their parents in three ways: in life, they care for them; in death, they mourn them; when mourning is over, they sacrifice to them. Caring for parents expresses accord; mourning expresses sorrow; sacrifice expresses reverence and timely attentiveness. Filial behavior lies in fulfilling these three criteria.

Upon fulfilling one's responsibilities within the family, one then seeks a helpmate from outside, and for this there are the rites of marriage. When a ruler seeks a wife, he says, "I ask from you this jadelike maiden to share with my humble self this poor state, to serve at the ancestral temple and at the altars of the land and grain." This is essentially how one seeks a helpmate. Husbands and wives must conduct sacrifices together, and each has his or her own respective duties, without and within. Only when these responsibilities are performed is there completion. Everything, of lesser and greater importance, must be prepared: minces and pickles made from the products of land and water, stands for the meats of the three sacrificial animals, condiments for the eight dishes, rare animals and plants—all the things of the yin and the yang forces. Everything, whether generated by heaven or grown upon the earth, is set forth. Outwardly, there is a complete profusion of things, and inwardly, there is a complete perfection of the will. This is the attitude appropriate to sacrificing.

Hence the Son of Heaven himself plows south of the city to provide grain for the sacrificial cauldrons, and the empress tends silkworms north of the city to supply ritual attire. The enfeoffed lords also plow east of the city to supply grain, and their wives likewise practice sericulture north of the city to supply caps and attire. It is not that the Son of Heaven and feudal lords have no one to do the plowing for them, or that the empress and the lords' wives have no one to do sericulture for them: it is just that they themselves want to express their sincerity and good faith. Such qualities are what is meant by perfection, and perfection means reverence; only when reverence is perfected can one serve the spiritual and the numinous. This is the way of sacrifice.

When it is time to perform sacrifices, the honorable person observes a vigil. Such observances give order to things and are conducted to give uniformity where none was before. They should only be observed if there is good reason and if one is respectful and reverent. When not in observance, one need not be so circumspect about things or lessen one's desires. When undergoing a vigil, however, one is cautious about baneful things, puts a stop to longings and desires, and closes one's ears to music. Therefore the texts say that for someone conducting a vigil, there is no music; that is, one dare not dissipate one's will with it. The mind entertains no trivial thoughts, but adheres to the Way; hands and feet make no heedless movements, but adhere to ritual. The honorable person's observance of vigils is solely directed toward pure, clear virtue. One observes a moderate vigil for seven days to secure it firmly and then a full vigil for three days to order it. Securing it firmly is what is meant by observing a vigil, and this is the epitome of pureness and clarity. Only having done this can one communicate with the spiritual and the numinous.

Eleven days prior to the sacrifice, the palace steward notifies the ruler's wife to observe the moderate vigil for seven days and the full vigil for three. The ruler observes the full vigil outside the palace, while his wife observes it within. Afterward they meet at the great ancestral temple. The ruler, in silken cap and gown, stands at the eastern steps, and his wife, in ritual attire, stands in the eastern chamber. Holding a jade scepter, he pours a libation from a goblet before the personator of the dead. The Grand Minister of the temple, holding a smaller jade scepter, offers a secondary libation. The sacrificial animal is brought in, the ruler holding the lead rope, and the ministers and officers follow, holding grasses to place beneath the animal. The married women of the ruler's clan, holding basins, follow the ruler's wife in presenting libations of clarified wine. With the sacrificial knife the ruler offers some of the organs of the sacrificial animal to the personator of the dead, as if to let him taste them, and his wife assists by holding the bronze cauldrons. Thus husbands and wives both personally participate in the rite.

Then the dancing begins, and the ruler takes up his shield and battle-ax and goes to the farthest eastern part of the dance area. Wearing his headdress, he strikes and parries, leading his ministers in an entertainment for the august personator of the dead. The sacrifices of the Son of Heaven bring joy to his realm; similarly, the rites of the enfeoffed lords bring joy to their regions when they too dance and entertain the personators of the dead, bringing joy to their lands.

Three aspects of sacrifice are especially important: of offerings, libations; of music, the high songs; and of dance performances, the "Night of the Battle of King Wu." These are the ways of the Chou, and they give outward expression to the will of the honorable person and enhance it. One's will is expressed in the advancing and retreating motion of one's steps, lighter and heavier, proportionate to the sentiment behind them. Even a sage cannot be inwardly lighthearted and outwardly serious. Honorable people conduct sacrifices in person to clarify what is important, and they follow the way of ritual. Emphasizing the three important aspects of sacrificing, they present offerings to the august personator of the dead. This is the way of the sage.

After sacrificing there are foodstuffs left over, and even though these are the most peripheral aspects of rites, one must still know what to do with them. As the ancient saying goes, the ending must be as fine as the beginning, and leftovers must be considered in the same vein. As a gentleman of antiquity once said, "The personator of the dead eats what the ghosts and spirits leave behind." This is a kind practice that illustrates the workings of governance. When the personator arises after eating, the ruler and three great ministers eat, and when the ruler arises, the six great officers eat, consuming what the ruler has left over. The great officers get up, and then the eight officers eat, those of lower rank eating what their superiors have left. Then the officers get up, and taking what is left, go out, placing it in the hall below. Finally the lesser officials come in and take it away, and the subordinate officials eat what their superiors have left. At each change there are more people, illustrating the degrees of higher and lower rank. Everyone shares in this beneficent custom, and this is what happens to the contents of the four vessels of millet in the ancestral temple. The ancestral temple is itself symbolic of the whole land.

Sacrifice is a great benefaction. When superiors receive some benefit, they then bestow it on those below them. It is just that superiors receive the beneficence first and subordinates receive it later; it is not that superiors accumulate excess while subordinates suffer from cold and hunger. When people of higher rank receive some boon, those below wait for it to flow down to them, knowing that beneficence will reach them. One can see all this by considering the distribution of leftovers from sacrifice, and hence it is said that this practice illustrates the workings of governance.

Sacrifice is the greatest of things when all its preparations are complete. What do such preparations teach? Through them the ruler can teach respect for rulers and ministers in the sphere outside of the family, and within the family sphere he can teach people to be filial. So if the sovereign is enlightened, the ministers will follow him. When he discharges his duties in the ancestral temple and to the altars of the land and grain, then his sons and grandsons will be filial. His teaching is brought forth because he perfects this Way and perfects this kind of deportment. Honorable people should act this way themselves in serving the ruler. Misunderstandings that occur between higher-ranking people should not be taken out on their subordinates, and subordinates should not direct their own animosities toward their superiors. Criticizing the actions of others but then doing the same thing oneself goes contrary to this teaching. So these are the fundamentals of the instruction of the honorable person. Is this not truly the epitome of concord? Is this not truly what is meant by sacrificing? So it is said that sacrifice is the basis of instruction.

In sacrifice there are ten proper norms: the ways appropriate to serving ghosts and spirits, the proper comportment of rulers and ministers, the relationships between parent and child, the distinctions between those of higher and lower

rank, the degrees of intimacy between close and distant relatives, the distributions of rank and emolument, the differences between husband and wife, fairness in the affairs of governance, the order of priorities between senior and junior, and the boundaries between higher and lower. These are the ten norms.

"Centrality and Equilibrium"

What heaven has mandated is called the nature. According with this nature is called the Way *(Tao).* Cultivating the Way is called instruction.

This Way cannot be departed from for even an instant, and if it can be, then it is not really the Way. Hence the honorable person is cautious about things as yet unseen and apprehensive about things as yet unheard.

Nothing is more visible than what is darkly hidden, and nothing is more evident than what can be barely detected. So the honorable person is cautious even when alone.

The condition when pleasure, anger, sorrow, and joy have not yet arisen is called centrality; the condition when these do arise and all reach a measured expression is called harmony. Centrality is the fundamental basis of the world, and harmony is the attainment of the Way throughout the world.

When centrality and harmony are perfected, everything in heaven and earth finds its place and all things flourish.

[1.1–5]

Spirits

The master said, "The virtue of ghosts and spirits is truly marvelous. One looks for them but they cannot be seen; one listens for them but they cannot be heard. They are at the marrow of things but they cannot be detected. They cause everyone in the world to observe vigils and purify themselves, dress in their richest attire, and present sacrificial offerings. Then the spirits seem to float just above the heads of the sacrificers, all around them. As it is said in the *Book of Odes,* 'The approaches of spirits are unfathomable. How could one be unmoved by this?' So it is said that what can barely be detected becomes evident, and that sincerity cannot be kept concealed."

[16.1–5]

The Five Relationships

So that the Way may be attained throughout the land, people must consider five things, and for enacting the Way, one must consider three. The five are the relationships between ruler and minister, parent and child, husband and wife, elder and younger brother, and friend and friend. These five constitute the attainment of the Way throughout the land. Understanding, humanity, and fortitude are the three aspects of attaining to virtue throughout the land, and one enacts them with a single-minded oneness. Some people understand all this from birth, others understand it through study, and still others understand it only through painful experience; nevertheless, once they understand it, those people are all the same. Some are able to enact all this with ease; others, with some effort; still others, with strenuous effort. Nevertheless, once they succeed, they are all the same.

[20.8–9]

Sincerity

Sincerity is the Way of heaven, and the attainment of sincerity is the Way of human beings. A person who is possessed of sincerity, who achieves things effortlessly and apprehends things without excessive deliberation, who goes along with things and attains the Way, is a sage. Those possessed of sincerity embrace what is good and hold fast to it.

They study widely and inquire extensively, ponder things carefully and make clear deliberations; they act with earnestness.

They do not rest lest there be something they have not studied or studied but not yet grasped, or lest there be something they have not inquired about or have inquired about but do not yet understand. Nor do they rest lest there be something they have not yet pondered or have pondered but not yet apprehended, or lest there be something they have not yet deliberated, or have deliberated but have not yet clarified. They do

not rest lest there be something they have not done or have done but without earnestness. If someone else accomplishes things after only one try, they will try a hundred times; if someone else accomplishes things after only ten attempts, they will try a thousand times.

If people are able to proceed in this way, then even if they are stupid they will become bright and intelligent, and even if they are weak they will become strong.

That this intelligence comes from sincerity is human nature itself. The fact that sincerity comes from intelligence is due to instruction. If there is sincerity there will be intelligence, and where there is intelligence there will be sincerity.

[20.18–20]

A Trinity with Heaven and Earth

In this world only those who have attained the epitome of sincerity can perfect their natures, and when they have perfected their own natures, they can then perfect the natures of other people. When they have perfected the natures of other people, they can then perfect the natures of things. When they have perfected the natures of things, they can then participate in the transforming and sustaining forces of heaven and earth and form a trinity with heaven and earth.

Next below these people are those who first develop themselves in small ways. When they are able to do that, they can attain to sincerity, and when they are sincere, they begin to take shape. Shape becomes lustrous and luster becomes brightness; brightness becomes vibrancy, vibrancy becomes change, and change becomes transformation. In this world when one attains sincerity, one can transform things.

Such is the Way of the perfection of sincerity that one can have foreknowledge of things before they happen. When a state is about to prosper, auspicious omens will appear, and when a state is about to perish, baneful prodigies become manifest. These can be seen in the milfoil stalks and the tortoiseshell, and they will vibrate within one's four limbs. When either misfortune or prosperity is about to happen, both the good and the bad will be foreknown. To perfect sincerity, then, is to become like a spirit.

[22–24]

Heaven and Earth

The ways of heaven and earth can be completely explained in one phrase: they are impartial to all things. How they generate things is unfathomable. The way of heaven and earth is expansive and generous, lofty and bright, far-reaching and enduring. Heaven seems to be but a glow of brightness, but if one gazes into its inexhaustible reaches, one will see the sun, moon, stars, and celestial bodies all suspended from it. It covers all things. The earth seems to be but a mass of soil, but if one looks farther into its breadth and depth, one will see that it effortlessly bears the weight of even the Hua peaks and carries the rivers and seas without their leaking away. It holds up all things. Mountains seem to be but lumps of rock, but looking at their breadth and height one sees plants and trees flourishing and birds and beasts thriving in their midst. Many treasures lie within them. Consider a spoonful of water, but then look at water's unfathomable depths where great turtles, sea tortoises, scaly creatures, dragons, fishes, and green turtles live. Precious things abound there.

[26.7–9]

"The Great Learning"

The Way of the great learning lies in clarifying bright virtue, loving the people, and abiding in the highest good.

Only if one knows where to abide can one develop resolve, and only with resolve can one become tranquil. Only tranquillity allows one to be restfully secure, and only with this security can one be reflective. Only by reflecting on things can one apprehend them.

Things have their roots and their branches, and affairs have their beginnings and their ends. If one knows what should be first and what should be last, then one can draw near the Way.

In antiquity, those who wanted to clarify their bright virtue throughout the entire realm first had to govern their states well. Those who wanted to govern their states well first had to manage their own families, and those who wanted to manage their families first had to develop their own selves. Those who wanted to develop themselves first rectified their own minds, and those who wanted to rectify their minds first made their thoughts sincere. Those who wanted to make their thoughts sincere first extended their knowledge. Those who wanted to extend their knowledge first had to investigate things.

Once things are investigated, knowledge can be extended. When knowledge is extended, thoughts can be made sincere; when thoughts are sincere, the mind can be rectified. When the mind is rectified, one can develop the self; once the self is developed, the family can be managed. When the family is managed, the state can be governed well; when the state is governed well, peace can prevail throughout the land.

From the Son of Heaven to the common people, everyone must consider developing the self to be the fundamental root of things. If the roots are confused, then the branches cannot be well governed. It should never happen that important things are trifled with, or that trifles are considered important.

The *Analects* of Confucius

Confucius (551–479 B.C.E.) is one of the first individuals in antiquity whose teachings were transmitted to later ages, and for this reason he is sometimes viewed as kind of founding figure of a tradition called "Confucianism." He perceived himself, however, not as a founder of a new tradition but as a perpetuator of the culture of the *History,* the *Odes,* and the ritual texts (known collectively as the *Rites*). The Chinese term translated as "Confucian" in English is *ju,* which means "learned person" or "scholar" and is not specifically limited to the disciples of Confucius. The term "Confucian" can nevertheless be used in a general way to refer to those people whose worldview is based on such ancient texts as the *History* and *Odes.* Confucius was not always considered the paramount teacher and sage of the Chinese tradition, and until the T'ang dynasty (618–907) his reputation was equaled if not overshadowed by that of the Duke of Chou. Passages attributed to Confucius were included in many texts of the late Chou and early Han, but those most likely to be actually his own are compiled in his *Analects* (literally "sayings"), an unsystematized collection of aphoristic sayings recorded and collected by his pupils.

Confucius focuses on the perfection of human conduct, a cultivation that can only take place by engaging and maintaining relationships with other people in a social context. Living the life of a recluse is thus unacceptable, and merely talking about ideals without practicing them is of little value. The person who understands the graces of human conduct he calls an "honorable person," or *chün-tzu,* a term that literally means "scion of a ruling family"; it is sometimes translated as "superior man," "noble man," or "gentleman," although the term might also apply to women. Honor, for Confucius, is not ascribed by birth but achieved by effort, through developing human relationships in compliance with such virtues as humanity *(jen),* consideration *(shu),* loyalty *(chung),* and understanding *(chih).* For him the Way lies in enacting these ideals. The term "Way," or *Tao,* literally means a path or road, and figuratively it means a way to act or the way the cosmos as a whole acts. For Confucius it is human endeavor that articulates the Tao, not the other way around. The most effective rulers are not those who emphasize administrative techniques but those who embody human values.

Many passages reveal Confucius's spiritual sensibilities toward heaven, ritual, sacrifice, and spirits. Heaven is but a vague and distant presence that he nevertheless senses very personally: it is the source of his own virtue and it understands him. He was versed in both the practice and theory of ritual, and he encouraged his students to conduct with great seriousness the sacrificial offerings due to spiritual beings without, however, forgetting obligations to the human realm. He spoke admiringly of the capabilities of shamans and participated in the seasonal Nuo exorcisms. Confucius's life was thus informed by a sensitivity toward different kinds of ideas and practices that Westerners would call religious. To ask whether "Confucianism" is a "religion" is a loaded question. "Confucians," or *jus,* were the learned people of their time, and like Confucius they adhered to various beliefs and practices, but their worldview need not be labeled a religion.

Confucius was from the state of Lu, now modern Shantung Province in northeast China; he held a number of official posts but is best known as a teacher. In modern times, in the spring and in the fall on September 28, which is observed as Confucius's birthday, sacrificial offerings to his spirit are still conducted by the mayors of the largest metropolitan cities of Taiwan.

Confucius's Character

The master said, "How delightful it is to study and to review from time to time what one has studied! How pleasant to have friends visit from afar!"

[1.1.1–2]

The master said, "At fifteen I was intent on study, at thirty I had established myself, at forty I had no uncertainty, at fifty I knew the mandate of heaven, at sixty I was in consonant accord with things, and at seventy I could follow my heart's desires without overstepping convention."

[2.4]

The master said, "One can still find happiness if one has only simple food to eat, water to drink, and a bent arm for a pillow. Wealth and high rank attained unrighteously are to me but floating clouds."

[7.15]

Tzu-kung said, "The master is congenial, pleasant, courteous, good tempered, and complaisant. Thus does he engage the world, and his way of engaging it is quite different from that of other people."

[1.10.2]

There were four things he was completely free of. He never showed a lack of forethought, he was not opinionated, he was not hidebound, and he was not egoistic.

[9.4]

The master offered instruction concerning four things: cultural refinement, proper conduct, loyalty, and good faith.

[7.24]

When the master was eating next to someone who was in mourning, he never ate to the full. He never sang on a day in which earlier he had been crying.

[7.9]

The master fished, but not with a net. When hunting he did not shoot at roosting birds.

[7.26]

Human Nature

Tzu-kung said, "One can apprehend the master's disquisitions on culture and refinement, but not his discussions of human nature or the way of heaven."

[5.12]

The master said, "In terms of human nature, people are much alike. But in terms of practice and effort, they are quite different."

[17.2]

Confucius said, "Those who are possessed of understanding from birth are the highest type of people. Those who understand things only after studying them are of the next lower type, and those who learn things from painful experience are yet the next. Those who have painful experiences but do not learn from them are the lowest type of people."

[16.9]

The Honorable Person

The master said, "Isn't one truly an honorable person if one is not acknowledged by others yet still does not resent it!"

[1.1.3]

The master said, "Honorable people are modest in what they say but surpassing in what they do."

[14.29]

The master said, "There are three aspects to the way of the honorable person, but I am incapable of them: to be possessed of humanity and have no anxieties, to be wise and have no doubts, and to be strong and have no fears." Tzu-kung said, "Master, those are your own ways."

[14.30]

The master said, "Honorable persons seek things within themselves. Small-minded people, on the other hand, seek things from others."

[15.20]

Confucius said, "There are three things of which the honorable person is in awe: the mandate of heaven, great people, and the words of the sages. Small-minded people do not understand the mandate of heaven and are not in awe of it; they are insolent toward great people and ridicule sages."

[16.8]

Humanity, Virtue, and Consideration

The master rarely spoke of profit, of one's mandated fate, or of humanity.

[9.1]

The master said, "Persons possessed of humanity are like this: wanting to develop themselves, they also develop others; wanting to achieve things themselves, they also allow others to achieve what they want. This is the direction humanity takes: to use what is close to oneself as an analogy to be extended to others."

[6.28.2–3]

Chung-kung asked about humanity. The master said, "In your social affairs behave as if you are meeting with important guests, and treat people as if you were participating in a great sacrificial offering. Do not impose on other people anything you yourself dislike. Let there be no animosity either in the state or in the family." Chung-kung said, "Even though I am not gifted, I will try to practice what you have just said."

[12.2]

Fan Ch'ih asked about humanity. The master said, "Be solicitous of others." Fan Ch'ih asked about understanding. The master said, "Be understanding toward others."

[12.22]

The master said, "Only persons possessed of humanity can truly like other people or truly dislike them."

[4.3]

The master said, "Is humanity something far away? If I want to be humane, then humanity has already been attained."

[7.29]

Someone asked, "What of repaying animosity with virtue?" The master said, "How could one repay that with virtue? Repay animosity with directness, and repay virtue with virtue."

[14.36]

Tzu-kung asked, "Is there one word by which one may live one's entire life?" The master said, "Isn't that word 'consideration'? Do not impose on other people anything you yourself dislike."

[15.23]

The Way

The master said, "It is enough that someone who dies in the evening has heard of the Way only that morning."

[4.8]

The master said, "Tseng-tzu, my way has only one theme that holds it all together." Tseng-tzu replied, "That is so." When the master went out, the other disciples asked Tseng-tzu what Confucius had meant. Tseng-tzu replied, "The master's way is simply loyalty and consideration."

[4.15]

It is that human beings glorify the Way, not that the Way glorifies human beings.

[15.28]

Governance

The master said, "Someone who governs with virtue is like the northern polar star, which stays in one place while all the other stars pay their respects to it."

[2.1]

Chi-k'ang Tzu asked Confucius about governance. Confucius replied, "To govern means to rectify. If you start by rectifying yourself, how would anyone else not do the same?"

[12.17]

The master said, "If you rectify your own self, then even if you give no orders they will still be carried out. If you don't rectify yourself, then even if you do give orders they will still not be followed."

[13.6]

The master said, "If one adopts administrative measures and implements punishments in a consistent fashion, the people will comply with them but will have no shame. But if one follows the Way of virtue and implements ritual consistently, the people will have a sense of shame and moreover will correct themselves."

[2.3]

Fan Ch'ih asked to study farming with him. The master said, "Better to ask an old farmer about it." He then asked to study gardening. "Better to ask an old gardener." When Fan Ch'ih left, the master said, "Fan Chih is such a small-minded person. If a superior loves ritual, then the people will be reverent. If a superior loves righteousness, the people will oblige him, and if he loves good faith, the people will respond to him. If he can be like this, then people from all directions will come to him, bearing their children on their backs. Why should he need to study farming?"

[13.4]

Heaven

The master said, "No one understands me." Tzu-kung said, "How can you say that no one understands you?" The master said, "I bear no animosity toward heaven and no ill-will toward human beings. My studies, while lowly, attain certain heights. It is heaven that understands me."

[14.37]

The master said, "I don't want to say anything." Tzu-kung said, "If you don't say anything, then what should we write down?" The master said, "Does heaven say anything? The four seasons proceed and all things are generated, but does heaven say anything?"

[17.19]

Confucius went to visit Madam Nan-tzu, which disturbed Tzu-lu. Confucius then swore, saying, "If I have done anything that can be proved wrong, may heaven despise me! May heaven despise me!"

[6.26]

The master said, "Heaven has generated the virtue within me. What can Huan T'ui do to me?"

[7.22]

A great minister asked Tzu-kung, saying, "Can't your master be considered a sage? He is a man of many different abilities." Tzu-kung replied, "Heaven has granted that he has very nearly become a sage, and, moreover, he is a man of many skills." The master heard this, and said, "The great minister understands me. When I was young, I was of very humble background, and hence I am capable at many different but nevertheless common things. But does the honorable person need this diversity? No."

[9.6]

Yen Yüan died. The master said, "Alas! Heaven has bereaved me! Heaven has bereaved me!"

[11.8]

Ssu-ma Niu lamented, "All people have brothers, but only I do not." Tzu-hsia said, "I have heard it said that 'Death and life are mandated, and wealth and high honor lie with heaven.' If the honorable person is reverential and well mannered, is respectful of others and follows ritual, then within the four seas all people will be brothers. How could the honorable person be worried that he have no brothers?"

[12.5]

Ritual

The master said, "People say 'ritual this' and 'ritual that.' But is ritual just jades and silks? They say 'music this' and 'music that.' But is music just bells and drums?"

[17.11]

Yen Yüan asked about humanity. The master said, "If one can prevail over the self and turn toward ritual, that is humanity. If one can do this for just a single day, the whole world will incline toward humanity. But is it that humanity just comes from one's own self alone, or from interacting with other people!" Yen Yüan said, "I would like to ask about the specific details of this." The master said, "Look at nothing contrary to ritual; hear nothing contrary to ritual, speak nothing contrary to ritual, do nothing contrary to ritual." Yen Yüan said, "Even though I am not gifted, I will try to practice what you have just said."

[12.1]

The master said, "What does someone not possessed of humanity have to do with ritual? What does someone not possessed of humanity have to do with music?"

[3.3]

Lin Fang asked about the fundamental basis of ritual. The master replied, "That is a good question! In performing rituals it is better to be simple rather than extravagant. For rites of mourning it is better to be sorrowful rather than casual."

[3.4]

When Fan Ch'ih was Confucius's charioteer, the master said, "Meng-sun asked me what filiality was and I said, 'Not being disobedient.' " Fan Ch'ih asked, "What did you mean by that?" The master replied, "I meant to serve one's parents with ritual when they are alive, to bury them with ritual when they die, and thereafter to sacrifice to them with ritual."

[2.5.2–3]

Tzu-kung wanted to eliminate the offering of the sacrificial sheep at the beginning of the lunar month. The master said, "Tzu-kung, you are concerned about the sheep, but I am concerned about the ritual."

[3.17]

The master said, "Honorable people, widely studied in cultured things and guided by ritual, will not overstep themselves."

[6.25]

The master discoursed eloquently on the *Book of Odes,* the *Book of History,* and on adherence to ritual. He discoursed eloquently on all of these.

[7.17]

The master said, "Respect without ritual becomes tiresome, circumspection without ritual becomes timidity, bold fortitude without ritual becomes unruly, and directness without ritual becomes twisted."

[8.2.1]

Sacrifice

Someone asked about the meaning of the great Ti sacrifice. The master said, "I do not know. Someone who knew how to explain it would find the whole realm in the palm of his hand."

[3.11]

The head of the Chi clan was about to perform the Lü sacrifice to Mount T'ai, a sacrifice that he had no prerogative to make. The master said to Tsan-yu, "Can you not keep him from doing this?" He replied, "I cannot." The master said, "Alas!"

[3.6]

The master was very circumspect about observing the vigils before sacrificing, about warfare, and about illness.

[7.12]

When observing the vigils before sacrifice, Confucius wore immaculately clean clothing. He altered his diet, and he moved from the place where he commonly sat.

[10.7]

The food was spare, with only soup and vegetables, but when sacrificing that was how he observed the vigils.

[10.8.10]

Spirits

The master said, "To sacrifice to a spirit with which one has no proper association is merely to curry favor with it."

[2.24]

When he sacrificed to the ancestral spirits, he did so as if they were actually present; when he sacrificed to other spirits, he did so as if they were actually present. The master said, "If I do not really take part in the sacrifice, it is as if I did not sacrifice at all."

[3.12]

Fan Ch'ih asked about wisdom. The master said, "To perform the obligations properly due to the people; and to pay reverence to ghosts and spirits, while keeping a distance from them—this may be called wisdom."

[6.20]

The master did not talk about strange marvels, the use of force, chaos and disorder, or spirits.

[7.20]

Prayer

When the master became very ill, Tzu-lu asked to be allowed to pray for him. The master asked, "Is this usually done?" and Tzu-lu replied, "It is. It is said in the eulogies that one prays to the spirits above and to the terrestrial divinities below." The master remarked, "Then I have been praying for a long time."

[7.34]

Wang-sun Chia asked, "What is meant by the expression 'Rather than supplicate the tutelary powers of the southwest corner of the house, supplicate those of the stove'?" The master replied, "That is not the case at all. Those who offend heaven have nothing to whom they might pray."

[3.13]

Shamanism, Divination, and Exorcism

The master said, "The people of the south say that unless someone is a steady person, they cannot become either a shaman or a healer. That is an excellent saying! Unless one is of steady virtue, one will invite disgrace. This would come simply from not divining properly."

[13.22]

When the villagers were performing the Nuo exorcism, he donned court dress and stood on the eastern steps.

[10.10.2]

Recluses

Once when Ch'ang Chü and Chieh Ni were out plowing their fields together, Confucius passed by and had Tzu-lu ask them where the ford was. Ch'ang Chü asked, "Who is that there in the carriage?"

"Confucius."

"Confucius from Lu?"

"Yes," Tzu-lu replied.

"Well, if that's who it is," Ch'ang added, "then he knows where the ford is."

Tzu-lu then asked Chieh Ni, who said, "Who are you?"

"I am Tzu-lu."

"You're a disciple of Confucius from Lu?"

"That is so."

"The whole world is flooded," Chieh stated, without interrupting his raking, "and who can change it? It's better to be a follower of someone who withdraws from the whole world than of someone who withdraws only from certain people."

When Tzu-lu got back he told Confucius what they said. Surprised, the master said, "One cannot flock together with birds and beasts. If I do not associate with human beings, then with whom should I associate? If the Way prevailed within the world, then I would not try to change it."

[18.6]

Tzu-lu, following at some distance behind the master, encountered an elderly man carrying a bamboo basket slung over his shoulder on a pole. Tzu-lu asked, "Have you seen my master?" The old man replied, "You don't look too hard-working, and you probably can't even tell one kind of grain from another. Just who might your master be?" The man stuck his staff in the ground and started weeding, but Tzu-lu just stood there respectfully with his hands clasped in front of his chest. In the end the old man invited Tzu-lu to stay over; he killed a chicken and prepared some millet to feed him, and he introduced him to his two children. The next day, Tzu-lu went on his way, and when he caught up with the master he told him what had happened. The master said, "He is a recluse." He had Tzu-lu go back so that he might meet him, but when they arrived, he had already gone out. Tzu-lu said, "Not to serve in office is not right. The proper customs between old and young cannot be set aside, but how much less can one set aside the righteousness between ruler and minister? By wanting to make himself pure, this man has thrown greater human relationships into disarray. When honorable persons serve in office, they enact this righteousness. When the Way is not enacted, they also know it of themselves."

[18.7]

Mo Tzu

The teachings of Confucius were actively propagated in Chinese society until modern times, but the teachings of his later rival, Mo Tzu (Mozi; floruit 479–438 B.C.E.), became subjects of only academic interest within a few hundred years after the latter's death. Almost nothing is known of Mo Tzu's life; his collected writings, like the writings of other ancient philosophers, are known simply by the name of their author and are called the *Mo Tzu*. Mo Tzu adheres to unique views on heaven, ghosts, and ritual, and he sets forth significant critiques of the Confucians (*jus*). Selections from his essays on these subjects are presented here.

Mo Tzu espouses a notion of universal love, a kind of mutual love between people and their counterparts in other families and states. People should regard the families of others as they regard their own, he asserts, and regard the states of others with the same solicitude they extend to their home state. To modern minds this notion might seem laudable, but it was anathema to Confucians, who severely criticized it and emphasized instead the unique and specific bonds between the "five relationships": the bond of love and filiality between parent and child, for example, could not be duplicated outside the family, and children could not be expected to love any parents more than their own. Mo Tzu claims that universal love will profit or benefit the world; Confucius, on the other hand, rarely speaks of profit. For Mo Tzu, mutual love between counterparts of equal station, however, is not tantamount to egalitarianism, and he never questions the hierarchical social and political order.

Confucius emphasizes humanity as a virtue to be extended toward others for its own sake, but Mo Tzu speaks of righteousness, a quality to be practiced for fear of retribution from heaven and in expectation of its rewards. These two values may in some contexts be distinguished as follows: humanity is a more specific virtue that informs particular individual relationships, whereas righteousness is a more general virtue that comprehensively informs all social behavior. For Mo Tzu, righteousness is monitored by heaven, who purviews the human realm as its judge and arbiter; its authority decides human affairs. Similarly, he claims that ghosts and spirits possess the power of retribution over human actions, and he supports his assertions with appeals to logical argument and to the authority of historical records. His criticisms of the hypocrisies of ritual and of people who fatalistically interpret the mandate of heaven are revealing of the realities, if not the ideals, of Confucian values.

"Universal Love"

Mo Tzu said: It is the business of the benevolent man to try to promote what is beneficial to the world and to eliminate what is harmful. Now at the present time, what brings the greatest harm to the world? Great states attacking small ones, great families overthrowing small ones, the strong oppressing the weak, the many harrying the few, the cunning deceiving the stupid, the eminent lording it over the humble—these are harmful to the world. So too are rulers who are not generous, ministers who are not loyal, fathers who are without kindness, and sons who are unfilial, as well as those mean men who, with weapons, knives, poison, fire, and water, seek to injure and undo each other.

When we inquire into the cause of these various harms, what do we find has produced them? Do they come about from loving others and trying to benefit them? Surely not! They come rather from hating others and trying to injure them. And when we set out to classify and describe those men who hate and injure others, shall we say that their actions are motivated by universality or partiality? Surely we must answer, by partiality, and it is this partiality in their dealings with one another that gives rise to all the great harms in the world. Therefore we know that partiality is wrong.

Mo Tzu said: Whoever criticizes others must have some alternative to offer them. To criticize and yet offer no alternative is like trying to stop flood with flood or put out fire with fire. It will surely have no effect. Therefore Mo Tzu said: Partiality should be replaced by universality.

But how can partiality be replaced by universality? If men were to regard the states of others as they regard their own, then who would raise up his state to attack the state of another? It would be like attacking his own. If men were to regard the cities of others as they regard their own, then who would raise up his city to attack the city of another? It would be like attacking his own. If men were to regard the families of others as they regard their own, then who would raise up his family to overthrow that of another?

It would be like overthrowing his own. Now when states and cities do not attack and make war on each other and families and individuals do not overthrow or injure one another, is this a harm or a benefit to the world? Surely it is a benefit.

When we inquire into the cause of such benefits, what do we find has produced them? Do they come about from hating others and trying to injure them? Surely not! They come rather from loving others and trying to benefit them. And when we set out to classify and describe those men who love and benefit others, shall we say that their actions are motivated by partiality or by universality? Surely we must answer, by universality, and it is this universality in their dealings with one another that gives rise to all the great benefits in the world. Therefore Mo Tzu has said that universality is right.

I have said previously that it is the business of the benevolent man to try to promote what is beneficial to the world and to eliminate what is harmful. Now I have demonstrated that universality is the source of all the great benefits in the world and partiality is the source of all the great harm. It is for this reason that Mo Tzu has said that partiality is wrong and universality is right.

"The Will of Heaven"

Now what does Heaven desire and what does it hate? Heaven desires righteousness and hates unrighteousness. Thus if I lead the people of the world to devote themselves to righteousness, then I am doing what Heaven desires. If I do what Heaven desires, then Heaven will do what I desire. Now what do I desire and what do I hate? I desire good fortune and prosperity and hate misfortune and calamity. If I do not do what Heaven desires and instead do what Heaven does not desire, then I will be leading the people of the world to devote themselves to what will bring misfortune and calamity.

How do I know that Heaven desires righteousness and hates unrighteousness? In the world, where there is righteousness there is life; where there is no righteousness there is death. Where there is righteousness there is wealth; where there is no righteousness there is poverty. Where there is righteousness there is order; where there is no righteousness there is disorder. Now Heaven desires life and hates death, desires wealth and hates poverty, desires order and hates disorder. So I know that Heaven desires righteousness and hates unrighteousness.

Moreover, righteousness is what is right. Subordinates do not decide what is right for their superiors; it is the superiors who decide what is right for their subordinates. Therefore the common people devote their strength to carrying out their tasks, but they cannot decide for themselves what is right. There are gentlemen to do that for them. The gentlemen devote their strength to carrying out their tasks, but they cannot decide for themselves what is right. There are ministers and officials to do that for them. The ministers and officials devote their strength to carrying out their tasks, but they cannot decide for themselves what is right. There are the three high ministers and the feudal lords to do that for them. The three high ministers and the feudal lords devote their strength to managing the affairs of government, but they cannot decide for themselves what is right. There is the Son of Heaven to do that for them. But the Son of Heaven cannot decide for himself what is right. There is Heaven to decide that for him. The gentlemen of the world have no difficulty in perceiving that the Son of Heaven decides what is right for the three high ministers, the feudal lords, the gentlemen, and the common people. But the people of the world are unable to perceive that Heaven decides what is right for the Son of Heaven. Therefore Yü, T'ang, Wen, and Wu, the sage kings of the Three Dynasties of antiquity, wishing to make it clear to the people of the world that it is Heaven that decides what is right for the Son of Heaven, all without exception fed their sacrificial oxen and sheep, fattened their dogs and pigs, prepared clean offerings of millet and wine, and sacrificed to the Lord on High and the spirits in order to

seek blessing and good fortune from Heaven. But I have never heard of Heaven seeking blessing and good fortune from the Son of Heaven! So I know that it is Heaven that decides what is right for the Son of Heaven.

The Son of Heaven is the most eminent person in the world and the richest in the world. He who desires riches and eminence must not fail to obey the will of Heaven. He who obeys the will of Heaven, loving all men universally and working for their benefit, will surely win reward. But he who disobeys the will of Heaven, showing partiality and hatred and working to injure others, will surely incur punishment.

"Explaining Ghosts"

Mo Tzu said: Now that the sage kings of the Three Dynasties of antiquity have passed away and the world has forgotten their principles, the feudal lords regard might as right. So we have rulers and superiors who are not generous and subordinates and subjects who are not loyal, fathers and sons, younger and older brothers who are not loving or filial, brotherly or respectful, virtuous or good. The leaders of the state do not diligently attend to affairs of government, and the humble people do not diligently pursue their tasks. The people give themselves up to evil, violence, thievery, and rebellion, using weapons, knives, poison, fire, and water to assault innocent persons on the roads and byways and seize their carriages and horses, robes and furs, for their own benefit. All of these conditions come about for the same reason, and as a result the world is in disorder.

Now why do we have this state of affairs? It all comes about because people are in doubt as to whether ghosts and spirits exist or not, and do not realize that ghosts and spirits have the power to reward the worthy and punish the wicked. If we could only make all the people in the world believe that the ghosts and spirits have the power to reward the worthy and punish the wicked, then how could there be any disorder in the world?

Those who claim that ghosts do not exist say:

"Of course there is no such thing!" and morning and evening they preach this doctrine to the world, spreading skepticism among the people and causing them to be in doubt as to whether ghosts and spirits exist or not. Thus the world becomes disordered. Therefore Mo Tzu said: If the rulers, ministers, and gentlemen of the world today truly desire to promote what is beneficial to the world and eliminate what is harmful, they must face this question of whether ghosts and spirits exist or not and examine it.

It is clear that one must examine this question of whether ghosts and spirits exist or not. Well then, if the examination is to be sound, what method should we use?

Mo Tzu said: The way to determine whether something exists or not is to find out whether people actually know from the evidence of their own ears and eyes whether it exists, and use this as a standard. If someone has actually heard it and seen it, then we must assume that it exists. But if no one has heard or seen it, then we must assume that it does not exist. If this is to be our method, then why don't we try going to some village or community and asking? If from antiquity to today, from the beginning of mankind to the present, there have been people who have seen ghostlike and spiritlike beings and heard their voices, then how can we say they don't exist? But if no one has seen or heard them, then how can we say they exist?

Now those who claim that ghosts do not exist say: "There are countless people in the world who say they have seen or heard ghostlike or spiritlike beings. But who among them has ever really seen or heard such a being?"

Mo Tzu said: If we are to go by what many people have jointly seen and what many people have jointly heard, then there is the case of Tu Po. King Hsüan [traditional dates 827–783 B.C.] of the Chou dynasty put to death his minister Tu Po, though he had committed no crime. Tu Po said, "My lord, you are going to put me to death, though I have committed no crime. If the dead have no consciousness, that will be the end of the matter. But if the dead have consciousness, then before three years are over I will

make you know it!" Three years later King Hsüan called together the feudal lords and went hunting at P'u. His party of several hundred hunting chariots and several thousand attendants filled the field. At midday Tu Po appeared, wearing a vermilion hat and robe, holding a vermilion bow and vermilion arrows, and riding in a plain chariot drawn by a white horse. He pursued King Hsüan and shot him in his chariot. The arrow pierced the king's heart and broke his back. He fell down in his chariot, slumped over his quiver, and died. At that time there were none among the Chou attendants who did not see what happened, and no one in distant regions who did not hear about it. It was recorded in the spring and autumn annals of Chou, rulers used it to instruct their subjects, and fathers to warn their sons, saying, "Be careful! Be circumspect! All those who kill innocent men will suffer misfortune and incur the punishment of the ghosts and spirits with just such rapidity!" If we examine what is written in the book, how can we doubt that ghosts and spirits exist?

"Against Confucians"

Moreover, the Confucians corrupt men with their elaborate and showy rites and music and deceive parents with lengthy mournings and hypocritical grief. They propound fatalism, ignore poverty, and behave with the greatest arrogance. They turn their backs on what is important, abandon their tasks, and find contentment in idleness and pride. They are greedy for food and drink and too lazy to work, but though they find themselves threatened by hunger and cold, they refuse to change their ways. They behave like beggars, stuff away food like hamsters, stare like he-goats, and walk around like castrated pigs. When superior men laugh at them, they reply angrily, "What do you fools know about good Confucians?" In spring and summer they beg for grain, and after the harvests have been gathered in they follow around after big funerals, with all their sons and grandsons tagging along. If they can get enough to eat and drink and get themselves put in complete charge of a few funerals, they are satisfied. What wealth they possess comes from other men's families, and what favors they enjoy are the products of other men's fields. When there is a death in a rich family, they are overwhelmed with joy, saying, "This is our chance for food and clothing!"

Mencius

Mencius (Mengzi; 371–289 B.C.E.?) spoke little of such religious themes as ritual, sacrifice, or spirits, and his teachings are noted instead for their focus on human nature and the development of innate predispositions. He was born in what is now Shantung Province in northeast China and spent his life traveling between various states counseling rulers on the administration of their kingdoms. In terms of style, his writings are dialogues with such figures as the rival philosopher Kao Tzu (ca. 420–ca. 350 B.C.E.), and his manner of argumentation often relies on analogies from the natural world—water, mountains, and plants. Whereas Confucius was virtually silent on the question of human nature, Mencius expounds on it at length, holding that human nature tends toward the good as surely as water flows downhill; the reason it does not always realize its potential is due only to external circumstances. People are moreover innately endowed with certain "minds," a term that in Mencius's philosophy suggests attitudes, senses, or predispositions rather than what in modern science is called the brain. The Chinese word for "mind" is the character *hsin,* which is thought to be a pictographic depiction of the four ventricles of the heart; that it can be translated as either "heart" or "mind" suggests an integrity between cognitive and affective faculties. Mencius articulates these minds—a mind of commiseration with others, a mind of shame and dislike, and so on—in various ways, but he essentially holds that all the qualities necessary to perfect human beings are already complete within themselves: they do not come from outside.

Confucius emphasized humanity, but Mencius focuses particularly on the idea of righteousness, which is for him a quality that begins with affections within the family that are then extended outward to the entire world. Mencius does not, however, provide any specific method for that development. Mencius, like Confucius, believes that the best ruler is one who prevails over others with virtue rather than force, but unlike Confucius he accords the people greater importance than the sovereign.

Yet while Confucius often referred to rites and sacrifice, Mencius reveals almost no interest in religious beliefs or practices. He spoke little of the mandate of heaven, and for him the proper way of serving heaven lies not in ritual offerings but in self-cultivation. His discourses on ritual consist of little more than an incidental allusion to women's rites; references to sacrifice, while rare, nevertheless describe the purifying qualities of presacrificial vigils. Mencius speaks approvingly of shamans, implying that they have a concern for prolonging human life. Yet his writings nevertheless do express sensibilities that some have called mystical, citing his statement that uncommonly sagelike people become spirits, for example, or noting also his ability to develop his inner flowing vital force, or *ch'i*. A vaguely defined kind of energy that suffuses all things, *ch'i* was understood in many different ways and became of great importance to philosophers, religious adepts, and medical practitioners alike up to modern times.

The Nature of Water

Kao Tzu said, "The nature is like swirling water. If there is a breach in the east, it will flow eastward; if there is a breach in the west, it will flow westward. Human nature has no differentiations of 'good' and 'not good,' just as water does not differentiate between east and west."

Mencius said, "Water indeed does not differentiate between east and west, but does it not distinguish between up and down? The good of human nature is like water's tendency always to flow downward. Humans all have this goodness, just as water always flows downward. Now if you smack the surface of the water you can send it higher than your forehead, and if you dam it up and direct it, you can send it up into the mountains. But does water do this because of its own nature, or because it has been forced? When people do what is not good, it is because a similar thing has happened to their own natures."

[6A.2]

Ox Mountain

Mencius said, "The trees on Ox Mountain were once beautiful, but since the mountain stood near a large state, the forests were cut down with axes and hatchets. How could the mountain stay beautiful? Nevertheless, under the breaths of day and night and with the moisture of rain and dew, the mountain sent forth sprouts and shoots, only to have oxen and sheep graze them away. Now the mountain is eroded and exposed, and people see it and never realize it was once forested. But how could this be the real nature of the mountain?

"Do not the minds of humanity and righteousness also exist within human beings? They let go of their good-hearted minds in the same way the trees are lost to axes and hatchets; cut down day after day, can they remain beautiful? The breaths of day and night and the vital forces of dawn allow people to be like one another in their loves and hates, but if the effects of those forces are too faint, then what people actually do between dawn and dusk shackles and destroys

them. The people are fettered again and again, and the vital forces of the night are insufficient to sustain them. When the vital forces of the night can no longer sustain them, then people almost become birds and beasts. And when others see those birds and beasts, they never realize that they had any natural gifts. But does this all really describe true human emotions? There is nothing that will not grow provided it obtains its proper sustenance; there is nothing that will not waste away if it loses that sustenance. Confucius once said, 'Hold fast to it and you can keep it; neglect it and you will lose it. Its comings and goings are not bounded by time, and no one knows whence it comes.' He was speaking of the mind when he said this."

[6A.8]

The Four Minds

Mencius said, "If people accord with their emotions, then they can do what is good; this is what is meant by goodness. Now if someone does what is not good, it is not due to a flaw in a person's own natural gifts. All people have a mind of commiseration; all have a mind of shame and dislike; all have a mind of respect and reverence; all have a mind that distinguishes right and wrong. The mind of commiseration is humanity; the mind of shame and dislike is righteousness; the mind of respect and reverence is ritual; the mind that distinguishes right and wrong is wisdom. Humanity, righteousness, ritual, and wisdom are not instilled in us from outside. It's just that we have them ourselves but do not usually think about them. Hence the saying 'Seek it and you will find it, neglect it and you will lose it.' Some people are twice what others are, some are five times what others are, still others differ to an incalculable degree. This is only because some people have not fully developed their natural gifts."

[6A.6–7]

The Child in the Well
and the Four Beginnings

Mencius said, "All people have a mind that cannot bear to see the suffering of others. The ancient kings had such minds and hence had governments that could not bear to see the suffering of others. If those with minds that cannot bear to see the suffering of others direct governments of the same type, then governing the realm will be for them as easy as turning something around in the palms of their hands.

"Now what I mean by saying that people have minds that cannot bear to see the suffering of others is this. Whenever people suddenly see a child about to fall into a well, they have a sense of apprehension for the child and sense commiseration with it. This is not because they want to earn the favor of the child's father and mother or make a good impression on neighbors and friends, or because they are annoyed by the child's cries.

"Looking at it this way, someone who lacks a mind of commiseration, of shame and dislike, of civility and courtesy, or of right and wrong is not a human being. The mind of commiseration is the beginning of humanity; the mind of shame and dislike is the beginning of righteousness; the mind of civility and courtesy is the beginning of ritual; the mind that distinguishes between right and wrong is the beginning of wisdom. People have these four beginnings just as they have their four limbs. People have these four, and when they say they are incapable of them, they are only stealing from themselves, and when they say their ruler is incapable of them, they are stealing from the ruler. If those people with these four beginnings within themselves know how to develop and fulfill them, they will be as fires beginning to burn or springs beginning to flow. Completely fulfilling these four allows them to embrace everything within the four seas, but if they cannot they will barely be able to care for their own parents."

[2A.6]

Great People and Sages

Mencius said, "A great person is one who has not lost the childlike mind."

[4B.12]

Mencius said, "In years of plenty the children are mostly well behaved, but in bad years they are unruly. This is not because heaven has given the latter different natural gifts but because their minds have been inundated and overwhelmed. Take for example the growing of wheat. Seeds are sown and raked over with the same soil and planted at the same time, and they grow and eventually ripen. But if they do not all turn out the same, we say it is because of the differences in the fertility of the soil or the amount of rain and moisture, or because they have been tended differently. Things of the same kind are all similar. How could human beings be any different? The sage and myself are of the same kind."

[6A.7.1-3]

Humanity and Righteousness

Mencius said, "All things are complete within ourselves. There is no greater happiness than daily to reflect within ourselves and be sincere. Nothing comes closer to seeking humanity than to be genuinely considerate in one's conduct."

[7A.4]

Mencius said, "Humanity is realized in the service of one's parents, and righteousness is realized in obedience to one's elder brothers; the fruits of wisdom are to understand these two things and never stray from them. The realization of ritual consists of their measured refinement; of music, in rejoicing in them. Where there is joy, then these two grow, and how can they desist from growing? When you too can no longer desist, then unconsciously your feet start tapping and your hands start dancing."

[4A.27]

Mencius said, "Humanity is the very mind of human beings, and righteousness is the road they must take. To neglect this road and not follow it is to lose one's mind and not know where to find it. Alas! When people lose a chicken or a dog, they know how to find it, but when they lose this mind, they do not. The way of study and inquiry is nothing more than seeking this lost mind."

[6A.11]

Mencius said, "That people can do something without having studied it first is innate capability. That they can understand something without deliberation is innate knowing. All small children know to love their parents and, when they grow up, to revere their elder brothers. To be affectionate toward one's parents is humanity, and to revere one's elder siblings is righteousness. Even with little else besides these, one can reach out to the whole world."

[7A.15]

Fish and Bear's Paw

Mencius said, "I want fish, and I also want bear's paw, but if I cannot have both of them at the same time, then I choose bear's paw over fish. I want to live, but I also want righteousness, but if I cannot have both of them at the same time, then I choose righteousness over life. I certainly want to live, but there are things I want more than life itself, and so I will not try to hold onto it by improper means. I certainly dislike death, but there are things I dislike even more than death itself, and so there are some hazards I will not try to avoid. Now if there really was nothing people wanted so much as life, then why do they not always try to hold onto it when they can? And if there really was nothing people disliked more than death, then why do they not always try to avoid it when they can? Life is not always sought after, and avoidable disasters are not always shunned. There is something more desirable than life, something more averse than death. Not only worthy people have this mind, for all people have it; it is just that worthy people cannot be bereft of it."

[6A.10.1–5]

The Way

Mencius said, "To be possessed of humanity is to be a human being. To express these two things in one word, then say it is the Way."

[7B.16]

Governance

Mencius said, "It is not enough to remonstrate with the ruler or criticize the government. Only a great person can draw out the flaws from the ruler's mind. If the ruler is possessed of humanity, everyone will be so; if the ruler is righteous, everyone will be righteous. If the ruler is rectified, then everyone will be upright also. As soon as the ruler is rectified, the entire state will be firmly secure."

[4A.20]

Mencius said, "Those who use force to avail themselves of humanity are hegemons, and these hegemons have large states indeed. Those who enact their virtue with humanity, however, are kings, and kings are not concerned with the largeness of their kingdoms. King T'ang, for example, had a state of only seventy leagues; King Wen, a state of only a hundred. If one should try to prevail over others with force, their minds do not submit even though the people outwardly succumb to force. But if one prevails over others with virtue, then their minds are inwardly joyful and they submit sincerely, just as the seventy disciples submitted to Confucius. As the *Odes* says, "From west and east, from south and north, everyone submitted.""

[2A.3]

The Mandate and Heaven

Mencius said, "There is nothing that does not have its mandate, and one should accord with the mandate and accept it in its uprightness. But those who truly understand what is mandated will not stand beneath a crumbling wall. Those who die having perfected the Way have rendered the mandate upright, but those who die in manacles and shackles have not."

[7A.2]

Mencius said, "Those who have completely developed their minds understand their natures, and those who understand their natures understand heaven. Those who care for their minds and sustain their natures serve heaven. Those people who stand unwavering between early death and long life and simply abide in the cultivation of the self establish the mandate."

[7A.1]

Ritual

Mencius said . . . , "Have you never studied the *Rites?* When a young man undergoes the capping rites into adulthood, his father admonishes him, and when a young woman is married off, her mother admonishes her. She sees her to the door and cautions her, saying, 'You are going to your new home, and you must be respectful and careful. Never disobey your husband.' Hence the way for women lies in developing the rectitude that consists in according with others."

[3B.2.2]

Sacrifice

If even the beautiful Lady Hsi had been dirty, then people would have passed her with their noses covered. But if even wicked people perform the sacrificial vigils and bathe, then they may sacrifice to the Lord on High.

[4B.25]

Mencius said, "The people rank the highest; next are the spirits of the land and grain, and the ruler is the least important. By gaining the people one can become a Son of Heaven, by gaining the Son of Heaven one can become an enfeoffed lord, and by gaining a lord one can become a great officer.

"When an enfeoffed lord imperils the spirits of the land and grain, then the location of their altars is moved.

"When the sacrificial animals have been prepared, the millet and dishes have been purified, and the sacrificial offerings are presented in their proper season, but there are still floods and droughts, move the location of the altars of the land and grain."

[8B.14]

Spirits

Hao-sheng Pu-hai asked, "What kind of a person is Yüeh Cheng?" Mencius replied, "He is a good

person, a person of good faith." "What is meant by 'good' and 'good faith,' " Hao-sheng continued. Mencius replied, "Someone who is likable is called good, and someone imbued with goodness is called a person of good faith. Those who can fully develop those qualities are called beautiful; those who can brilliantly manifest that development are called great. Someone who is great and can transform things is called a sage, and those who are sagelike beyond ordinary understanding are called spirits."

[7B.25.7–8]

The Shaman's Profession

Mencius said, "How could it be that the arrow maker is possessed of less humanity than the maker of shields? Arrow makers are only worried about wounding people; shield makers are only concerned lest people become wounded. Such is the case also with the shaman and the coffin maker. Hence one must be cautious about choosing a profession."

[2A.7]

The Unmoving Mind
and Vital Force

K'ung-sun Ch'ou asked, "May I ask about your unmoving mind, and about the unmoving mind of Kao Tzu?" Mencius replied, "Kao Tzu says, 'What cannot be apprehended in words cannot be sought for in the mind, and what cannot be apprehended by the mind should not be sought for in the vital force.' Now I would allow that what cannot be apprehended by the mind should not be sought for in the vital force, but I would not allow that what cannot be apprehended in words cannot be sought for in the mind. The will is the captain of the vital force, and vital force suffuses the entire body. The will is of greater importance and is seconded by vital force. So I say maintain your will firmly without disrupting the vital force."

Ch'ou said, "Why do you say that the will is of greater importance and is seconded by vital force? And why should one maintain one's will firmly without disrupting the vital force?"

"If will is unified," Mencius replied, "then it

moves the vital force. When the vital force is unified, then it moves the will. For example, when people fall or run, the vital force turns and moves the mind."

"What are your strong points?" Ch'ou asked.

"I understand words," he replied, "and I am good at sustaining my flowing vital force."

"What is meant by 'flowing vital force'?"

"It is difficult to say," Mencius replied. "Vital force is exceedingly great and exceedingly strong. If one sustains it consistently and does not injure it, then it is suffused everywhere between heaven and earth. Vital force is espoused to righteousness and the Way, and without them it wastes away. It is generated by the accumulation of righteousness, but it is not derived from desultory acts of righteousness. If in the mind one has misgivings about one's actions, then one will waste away. Hence I have said that Kao Tzu has never understood righteousness, for he considers it something external."

[2A.9–16]

Hsün Tzu

Ritual is of central importance to the thought of Hsün Tzu (Xunzi; born ca. 312 B.C.E.?), a later contemporary of Mencius. His discourses on such subjects as governmental administration, ritual theory, and self-cultivation, unlike the aphorisms of Confucius or the dialogues of Mencius, are coherent and systematic treatises of some length. A native of the state of Chao near modern Shansi Province in north-central China, he later moved to the court of the intellectual center of Ch'i on the Shantung peninsula, where he was respected as one of its most distinguished scholars.

Like Mencius, Hsün Tzu draws on analogies from nature, but whereas Mencius had employed them to suggest the innate endowments of human beings, Hsün Tzu focuses instead on the unlimited possibilities of self-development. Frequent allusions to artisanry and crafts suggest the importance of the careful fashioning of the self. He presents an urgent curriculum that espouses embodying ancient learning in a contemporary context and that results in nothing less than sagehood. Rites, understood conceptually, are a vital aspect of both personal perfection and good governance; they allow human expressions of emotion and refinement to participate in the orderly progressions of the celestial and terrestrial realms. Humans may form a trinity with heaven and earth, but such a relationship involves the full realization of human potential, not the manipulation of the other two with mantic arts, that is, arts of divination. Sacrifice and divination are nothing more, and nothing less, than expressions of human refinement. Preternatural manifestations that prompted deprecatory exorcisms in earlier times need not concern those who live a measured life.

Human beings do not pray to heaven but complete it by according with their own heavenly endowments. Employing the vocabulary of bureaucratic administration, Hsün Tzu describes the human body as a government in miniature, ruled by the mind (the heavenly ruler), informed by the faculties (literally, "heavenly ministers"), and guided by a heavenly directive. It is the mind and its qualities of emptiness, tranquillity, and unity that allow human beings to apprehend the Way, a notion Hsün Tzu does not otherwise explain clearly. The Way is for the sage a balance, an implement that suggests centrality, a tool that frees the sage's vision from the impediments of opposites and distinctions.

Hsün Tzu is perhaps best known for propounding the view that human nature is evil, but as his essay on that topic falls toward the end of his collected writings, its importance should not be overstated. To say that human nature is evil is not to say that humans are entirely evil, for they still are possessed of a goodness that comes from conscious effort; they nevertheless require the transformations of learning. While Hsün Tzu and Mencius disagree on the beginnings of human existence, they nevertheless both agree that external circumstances influence its outcome.

These readings are selections from his treatises "Encouraging Learning," "On Heaven," "On Ritual," "Dispelling Obfuscation," and "Human Nature Is Evil."

"Encouraging Learning"

Honorable persons say that learning must never cease. Blue comes from the indigo plant but is bluer than the plant itself; ice comes from water but is colder than water itself. A piece of wood as straight as a marking line can be bent into a wheel with curves as round as those made by a compass, and when it dries out it does not become straight again; bending makes it so. Wood fashioned with a marking line can be straightened, and metal fashioned with a whetstone can be sharpened. If honorable persons study widely and daily reflect within themselves, then they can clarify their understanding and their conduct will be faultless. Unless one climbs a high mountain, one will never understand the height of heaven, and unless one looks down into deep valleys, one will never understand the depth of the earth. Unless one hears the words passed down from the ancient kings, one will never understand the greatness of study and inquiry. The children of the foreign people of the Han, Yüeh, and Mo cry at birth just as we do, but as they grow they develop different customs. It is what they are taught that makes them so. As the *Odes* says,

Ah, you honored ones!
Do not be always placidly secure,
Complacently respectful at your stations,
But hold dear what is upright and direct
And spirits will hear of it
And grant you great blessings.

No spirit is greater than the transformative Way; no blessing is more enduring than to have no misfortunes.

I once spent an entire day thinking, but it could not compare to one moment of study; I once stood on tiptoe to see afar, but it could not compare to climbing a mountain to see farther. If one waves from atop a high mountain, then even though one's arm is not actually any longer, one can still be seen from farther away. If one shouts in the same direction the wind is blowing, then even though one's voice is not actually any more forceful, one can be heard

much more clearly. If one avails oneself of carriages or horses, one will not have actually improved one's own feet by doing so, yet one can travel a thousand leagues. If one uses a boat or a ship, then even though one cannot swim, one can traverse rivers and streams. Honorable people are not different from other people at birth: it is just that they are better at making use of things. . . .

Where does learning begin? Where does it end? In terms of particulars, one begins by reciting the classics and ends by reading the *Rites;* in terms of larger meanings, one begins by being a civil person and ends by becoming a sage. If one genuinely accumulates effort over a long period of time, then one can enter into things. Learning continues until death, and only then does one stop. The particulars of study end within certain parameters, but the larger meanings cannot be set aside even for an instant. Those who follow this course can really be considered human beings; those who do not are like birds and beasts. The *Book of History* relates matters of governance, the *Book of Odes* describes the articulation of sounds, and the *Rites* is the fundamental record of basic standards and their many different applications. Learning extends to the *Rites* and stops there: this is called the epitome of the Way and of virtue. The reverence and refinement of the *Rites,* the centrality and harmony of the *Book of Music,* the breadth of the *Odes* and *History,* and the subtlety of the *Spring and Autumn Annals* constitute a finished completeness in heaven and earth.

The learning of honorable persons enters their ears, accumulates in their minds, spreads throughout their four limbs, and takes shape in both action and tranquillity. Their slightest words and subtlest movements can be considered standards worth emulating. The learning of small-minded people, however, enters their ears and comes out their mouths. Since only four inches separate mouth and ear, how can that learning suffice to enhance a seven-foot frame? In antiquity, learning was done for one's own self, but today it is done only for the approbation of others. The learning of an honorable person is to enhance one's own self, but the learning of the small-minded person is like that of birds and animals. . . .

For learning, nothing is more advantageous than associating closely with others. The *Rites* and *Music* provide standards but few explanations; the *Odes* and *History* are ancient but not always relevant; the *Spring and Autumn Annals* is concise but not engaging. If one models oneself on the practices of others and on the explanations of honorable people, then one will be widely respected in the world. So I say that for learning, nothing is more advantageous than associating closely with others.

Of the paths of learning, nothing is quicker than to love such people; the next best is to value ritual. If one can do neither, then one's learning will be nothing but a fragmented miscellany derived from the *Odes* and *History,* and one would die as nothing more than a vulgar scholar. For those who want to model themselves on the ancient kings and base themselves on humanity and righteousness, then ritual is the warp and woof of the path they must take. Consider picking up a fur coat by the collar: it is immeasurably easier if one grasps it with all five fingers. Following not ritual formulations but only the *Odes* and *History* is like fathoming the depth of a river with one's finger, pounding grain with the point of a lance, or eating out of a tall pot with a pointed awl. It simply cannot be done. Those who value ritual, even though they might not yet clearly understand it, can emulate people of civility. But those who do not value ritual, then even though they may be otherwise perceptive, merely become pedantic scholars.

"On Heaven"

Heaven's acts are constant: they did not make Emperor Yao prevail, and they did not make Emperor Chieh perish. Those who respond to heaven with good governance will find auspiciousness; those who respond to it with chaos will experience calamities. Those who are strong in fundamental things and are measured in their expenditures cannot be impoverished by heaven,

and those who manage their sustenance and provisions in a diligent and timely way cannot be indisposed by it. Those who cultivate the Way consistently cannot be beset by misfortunes from heaven: floods and droughts cannot cause famine; excessive cold and heat cannot bring epidemics; preternatural manifestations cannot cause calamities. But those who are confused about what is fundamentally important and who make extravagant expenditures cannot be enriched by heaven: even if they live frugally and their exertions are few, heaven cannot make them whole. When they try to follow two ways at the same time or tread mistaken byways, heaven cannot bring them auspiciousness. Neither floods nor droughts occur, yet famine appears; neither cold nor heat spreads across the land, but epidemics begin; no preternatural signs manifest themselves, yet calamities happen. These people experience the same seasons that well-governed ages do, but the misfortunes and disasters they encounter are uniquely their own. Yet they cannot revile heaven, for it is just their own actions that have made things so. One who clearly discerns what is of heaven and what is of the human realm can be called a perfected person.

To accomplish without action and to apprehend without striving: such are the operations of heaven. This being the case, perfected persons are profound yet not excessively deliberative, great yet not excessively proficient, sensitive yet not excessively perspicacious. So it is said that they do not compete with the operations of heaven. Heaven has its seasons; the earth, its resources; and human beings, good governance. Hence it is said that they can constitute a trinity. But if human beings reject their own part of the triad and covet the prerogatives of the other two, then they are greatly mistaken.

Stars follow one another in array as they revolve, the sun and moon shine in oscillation, and the seasons wait their turn; yin and yang undergo great transformations, wind and rain spread through all quarters, and all things attain a fullness and are generated forth, each obtaining the sustenance for its own completion. One does not actually see these processes but sees only their fruition, and thus these are known as spirits. One knows that something completes things, but no one understands its formless powers, and this something is called heaven. Only the sage makes no attempt to understand heaven.

When the operations of heaven are established and its efforts come to fruition, then form is complete and the spirit is generated. Like, dislike, pleasure, anger, sorrow, and joy are lodged there, and these are called the heavenly emotions. Ear, eye, nose, mouth, and bodily form are connected, yet each has unique capabilities; these are the heavenly faculties. The mind abides in the central cavity and governs the five faculties, and it is called the heavenly ruler. Resources of different kinds are used to sustain one's own kind, and this is known as heavenly sustenance. To accord with one's own kind is a blessing; to go against it, misfortune. This is the heavenly directive. To becloud the heavenly ruler, confuse the heavenly faculties, spurn heavenly sustenance, turn against the heavenly directive, and reject the heavenly emotions is to destroy the efforts of heaven. This is a great calamity. Sages clarify the heavenly ruler, rectify the heavenly faculties, provide for heavenly sustenance, follow the heavenly directive, sustain the heavenly emotions, and complete the efforts of heaven. Thus they understand both what should be done and what should be left undone, and heaven and earth minister to them and all things serve them. Their conduct is well ordered, their sustenance is provided, and they live unharmed. This is what is meant by understanding heaven. . . .

When stars fall or trees cry out, everyone becomes afraid, saying, "What was that?" Nothing, I say, for they are only the mutations of heaven and earth, the transformations of yin and yang, or things that simply rarely happen. They may be considered strange, but not fearful. Eclipses of the sun and moon, untimely wind and rain, and occasional appearances of strange stars have occurred continually throughout every age. But if leaders are clear-minded and their directives are fair, then even if all these things

occur at once, no harm will result. If leaders are unenlightened and their directives are unsound, however, they will not be advantaged even if none of them occurs. Stars falling or trees crying out are only the mutations of heaven and earth, the transformations of the yin and yang, or are simply things that rarely happen. They may be considered strange, but not fearful. . . .

One might ask why it rains when the Yü rain sacrifice is performed. I say that there is no reason, for even if one does not perform the sacrifice it still will rain. When people try to rescue the sun or moon from being eclipsed, perform the rain sacrifice when there are floods or droughts, or make great decisions only after divining with the tortoiseshell or milfoil stalks, it is not because they are trying to get actual results by doing so, for these are just expressions of refined culture. The honorable person considers these expressions of refined culture, but the common people believe them the work of spirits. Considering it culture is auspicious; considering it the work of spirits is inauspicious.

Nothing in heaven shines brighter than the sun and moon; nothing on earth shines brighter than water and fire; no objects shine brighter than pearls and jade; and in the human realm, nothing shines brighter than rites and righteousness. Unless the sun and moon are on high, their light does not shine brightly; unless water and fire accumulate in sufficient quantity, they shed only a weak glow; unless pearls and jade are lustrous, kings and dukes will not treasure them. If a state does not enhance itself with rites and righteousness, then its accomplishments and reputation will remain unknown. Human beings' mandated fate lies with heaven, but a state's mandate lies in ritual. Leaders become true kings by valuing ritual and respecting worthy people; they become only hegemons if they value administrative standards and care for the people. But if they covet profit and are merely cunning, they perish, completely lost in the perils of intrigues and plots.

Should one glorify heaven and yearn for it? Better to cultivate things and manage them. Should one comply with heaven and praise it?

Better to manage the mandate of heaven and avail oneself of it. Should one await the seasons in anticipation? Better to resonate with them and accelerate their productivity. Should one rely on things to multiply of themselves? Better to transform them with one's own skills and abilities. Should one consider things only at face value? Better to understand them from within and thus not lose them. Should one find the source that generates all things? Better to find what brings them to completion. If one misjudges what is appropriate for human beings and yearns for what is of heaven, one will lose emotional resonances with the ten thousand things of this world.

"On Ritual"

How did rites originate? I say that people are born with desires, and if they do not obtain what they desire at first, they will continue to pursue them. But if in this pursuit they follow no limitations or parameters, they will invariably begin struggling with one another, and conflict leads to chaos, and chaos brings impoverishment. The ancient kings, abhorring chaos, created the formulations of ritual and righteousness to distribute things among the people, to give sustenance to their desires, and to give them the means for satisfying them. So desires did not suffer because of a lack of material things, and material things were not depleted because of desires, and both desires and material things were sustained and developed. This is how rights originated.

Ritual is sustenance. The mouth is sustained by the meat of livestock fed on hay and grain, and by the taste of grain and millet, all flavored and seasoned with spices. The nose is sustained by aromatic orchids and fragrant plants; the eye, by the ornamentation of sculpture, inlay, and embroidery. The ear is sustained by drums, bells, flutes, stone chimes, zithers, and pipes; the body, by capacious rooms and chambers, beds, mats, and armrests. Thus ritual is sustenance. . . .

Ritual has three fundamental bases. Heaven and earth are the basis of life; ancestors, the basis of one's own kin; and rulers and teachers, the basis of good governance. Without heaven and earth, how could there be life? Without ancestors, where would one come from? Without rulers and teachers, how could there be good governance? If any of these three is absent, human beings will have no rest. With ritual one serves heaven above and earth below, reveres one's ancestors, and esteems rulers and teachers. These are the three bases of ritual. . . .

Rites begin with plainness, are completed with cultured refinement, and conclude with joyfulness. When everything is prepared to perfection, emotions and refinement are both fully expressed. In the next best kind of ritual, emotions and refinement alternate, and yet the next best kind inclines toward emotion and everything returns to a great unity. Heaven and earth are in harmony, the sun and moon shine, the four seasons find their proper order, stars and planets move, rivers flow, all things prosper, like and dislike find their due measure, and pleasure and anger find appropriate expression. Everything below is in accord, everything above is bright, all things change but are not disordered. Those who depart from this are lost. Such are the perfections of ritual! When rites are highly valued and are developed to the epitome of perfection, nothing in the world can detract from or add to them, and roots and branches are in accord and ends resonate with their beginnings. Refinement, when perfected, can be expressed in its varied distinctions, and perceptions, when perfected, can explain all things. Those in this world who follow ritual will govern well, but those who do not will find chaos; those who follow it will be restfully secure, but those who do not will find themselves in great danger. Those who follow it will survive, but those who do not will perish. Small-minded people cannot fathom these things.

"Dispelling Obfuscation"

Sages understand the hazards of the development of the mind and see the perils of various obfuscations and hindrances. But for sages there is no desire or hatred, beginning or end, near or far, broad or shallow, ancient or modern. They purvey all things and suspend them from a balance, and thus the many differences between things create no obfuscations to confuse their formulations. What is this balance? It is the Way. The mind must understand the Way, for if it does not, then it will not accept the Way but will accept what is contrary to the Way. . . .

The essentials of good governance lie in understanding the Way. How do people understand the Way? With the mind, which is empty, unified, and tranquil. The mind always has things stored in it yet can be considered empty; it is always full yet can be considered unified; the mind is always active yet can be considered tranquil. People are born with understanding, and this understanding has various intentions. Even though intentions are stored within the mind it is still considered empty, for what has already been stored does not impede the reception of new things. When the mind is born it has understanding, and this understanding encompasses many different things. Different things can be known at the same time, and when two things are known at the same time, they become one. That they do not interfere with one another is called unity. When the mind sleeps it dreams, and in daydreams it wanders about, creating its own imaginings; it is always active. Nevertheless, it can be considered tranquil, for it does not allow dreams and imaginings to confuse its own understanding. If there are those who have not yet attained the Way but are still seeking it, explain emptiness, unity, and tranquillity to them.

"Human Nature Is Evil"

Human nature is evil; its goodness is conscious effort. The nature of people today is such that from birth they covet profit. To accommodate their covetousness they struggle and fight for their lives, and courtesy and civility vanish. From birth they bear violent hatreds, and to accommodate those hatreds they resort to violence and banditry, and loyalty and good faith disappear. From birth they have the desires of the ear and eye and fondness for sound and color; to accommodate those desires they resort to wanton behavior, and refined principles of ritual and righteousness evaporate. If people follow their natures and accommodate their emotions, struggling and fighting will invariably ensue, and they will transgress their stations in life, upset principles, and turn to violence. Only with the transformations of standards and teachers and the ways of ritual and righteousness can courtesy and civility appear, and under those circumstances people can develop refined culture and principles and turn to good governance. If one looks at it this way, then it is clear that human nature is evil, and that goodness is conscious effort.

A bent piece of wood can only be straightened by steaming, and a dull piece of metal can only be sharpened by grinding it against a whetstone. Now considering that human nature is evil, it can only be rectified with standards and teachers, and it can only be well governed with the application of ritual and righteousness. If people have no standards or teachers, they will waver perilously and lack rectitude; without rites or righteousness they will be intractable, disorderly, and badly governed. In antiquity the sage kings perceived all this. They initiated rituals and righteousness and formulated standards and various measures to straighten and enhance human nature and emotions; they did this to rectify them, to train and transform them, and to guide them. Thus everything was well governed and everything accorded with the Way. People today who are transformed by teachers and standards, who develop refined culture and learning, who follow the ways of ritual and righteousness, become honorable persons. Those who just go along with their natures and emotions, are satisfied with wantonness, and go contrary to ritual, are small-minded people. If one looks at it this way, it is clear that human nature is evil.

Mencius said the fact that human beings learn is because the nature is good. I say this is not so, and this indicates that he did not understand human nature and did not perceive the differences between human nature and conscious effort. The nature is given by heaven; it can be neither learned nor devised. But rites and righteousness were produced by the sages, and hence are things that human beings can learn and do; they can be devised and brought to completion. What is within human beings that can be neither learned nor devised is called the nature; what is within human beings that can be learned and done, that can be devised and brought to completion, is called conscious effort. These are the differences between the nature and conscious effort. . . .

Someone once asked, "If human nature is evil, then how were ritual and righteousness generated?" I responded by saying that ritual and righteousness were produced by the conscious effort of sages, not by human nature. Now a ceramist molds clay into utensils, but these objects are generated by the artisan's conscious effort, not by human nature. Some artisans carve wood into utensils, but these also are produced by the artisan's conscious effort, not by human nature. Sages brought together their thoughts and reflections and fashioned conscious effort to develop general principles; they then produced rites and righteousness and originated standards and measures. Thus rituals, righteousness, standards, and measures were produced by the conscious effort of the sages, not by human nature.

The *Tao-te ching* of Lao Tzu

Perhaps no other classic is as well known outside of China as the *Tao-te ching*, the "Classic of the Way and of Virtue," a work traditionally attributed to a legendary figure named Lao Tzu (Laozi). "Tao" means "the Way"; a term that appears in many ancient texts, it is the main focus of this particular one. "Te" is virtue, an inner power and integrity; "ching" means simply a classical text. Tradition holds that the work was written in the sixth century B.C.E., but other estimates place it as late as three centuries thereafter. The identity of Lao Tzu is equally uncertain, and while some believe he is a fabrication of legend, others accept the traditional biography of his life. According to that account, he was a native of Ch'u, now modern Honan Province in south-central China. He served as the keeper of an archives but in later life took leave of the world and headed west for parts unknown. At the outer gateposts of civilization, the gatekeeper asked Lao Tzu to write a book for him, and in response Lao Tzu composed the *Tao-te ching*.

The passages selected here relate some of the most important concepts of the *Tao-te ching*: the qualities of the Tao itself, complementary "opposites," water, the sage, nonaction, the "uncarved block," the valley, and the female. The opening passage might be compared with the opening lines of Genesis, where a divinity creates a universe by separating night from darkness, land from water, and heaven from earth; it creates forms from the formless by the act of speaking, by in a sense creating names. A world is thus fashioned by creating separations, divisions, and distinctions. The world of the *Tao-te ching*, however, has no creator divinities but only a Nameless origin; the Named, however, is also acknowledged. According to the *Tao*, even now the world actually entertains no separations and distinctions, for there is at once being and nonbeing, which are but different names for the same thing. Seeming opposites are not produced by a third party but produce and define one another, and as they produce one another, they cannot truly be opposites.

The primal void of Genesis became dry land and water, but Lao Tzu enjoys voidness and nonbeing for their own sakes and even finds them useful: the utility of a vessel lies not in the clay of a pot but in the empty space that allows it to hold water. Hsün Tzu found in the potter's ability to make clay vessels a metaphor for conscious activity, but Lao Tzu finds in clay vessels a metaphor for the entire world.

The best person, for Lao Tzu, is like water, which benefits all things and does not shun the lowest places of the world. To Mencius, water was a metaphor for the goodness of human nature, but Lao Tzu questions even the notion of goodness and sees potential disaster stemming from conventional understandings of humanity, righteousness, and propriety (ritual). Lao Tzu praises the sage who mysteriously accomplishes things by *wu-wei,* or "nonaction," the ability to act without competing with things, just as water, the softest of all things, wears away rock. He advocates not Hsün Tzu's straightening and steaming of wood but instead advocates returning to the simplicity of the "uncarved block," or "uncarved wood," a wholeness without distinctions. Lao Tzu praises those who, instead of seeking prominence, become the low ravines and valleys of the world and thus maintain their inner virtue. The spirit of the valley is the female, the soft and yielding force that overcomes the male force of direct action.

The *Tao-te ching* is commonly divided into eighty-one verses, and the passages here follow that numbering system.

1

The Tao that can be told of is not the
  eternal Tao;
The name that can be named is not the
  eternal name.
The Nameless is the origin of Heaven
  and Earth;
The Named is the mother of all things.

Therefore let there always be non-being,
  so we may see their subtlety,
And let there always be being, so we
  may see their outcome.
The two are the same,
But after they are produced, they have
  different names.
They both may be called deep and
  profound.
Deeper and more profound,
The door of all subtleties!

2

When the people of the world all know
  beauty as beauty,
  There arises the recognition of
  ugliness.
When they all know the good as good,
  There arises the recognition of evil.
Therefore:

  Being and non-being produce each
  other;
  Difficult and easy complete each
  other;
  Long and short contrast each other;
  High and low distinguish each other;
  Sound and voice harmonize each
  other;
  Front and behind accompany each
  other.

  Therefore the sage manages affairs
  without action
  And spreads doctrines without words.
  All things arise, and he does not turn
  away from them.
  He produces them but does not take
  possession of them.

He acts but does not rely on his own
  ability.
He accomplishes his task but does not
  claim credit for it.
It is precisely because he does not
  claim credit that his
  accomplishment remains with
  him.

4

Tao is empty (like a bowl).
It may be used but its capacity is never
  exhausted.
It is bottomless, perhaps the ancestor of
  all things.
It blunts its sharpness,
It unties its tangles.
It softens its light.
It becomes one with the dusty world.
Deep and still, it appears to exist
  forever.
I do not know whose son it is.
It seems to have existed before the Lord.

6

The spirit of the valley never dies.
  It is called the subtle and profound
  female.
The gate of the subtle and profound
  female
  Is the root of Heaven and Earth.
It is continuous, and seems to be always
  existing.
Use it and you will never wear it out.

8

The best (man) is like water.
Water is good; it benefits all things and
  does not compete with them.
It dwells in (lowly) places that all
  disdain.
This is why it is so near to Tao.
(The best man) in his dwelling loves the
  earth.
In his heart, he loves what is profound.

In his associations, he loves humanity.
In his words, he loves faithfulness.
In government, he loves order.
In handling affairs, he loves
    competence.
In his activities, he loves timeliness.
It is because he does not compete that he
    is without reproach.

11

Thirty spokes are united around the hub
    to make a wheel,
    But it is on its non-being that the
        utility of the carriage depends.
Clay is molded to form a utensil,
    But it is on its non-being that the
        utility of the utensil depends.
Doors and windows are cut out to make
    a room,
    But it is on its non-being that the
        utility of the room depends.
Therefore turn being into advantage, and
    turn non-being into utility.

14

We look at it and do not see it;
    Its name is The Invisible.
We listen to it and do not hear it;
    Its name is The Inaudible.
We touch it and do not find it;
    Its name is The Subtle (formless).
These three cannot be further inquired
    into,
And hence merge into one.
Going up high, it is not bright, and
    coming down low, it is not
    dark.
Infinite and boundless, it cannot be
    given any name;
It reverts to nothingness.
This is called shape without shape,
Form without objects.
It is The Vague and Elusive.
Meet it and you will not see its head.
Follow it and you will not see its back.
Hold on to the Tao of old in order to

master the things of the
    present.
From this one may know the primeval
    beginning (of the universe).
This is called the bond of Tao.

21

The all-embracing quality of the great
    virtue follows alone from the
    Tao.
The thing that is called Tao is eluding
    and vague.
    Vague and eluding, there is in it the
        form.
    Eluding and vague, in it are things.
Deep and obscure, in it is the essence.
The essence is very real; in it are
    evidences.
From the time of old until now, its name
    (manifestations) ever remains.
By which we may see the beginning of
    all things.
How do I know that the beginnings of
    all things are so?
Through this (Tao).

28

He who knows the male and keeps to
    the female
Becomes the ravine of the world.
Being the ravine of the world,
He will never depart from eternal virtue,
But returns to the state of infancy.
He who knows the white and yet keeps
    to the black
Becomes the model for the world.
Being the model for the world,
He will never deviate from eternal
    virtue,
But returns to the state of the non-
    ultimate.
He who knows glory but keeps to
    humility
Becomes the valley of the world.
Being the valley of the world,
He will be proficient in eternal virtue,

And returns to the state of simplicity
(uncarved wood).
When the uncarved wood is broken up,
it is turned into concrete
things.
But when the sage uses it, he becomes
the leading official.
Therefore the great ruler does not cut
up.

38

The man of superior virtue is not
(conscious of) his virtue,
And in this way he really possesses
virtue.
The man of inferior virtue never loses
(sight of) his virtue,
And in this way he loses his virtue.
The man of superior virtue takes no
action, but has no ulterior
motive to do so.
The man of inferior virtue takes action,
and has an ulterior motive to
do so.
The man of superior humanity takes
action, but has no ulterior
motive to do so.
The man of superior righteousness takes
action, but has no ulterior
motive to do so.
The man of superior propriety takes
action,
And when people do not respond to it,
he will stretch his arms and
force it on them.
Therefore when Tao is lost, only then
does the doctrine of virtue
arise.
When virtue is lost, only then does the
doctrine of humanity arise.
When humanity is lost, only then does
the doctrine of righteousness
arise.
When righteousness is lost, only then
does the doctrine of propriety
arise.

Now, propriety is a superficial
expression of loyalty and
faithfulness, and the beginning
of disorder.
Those who are the first to know have the
flowers of Tao but are the
beginning of ignorance.
For this reason the great man dwells in
the thick, and does not rest
with the thin.
He dwells in the fruit, and does not rest
with the flower.
Therefore he rejects the one, and accepts
the other.

43

The softest things in the world overcome
the hardest things in the world.
Non-being penetrates that in which there
is no space.
Through this I know the advantage of
taking no action.
Few in the world can understand the
teaching without words
and the advantage of taking no action.

81

True words are not beautiful;
Beautiful words are not true.
A good man does not argue;
He who argues is not a good man.
A wise man has no extensive
knowledge;
He who has extensive knowledge is
not a wise man.
The sage does not accumulate for
himself.
The more he uses for others, the more
he has himself.
The more he gives to others, the more
he possesses of his own.
The Way of Heaven is to benefit others
and not to injure.
The Way of the sage is to act but not to
compete.

Chuang Tzu

Chuang Tzu's (Zhuangzi; 369?–286? B.C.E.) world is not an ordered and measured realm of righteousness and humanity but a world of infinitely transformed perspectives, of perceptions that see a cosmos hidden within the cosmos, of perceptions that find true values in the remnants and cast-offs discounted by those who entertain conventional values. The enigmatic anecdotes of the *Chuang Tzu* evoke a vision of perception found not in some transcendent realm but in the very cracks of ordinary existence. This vision can be apprehended in the natural world with the ears and eyes, but those blinded and deafened by a fragmented understanding that distinguishes between the words "this" and "that" can never find the hinge of the Way that lies between them, never hear the piping of heaven, and never understand the virtue of the holy person. Virtually nothing is known of Chuang Tzu's life, except that his given name was Chou and that he was a contemporary of Mencius.

Confucius's encounters with recluses only reconfirmed his own view that human society, no matter how troubled, was his proper environment; Chuang Tzu's ideal person was a holy man (*shen jen,* literally, "spirit person"), one who leaves the human realm far behind in celestial journeys, mounted on clouds and dragons. In the chapter "Free and Easy Wandering," Chuang Tzu describes the holy man. Unbound by the five relationships and not engaged in government service, such persons do not eat the millet and grain bestowed by Hou Chi and thus are free of both the labors and the ritual obligations of the material world in an agricultural society. Their powers stem from the development of nonmaterial forces by which they nevertheless benefit society. Such spiritlike people are perhaps what Mencius meant by sages who were sagelike beyond all understanding. Figures similar to Chuang Tzu's holy man appear frequently throughout the spiritual literature of China.

Hsün Tzu had assured people that the strange cries of trees were no cause for alarm, but Chuang Tzu hears in them the piping of heaven and earth that sounds through all things and gives each thing its own identity; its movements recall the restorative breaths of night and day on Mencius's Ox Mountain. For Chuang Tzu, trees not only cry but talk and communicate true values to human beings; the serrate oak at the village shrine, a cast-off whose wood is rejected by carpenters such as those who in the *Hsün Tzu* might otherwise steam and straighten it, appears in a dream to Carpenter Shih to reveal the usefulness of being useless. People who make themselves useful for government service risk the dangers of intrigue and unjust punishment; better to be useless to others, useful to oneself, and thus survive. Lao Tzu advocated the sage who governed by nonaction, but Chuang Tzu favored leaving politics altogether. That the oak appears to the carpenter in a dream is not necessarily unusual, for in the *Tso Chuan* a spirit talks to Duke Ch'eng in a dream, and dream divination was a profession recorded in the *Rites of Chou*. The counsel given by the oak tree is in a sense similar to the advice that might be offered by the hexagram "Retreat" in the *Book of Changes:* disengage from social activity.

The *Chuang Tzu* is peopled not with Confucius's honorable persons but with fictional characters such as Shu-shan No-Toes, an outcast who has suffered the punitive amputations imposed by the legal system. Thinkers such as Hsün Tzu offered ritual and education as preventive measures to curb potential violence but provided no solace for its actual victims. Shu-shan No-Toes's personal encounter with brutality has given him insight into what is more valuable than a foot, perhaps into what it was that Mencius considered more valuable than life itself. In an imaginary encounter with Confucius, Shu-shan becomes disenchanted with the sage's limited conventionality and complains to Lao Tan (Lao Tzu), who suggests that Confucius is still shackled by a limited perspective that does not see the wholeness underlying both death and life; Confucius has thus been "punished" by heaven. Through the character of Lao Tan, Chuang Tzu contrasts the sagelike ideal of Confucius with the idea of the perfected man, or perfected person, which may be understood as another name for the holy man. Chuang Tzu creates another unlikely role model in the figure of Cook Ting, who has found the Way in the spaces between the joints of the oxen he butchers for a living. His extraordinary perception and skills allow him to move effortlessly through life and become a model for kings to emulate. The *Book of Rites* in the "General Principles of Sacrifice" had described learning and instruction as qualities that rulers dispense to their subordinates, but here the hierarchy of student and teacher is completely reversed.

Chuang Tzu's vision of undifferentiated wholeness is epitomized by the character of Hun-tun, or "wonton," whose name suggests a dumpling-shaped character. When his friends Sudden and Brief try to bring order, conformity, and symmetry to his unbroken shape, he perishes. Order and symmetry hence become associated with death; formless disarray, with life, and the discrete order and progression characteristic of texts such as the "Great Learning" become threats to life itself. Chuang Tzu values not the polish of refined culture taught by Confucius but instead esteems the Great Clod, a mysterious force that breathes out wind, or vital force *(ch'i)*, whose name recalls the "uncarved block" of Lao Tzu.

Chuang Tzu, also known as Chuang Chou, perceives that this undifferentiated wholeness undergoes constant transformations, and thus he is not surprised to find himself suddenly transformed into a butterfly in a dream where he is unable to distinguish between waking and dreaming life, or between his own identity and that of a butterfly. The transformation of self accomplished with study, inquiry, deliberation, and earnest effort in the "Centrality and Equilibrium" is achieved here with the natural effortlessness of a caterpillar becoming a butterfly.

The Holy Man

Chien Wu said to Lien Shu, "I was listening to Chieh Yü's talk—big and nothing to back it up, going on and on without turning around. I was completely dumfounded at his words—no more end than the Milky Way, wild and wide of the mark, never coming near human affairs!"

"What were his words like?" asked Lien Shu.

"He said that there is a Holy Man living on faraway Ku-she Mountain, with skin like ice or snow, and gentle and shy like a young girl. He doesn't eat the five grains, but sucks the wind, drinks the dew, climbs up on the clouds and mist, rides a flying dragon, and wanders beyond the four seas. By concentrating his spirit, he can protect creatures from sickness and plague and make the harvest plentiful. I thought this was all insane and refused to believe it."

"You would!" said Lien Shu. "We can't expect a blind man to appreciate beautiful patterns or a deaf man to listen to bells and drums. And blindness and deafness are not confined to the body alone—the understanding has them too, as your words just now have shown. This man, with this virtue of his, is about to embrace the ten thousand things and roll them into one. Though the age calls for reform, why should he wear himself out over the affairs of the world? There is nothing that can harm this man. Though flood waters pile up to the sky, he will not drown. Though a great drought melts metal and stone and scorches the earth and hills, he will not be burned. From his dust and leavings alone you could mold a Yao or a Shun! Why should he consent to bother about mere things?"

The Piping of Heaven

Tzu-ch'i of South Wall sat leaning on his armrest, staring up at the sky and breathing—vacant and far away, as though he'd lost his companion. Yen Ch'eng Tzu-yu, who was standing by his side in attendance, said, "What is this? Can you really make the body like a withered tree and the mind like dead ashes? The man leaning on the armrest now is not the one who leaned on it before!"

Tzu-ch'i said, "You do well to ask the question, Yen. Now I have lost myself. Do you understand that? You hear the piping of men, but you haven't heard the piping of earth. Or if you've heard the piping of earth, you haven't heard the piping of Heaven!"

Tzu-yu said, "May I venture to ask what this means?"

Tzu-ch'i said, "The Great Clod belches out breath and its name is wind. So long as it doesn't come forth, nothing happens. But when it does, then ten thousand hollows begin crying wildly. Can't you hear them, long drawn out? In the mountain forests that lash and sway, there are huge trees a hundred spans around with hollows and openings like noses, like mouths, like ears, like jugs, like cups, like mortars, like rifts, like ruts. They roar like waves, whistle like arrows, screech, gasp, cry, wail, moan, and howl, those in the lead calling out *yeee!*, those behind calling out *yuuu!* In a gentle breeze they answer faintly, but in a full gale the chorus is gigantic. And when the fierce wind has passed on, then all the hollows are empty again. Have you never seen the tossing and trembling that goes on?"

Tzu-yu said, "By the piping of earth, then, you mean simply [the sound of] these hollows, and by the piping of man [the sound of] flutes and whistles. But may I ask about the piping of Heaven?"

Tzu-ch'i said, "Blowing on the ten thousand things in a different way, so that each can be itself—all take what they want for themselves, but who does the sounding?"

This and That

Words are not just wind. Words have something to say. But if what they have to say is not fixed, then do they really say something? Or do they say nothing? People suppose that words are different from the peeps of baby birds, but is there any difference, or isn't there? What does the Way rely upon, that we have true and false? What do words rely upon, that we have right and wrong? How can the Way go away and not exist? How can words exist and not be acceptable? When the Way relies on little accomplishments and words rely on vain show, then we have the rights and wrongs of the Confucians and the Mo-ists. What one calls right the other calls wrong; what one calls wrong the other calls right. But if we want to right their wrongs and wrong their rights, then the best thing to use is clarity.

Everything has its "that," everything has its "this." From the point of view of "that" you cannot see it, but through understanding you can know it. So I say, "that" comes out of "this" and "this" depends on "that"—which is to say that "this" and "that" give birth to each other. But where there is birth there must be death; where there is death there must be birth. Where there is acceptability there must be unacceptability; where there is unacceptability there must be acceptability. Where there is recognition of right there must be recognition of wrong; where there is recognition of wrong there must be recognition of right. Therefore the sage does not proceed in such a way, but illuminates all in the light of Heaven. He too recognizes a "this," but a "this" which is also "that," a "that" which is also "this." His "that" has both a right and a wrong in it; his "this" too has both a right and a wrong in it. So, in fact, does he still have a "this" and "that"? Or does he in fact no longer have a "this" and "that"? A state in which "this" and "that" no longer find their opposites is called the hinge of the Way. When the hinge is fitted into the socket, it can respond endlessly. Its right then is a single endlessness and its wrong too is a single endlessness. So I say, the best thing to use is clarity.

Butterfly Dream

Once Chuang Chou dreamt he was a butterfly, a butterfly flitting and fluttering around, happy with himself and doing as he pleased. He didn't know he was Chuang Chou. Suddenly he woke up and there he was, solid and unmistakable Chuang Chou. But he didn't know if he was Chuang Chou who had dreamt he was a butterfly, or a butterfly dreaming he was Chuang Chou. Between Chuang Chou and a butterfly there must be *some* distinction! This is called the Transformation of Things.

Cook Ting

Cook Ting was cutting up an ox for Lord Wen-hui. At every touch of his hand, every heave of his shoulder, every move of his feet, every thrust of his knee—zip! zoop! He slithered the knife along with a zing, and all was in perfect rhythm, as though he were performing the dance of the Mulberry Grove or keeping time to the Ching-shou music.

"Ah, this is marvelous!" said Lord Wen-hui. "Imagine skill reaching such heights!"

Cook Ting laid down his knife and replied, "What I care about is the Way, which goes beyond skill. When I first began cutting up oxen, all I could see was the ox itself. After three years I no longer saw the whole ox. And now—now I go at it by spirit and don't look with my eyes. Perception and understanding have come to a stop and spirit moves where it wants. I go along with the natural makeup, strike in the big hollows, guide the knife through the big openings, and follow things as they are. So I never touch the smallest ligament or tendon, much less a main joint.

"A good cook changes his knife once a year—because he cuts. A mediocre cook changes his knife once a month—because he hacks. I've had this knife of mine for nineteen years and I've cut up thousands of oxen with it, and yet the blade is as good as though it had just come from the grindstone. There are spaces between the joints, and the blade of the knife has really no thickness. If you insert what has no thickness into such spaces, then there's plenty of room—more than enough for the blade to play about in. That's why after nineteen years the blade of my knife is still as good as when it first came from the grindstone.

"However, whenever I come to a complicated place, I size up the difficulties, tell myself to watch out and be careful, keep my eyes on what I'm doing, work very slowly, and move the knife with the greatest subtlety, until—flop! the whole thing comes apart like a clod of earth crumbling to the ground. I stand there holding the knife and look all around me, completely satisfied and reluctant to move on, and then I wipe off the knife and put it away."

"Excellent!" said Lord Wen-hui. "I have heard the words of Cook Ting and learned how to care for life!"

Carpenter Shih and the Usefulness of Uselessness

Carpenter Shih went to Ch'i and, when he got to Crooked Shaft, he saw a serrate oak standing by the village shrine. It was broad enough to shelter several thousand oxen and measured a hundred spans around, towering above the hills. The lowest branches were eighty feet from the ground, and a dozen or so of them could have been made into boats. There were so many sightseers that the place looked like a fair, but the carpenter didn't even glance around and went on his way without stopping. His apprentice stood staring for a long time and then ran after Carpenter Shih and said, "Since I first took up my ax and followed you, Master, I have never seen timber as beautiful as this. But you don't even bother to look, and go right on without stopping. Why is that?"

"Forget it—say no more!" said the carpenter. "It's a worthless tree! Make boats out of it and they'd sink; make coffins and they'd rot in no time. Use it for doors and it would sweat sap like pine; use it for posts and the worms would eat them up. It's not a timber tree—there's nothing it can be used for. That's how it got to be that old!"

After Carpenter Shih had returned home, the oak tree appeared to him in a dream and said, "What are you comparing me with? Are you comparing me with those useful trees? The cherry apple, the pear, the orange, the citron, the rest of those fructiferous trees and shrubs—as soon as their fruit is ripe, they are torn apart and subjected to abuse. Their big limbs are broken off, their little limbs are yanked around. Their utility makes life miserable for them, and so they don't get to finish out the years Heaven gave them, but are cut off in mid-journey. They bring it on themselves—the pulling and tearing of the common mob. And it's the same way with all other things.

"As for me, I've been trying a long time to be of no use, and now that I'm about to die, I've finally got it. This is of great use to me. If I had been of some use, would I ever have grown this large? Moreover you and I are both of us things. What's the point of this—things condemning things? You, a worthless man about to die—how do you know I'm a worthless tree?"

When Carpenter Shih woke up, he reported his dream. His apprentice said, "If it's so intent on being of no use, what's it doing there at the village shrine?"

"Shhh! Say no more! It's only *resting* there. If we carp and criticize, it will merely conclude that we don't understand it. Even if it weren't at the shrine, do you suppose it would be cut down? It protects itself in a different way from ordinary people. If you try to judge it by conventional standards, you'll be way off!"

Shu-shan No-Toes and Confucius

In Lu there was a man named Shu-shan No-Toes who had had his foot cut off. Stumping along, he went to see Confucius.

"You weren't careful enough!" said Confucius. "Since you've already broken the law and gotten yourself into trouble like this, what do you expect to gain by coming to me now?"

No-Toes said, "I just didn't understand my duty and was too careless of my body, and so I lost a foot. But I've come now because I still have something that is worth more than a foot and I want to try to hold on to it. There is nothing that heaven doesn't cover, nothing that earth doesn't bear up. I supposed, Master, that you would be like heaven and earth. How did I know you would act like this?"

"It was stupid of me," said Confucius.

"Please, sir, won't you come in? I'd like to describe to you what I have learned."

But No-Toes went out.

Confucius said, "Be diligent, my disciples! Here is No-Toes, a man who has had his foot cut off, and still he's striving to learn so he can make up for the evil of his former conduct. How much more, then, should men whose virtue is still unimpaired!"

No-Toes told the story to Lao Tan. "Confucius certainly hasn't reached the stage of a Perfect Man, has he? What does he mean coming around so obsequiously to study with you? He is after the sham illusion of fame and reputation and doesn't know that the Perfect Man looks on these as so many handcuffs and fetters!"

Lao Tan said, "Why don't you just make him see that life and death are the same story, that acceptable and unacceptable are on a single string? Wouldn't it be well to free him from his handcuffs and fetters?"

No-Toes said, "When Heaven has punished him, how can you set him free?"

The Death of Hun-tun

The emperor of the South Sea was called Shu [Brief], the emperor of the North Sea was called Hu [Sudden], and the emperor of the central region was called Hun-tun [Chaos]. Shu and Hu from time to time came together for a meeting in the territory of Hun-tun, and Hun-tun treated them very generously. Shu and Hu discussed how they could repay his kindness. "All men," they said, "have seven openings so they can see, hear, eat, and breathe. But Hun-tun alone doesn't have any. Let's trying boring him some!"

Every day they bored another hole, and on the seventh day Hun-tun died.

The *Songs of the South*

Personal encounters with the divine are the focus of poems from the state of Ch'u, a kingdom above the Yangtze River that was the southernmost of the states of northern China. Compiled in the second century C.E. into the anthology the *Songs of the South,* the poems are of unknown authorship and are of different provenances, although many are traditionally attributed to the poet Ch'ü Yüan (Qu Yuan; 340?–278 B.C.E.). A conscientious minister of Ch'u, Ch'ü Yüan was slandered and banished from court; despairing at the corruptness of the world, he drowned himself in the Mi-lo River. Ch'ü Yüan's death is today commemorated on the midsummer Dragon Boat Festival, where boat races reenact fishermen's attempts to save Ch'ü Yüan's life, according to one version of the story, or reenact riverine offerings to water spirits to divert them from eating Ch'ü Yüan's body.

Whether the poems were enjoyed primarily for their literary qualities or whether they were part of ritual liturgies and invocations is likewise unknown; in many cases even the gender of the speakers is unclear and has been interpreted by the translator. Most poems probably date to the third or second centuries B.C.E.

"The August Lord of the East," "Lady of the Hsiang," "Greater Master of Fate," "River Earl," and "Mountain Spirit" belong to a song cycle called "The Nine Songs," and although scholars have devised several theories to provide a context for the "Songs," none can be proved definitively. Clearly anthropomorphic and far removed from the notion of heaven held by Confucius or Hsün Tzu, the divinities of the "Nine Songs" are celestial, terrestrial, and riverine gods. Sacrifices performed to distant celestial phenomena, mountains, and rivers are recorded in such texts as the *Book of History,* but the recipients of those rites were natural forces devoid of human form. The gods and spirits of the "Songs," on the other hand, are personalities with whom humans can develop relationships of companionship, love, and even marriage. Narrators of the poems seek out divine company in restive celestial journeys but rarely overtake the object of their longing.

The August Lord of the East, the Great Oneness, was the most important of these deities, and the poem of that title suggests he was identified with the Lord on High. Whereas in some traditions such verses might describe the characteristics of the deity or associate it with the powers of dawn or of the sky, for example, "The August Lord" focuses instead on the activities of the human devotees. And whereas sky gods in other cultures might prefer blood sacrifices or penitence on the part of the sacrificer, the August Lord prefers dramatic performances and fragrant smells. Aromatic flowers and scents appear repeatedly throughout the *Songs of the South* as enticements to invoke numinous presences, while sacrifices in the *Book of Odes* composed farther north, on the other hand, feature the smells of cooked meats and grains.

Goddesses of the "Nine Songs" are not mother figures, fertility deities, or abstractions of femininity but idealized creations of sexually available women who are the objects of the poet's desire. In later Chinese literature and painting, allusions to mountain goddesses and depictions of riverine deities are often suggestive of sexual love. Originally, however, the associations of the Lady of the Hsiang were more chaste, as she was one of two goddesses of the Hsiang (Xiang) River who were traditionally believed to have been the daughters of the legendary emperor Yao (third millennium B.C.E.), who gave them both to his successor Shun in marriage. Hoping to invoke the distant goddess, seemingly unattainable yet hinting at promises of love fulfilled, the poet of "The Lady of the Hsiang" envisions a chamber of scented plants to lure her. Yearning and hesitation also pervade "The Mountain Spirit," an account of a female divinity who lives at the juncture of earth and sky and controls the wind and rain. In the *Book of Rites,* mountains were propitiated for their abilities to produce rains that benefited the crops, but here the theme is sexual love.

Bridal imagery at the close of "The River Earl" suggests the narrator is perhaps female. The River Earl was the divinity of the Ho River, the Yellow River of northern China, which King Chao of Ch'u of the *Tso chuan* had earlier refused to placate. Later popular legend relates that humans beings were sacrificed to the Ho to calm its torrents, and the *Rites of Chou* does record that the Grand Minister of Rites drowned sacrificial animals as offerings to rivers and lakes. But the narrator of "The River Earl" reveals no fear of imminent death and instead describes an exhilarating journey that begins above the surface of the waters and passes over the peaks of the K'un-lun Mountains in central China.

Human beings might aspire to become the traveling companions of even the Greater Master of Fate, who decided human life-span and guided the forces of yin and yang. In earlier philosophical texts, one's mandated fate was rarely understood so starkly, and yin and yang were mentioned but rarely. The origin and development of the notions of yin and yang are unclear, but by very late Chou and early Han times they were considered complementary cosmic forces that infused all things in ever-changing proportions. Yin was associated with the ideas of the female, passivity, darkness, cold, and wetness, whereas yang was considered male, active, bright, hot, and dry. Of no great antiquity, however, are the well-known interlocking tadpole-shaped yin-yang symbols, which probably date only to the fourth or fifth centuries C.E. The Greater Master of Fate was eventually associated with the god of the kitchen hearth, one of the five tutelary deities of the house, and even in modern times people keep statues of him in their kitchens. He continually purviews conduct within the household, and before he is sent off to convey his observations to the spiritual authorities at the end of the year to decide due reward or punishment, his mouth is smeared with honey to sweeten his report.

Perhaps somewhat later than the "Nine Songs" is the "Far-Off Journey," whose anonymous poet might have been one of the literati who gathered under the patronage of Liu An (ca. 170–122 B.C.E.), the Prince of Huai-nan, who was himself a poet and thinker of some renown. Drawing upon imagery from both the *Tao-te ching* and the *Chuang Tzu* while transcending even their idea of nonaction, or inaction, "Far-Off Journey" relates a series of vivid visionary journeys into a soundless, invisible nowhere called the Great Beginning. Encounters with divinities, the goal of the "Nine Songs," are thus of incidental importance in the "Journey," which sets subtler spiritual goals.

The journey is initially inspired not by a desire to converse with gods or communicate with the dead, as such journeys are in some cultures, but by disenchantment with the sorrows of this world. In many traditions, spiritual journeys are professional responsibilities common to shamans, religious adepts of many different specialties who might generally be described as people who can communicate at will with the realm of the spirits. In some cultures people become shamans by choice and by training, but in others they must be chosen by a spirit, usually at some psychological cost to the person involved; some can make their souls leave their body at will and send them on journeys for information to benefit the human community or conduct the dead to the afterlife; others become vessels for spirits who possess them, and are often called spirit mediums. In some traditions, symptoms of someone who has been called to become a shaman are mental instability, restlessness, anxiety, or even nervous breakdown.

These latter states describe the condition of the poet at the beginning of "Far-Off Journey," who soon experiences death and regeneration as his (or her) spirit temporarily, and perhaps involuntarily, leaves his body. He appears initially to be a novice rather than a professional, for he decides to embark on an ecstatic quest for knowledge concerning the origins of the vital force, or *ch'i.* Knowledge or healing for the benefit of the community is not his goal: the spiritual guides he seeks to emulate are famous adepts who have left the world altogether. Troubled by thoughts of the transience of life, he imbibes celestial essences as did Chuang Tzu's holy man, and he sets out on a journey that brings him into contact with many accomplished adepts and sources of power; his spiritual capabilities accelerate swiftly and he soon commands gods and deities to do his bidding. He races across the cosmos in all directions, horizontally and vertically, and surveys all its marvels, until finally he enters the blank silence of the Great Beginning.

"Summons of the Soul" relates the efforts of the shaman Yang to summon a *hun* anima soul to return to the world of the living, perhaps to provide the soul a resting place, as Tzu-ch'an did for the wraith of Po-yü in the *Tso chuan,* or, more likely, to revive a dead body. Mencius's statement that shamans were concerned lest people die suggests their role in prolonging human life. The first few lines of the poem are possibly unrelated to the rest of the verse, which ends with a "luan," or concluding refrain; the summons otherwise begins with the Lord God directly commissioning Shaman Yang to find the soul. Shaman Yang describes a cosmology where a central city of joy and bodily comfort is surrounded on all sides by fearsome regions, each with its own unique terrors and physical hardships; subterranean regions offer carnal torment, and heaven is no paradise. Spiritual and terrestrial geography overlap, for while the regions to the north, south, east, and west possibly describe actual locations, the realms at the zenith and nadir are purely imaginary. Clearly the afterlife is not preferable to earthly existence, whose sensual delights are the antithesis of the Great Beginning of the "Far-Off Journey."

"The August Lord of the East, the Great Oneness"

On an auspicious day at a propitious
    time
We reverently draw nigh to entertain the
    August One on High.
We grip the long swords by their hilts of
    jade,
And chalcedon pendants resound ajangle;
Here are tablets of nephrite for jade
    talismans.
Now let us proffer precious fragrances:
Meats steamed in pungent leaves and
    aromatic wrappings,
Libations of cassia wine and spiced
    broths.
Raise up the drumsticks and beat the
    drums!
Soft, slow rhythms mark the gentle airs,
Then winds and strings join in a grand
    concord.
Shamans dance in resplendent array
And fragrant perfumes fill the halls;
The musical strains all blend in concert.
The Lord is pleased and happily content.

"The Lady of the Hsiang"

A child of the lord descends upon the
    northern shore;
Her eyes' subtle glances yearn for me.
Rustling and soughing on the autumn
    winds,
Leaves settle on the waves of Lake
    Tung-t'ing.
Over the white sedge I peer across the
    distance
Toward a rendezvous with the fair one
    when the moon is high
And the birds roost in the marsh-grass.
But why are the fishing nets up in the
    trees?
Heraclea grows on the River Yuan;
    orchids grow on the Li.
My thoughts are of the lady, but I dare
    not voice them.

Wildly reeling I peer into the distance,
Keeping lookout over the current,
    rushing and roiling.
But why do the deer graze down in the
    courtyard?
And the sea-dragons dart up in the
    shallows?
At dawn I pace my steeds at the river's
    brink,
At dusk I ford over to the western
    shoals,
For I hear my fair one beckoning me;
Mounting her chariot together we will
    roam.
I will build a bower among the waters,
Roof fashioned of water lilies,
Walls of iris, purple cowrie floors;
Scented spices sprinkled through the
    halls,
Cassia crossbeams, wood-orchid rafters,
Magnolia lintels, chambers of white-flag;
Lattices of fig weaved as screens,
Sprigs of march-orchid for an arbor.
White jades as talismans,
Stone-orchids for fragrance,
Iris-wrought water-lily halls,
Bunched nosegays of asarum:
A myriad scents fill the courtyard,
And perfumed fragrances waft through
    corridor and gate.
From Mount Chiu-i a vast host is
    ushered in welcome;
Ethereal presences come like clouds.
Tossing my cloak into the waters,
Leaving my robes on the banks of the
    Li,
I pluck asarum from these islets
To give to the one far away.
The seasons of time allow but a fleeting
    encounter:
Would that I might wander freely,
    enraptured.

"The Mountain Spirit"

There seems to be someone on the
    mountain slope,

Shawled in fig leaves, skirted in rabbit
 fur;
Someone with telling glances and a
 ready smile.
"You love me, then; you who are so
 beautiful."
She drives red leopards, spotted lynxes
 behind,
A magnolia chariot fit with cassia
 pennants.
Wrapped in stone-orchids and sashed
 with asarum,
She plucks scented sprigs for the one she
 thinks of.
I am here in the covering bamboo,
 whose depths never see the
 light of heaven;
Dangerous and difficult the road, but I
 have come, alone and late.
I see her standing alone on the
 mountain:
Billowing clouds roil beneath her,
Lowering shadows darken the
 daylight,
And the east winds gale as the spirit
 ethereal brings the rain.
Lingering with this numinous creature,
 blissful, I forget to return
 home.
But it is already late in the year: how
 can I adorn myself for her?
I pluck trefoil orchids in the mountains
 depths
From bouldered clefts entwined with
 tendrils.
Yearning for this fair one, restive, I
 forget to return home.
The lady thinks of me, but she does not
 stay.
In the mountains, this man, scented with
 asarum,
Drinks at stony springs shadowed among
 the pines and cypress.
The lady thinks of me but hesitates,
 uncertain.
Thunder resounds from the darkening
 rains

And monkeys jabber at the cries of
 night;
Winds sough and sigh to the whispering
 groves.
Thinking of her, I walk away, dejected.

"The River Earl"

With you I roam the nine rivers,
Balanced on the rising winds and poised
 above the waves;
Riding a water-chariot canopied with
 lotus,
Drawn by a brace of dragons, sea-
 serpents at their sides.
Ascending the K'un-lun Mountains I
 gaze into the four directions,
My mind soaring out into the vast
 expanse.
But the sun is about to set: unsettled, I
 forget to return home,
And thinking of those distant shores, I
 am lost in thought.
In fish-scale chambers and dragon halls,
Purple cowrie gate-towers, palaces of
 pearl;
That ethereal creature—what is he doing
 in the water's depths?
Riding a white sea-turtle with an
 entourage of speckled fishes!
With you I roam the banks of the river,
The rushing, thawing waters churning as
 they descend.
You hold out your hand and head
 eastward,
Taking your fair one to the southern
 reaches.
Waves in torrents come to welcome me;
Fishes, shoal upon shoal, are my
 bridesmaids.

"The Greater Master of Fate"

Fling open the gate of heaven!
Surging forward, driving the lowering
 clouds,
Commanding the whirlwind to gallop
 onward,

Sending showers of rain to spatter the
    dust,
The Master wheels in flight as he soars
    downward.
"Across the K'ung-san Mountains I
    follow you.
For all and sundry in the Nine Lands,
Long life and early death depend on
    you."
Flying high, gliding softly,
Mounting pure vital forces and driving
    the yin and yang,
The Master and I in vigilant haste
Conduct the Lord to the Nine
    Mountains.
Medium's robes ethereal, billowing in
    waves,
Pendant jades jangling a yin and a yang;
The multitudes do not understand what
    is happening.
I pluck rare hemp in lustrous hues
To give to the one who lives far away.
Old and feeble, I'm nearing the end;
Not growing closer but ever more
    distant.
Driving dragons in a rumbling tumult
He lurches aloft into the dark heavens.
Twirling a wand of cassia, I stand here a
    long while,
The more I think of him, the greater my
    sorrow.
This sadness—how can I bear it?
Would that I could be as I am today,
    never to weaken and wane.
But human fate has its meted course;
Of its sunderings and couplings, what
    can be done?

"Far-Off Journey"

Wrought with afflictions of the wonts of
    this age
I long to rise softly and journey afar,
But my meager powers are of trifling
    avail.
On what might I ride to soar upwards?
Confronting sunken depravity, a morass
    of corruption,

Alone and depressed, in whom might I
    confide?
Through the night I am wakeful and
    sleepless,
And my soul is restive until dawn;
I ponder the unfathomable reaches of
    heaven and earth,
Mourn the endless travails of human
    existence,
Lament those people already departed,
    whom I had never met,
And those yet to come, whom I would
    never know.
Pacing about, my thoughts adrift,
Nervously anxious and oddly pensive,
My thoughts run wild and unsettled,
And my heart is sadly despondent.
My spirit flashes forth and does not
    return,
And my physical frame withers and is
    left behind.
Reflecting inwardly I remain steadfast,
Searching for the source of the true vital
    force.
In silent vacuity and tranquillity I find
    quiet joy;
With still nonaction I accomplish things
    naturally.
I hear how Red Pine cleansed himself of
    dust,
And aspire to emulate his example.
I marvel at how the perfected ones
    developed virtue,
And admire those of ages past who
    ascended as immortals.
They are transformed, gone, visible no
    longer,
But their names still resound vividly to
    this very day.
I marvel at Fu Yüeh, who consigned
    himself to the stars,
And admire Han Chung's attainment of
    the one.
Their physical frames, sublime, were
    absorbed into the distance.
Far from the throngs of humanity, they
    entered seclusion,

And relying on the shiftings of the vital
forces, they ascended ever
higher.
Fleetingly, swift as spirits and wondrous
as ghosts,
At times they seem to appear, remotely
seen,
As subtle effulgences, moving back and
forth.
Transcending miasmas and dusts,
becoming extremely pure,
At death they did not return to their old
abodes;
Having escaped all misfortunes, they
were free of anxiety.
But those of this world do not
understand them.
I am in awe of the regularity of heaven's
seasons,
Of that shining ethereal brightness, in its
westward journey;
But a light frost is settling, sinking
downward,
And I worry lest my fragrant flowers fall
early.
Would that I could drift and roam,
Forever passing the years with no
particular design.
But with whom might I enjoy my few
remaining fragrances?
At dawn, I unloose my feelings into the
prevailing winds.
But Kao Yang is far away, so distant:
what am I to do?
I remark again how springs and autumns
rush by without respite;
How can I remain long in this old
abode?
I cannot reach Hsüan Yüan,
But I can follow Wang Ch'iao and sport
with him.
I dine on the six vital forces and drink
mists and vapors,
Rinse my mouth with the principal yang
forces and imbibe the morning
haze.

I safeguard the halcyon clarity of the
spiritual and numinous,
And refined vital forces enter and
coarser dregs are expelled.
Flowing with the gentle breezes, I roam
about with them;
Arriving at the Southern Aerie, I stop at
once,
And seeing Master Wang, I stay the
night.
I ask him how the one vital force can be
harmonized with virtue,
And he says, "The way can be received,
but it cannot be transmitted to
others.
It is so small that it has no inner space,
so large that it has no outer
limits.
When the soul is without artifice, one
can deal with things naturally;
When the unitary vital force permeates
the spirit, sustain it throughout
the night.
Abide in vacuity prior to nonaction,
And everything will come to completion.
This is the gate of virtue."
I hear this and treasure it; I continue on,
Quickly preparing to set out.
I soon see the Feathered People of the
Cinnabar Hills
And linger in that ancient deathless land.
I wash my hair in Boiling Valley,
And at night dry my bodily self at Nine
Yang Forces;
I inhale the subtle secretions of the
Flying Springs,
And embrace the shining emblems of the
jade regalia.
The jade's colors radiate, casting a luster
on my face;
My subtle essences, purified, start to
strengthen;
My material self melts and dissolves,
frothing away,
And my spirit floats about, loose and
free.

I admire the warm, radiant virtues of the
southern land,
And the winter blossoming of the
beautiful cassia tree.
There desolate mountains are
uninhabited by beasts,
And silent wildernesses harbor no human
beings.
Bearing my corporeal soul, I ascend the
mists of dawn,
And spread upon a floating cloud, I
journey upward.
I order the porter of the gates of heaven
to open his doors,
Swing back the gates, and keep a look-
out for me.
I summon Feng Lung and place him in
my vanguard
And ask him where Great Subtlety lies.
Collecting my redoubled yang forces, I
enter the palace of the Lord;
I visit Temporal Origins and purview the
City of Clarity.
Setting out at dawn, I stop at the Court
of Grand Ceremony,
And by evening draw nigh to the Gate
of Subtlety.
Marshalling a company of ten thousand
chariots,
Rolling forward en masse at an even
gallop,
I drive eight dragons, beautiful and
sleek,
In a chariot strung with waving
serpentine cloud banners
And mounted with bold rainbows of
multicolored streamers,
Their five colors arrayed in dazzling
brightness.
My inside steeds arch proudly, lowering
and tossing;
The outside team writhes spiritedly,
prancing.
Charging off, we ride tightly bunched
and then fan out in a fray,
And the colorful stampede takes off.

Taking up the reins and unleashing the
whip,
I set off to see Kou Mang.
Passing Grand Luminosity, I wheel to
the right,
Sending Fei Lien ahead to clear the way.
As the light brightens just before
sunrise,
I traverse the diameter of heaven and
earth;
The Earl of the Wind courses ahead as
my vanguard,
Sweeping away the dusts and ushering in
clear coolness;
Soaring phoenixes bear my banners
aloft,
And I encounter Ju Shou at the Western
August Heavens.
Grasping a broom-star as my standard
And wielding aloft the Dipper's handle
as my ensign,
In a glittering coruscation wending high
and low,
I roam onward, scattering the flowing
waves of mist.
Daylight clouds into darkness
As I summon Hsüan Wu to race in my
retinue,
Charge Wen Ch'ang to direct the
maneuvers at the rear guard,
And appoint a host of spirits to flank me
on both sides.
The road spans far into the distance,
And I check the pace as I veer sharply
upward.
At my right the Master of Rains serves
as my scout,
And on the left, the Duke of Thunder is
my escort.
Wanting to traverse the entire world, I
forget to return home;
My thoughts are carefree and
unconstrained,
And inwardly I rejoice and am at peace
with myself,
Delighting in my own contentment.

But pacing the azure clouds, drifting and
    roaming,
I suddenly catch a glimpse of my old
    homeland;
My charioteers and grooms long for it,
    and my own heart grows sad.
Even the outside horses, turning back to
    look, do not go on.
Thinking of my old home, I envision it
    in my thoughts,
Drawing a deep breath as I hide my
    tears.
With a troubled countenance, I still
    advance upward,
Restraining my will and regaining
    composure.
Aiming for the Flaming Spirit, I gallop
    straight for it,
Heading toward the Southern Mountains.
I survey the barren reaches beyond
    space,
The floating mirages that drift of their
    own accord,
But Chu Jung warns me to turn back.
So I remount, bidding the simurgh to
    invite Fu Fei;
Strumming "In Many Ponds" and
    playing "Uplifting the Clouds,"
Two maidens present the Nine Shao
    Songs.
I bid the spirits of the Hsiang River to
    play the drum and zither,
And order the God of the Sea to dance
    with P'ing-i.
Lines of black dragons and sea-serpents
    weave in and out,
Their bodies wriggling and swaying in
    serpentines.
Lady Rainbow brightens ever more
    beautifully
As the simurgh soars and flies
    above
And the music rises in limitless
    crescendos.
I roam again, sporting to and fro,
Rolling onward at an even pace,
    galloping excitedly,

Striding ahead to the boundary limits at
    the Gate of Coldness;
Rushing forth swiftly with the wind at
    Clear Springs,
I follow Chuan Hsü over tiers of ice.
Crossing the land of Hsüan Ming, I
    diverge from my path;
Mounting the latitudes, I turn to look
    back,
Summoning Ch'ien Lei to manifest
    himself
To go before me and level the road.
I have traversed the Four Vastnesses,
Made a circuit of the Six Deserts,
Ascended to the lightning's cracks,
And descended into the Great Ravine.
Peaks rise high below, but there is no
    earth;
Empty vastness soars above, but there is
    no heaven.
Glancing this way and that, I see nothing;
Listening anxiously, I hear nothing.
Going beyond nonaction, I attain clarity,
And dwell in the Great Beginning.

"Summons of the Soul"

[As a youth, I was pure and innocent,
The very embodiment of righteousness,
    possessed of selfless character;
I adhered to great virtue, even when I
    might have been ensnared in
    commonness and corruption.
But those above me did not admit of my
    great virtue,
And I long sustained misfortune and
    despondent bitterness.]

The Lord enjoined Shaman Yang,
    saying,
"There is someone below whom I want
    to help.
His corporeal and anima souls have left
    him and are dissipating.
Perform a divination with milfoil stalks
    concerning this."
Shaman Yang replied, "A divination of
    dreams can be done.

Complying with the behest of the Lord
    on High would otherwise be
    difficult, for
If I only divine with milfoil stalks, I fear
    that this man may still die,
And that you would no longer avail
    yourself of Shaman Yang."
Then he went down to perform the
    summoning, and said,

"O soul, come back! You have fled your
    usual abode.
But why run off to the four quarters?
You have deserted your favorite haunts,
    only to encounter baleful woes.

"Oh soul, come back! You cannot linger
    in the east,
Where people a thousand fathoms tall
    snatch souls.
Ten suns shine in turn, liquefying metal
    and melting stone.
Those people are used to it, but if you
    go there, soul,
You would be undone.
Oh soul, come back! You cannot linger
    there.

"Oh soul, come back! You cannot stay
    in the south,
Where people with painted faces and
    blackened teeth
Sacrifice with human flesh and save the
    bones for soup.
Here live writhing coils of vipers and
    pythons,
A great fox that runs a thousand
    leagues,
A vicious nine-headed serpent that
    strikes suddenly,
Swallowing human beings to sate its
    appetite.
Come back! You cannot stay there long.

"Oh soul, come back! In the west stretch
    a thousand leagues of perilous
    shifting sands
Where you may fall into a thundering
    abyss
And continually be ground to bits.

Even should you happen to escape,
    beyond is a vast wasteland
Where live red ants the size of elephants
And black hornets as big as pitchers.
Crops cannot grow there; briars and
    stalks suffice for food.
The land sears human beings, who
    search in vain for water.
Fearful, you will find no rest, for those
    vast reaches are endless.
Come back, lest you invite danger.

"Oh soul, come back! You cannot stay
    in the north,
With its towering tiers of ice and
    flurrying snows that fall for a
    thousand leagues around.
Come back! You cannot stay there long.

"Oh soul, come back! Do not ascend to
    the heavens.
Tigers and leopards at the nine gates
    devour human beings,
And a nine-headed man uproots nine
    thousand trees.
Hyenas and wolves follow you with their
    eyes, howling as they prowl
    about,
Dangling human beings in the air to
    amuse themselves, then tossing
    them into deep crevasses.
Only at the bidding of the Lord do they
    close their eyes.
Come back, lest you invite harm.

"Oh soul, come back! Do not descend
    into the hidden realm.
There lives the nine-curled Earl of the
    Earth: sharp-horned,
Humpbacked, with bloodied thumbs, he
    trails human beings apace,
Sporting a three-eyed tiger's head upon
    the body of an ox.
To him, humans are but sweetmeats.
Come back, lest you invite misfortune.

"Oh soul, come back! Enter the city
    gates.
Adept invocators summon you, walking
    ahead in pairs.

Baskets from Ch'in, Ch'i weavings,
    silks from Cheng:
Everything for the summoning is
    prepared; the sustained cries of
    the invocators resound.
"Oh soul, come back! Return to your old
    abode.
Heaven, earth, and the four quarters are
    rife with baseness and
    depravity.
But envision your own house: tranquil
    and peaceful,
With lofty halls and spacious rooms,
    tiered balconies rimmed with
    railings,
Layered terraces and storied pavilions
    with views of distant
    mountains,
Latticed doors and vermillion curtains,
    crossbeams ranged with
    carvings;
Chambers heated in winter and cooled in
    summer.
The grounds are wound about with glens
    and streams, babbling and
    burbling;
Warm breezes bend the lilies and gently
    sway the orchids.
Here are halls and alcoves laid with
    vermillion dust mats,
Rooms floored in nephrite and curtained
    on hooks of jade,
Quilts of kingfisher feathers and pearls,
    glimmering brightly;
Walls covered with rush weavings and
    draped in light silk,
And hung with tasseled embroideries,
    knotted openwork, and jade
    ornaments.
In chambers decorated with rare and
    precious things,
Bright orchid-musk candles cast a
    shimmering incandescence.
Two shifts of eight chambermaids take
    turns attending you:
Good daughters of the nine princely
    clans, they far surpass ordinary
    women.

Women in beautiful coiffures, each
    uniquely styled, fill your halls;
Possessed of graceful demeanor and
    unruffled complaisance,
Seemingly delicate, they are yet strong
    and straightforward, and speak
    their minds.
Beautiful and refined, they grace your
    bedchamber
With their mothlike eyebrows, limpid
    gazes, and stirring eyes,
With lovely faces, carefully made up,
    that sparkle silken glances.
They attend you at your leisure among
    the curtained bowers,
In lofty chambers draped with kingfisher
    reds and blues,
Inside vermillion walls set with scarlet
    moldings and black-jade
    beams.
Gaze up to the carved rafters limned
    with dragons and serpents;
Sit in the pavilions, resting against the
    railings above the winding
    pools
Where water lilies have just started to
    blossom among the caltrops,
Purplish stalks rising in the wind over
    rippling leaves of green.
Servants exotically garbed in spotted-
    leopard skins await you at the
    bank;
Lowering the carriage, grooms and
    livery stand in attendance.
Orchids carpet the grove's edge; fine
    trees line the garden fence.
"Oh soul, come back! Why travel afar?
People of your household have come to
    pay their respects with
    plenteous viands of every sort:
Rice, millet, barley, and wheat mixed
    with yellow millet;
Foods seasoned to taste: bitter, salty,
    sour, spicy, and sweet.
Here are marbled roasts of beef and
    savory steaks
In tangy, pungent seasonings, served
    with Wu soup;

Turtle casserole and roast lamb with yam
    sauce,
Heron in piquant sauce, stewed wild
    duck, fried swan and crane,
Dewdrop chicken, and tortoise simmered
    in broth, spicy but not too
    hot;
Honeyed rice cakes and sugared pastries
    of flour,
Crystalline measures of sweetened
    libations served in winged
    goblets,
Drinks cooled with crushed ice; and
    chilled, translucent liquors.
Fine ewers are set out, filled with clear-
    bodied broths.
Come back! Return to your old home,
    where you will be revered and
    find repose.

"Before the sacrificial meats and
    delicacies are finished, women
    musicians come forward,
Setting up chimes, beating drums, and
    performing new songs:
'Fording the River,' 'Picking Caltrops,'
    and 'Scattering Water Lilies.'
Beautiful women grow tipsy, their faces
    blushing red;
Maids flash glancing looks from eyes
    that grow ever more dazzling.
They are shawled in silk and robed in
    fine embroidered gowns,
    exquisite yet understated;
Their long hair and thick tresses now fall
    in splendid disarray.
Two lines of eight dancers in perfect
    symmetry begin the dance of
    Wu,
Their outspread sleeves as straight as
    bamboo, swaying downwards.
Winds and strings crescendo wildly to
    the drum beat,
And the palace halls rock and shake as
    the musicians begin the
    exhilarating airs of Ch'u;
Songs of Wu and ballads from Ts'ai
    resound to the grand pitch-
    scales.

Men and women now sit together
    openly, without reserve;
And loosened sashes and hat strings lie
    in tangled disarray.
Bewitching sylphs from Cheng and Wei
    mingle here and there,
But the troops of those exhilarating airs
    of Ch'u,
Admired for their coiffures, are singled
    out from the rest.
Jade markers and ivory boards are
    brought for a game of sixes:
Players pair off and make their moves,
    marshalling and advancing,
Capturing pieces with each high throw,
    shouting 'five whites!'
It grows ever late as they parry, and the
    daylight hours are nearly
    spent.
Chiming bells rock in their stands;
    catalpa zithers hum.
The guests delight in wine, but not
    wantonly, as the suns sinks
    into the night,
And orchid-musk candles glow from
    ornamental lamps.
Collecting their thoughts as they set
    down verses amidst the wafts
    of orchid scent,
Those who have found a perfect mate
    write poems of their mutual
    love.
Drinking wine, they find complete
    happiness and bring joy to the
    recently departed.
Oh soul, come back! Return to your old
    home."

The refrain says,
"At the new year's rites at the beginning
    of spring, restive, you journey
    south,
When the watercress unfurls its leaves
    and the white iris grows.
The road winds through Lu-chiang, with
    Chang-po on the right.
Drawing near the shore and its vast
    expanse of water, you survey
    the distant reaches, and see

Four-horse braces of blue-black steeds, a
    line-up of a thousand chariots,
Rising flames of torches, flickering
    shadowed faces.
Breaking into a run you take your
    position, and now in the
    vanguard you course ahead;
Curbing the gait to a steady pace, you
    rein in the carriage and wheel
    to the right,
Galloping with the king among the
    lowlands, directing the feints
    and advances;
Your king himself shoots, flushing out a
    grey tapir.

But a red horizon now bears up the night
    sky above, and there is no time
    to lose.
Here marsh-orchids cover the trail: the
    path is too swampy.
Deep, so deep run the waters of the
    river, overspread with groves
    of maple.
But the eye that sees a thousand leagues
    ahead
Wounds the springtime of one's very
    heart.
Oh soul, come back! Alas for this land
    south of the river!"

HAN
(202 B.C.E.–220 C.E.)

AND WEI
(220–264)

DYNASTIES

Wang Fu's *Discourses of a Recluse*

Briefly unified under the short-lived Ch'in dynasty (221–207 B.C.E.), the various states of northern China were more firmly consolidated under one emperor in the Han dynasty (202 B.C.E.–220 C.E.), an era of such cultural achievement that the Chinese still refer to themselves as "people of the Han." Han thinkers developed a variety of new cosmologies, ritual usages, spiritual beliefs, and theories of governance, influenced to varying degrees by the writings of Chou philosophers.

Wang Fu (ca. 78–163), for example, appeals to the authority of such classical texts as the *Tso chuan* and the writings of Confucius and Mencius in his discussion of the principles governing human attitudes toward the spirit world. Some of these concerns are elaborated in his "Spirit Mediums Set Forth," chapter 26 of his *Discourses of a Recluse (Ch'ien-fu lun)*, a work that also includes his views on divination, physiognomy, and the interpretation of dreams. Wang was himself a recluse; Confucius and his student Tzu-lu had censured those whom they thus believed ignored human relationships, but Wang avails himself of his position to critique society from the outside and thus plays an active yet indirect role in forming its values and norms. In Chinese culture, people who lived as so-called recluses or hermits did not necessarily cut off all ties with the outside world: historical accounts over the centuries note famous literati and painters who retired to rural retreats or villas and there maintained intellectual coteries of their own and corresponded actively with the outside world.

Wang's "Spirit Mediums Set Forth" appeals to sentiments articulated in Chou texts and reveals how those texts were employed to critique contemporary Han values. He turns particularly to the narratives of the *Tso chuan,* and the fact that he can briefly allude to a name or incident from that text and be assured that his readers will understand his meaning reflects the widespread influence of the *Tso* in Han times. "Spirit Mediums" also reveals how the ambiguities of respecting spirits but keeping them at a distance were still problematic in the Han, as were issues of the relative importance of human effort and divine intervention.

Wang perhaps does not value the effectiveness of human effort as highly as did Hsün Tzu, who spoke of knowing of no greater "spirit" than the transformative Way, a Way that could be directly apprehended by the human mind. While Wang seems somewhat more credulous of spirits and of uncanny powers than did Hsün Tzu, he also tries to allay the people's fears of preternatural manifestations and is likewise concerned that human beings turn inward to find the true source of their fortunes and misfortunes. Although he does not deny that shamans (*wu,* a term also sometimes translated as "spirit mediums") and other professionals communicate with spirits, he does not believe that either the ruler or the common people should shirk their moral obligations by relying upon the external performative arts of shamans or upon arbitrary taboos placed on certain words or actions.

"Spirit Mediums Set Forth"

The good or bad fortune of human beings is directed by their behavior and decided by fate. Behavior is self-determined; fate is regulated by heaven. People are definitely in control of their own affairs, but those things within heaven's power cannot be known. The prayers and invocations of shamanesses and shamans can sometimes be of help, but they cannot mediate when one offends against virtue. Shamans, historians, and those who offer prayers and invocations no doubt enable one to commune with spirits and ghosts, but they can only be of help in trivial matters. When it comes to the great course of fate, there is really nothing one can do. This can be compared with a common man's appeals to a higher authority: though he can extricate himself from the consequences of some obscure offense, in clear-cut cases of wrongdoing he is helpless.

Imagine, for example, a man who disparages the teachings of his ruler and father day and night, who willfully offends against the restrictions of the sage kings, and who gives free rein to his heart's desires. Suppose a man decides to correct his errors and [lacuna] reform, then abruptly requests an audience with the authorities and begs to be pardoned. It would be of no use. Wouldn't it have been better if he had cultivated himself, if he had been cautious and fearful without any offense against his superiors for which he must be reported? This is why Confucius objected to Tzu-lu's prayers on his behalf and said, "I have been praying for a long time" [*Analects* 7.34]. The *Classic of Filial Piety* says, "Now in such a case, if in life people are cared for, then in death when sacrifices are offered to their spirits, they will receive them" [*Hsiao ching* 4.14b]. From this perspective, when virtue and righteousness have not been disregarded, the spirits and departed ancestors will accept sacrifices. When the spirits and departed ancestors receive and enjoy them, good fortune and blessings will be abundant. The *Odes* [ode no. 274] says,

Blessings are sent down abundantly,
Blessings are sent down bountifully.
Careful and decorous in comportment,
Drinking and eating to the full,
Blessings and distinctions continue on.

This means that when human virtue and righteousness are flourishing and bounteous, the spirits will accept and enjoy sacrifices, drinking and eating to the full, and will then reciprocate with blessings.

The Duke of Kuo beckoned spirits and perished soon afterward [*Tso chuan*, Duke Chuang 32]. Chao Ying sacrificed to heavenly beings and was quickly destroyed [*Tso*, Duke Ch'eng 5]. No doubt this is what is meant when it was said, "The spirits refuse their offerings, and the people refuse to attend to their affairs" [*Tso*, Duke Chao 1]. Thus, as the *History of Lu* recounts, "When a state is about to flourish, the ruler listens to the people; when it is about to perish, he listens to the spirits" [*Tso*, Duke Chuang 32].

But Duke Chao of Ch'u refrained from sacrificing to clouds [*Tso*, Duke Ai 6]; Duke Ching of Sung would not transfer his bad fate to a scapegoat [*Lü-shih ch'un-ch'iu*, 6.8b]; Tzu-ch'an opposed Pei Tsao [*Tso*, Duke Chao 17]; and Duke Wen of Chu disregarded the tortoise-shell and his historian [*Tso*, Duke Wen 13]. These were all men who examined themselves and knew the Way; they cultivated themselves and awaited their destinies [*Mencius* 7A.1]. Yen P'ing-chung said, "Prayers bring benefits; curses likewise bring harm" [*Tso*, Duke Chao 20]. Chi Liang's admonition of the Marquis of Sui and Kung Chih-chi's persuasion of Duke Yu exemplify an enlightened grasp of the Way of Heaven and humankind and a penetrating knowledge of the activities of the spiritual and numinous [*Tso*, Duke Hsi 5 and Duke Huan 6]. That evil influences cannot conquer virtue, and that heresy cannot overcome truth is Heaven's law. Although there may be transgressions from time to time, the wise hold fast to the true path and keep their distance from wicked ghosts. That which is called a "wicked ghost" is an unrestrained and evil elemental being; they are not faithful guardians, nor are they truly spiritual and numinous. Yet there are such ghosts, just as in the world of men there are those who falsely claim to sell items at adjusted prices in order to make unlawful demands. If some are tempted by this scheme, then others will throng from afar without ceasing, and calamity will be certain. Ghosts and spirits are also like this. Thus, Shen Hsü said, "When people have cause to feel fearful, their vital force becomes brilliant and summons forth monstrosities. If a person affords no cause for them, then monstrosities will not appear by themselves" [*Tso, Duke Chuang* 14]. This means that people should not be overly fearful. If they are overly fearful and anxious without reason, they really will summon forth monstrous omens.

Furthermore, just as ranks of nobility exist among human beings, there are honorable and base spirits. The sacrifices to Heaven, earth, mountains, and streams, to the altars of the land and grain, to the five deities, and to all appointed ministers who have been of service to the people are those prescribed for the Son of Heaven and the enfeoffed lords. As for the seven spirits that female and male shamans pray to and speak of and whom petty people entreat and fear—the Earth Duke, the Flying Corpse, Baleful Bogies, the Lord of the North, Hsien-chu, Roadthwart, and "direct correspondences," as well as the worthless and vulgar taboos observed by the common people when constructing houses—

these have never been feared by the Son of Heaven.

In the capital of olden times, no precautions were taken to influence results, but since establishing various taboos, the auspicious omens, and felicitous responses, the illustriousness and prosperity of sons and grandsons do not surpass those of former times. Moreover, if because of these taboos rulers fear subjects and superiors doubt inferiors, then this will surely create a display of weakness and invite insult. I fear this is not the aim of eliciting blessings.

I have read in the records of antiquity that when the lord of humankind perfects himself and when he is enlightened as to punishments and rewards, the kingdom will be well governed and the people will be at peace. When the people are content, heaven is pleased and increases the number of their days. Therefore, the *Book of History* says, "The king will receive an everabiding mandate from Heaven through the common people" [*Shao kao*]. Confucius said: "The one whom heaven assists is obedient. The one whom human beings assist is trustworthy. He treads the path of trustworthiness, he takes care to be obedient and to exalt the worthy—therefore 'from Heaven he receives assistance and there is good fortune; there is advantage in all endeavors' " [*Book of Changes, Hsi-tz'u* 1.12, quoting passages from the hexagram *Ta yu*]. This is the most fundamental way to avert evil and summon forth good fortune.

Pan Chao's Perfected Woman

Ritual texts of the Chou period recorded ceremonies and forms of etiquette that circumscribed the behavior of both men and women. The "Principles of Sacrifice" in the *Book of Rites,* for example, related how the public performance of ceremonies, in which members of both sexes took part, exemplified the norms that governed the relationships between husband and wife. Hierarchy, differentiation, and distinction were principles valued in early Chinese thought, and a harmony of differences, rather than egalitarianism, was the paradigm applied to familial as well as governmental relations. Dissolution of distinctions, on the other hand, was associated with chaos and social disorder.

Similar distinctions applied in ancient times to relations between the sexes, as is explained in the "Inner Maxims" *(Nei tse),* a chapter of the *Book of Rites* that describes relations within the household. From the age of seven, boys and girls did not eat together or sit on the same mat; at ten, girls were discouraged from leaving the house, while boys were sent out to study reading and writing with a teacher and continued their education throughout their adult lives. As teenagers, boys learned archery and chariot driving and at twenty underwent the capping rites of adulthood and began to study ceremonial proceedings; they married at thirty. Girls, on the other hand, from the age of ten studied at home with governesses who taught them weaving, sewing, etiquette, and the preparation and arrangement of foods and dishes for sacrificing. At fifteen girls pinned up their hair, signaling their availability for marriage, and they married at about the age of twenty. Spouses had different but complementary responsibilities and obligations to one another. Men resided in the exterior apartments of the house, women the interior; both inside and outside of the house, men and women were encouraged to maintain a circumspect formality of behavior. Such were the ideals expressed in the *Book of Rites,* but the realities of social conduct are difficult to measure.

Lessons for Women (Nü chieh), a primer of female virtues compiled by the historian Pan Chao (ca. 48–ca. 112), builds upon the ancient norms of texts such as the *Rites* and describes the ritualized kinds of behavior women should follow in their responsibilities as wives. She intended the work as a guide of wifely conduct for her own daughters, who were of marriageable age. Marriage presented unique problems for women, who left the household of their natal extended family to join that of their husbands, a custom that placed young brides at the service of their in-laws and obliged them to contend with their spouse's siblings and other relatives. Pan Chao's *Lessons* suggests general principles for negotiating this new set of relationships, and in many respects they parallel the qualities of consideration, loyalty, and harmony that Confucius and Mencius espoused for all people; the *Lessons,* however, places a heavier premium on acquiescence, humility, and service to others. Philosophically, Pan bases her conceptions of female and male behavior on the ideas of yin and yang, which are yielding and strong, respectively. Although her *Lessons* perhaps suggests a view of womanhood defined by yielding and complaisance, one might also note that these were the values that allowed Lao Tzu's sage to govern the world by nonaction, and that they were principles long espoused by statecraft experts and military strategists for overthrowing neighboring kingdoms by subterfuge. Pan Chao's admonitions need not be understood as weakening the position of women: the softest things in the world, noted the *Tao-te ching,* overcome the hardest.

Pan Chao's laments concerning her daughters' lack of education may be only pious self-effacement, yet it is possible that her professional responsibilities prevented her from spending much time at home. She hailed from a prominent scholarly family, and her career indicates the breadth of her own education. Her father Pan Piao (3–54) had begun compiling the *Han shu,* or *History of the Former Han Dynasty* (206 B.C.E.–8 C.E.), a work that upon his death was completed only with the continued efforts of his son Pan Ku (32–92) and then of his daughter Pan Chao. Her precise role in its compilation is uncertain, although according to a fifth-century biography, she supervised the editing of the treatises on astronomy and of the chronological tables of nobility, conducting her work at one of the imperial libraries. The same biography notes that she served as tutor to the empress and women of the court and acted as an advisor to Empress Teng, who became regent in 106 and controlled political power for the next fifteen years. The noted Han scholar Ma Jung (79–166) was Pan's student.

Over the following centuries, Pan Chao's name became synonymous with womanly erudition, and her *Lessons for Women* was well known. In the T'ang dynasty, her name was included in the list of exemplary women who received imperial sacrifices, and in later centuries she was often depicted in wood-block prints and paintings.

Lessons for Women
Introduction

I, the unworthy writer, am unsophisticated, un-enlightened, and by nature unintelligent, but I am fortunate both to have received not a little favor from my scholarly father, and to have had a (cultured) mother and instructresses upon whom to rely for a literary education as well as for training in good manners. More than forty years have passed since at the age of fourteen I took up the dustpan and the broom in the Ts'ao family. During this time with trembling heart I feared constantly that I might disgrace my parents, and that I might multiply difficulties for both the women and the men (of my husband's family). Day and night I was distressed in heart, (but) I labored without confessing weariness. Now and hereafter, however, I know how to escape (from such fears).

Being careless, and by nature stupid, I taught and trained (my children) without system. Consequently I fear that my son Ku may bring disgrace upon the Imperial Dynasty by whose Holy Grace he has unprecedentedly received the extraordinary privilege of wearing the Gold and the Purple, a privilege for the attainment of which (by my son, I) a humble subject never even hoped. Nevertheless, now that he is a man and able to plan his own life, I need not again have concern for him. But I do grieve that you, my daughters, just now at the age for marriage, have not at this time had gradual training and advice; that you still have not learned the proper customs for married women. I fear that by failure in good manners in other families you will humiliate both your ancestors and your clan. I am now seriously ill, life is uncertain. As I have thought of you all in so untrained a state, I have been uneasy many a time for you. At hours of leisure I have composed in seven chapters these instructions under the title, "Lessons for Women." In order that you may have something wherewith to benefit your persons, I wish every one of you, my daughters, each to write out a copy for yourself.

From this time on every one of you strive to practise these (lessons).

Chapter I Humility

On the third day after the birth of a girl the ancients observed three customs: (first) to place the baby below the bed; (second) to give her a potsherd with which to play; and (third) to announce her birth to her ancestors by an offering. Now to lay the baby below the bed plainly indicated that she is lowly and weak, and should regard it as her primary duty to humble herself before others. To give her potsherds with which to play indubitably signified that she should practise labor and consider it her primary duty to be industrious. To announce her birth before her ancestors clearly meant that she ought to esteem as her primary duty the continuation of the observance of worship in the home.

These three ancient customs epitomize a woman's ordinary way of life and the teachings of the traditional ceremonial rites and regulations. Let a woman modestly yield to others; let her respect others; let her put others first, herself last. Should she do something good, let her not mention it; should she do something bad, let her not deny it. Let her bear disgrace; let her even endure when others speak or do evil to her. Always let her seem to tremble and to fear. (When a woman follows such maxims as these,) then she may be said to humble herself before others.

Let a woman retire late to bed, but rise early to duties; let her not dread tasks by day or by night. Let her not refuse to perform domestic duties whether easy or difficult. That which must be done, let her finish completely, tidily, and systematically. (When a woman follows such rules as these,) then she may be said to be industrious.

Let a woman be correct in manner and upright in character in order to serve her husband. Let her live in purity and quietness (of spirit), and attend to her own affairs. Let her love not gossip and silly laughter. Let her cleanse and purify and arrange in order the wine and the food for the offerings to the ancestors. (When a woman observes such principles as these,) then she may be said to continue ancestral worship.

No woman who observes these three (fundamentals of life) has ever had a bad reputation or has fallen into disgrace. If a woman fail to observe them, how can her name be honored; how can she but bring disgrace upon herself?

Chapter II Husband and Wife

The Way of husband and wife is intimately connected with *Yin* and *Yang,* and relates the individual to gods and ancestors. Truly it is the great principle of Heaven and Earth, and the great basis of human relationships. Therefore the "Rites" honor union of man and woman; and in the "Book of Poetry" the "First Ode" manifests the principle of marriage. For these reasons the relationship cannot but be an important one.

If a husband be unworthy, then he possesses nothing by which to control his wife. If a wife be unworthy, then she possesses nothing with which to serve her husband. If a husband does not control his wife, then the rules of conduct manifesting his authority are abandoned and broken. If a wife does not serve her husband, then the proper relationship (between men and women) and the natural order of things are neglected and destroyed. As a matter of fact the purpose of these two (the controlling of women by men, and the serving of men by women) is the same.

Now examine the gentlemen of the present age. They only know that wives must be controlled, and that the husband's rules of conduct manifesting his authority must be established. They therefore teach their boys to read books and (study) histories. But they do not in the least understand that husbands and masters must (also) be served, and that the proper relationship and the rites should be maintained.

Yet only to teach men and not to teach women,—is that not ignoring the essential relation between them? According to the "Rites," it

is the rule to begin to teach children to read at the age of eight years, and by the age of fifteen years they ought then to be ready for cultural training. Only why should it not be (that girls' education as well as boys' be) according to this principle?

Chapter III Respect and Caution

As *Yin* and *Yang* are not of the same nature, so man and woman have different characteristics. The distinctive quality of the *Yang* is rigidity; the function of the *Yin* is yielding. Man is honored for strength; a woman is beautiful on account of her gentleness. Hence there arose the common saying: "A man though born like a wolf may, it is feared, become a weak monstrosity; a woman though born like a mouse may, it is feared, become a tiger."

Now for self-culture nothing equals respect for others. To counteract firmness nothing equals compliance. Consequently it can be said that the Way of respect and acquiescence is woman's most important principle of conduct. So respect may be defined as nothing other than holding on to that which is permanent; and acquiescence nothing other than being liberal and generous. Those who are steadfast in devotion know that they should stay in their proper places; those who are liberal and generous esteem others, and honor and serve (them).

If husband and wife have the habit of staying together, never leaving one another, and following each other around within the limited space of their own rooms, then they will lust after and take liberties with one another. From such action improper language will arise between the two. This kind of discussion may lead to licentiousness. Out of licentiousness will be born a heart of disrespect to the husband. Such a result comes from not knowing that one should stay in one's proper place.

Furthermore, affairs may be either crooked or straight; words may be either right or wrong. Straightforwardness cannot but lead to quarreling; crookedness cannot but lead to accusation. If there are really accusations and quarrels, then undoubtedly there will be angry affairs. Such a result comes from not esteeming others, and not honoring and serving (them).

(If wives) suppress not contempt for husbands, then it follows (that such wives) rebuke and scold (their husbands). (If husbands) stop not short of anger, then they are certain to beat (their wives). The correct relationship between husband and wife is based upon harmony and intimacy, and (conjugal) love is grounded in proper union. Should actual blows be dealt, how could matrimonial relationship be preserved? Should sharp words be spoken, how could (conjugal) love exist? If love and proper relationship both be destroyed, then husband and wife are divided.

Chapter IV Womanly Qualifications

A woman (ought to) have four qualifications: (1) womanly virtue; (2) womanly words; (3) womanly bearing; and (4) womanly work. Now what is called womanly virtue need not be brilliant ability, exceptionally different from others. Womanly words need be neither clever in debate nor keen in conversation. Womanly appearance requires neither a pretty nor a perfect face and form. Womanly work need not be work done more skillfully than that of others.

To guard carefully her chastity; to control circumspectly her behavior; in every motion to exhibit modesty; and to model each act on the best usage, this is womanly virtue.

To choose her words with care; to avoid vulgar language; to speak at appropriate times; and not to weary others (with much conversation), may be called the characteristics of womanly words.

To wash and scrub filth away; to keep clothes and ornaments fresh and clean; to wash the head and bathe the body regularly, and to keep the person free from disgraceful filth, may be called the characteristics of womanly bearing.

With whole-hearted devotion to sew and to weave; to love not gossip and silly laughter; in cleanliness and order (to prepare) the wine and food for serving guests, may be called the characteristics of womanly work.

These four qualifications characterize the greatest virtue of a woman. No woman can afford to be without them. In fact they are very easy to possess if a woman only treasure them in her heart. The ancients had a saying: "Is Love afar off? If I desire love, then love is at hand!" So can it be said of these qualifications.

Chapter V Whole-hearted Devotion

Now in the "Rites" is written the principle that a husband may marry again, but there is no Canon that authorizes a woman to be married the second time. Therefore it is said of husbands as of Heaven, that as certainly as people cannot run away from Heaven, so surely a wife cannot leave (a husband's home).

If people in action or character disobey the spirits of Heaven and of Earth, then Heaven punishes them. Likewise if a woman errs in the rites and in the proper mode of conduct, then her husband esteems her lightly. The ancient book, "A Pattern for Women" (*Nü Hsien*), says: "To obtain the love of one man is the crown of a woman's life; to lose the love of one man is to miss the aim in woman's life." For these reasons a woman cannot but seek to win her husband's heart. Nevertheless, the beseeching wife need not use flattery, coaxing words, and cheap methods to gain intimacy.

Decidedly nothing is better (to gain the heart of a husband) than whole-hearted devotion and correct manners. In accordance with the rites and the proper mode of conduct, (let a woman) live a pure life. Let her have ears that hear not licentiousness; and eyes that see not depravity. When she goes outside her own home, let her not be conspicuous in dress and manners. When at home let her not neglect her dress. Women should not assemble in groups, nor gather together, (for gossip and silly laughter). They should not stand watching in the gateways. (If a woman follows) these rules, she may be said to have whole-hearted devotion and correct manners.

If, in all her actions, she is frivolous, she sees and hears (only) that which pleases herself. At home her hair is dishevelled, and her dress is slovenly. Outside the home she emphasizes her femininity to attract attention; she says what ought not to be said; and she looks at what ought not to be seen. (If a woman does such as) these, (she may be) said to be without whole-hearted devotion and correct manners.

Chapter VI Implicit Obedience

Now "to win the love of one man is the crown of a woman's life; to lose the love of one man is her eternal disgrace." This saying advises a fixed will and a whole-hearted devotion for a woman. Ought she then to lose the hearts of her father- and mother-in-law?

There are times when love may lead to differences of opinion (between individuals); there are times when duty may lead to disagreement. Even should the husband say that he loves something, when the parents-in-law say "no," this is called a case of duty leading to disagreement. This being so, then what about the hearts of the parents-in-law? Nothing is better than an obedience which sacrifices personal opinion.

Whenever the mother-in-law says, "Do not do that," and if what she says is right, unquestionably the daughter-in-law obeys. Whenever the mother-in-law says, "Do that," even if what she says is wrong, still the daughter-in-law submits unfailingly to the command.

Let a woman not act contrary to the wishes and the opinions of parents-in-law about right and wrong; let her not dispute with them what is straight and what is crooked. Such (docility) may be called obedience which sacrifices personal opinion. Therefore the ancient book, "A Pattern for Women," says: "If a daughter-in-law (who follows the wishes of her parents-in-law) is like an echo and a shadow, how could she not be praised?"

Chapter VII Harmony with Younger Brothers- and Sisters-in-law

In order for a wife to gain the love of her husband, she must win for herself the love of her parents-in-law. To win for herself the love of her parents-in-law, she must secure for herself the good will of younger brothers- and sisters-in-law. For these reasons the right and the wrong, the praise and the blame of a woman alike depend upon younger brothers- and sisters-in-law. Consequently it will not do for a woman to lose their affection.

They are stupid both who know not that they must not lose (the hearts of) younger brothers- and sisters-in-law, and who cannot be in harmony with them in order to be intimate with them. Excepting only the Holy Men, few are able to be faultless. Now Yen Tzŭ's greatest virtue was that he was able to reform. Confucius praised him (for not committing a misdeed) the second time. (In comparison with him) a woman is the more likely (to make mistakes).

Although a woman possesses a worthy woman's qualifications, and is wise and discerning by nature, is she able to be perfect? Yet if a woman live in harmony with her immediate family, unfavorable criticism will be silenced (within the home. But) if a man and woman disagree, then this evil will be noised abroad. Such consequences are inevitable. The "Book of Changes" says:

Should two hearts harmonize,
The united strength can cut gold,
Words from hearts which agree,
Give forth fragrance like the orchid.

This saying may be applied to (harmony in the home).

Though a daughter-in-law and her younger sisters-in-law are equal in rank, nevertheless (they should) respect (each other); though love (between them may be) sparse, their proper relationship should be intimate. Only the virtuous, the beautiful, the modest, and the respectful (young women) can accordingly rely upon the sense of duty to make their affection sincere, and magnify love to bind their relationships firmly.

Then the excellence and the beauty of such a daughter-in-law becomes generally known. Moreover, any flaws and mistakes are hidden and unrevealed. Parents-in-law boast of her good deeds; her husband is satisfied with her. Praise of her radiates, making her illustrious in district and in neighborhood; and her brightness reaches to her own father and mother.

But a stupid and foolish person as an elder sister-in-law uses her rank to exalt herself; as a younger sister-in-law, because of parents' favor, she becomes filled with arrogance. If arrogant, how can a woman live in harmony with others? If love and proper relationships be perverted, how can praise be secured? In such instances the wife's good is hidden, and her faults are declared. The mother-in-law will be angry, and the husband will be indignant. Blame will reverberate and spread in and outside the home. Disgrace will gather upon the daughter-in-law's person, on the one hand to add humiliation to her own father and mother, and on the other to increase the difficulties of her husband.

Such then is the basis for both honor and disgrace; the foundation for reputation or for ill-repute. Can a woman be too cautious? Consequently to seek the hearts of young brothers- and sisters-in-law decidedly nothing can be esteemed better than modesty and Acquiescence.

Modesty is virtue's handle; acquiescence is the wife's (most refined) characteristic. All who possess these two have sufficient for harmony with others. In the "Book of Poetry" it is written that "here is no evil; there is no dart." So it may be said of (these two, modesty and acquiescence).

The Unattainable Goddess

Even divinities seem to have taken Pan Chao's ideals of womanly behavior to heart, for the Goddess of the Lo, unlike the Lady of the Hsiang or the Mountain Spirit of Ch'u poetry, is skilled in ritual and versed in the *Book of Odes;* a model of loyalty, she discourses on the proper principles of friendship that should obtain between humans and the divine. In the "Rhyme-Prose on the Goddess of the Lo," values of idealized comportment expounded by Chou philosophers have commingled with the visionary yearnings of the poets of the South. The "Goddess" was composed around the year 222 by Ts'ao Chih (192–232), whose eldest brother was the first ruler of the Wei dynasty (220–264). Written as a rhyme-prose, or rhapsody *(fu),* it displays the elaborate descriptive passages characteristic of that genre, whose poems more often describe entire capital cities or lavish imperial hunts. That a poem of this type describes but one woman suggests a remarkable intensity of focus. Only the objects of the male gaze interest the author of the poem, however, who offers no visual clues to the narrator's own appearance. Ts'ao Chih's short prose preface to the work indicates that he modeled it on an earlier verse by the poet Sung Yü (third century B.C.E.), which describes a woman Sung saw in a dream.

In the earlier "Lady of the Hsiang," the narrator had thought only of attracting the divinity into an imaginary dwelling for a tryst, but in the "Goddess of the Lo" the narrator, although clearly infatuated, thinks first of the proprieties of prenuptial rites, and he gives the goddess a jade token of his sincerity. She reciprocates with a garnet stone but eventually leaves, not out of fickleness but again because of propriety: the human and spirit worlds must never touch, she claims. Her personal passion for the mortal accedes to larger principles, and she thus in a sense makes him comply with Confucius's advice to respect spirits, but keep them at a distance. Neither the goddess nor the mortal, however, finds joy in this wisdom.

"Rhyme-Prose on the Goddess of the Lo"

In the third year of the Huang-ch'u era, I attended court at the capital and then crossed the Lo River to begin my journey home. Men in olden times used to say that the goddess of the river is named Fu-fei. Inspired by the example of Sung Yü, who described a goddess to the king of Ch'u, I eventually composed a *fu* which read:

Leaving the capital
to return to my fief in the east,
Yi Barrier at my back,
up over Huan-yüan,
passing through T'ung Valley,
crossing Mount Ching;
the sun had already dipped in the west,
the carriage unsteady, the horses
    fatigued,
and so I halted my rig in the spikenard
    marshes,
grazed my team of four at Lichen Fields,
idling a while by Willow Wood,
letting my eyes wander over the Lo.
Then my mood seemed to change, my
    spirit grew restless;
suddenly my thoughts had scattered.
I looked down, hardly noticing what was
    there,
looked up to see a different sight,
to spy a lovely lady by the slopes of the
    riverbank.

I took hold of the coachman's arm and asked, "Can you see her? Who could she be—a woman so beautiful!"

The coachman replied, "I have heard of the goddess of the River Lo, whose name is Fu-fei. What you see, my prince—is it not she? But what does she look like? I beg you to tell me!"

And I answered:

Her body soars lightly like a startled
    swan,
gracefully, like a dragon in flight,
in splendor brighter than the autumn
    chrysanthemum,
in bloom more flourishing than the pine
    in spring;
dim as the moon mantled in filmy
    clouds,
restless as snow whirled by the driving
    wind.
Gaze far off from a distance:
she sparkles like the sun rising from
    morning mists;
press closer to examine:
she flames like the lotus flower topping
    the green wave.
She strikes a balance between plump and
    frail;
the tall and short of her are justly
    proportioned,
with shoulders shaped as if by carving,
waist narrow as though bound with
    white cords;
at her slim throat and curving neck
the pale flesh lies open to view,
no scented ointments overlaying it,
no coat of leaden powder applied.
Cloud-bank coiffure rising steeply,
long eyebrows delicately arched,
red lips that shed their light abroad,
white teeth gleaming within,
bright eyes skilled at glances,
a dimple to round off the base of the
    cheek—
her rare form wonderfully enchanting,
her manner quiet, her pose demure.
Gentle-hearted, broad of mind,
she entrances with every word she
    speaks;
her robes are of a strangeness seldom
    seen,
her face and figure live up to her
    paintings.
Wrapped in the soft rustle of silken
    garments,
she decks herself with flowery earrings
    of jasper and jade,
gold and kingfisher hairpins adorning her
    head,

strings of bright pearls to make her body
    shine.
She walks in figured slippers fashioned
    for distant wandering,
airy trains of mistlike gauze in tow,
dimmed by the odorous haze of unseen
    orchids,
pacing uncertainly beside the corner of
    the hill.
Then suddenly she puts on a freer air,
ready for rambling, for pleasant
    diversion.
To the left planting her colored
    pennants,
to the right spreading the shade of cassia
    flags,
she dips pale wrists into the holy river's
    brink,
plucks dark iris from the rippling
    shallows.
My fancy is charmed by her modest
    beauty,
but my heart, uneasy, stirs with distress:
without a skilled go-between to join us
    in bliss,
I must trust these little waves to bear my
    message.
Desiring that my sincerity first of all be
    known,
I undo a girdle-jade to offer as pledge.
Ah, the pure trust of the lovely lady,
trained in ritual, acquainted with the
    Odes;
she holds up a garnet stone to match my
    gift,
pointing down into the depths to show
    where we should meet.
Clinging to a lover's passionate faith,
yet I fear that this spirit may deceive
    me;
warned by tales of how Chiao-fu was
    abandoned,
I pause, uncertain and despairing;
then, stilling such thoughts, I turn a
    gentler face toward her,
signaling that for my part I abide by the
    rules of ritual.

The spirit of the Lo, moved by my
    action,
paces to and fro uncertainly,
the holy light deserting her, then
    reappearing,
now darkening, now shining again;
she lifts her light body in the posture of
    a crane,
as though about to fly but not yet taking
    wing.
She walks the heady perfume of pepper-
    scented roads,
strides through clumps of spikenard,
    scattering their fragrance,
wailing distractedly, a sign of endless
    longing,
her voice, sharp with sorrow, growing
    more prolonged.
Then a swarm of milling spirits appears,
calling companions, whistling to their
    mates,
some sporting in the clear current,
some hovering over sacred isles,
some searching for bright pearls,
some collecting kingfisher plumes.
The goddess attends the two queens of
    Hsiang in the south,
joins hands with Wandering Girl from
    the banks of the Han,
sighs that the Gourd Star has no spouse,
laments that the Herdboy must live
    alone.
Lifting the rare fabric of her thin jacket,
she makes a shield of her long sleeve,
    pausing in hesitation,
body nimbler than a winging duck,
swift, as befits the spirit she is;
traversing the waves in tiny steps,
her gauze slippers seem to stir a dust.
Her movements have no constant
    pattern,
now unsteady, now sedate;
hard to predict are her starts and pauses,
now advancing, now turning back.
Her roving glance flashes fire;
a radiant warmth shines in her jadelike
    face.

Her words, held back, remain unvoiced,
her breath scented as though with hidden
    orchids;
her fair face all loveliness—
she makes me forget my hunger!
Then the god P'ing-i calls in his winds,
the River Lord stills the waves,
while P'ing-i beats a drum
and Nü-kua offers simple songs.
Speckled fish are sent aloft to clear the
    way for her carriage,
jade bells are jangled for
    accompaniment;
six dragon-steeds, solemn, pulling neck
    to neck,
she rides the swift passage of her cloudy
    chariot.
Whales dance at the hubs on either side,
water birds fly in front to be her guard.
And when she has gone beyond the
    northern sandbars,
when she has crossed the southern
    ridges,
she bends her white neck,
clear eyes cast down,
moves her red lips,
speaking slowly;
discussing the great principles that
    govern friendship,
she complains that men and gods must
    follow separate ways,
voices anger that we cannot fulfill the
    hopes of youth,
holding up her gauze sleeve to hide her
    weeping,
torrents of teardrops drowning her
    lapels.
She laments that our happy meeting
    must end forever,

grieves that, once departed, we go to
    different lands.
"No way to express my unworthy love,
I give you this bright earring from south
    of the Yangtze.
Though I dwell in the Great Shadow
    down under the waters,
my heart will forever belong to you, my
    prince!"
Then suddenly I could not tell where she
    had gone;
to my sorrow the spirit vanished in
    darkness, veiling her light.
With this I turned my back on the
    lowland, climbed the height;
my feet went forward but my soul
    remained behind.
Thoughts taken up with the memory of
    her image,
I turned to look back, a heart full of
    despair.
Hoping that the spirit form might show
    itself again,
I embarked in a small boat to journey
    upstream,
drifting over the long river, forgetting to
    return,
wrapped in endless remembrances that
    made my longing greater.
Night found me fretful, unable to sleep;
heavy frosts soaked me until the break
    of day.
I ordered the groom to ready the
    carriage,
thinking to return to my eastern road,
but though I seized the reins and lifted
    up my whip,
I stayed lost in hesitation and could not
    break away.

SIX DYNASTIES PERIOD

(220-589)

The Buddhist Pure Land

Around the first century of the common era, and possibly much earlier, the teachings of Buddhism were gradually transmitted from India to China via the silk routes of Central Asia. Buddhism's novel cosmologies and spiritual practices were not well understood until some centuries later, but by the Six Dynasties era (220–589) scholars had translated many Buddhist scriptures into Chinese.

By the time Buddhism reached China, it was an established tradition with a history of over five hundred years, and since it is impossible to understand Chinese Buddhism without some background knowledge of its Indian roots, a brief explanation of the basic tenets of the early teachings of Buddhism is presented here. Originating south of the Himalayan mountains in what is now Nepal, Buddhism traces its origins to the teachings of Siddhārtha Gautama (ca. 566–ca. 486 B.C.E.?), a historical figure about whom little is actually known. According to traditional accounts of his life, he was born into a wealthy family, married, and had a son; disaffected by the sufferings of human life, however, he left home in his late twenties or early thirties and became a forest-dwelling wandering ascetic, a common enough practice at that time. After five or six years of spiritual exercises, he experienced a new, enlightened perspective on reality and thereafter was known as "the Buddha," an epithet that literally means "the awakened one" or "the enlightened one." He spent the rest of his life articulating that experience in his teachings, and he acquired many followers, both male and female. The community of followers, who were originally mendicant wanderers but later adopted a sedentary monastic life-style, was called the *sangha* (Sanskrit) and included both monastics and lay followers.

The content of that teaching is now somewhat difficult to define, since it was communicated verbally, transmitted orally from disciple to disciple, and only consigned to writing sometime around the third century B.C.E. Essential truths of that teaching, however, are expressed in the Buddha's "Four Noble Truths," which might be understood as a medical diagnosis of the ills of human existence. These truths are as follows: (1) life is unsatisfactory, (2) unsatisfactoriness is caused by inordinate craving, (3) craving can cease, (4) the route to cessation is an eightfold path. Life is unsatisfactory in the sense that all things are subject to grosser and subtler kinds of suffering; all things are transient and have no permanent self-nature. Even human beings have no permanent self-nature or everlasting soul: they are only temporary, ever-changing composites of five "aggregates" (Sanskrit *skandhas*): material form, sensations, perceptions, volitions and attitudes, and consciousness. Unsatisfactoriness is augmented by inordinate cravings or thirsts to possess, contain, and own permanently those things that are by their very nature impermanent and always changing. Craving, however, can cease, and this cessation is called nirvana. Cessation may be sought through an eightfold path divided into three larger categories: wisdom, ethical behavior, and mental discipline. Wisdom entails (1) right thoughts of unselfish detachment from the world and (2) right understanding and insight into the nature of reality. Ethical behavior requires (3) right speech, (4) right action, (5) and right livelihood, that is, refraining from harming all creatures in word and action and developing sentiments of selfless compassion toward them. Mental discipline involves (6) right efforts to develop oneself mentally, (7) right mindfulness and awareness of things, and (8) right concentration, the development of concentrative or meditative states (Sanskrit *dhyāna*). In the few hundred years after Siddhārtha Gautama's death, a large tripartite body of literature was compiled to record the Buddha's teaching, or *Dharma*. This Buddhist canon, or Tripiṭaka (literally "three baskets"), consists of the Buddha's own discourses, or *sūtras*, which became the scriptures of the tradition; the monastics' code of discipline; and philosophical commentaries by various thinkers.

Originally, the teachings of Siddhārtha Gautama were not theistic, and the Buddha was revered as an extraordinary human being but was not considered a god or divinity. Questions regarding the purported origins or structure of the cosmos were dismissed as issues not conducive to the more urgent problem of the alleviation of human suffering. Those who sought to recapture the enlightenment experience of the Buddha did so by virtue of their own efforts, for there existed no supranormal forces or deities to assist them.

The Four Noble Truths and other teachings of the Buddha, however, accommodated varied interpretations, and they generated much philosophical speculation and contention. Beginning around the third century B.C.E., novel trends of

Buddhist thought, which might only very loosely be called "schools" of thought, developed in India. Some thinkers particularly emphasized certain aspects of the eightfold path, such as wisdom or mental discipline; other, more conservative, thinkers adhered more closely to the original teachings. Yet others proposed new cosmologies and asserted, for example, that Siddhārtha Gautama, the historical Buddha, was in fact but one particular earthly manifestation of a timeless cosmic Buddha or Buddha essence that manifested itself in innumerable universes simultaneously; hence, there is not one but many Buddhas throughout the past, present, and future. New scriptures purporting to be the words of the historical Buddha promulgated new spiritual paths and soteriological techniques, and some held that all people, even those not well versed in the eightfold path, could themselves attain Buddhahood. (Those scriptures did not, however, necessarily clearly explain what Buddhahood actually was.) Moreover, human beings could call on the assistance of various Buddhas and *bodhisattvas*, literally "enlightened beings," to assist them in their spiritual progress. So when Buddhist teachings and scriptures entered China around the first century of the common era, they presented a very heterogeneous and unsystematized mix of ideas. Selections from some of the most important scriptures to influence the Chinese Buddhist tradition are presented here.

One of these is the *Scripture of the Pure Land (Sukhāvatīvyūha)*, which describes a sweet or happy realm that is the antithesis of the world of human suffering. Both longer and shorter versions of the sutra exist, and this is a selection from the former. The *Scripture of the Pure Land* was translated into Chinese a number of times beginning in the third century, and, at least as early as the fifth century, societies formed in China to practice its teachings; it remains extremely popular to the present day.

The scripture takes the form of an imaginary conversation between the historical Buddha and one of his disciples, Ānanda, as the Buddha explains the Pure Land of the Buddha Amitābha, the Buddha of Light, also known as the Buddha Amitāyus, the Buddha of Life. In a previous lifetime in eons past, Amitābha was once the monk Dharmākara, who made a vow before a Buddha of the past to save all beings; through the powers of concentration, Dharmākara created in his mind a perfect world. Dharmākara kept his vow and now abides in that perfect world-system as Amitābha, and in that Pure Land saves countless sentient beings. The geography of the Pure Land is scaled to provide a comfortable environment ideally suited to the attainment of enlightenment; every imaginable physical and conceptual aid to spiritual perfection is provided by the Tathāgata, or "Thus Come One," a honorific epithet of a Buddha. Here are the three refuges where one may find safety: the Buddha, the Dharma, and the sangha. Here also are the six perfections of a bodhisattva: the perfections of the qualities of giving, ethics, renunciation, wisdom, effort, and patience.

Buddhism espoused a notion of rebirth, which may be understood literally or figuratively. The Pure Land scripture asserted that humans unable to attain nirvana in this life may be reborn into the Pure Land in the next provided they are reverently devoted to Amitābha, accumulate a store of spiritual merit by the performance of good works, try to attain enlightenment, and make a vow to be reborn in Amitābha's happy land. Enlightenment is assured for those who hear the name of Amitābha and resolutely devote themselves to him with even a single thought. Amitābha can be directly seen at the time of death; paintings of him sometimes were equipped with strings that the dying might grasp to facilitate ascension into the Pure Land. Pure Land Buddhism, which adopts the religious practices recommended in the sutra, is sometimes considered a devotional as opposed to a philosophical tradition, yet the scripture describes a realm where the practitioner may joyfully hear the most abstruse analytical discourses. The Pure Land may be understood literally as a place of sensual comforts or figuratively as a realm of perfect concentration like that conceived in Dharmākara's mind.

Selection from the *Scripture of the Pure Land*

This world Sukhavati, Ananda, which is the world system of the Lord Amitabha, is rich and prosperous, comfortable, fertile, delightful and crowded with many Gods and men. And in this world system, Ananda, there are no hells, no animals, no ghosts, no Asuras and none of the inauspicious places of rebirth. And in this our world no jewels make their appearance like those which exist in the world system Sukhavati.

And that world system Sukhavati, Ananda, emits many fragrant odours, it is rich in a great variety of flowers and fruits, adorned with jewel trees, which are frequented by flocks of various birds with sweet voices, which the Tathagata's miraculous power has conjured up. And these jewel trees, Ananda, have various colours, many colours, many hundreds of thousands of colours. They are variously composed of the seven precious things, in varying combinations, i.e. of gold, silver, beryl, crystal, coral, red pearls, or emerald. Such jewel trees, and clusters of banana trees and rows of palm trees, all made of precious things, grow everywhere in this Buddha-field. On all sides it is surrounded with golden nets, and all round covered with lotus flowers made of all the precious things. Some of the lotus flowers are half a mile in circumference, others up to ten miles. And from each jewel lotus issue thirty-six hundred thousand kotis of rays. And at the end of each ray there issue thirty-six hundred thousand kotis of Buddhas, with golden-coloured bodies, who bear the thirty-two marks of the superman, and who, in all the ten directions, go into countless world systems, and there demonstrate Dharma.

And further, Ananda, in this Buddha-field there are nowhere any mountains—black mountains, jewel mountains, Sumerus, kings of mountains, circular mountains and great circular mountains. But the Buddha-field is everywhere even, delightful like the palm of the hand, and in all its parts the ground contains a great variety of jewels and gems.

And many kinds of rivers flow along in this world system Sukhavati. There are great rivers there, one mile broad, and up to fifty miles broad and twelve miles deep. And all these rivers flow along calmly, their water is fragrant with manifold agreeable odours, in them there are bunches of flowers to which various jewels adhere, and they resound with various sweet sounds. And the sound which issues from these great rivers is as pleasant as that of a musical instrument, which consists of hundreds of thousands of kotis of parts, and which, skilfully played, emits a heavenly music. It is deep, commanding, distinct, clear, pleasant, and one never tires of hearing it, it always agrees with one and one likes to hear it, like the words "Impermanent, peaceful, calm, and not-self." Such is the sound that reaches the ears of those beings.

And, Ananda, both the banks of those great rivers are lined with variously scented jewel trees, and from them bunches of flowers, leaves, and branches of all kinds hang down. And if those beings wish to indulge in sports full of heavenly delights on those river-banks, then, after they have stepped into the water, the water in each case rises as high as they wish it to—up to the ankles, or the knees, or the hips, or their sides, or their ears. And heavenly delights arise. Again, if beings wish the water to be cold, for them it becomes cold; if they wish it to be hot, for them it becomes hot; if they wish it to be hot and cold, for them it becomes hot and cold, to suit their pleasure. And those rivers flow along, full of water scented with the finest odours, and covered with beautiful flowers, resounding with the sounds of many birds, easy to ford, free from mud, and with golden sand at the bottom. And all the wishes those beings may think of, they all will be fulfilled, as long as they are rightful.

And as to the pleasant sound which issues from the water (of these rivers), that reaches all the parts of this Buddha-field. And everyone hears the pleasant sound he wishes to hear, i.e. he hears of the Buddha, the Dharma, the Samgha, of the (six) perfections, the (ten) stages, the powers, the grounds of self-confidence, of the special dharmas of a Buddha, of the analytical knowledges, of emptiness, the signless, and the wishless, of the uneffected, the unborn, of non-production, non-existence, non-cessation, of calm, quietude, and peace, of the great friendliness, the great compassion, the great sympathetic joy, the great evenmindedness, of the patient acceptance of things which fail to be produced, and of the acquisition of the stage where one is consecrated (as a Tathagata). And, hearing this, one gains the exalted zest and joyfulness, which is associated with detachment, dispassion, calm, cessation, Dharma, and brings about the state of mind which leads to the accomplishment of enlightenment. And nowhere in this world-system Sukhavati does one hear of anything unwholesome, nowhere of the hindrances, nowhere of the states of punishment, the states of woe and the bad destinies, nowhere of suffering. Even of feelings which are neither pleasant nor unpleasant one does not hear there, how much less of suffering! And that, Ananda, is the reason why this world-system is called the "Happy Land" (Sukhavati). But all this describes it only in brief, not in detail. One aeon might well reach its end while one proclaims the reasons for happiness in the world-system Sukhavati, and still one could not come to the end of (the enumeration of) the reasons for happiness.

Moreover, Ananda, all the beings who have been reborn in this world-system Sukhavati, who are reborn in it, or who will be reborn in it, they will be exactly like the Paranirmitavasavartin Gods; of the same colour, strength, vigour, height and breadth, dominion, store of merit, and keenness of superknowledges; they enjoy the same dresses, ornaments, parks, palaces, and pointed towers, the same kind of forms, sounds, smells, tastes, and touchables, just the same kinds of enjoyments. And the beings in the world-system Sukhavati do not eat gross food, like soup or raw sugar; but whatever food they may wish for, that they perceive as eaten, and they become gratified in body and mind, without there being any further need to throw the food into the body. And if, after their bodies are gratified, they wish for certain perfumes, then the whole of that Buddha-field becomes scented with just that kind of heavenly perfumes. But if someone does not wish to smell that perfume, then the perception of it does not reach him. In the same way, whatever they may wish for comes to them, be it musical instruments, banners, flags, etc.; or cloaks of different colours, or ornaments of various kinds. If they wish for a palace of a certain colour, distinguishing marks, construction, height, and width, made of various precious things, adorned with hundreds of thousands of pinnacles, while inside it various heavenly woven materials are spread out, and it is full of couches strewn with beautiful cushions—then just such a palace appears before them. In those delightful palaces, surrounded and honoured by seven times seven thousand Apsarases, they dwell, play, enjoy, and disport themselves.

And the beings who are touched by the winds, which are pervaded with various perfumes, are filled with a happiness as great as that of a monk who has achieved the cessation of suffering.

And in this Buddha-field one has no conception at all of fire, sun, moon, planets, constellations, stars, or blinding darkness, and no conception even of day and night, except (where they are mentioned) in the sayings of the Tathagata. There is nowhere a notion of monks possessing private parks for retreats.

And all the beings who have been born, who are born, who will be born in this Buddha-field, they all are fixed on the right method of salvation, until they have won Nirvana. And why? Because there is here no place for and no conception of the two other groups, i.e. of those who are not fixed at all, and those who are fixed on wrong ways. For this reason also that world-system is called the "Happy Land."

And further again, Ananda, in the ten directions, in each single direction, in Buddha-fields countless like the sands of the river Ganges, Buddhas and Lords countless like the sands of the river Ganges glorify the name of the Lord Amitabha, the Tathagata, praise him, proclaim his fame, extol his virtue. And why? Because all beings are irreversible from the supreme enlightenment if they hear the name of the Lord Amitabha, and, on hearing it, with one single thought only raise their hearts to him with a resolve connected with serene faith.

And if any beings, Ananda, again and again reverently attend to this Tathagata, if they will plant a large and immeasurable root of good, having raised their hearts to enlightenment, and if they vow to be reborn in that world system, then, when the hour of their death approaches, that Tathagata Amitabha, the Arhat, the fully Enlightened One, will stand before them, surrounded by hosts of monks. Then, having seen that Lord, and having died with hearts serene, they will be reborn in just that world-system Sukhavati. And if there are sons or daughters of good family, who may desire to see that Tathagata Amitabha in this very life, they should raise their hearts to the supreme enlightenment, they should direct their thought with extreme resoluteness and perseverance unto this Buddha-field and they should dedicate their store of merit to being reborn therein.

The *Lotus Sutra*

One of the most influential texts in all of Asia is the *Lotus Sutra,* a scripture that promises universal salvation for all beings and assures the assistance of benevolent Buddhas and bodhisattvas. Compiled in India between around 50 to 150 C.E., the scripture was rendered into Chinese at least six times from the third to the sixth centuries. This selection, chapter 25 of the sutra, is based on a version completed under the noted translator Kumārajīva (ca. 350–410); it describes the bodhisattva known in Sanskrit as Avalokiteśvara, the Regarder of the Cries of the World, the bodhisattva of compassion.

Descriptions of Avalokiteśvara's manifold powers reveal clearly the distinctions between Buddhism's human founder, Siddhārtha Gautama, and the suprahuman savior-divinities of later Buddhism. Couched as a dialogue between the historical Buddha and the bodhisattva Infinite Thought, this chapter describes the merciful attentiveness of Avalokiteśvara, who watches the world from all sides and in all directions. The Four Noble Truths had asserted the importance of personally applying oneself to an eightfold course toward spiritual emancipation, but here both the means and the goals of salvation are somewhat different: devotion, reverence, and homage to the bodhisattva, as well as offerings and the invocation of his name, ensure deliverance from personal danger, mental vexation, or want. Yet both the earlier and later traditions emphasize the alleviation of human suffering. The bodhisattva also acts as a teacher of the Law, or Dharma, by appearing in this world in many manifestations. These manifestations are one aspect his tactfulness, or skill in liberative techniques (*upāya*), for freeing all sentient beings from the pains of this world.

Avalokiteśvara's name was translated into Chinese as Kuan-yin, literally, the One Who Perceives Sounds. Kuan-yin became one of the most popular divinities of Chinese Buddhism and appears in many iconographic forms: originally male in India, the bodhisattva of compassion is also depicted in female form in Chinese painting and sculpture. Ultimately, however, Kuan-yin is beyond all conceptions of male and female; many visual depictions of her, like those of other Buddhist divinities, are deliberately ambiguous in terms of gender. She is often considered an associate of the Buddha Amitābha, whose Pure Land lies in the west. Kuan-yin, however, was also believed to preside over her own world-system, called Potalaka (Chinese P'u-t'o), in the south. By the eleventh century, this realm was identified with the island of Mount P'u-t'o off the southern coast of China, which became a well-known pilgrimage site for devotees of Kuan-yin.

"The All-Sidedness of the Bodhisattva Regarder of the Cries of the World"

At that time the Bodhisattva Infinite Thought rose up from his seat, and baring his right shoulder and folding his hands toward the Buddha, spoke thus: "World-honored One! For what reason is the Bodhisattva Avalokiteśvara named Regarder of the Cries of the World?"

The Buddha answered the Bodhisattva Infinite Thought: "Good son! If there be countless hundred thousand myriad koṭis of living beings suffering from pain and distress who hear of this Bodhisattva Regarder of the Cries of the World, and with all their mind call upon his name, the Bodhisattva Regarder of the Cries of the World will instantly regard their cries, and all of them will be delivered.

"If there be any who keep the name of that Bodhisattva Regarder of the Cries of the World, though they fall into a great fire, the fire will not be able to burn them, by virtue of the supernatural power of that bodhisattva's majesty. If any, carried away by a flood, call upon his name, they will immediately reach the shallows. If there be hundreds of thousands of myriads of koṭis of beings who in search of gold, silver, lapis lazuli, moonstones, agate, coral, amber, pearls, and other treasures go out on the ocean, and if a black gale blows their ships to drift upon the land of the rākṣasa demons, and if amongst them there be even a single person who calls upon the name of the Bodhisattva Regarder of the Cries of the World, all those people will be delivered from the throes of the rākṣasas. It is for this reason that [he] is named Regarder of the Cries of the World.

"If, again, there be any man on the verge of [deadly] harm who calls upon the name of the Bodhisattva Regarder of the Cries of the World, the sword of the attacker will instantly snap asunder and he will be set free. Even if the three-thousand-great-thousandfold world were full of yakshas and rākṣasas seeking to afflict people, these wicked demons, hearing them call upon the name of the Bodhisattva Regarder of the Cries of the World, would not be able to see them with [their] wicked eyes, how much less to hurt them.

"If, moreover, there be anyone, guilty or not guilty, loaded with manacles, fetters, cangues, or chains, who calls on the name of the Bodhisattva Regarder of the Cries of the World, they shall all be snapped and broken off and he shall be freed.

"If the three-thousand-great-thousandfold world were full of enemies and robbers, and there were a merchant chief who led many merchants having charge of costly jewels along a perilous road, and among them one man speaks forth: 'Good sons! Be not afraid. With one mind do you invoke the title of the Bodhisattva Regarder of the Cries of the World, for this bodhisattva is able to give courage to all the living. If you invoke his name, you will be freed from these enemies and robbers.' On hearing this, if all the traders together with one voice cry, 'Namaḥ! Bodhisattva Regarder of the Cries of the World!' then, by invoking his name, they will be relieved. Infinite Thought! Such is the awe-inspiring supernatural power of the Bodhisattva Regarder of the Cries of the World.

"If any living beings much given to carnal passion keep in mind and revere the Bodhisattva Regarder of the Cries of the World, they will be set free from their passion. If any much given to irascibility keep in mind and revere the Bodhisattva Regarder of the Cries of the World, they will be set free from their irascibility. If any much given to infatuation keep in mind and revere the Bodhisattva Regarder of the Cries of the World, they will be set free from their infatuation. Infinite Thought! Such are the abundant benefits conferred by the supernatural power of the Bodhisattva Regarder of the Cries of the World. Consequently, let all the living ever keep him in mind.

"If any woman desiring a son worships and pays homage to the Bodhisattva Regarder of the Cries of the World, she will bear a son happy, virtuous, and wise. If she desires a daughter, she will bear a daughter of good demeanor and looks, who of old has planted virtuous roots, beloved and respected by all. Infinite Thought! Such is the power of the Bodhisattva Regarder of the Cries of the World. If any of the living revere and worship the Bodhisattva Regarder of the Cries of the World, blessings will not be rudely rejected.

"Therefore, let all the living cherish the title of the Bodhisattva Regarder of the Cries of the World. Infinite Thought! Suppose anyone cherishes the names of bodhisattvas [numerous as] the sands of sixty-two koṭis of the Ganges, who all his life makes them offerings of food, drink, garments, bedding, and medicaments—what is your opinion—are not the merits of that good son or good daughter abundant?" Infinite Thought replied: "Extremely abundant!" The World-honored One, the Buddha, proceeded: "But if [any]one cherishes the title of the Bodhisattva Regarder of the Cries of the World, or only for a moment worships and reveres him, the blessings of these two men will be exactly equal without difference, and cannot be exhausted in hundreds of thousands of myriads of koṭis of kalpas. Infinite Thought! Such is the immeasurable, boundless degree of blessedness he will obtain who cherishes the name of the Bodhisattva Regarder of the Cries of the World."

The Bodhisattva Infinite Thought [again] said to the Buddha: "World-honored One! How is it that the Bodhisattva Regarder of the Cries of the World wanders in this sahā-world? How does he preach the Law to the living? What is the character of his tactfulness?"

The Buddha replied to the Bodhisattva Infinite Thought: "Good son! If the living in any realm must be saved in the body of a buddha, the Bodhisattva Regarder of the Cries of the World appears as a buddha and preaches to them the Law. To those who must be saved in the body of a pratyekabuddha, he appears as a pratyekabuddha and preaches to them the Law. To those who must be saved in the body of a śrāvaka, he appears as a śrāvaka and preaches to them the Law. To those who must be saved in the body of Brahma, he appears as Brahma and preaches to them the Law. To those who must be saved in the body of Śakra, he appears

as Śakra and preaches to them the Law. To those who must be saved in the body of Īśvara, he appears as Īśvara and preaches to them the Law. To those who must be saved in the body of Maheśvara, he appears as Maheśvara and preaches to them the Law. To those who must be saved in the body of a great divine general, he appears as a great divine general and preaches to them the Law. To those who must be saved in the body of Vaiśravaṇa, he appears as Vaiśravaṇa and preaches to them the Law. To those who must be saved in the body of a minor king, he appears as a minor king and preaches to them the Law. To those who must be saved in the body of an elder, he appears as an elder and preaches to them the Law. To those who must be saved in the body of a citizen, he appears as a citizen and preaches to them the Law. To those who must be saved in the body of a minister of state, he appears as a minister and preaches to them the Law. To those who must be saved in the body of a Brahman, he appears as a Brahman and preaches to them the Law. To those who must be saved in the body of a bhikshu, bhikshuṇī, upāsaka, or upāsikā, he appears as a bhikshu, bhikshuṇī, upāsaka, or upāsikā and preaches to them the Law. To those who must be saved in the body of the wife of an elder, citizen, minister, or Brahman, he appears as a woman and preaches to them the Law. To those who must be saved in the body of a youth or maiden, he appears as a youth or maiden and preaches to them the Law. To those who must be saved in the body of a god, dragon, yaksha, gandharva, asura, garuḍa, kiṃnara, mahoraga, human or nonhuman being, he appears in every such form and preaches to them the Law. To those who must be saved in [the shape of] a diamond-holding god, he appears as a diamond-holding god and preaches to them the Law. Infinite Thought! Such are the merits acquired by this Bodhisattva Regarder of the Cries of the World and the various forms in which he rambles through many lands to save the living. Therefore, do you with single mind pay homage to the Bodhisattva Regarder of the Cries of the World. This Bodhisattva-Mahāsattva Regarder of the Cries of the World is able to make fearless those in anxiety and distress. For this reason all in this sahā-world give him the title Bestower of Fearlessness."

The Bodhisattva Infinite Thought said to the Buddha: "World-honored One! Let me now make an offering to the Bodhisattva Regarder of the Cries of the World."

Thereupon he unloosed from his neck a necklace of pearls worth a hundred thousand pieces of gold and presented it to him, making this remark: "Good sir! Accept this pious gift of a pearl necklace." But the Bodhisattva Regarder of the Cries of the World would not accept it.

Again the Bodhisattva Infinite Thought addressed the Bodhisattva Regarder of the Cries of the World: "Good sir! Out of compassion for us, accept this necklace." Then the Buddha said to the Bodhisattva Regarder of the Cries of the World: "Out of compassion for this Bodhisattva Infinite Thought and the four groups, and for the gods, dragons, yakshas, gandharvas, asuras, garuḍas, kiṃnaras, mahoragas, human and non-human beings, and others, accept this necklace." Then the Bodhisattva Regarder of the Cries of the World, having compassion for all the four groups and the gods, dragons, human and non-human beings, and others, accepted the necklace, and dividing it into two parts, offered one part to Sakyamuni Buddha and offered the other to the stupa of the Buddha Abundant Treasures.

"Infinite Thought! With such sovereign supernatural powers does the Bodhisattva Regarder of the Cries of the World wander through the sahā-world."

Then the Bodhisattva Infinite Thought made inquiry thus in verse:

The World-honored One with all the mystic
     signs!
Let me now again inquire of him:
For what cause is this Buddha-son named
Regarder of the Cries of the World?

The Honored One with all the mystic signs answered Infinite Thought in verse:

Listen to the deeds of the Cry Regarder,
Who well responds to every quarter;
His vast vow is deep as the sea,
Inconceivable in its eons.

Serving many thousands of koṭis of buddhas,
He has vowed a great pure vow.
Let me briefly tell you.
[He who] hears his name, and sees him,
And bears him unremittingly in mind,
Will be able to end the sorrows of existence.
Though [others] with harmful intent
Throw him into a burning pit,
Let him think of the Cry Regarder's power
And the fire pit will become a pool.
Or driven along a great ocean,
In peril of dragons, fishes, and demons,
Let him think of the Cry Regarder's power
And waves cannot submerge him.
Or if, from the peak of Sumeru,
Men would hurl him down,
Let him think of the Cry Regarder's power
And like the sun he will stand firm in the
     sky.
Or if, pursued by wicked men,
And cast down from Mount Diamond,
He thinks of the Cry Regarder's power,
Not a hair shall be injured.
Or if, meeting with encompassing foes,
Each with sword drawn to strike him,
He thinks of the Cry Regarder's power,
All their hearts will turn to kindness.
Or if, meeting suffering by royal [command],
His life is to end in execution,
[And] he thinks of the Cry Regarder's power,
[The executioner's] sword will break in
     pieces.
Or if, imprisoned, shackled, and chained,
Arms and legs in gyves and stocks,
He thinks of the Cry Regarder's power,
Freely he shall be released.
Or if by incantation and poisons
One seeks to hurt his body,
And he thinks of the Cry Regarder's power,
All will revert to their originator.
Or if, meeting evil rākshasas,
Venomous dragons, and demons,
He thinks of the Cry Regarder's power,
At once none will dare to hurt him.
If, encompassed by evil beasts,
Tusks sharp and claws fearful,
He thinks of the Cry Regarder's power,
They will flee in every direction.
If, scorched by the fire-flame
Of the poisonous breath
Of boas, vipers, and scorpions,
He thinks of the Cry Regarder's power,
Instantly at his voice they will retreat.

Clouds thunder and lightning flashes,
Hail falls and rain streams:
He thinks of the Cry Regarder's power
And all instantly are scattered.
The living, crushed and harassed,
Oppressed by countless pains:
The Cry Regarder with his mystic wisdom
Can save [such] a suffering world.
Perfect in supernatural powers,
Widely practiced in wisdom and tact,
In the lands of the universe there is no place
Where he does not manifest himself.
All the evil states of existence,
Hells, ghosts, and animals,
Sorrows of birth, age, disease, death,
All by degrees are ended by him.
True regard, serene regard,
Far-reaching wise regard,
Regard of pity, compassionate regard,
Ever longed for, ever looked for!
Pure and serene in radiance,
Wisdom's sun destroying darkness,
Subduer of woes of storm and fire,
Who illumines all the world!
Law of pity, thunder quivering,
Compassion wondrous as a great cloud,
Pouring spiritual rain like nectar,
Quenching the flames of distress!
In disputes before a magistrate,
Or in fear in battle's array,

If he thinks of the Cry Regarder's power
All his enemies will be routed.
His is the wondrous voice, voice of the
    world-regarder,
Brahma-voice, voice of the rolling tide,
Voice all world-surpassing,
Therefore ever to be kept in mind,
With never a doubting thought.
Regarder of the World's Cries, pure and
    holy,
In pain, distress, death, calamity,
Able to be a sure reliance,
Perfect in all merit,
With compassionate eyes beholding all,
Boundless ocean of blessings!
Prostrate let us revere him.

Thereupon the Bodhisattva Stage Holder rose from his seat, and went before and said to the Buddha: "World-honored One! If any living being hears of the sovereign work and the all-sided transcendent powers [shown in] this chapter of the Bodhisattva Regarder of the Cries of the World, it should be known that the merits of this man are not a few."

While the Buddha preached this chapter of the All-sided One, the eighty-four thousand living beings in the assembly all set their minds upon Perfect Enlightenment, with which nothing can compare.

Emptiness Is Form

The *Heart Sutra*'s brevity belies its great importance in Buddhist philosophy. It epitomizes the perfection of the wisdom aspect of the eightfold path and belongs to a type of literature appropriately called *Prajñāpāramitā*, the literature of the perfection *(pāramitā,* literally "to go beyond to the other shore") of wisdom *(prajñā).* Such literature originated in India around the first century B.C.E. and enjoyed popularity in China particularly during the fourth century of the common era. The *Heart Sutra* is of Indian provenance and dates perhaps to the fourth century; it is regarded as one of the most philosophically subtle works in the Buddhist canon. Extant in several versions, this is the smaller version, presented in its entirety.

In Buddhist iconography, wisdom, sometimes viewed as insight or understanding, is depicted as a female divinity and is thus invoked as "the lovely." Such deities may be understood either as divine beings or as aspects of the human mind. The bodhisattva Avalokita, or Avalokiteśvara, is engaged in contemplating the wisdom or insight that has gone beyond to another shore or dimension, and he tries to convey this insight to Śāriputra, a disciple of the Buddha. Avalokita takes as his theme of contemplation the five aggregates *(skandhas)* that constitute a human being, here translated as the five "heaps" of form, feelings (sensation), perceptions, impulses (volitions or attitudes), and consciousness. He realizes that all *dharmas,* or phenomena, are empty. ("Dharma" capitalized means the teaching of Buddhism; *dharma* in lowercase refers to phenomena or things.) Beginning with the aggregate of form, Avalokita perceives that form has no permanent abiding self-nature that allows it to exist independently of other conditions; a particular form is not a permanent, self-existent entity but an ephemeral resting point within a larger reality that is constantly in flux. From the temporal perspective of a particular resting point, there is form; but from the timeless perspective of the larger reality, there is no single form that exists eternally. Thus forms are empty *(śūnyatā)* of independent self-nature.

To say that forms are empty is not to say that things do not exist at all; it merely suggests that no particular thing exists in one state forever, for if that were the case the world would become completely static. To make a comparison with the thought of the Chou philosophers, Hsün Tzu in his view of the human mind had implied that emptiness was not nothingness but was the unlimited capacity of the mind to always absorb more things, no matter how many ideas it always contained. Similarly, the Buddhist view of emptiness is not nothingness but is the unlimited and boundless openness of a universe always in motion and transformation. Such metaphors suggest Chuang Tzu's transformation of things, and in fact the Chinese often appealed to ideas from texts such as the *Chuang Tzu* and the *Tao-te ching* when first trying to translate Buddhist concepts into their own way of thinking.

Those who understand that form is emptiness and emptiness is form are well on the way to becoming bodhisattvas themselves and to attaining nirvana. Such beings, however, realize that there is ultimately nothing to attain or even think about (no "thought coverings"); paradoxically, this realization liberates them into an awakened perception of reality. The scripture closes with a spell, or mantra, that evokes the blissful apprehension of subtle insight.

The *Heart Sutra*

I. The Invocation

Homage to the Perfection of Wisdom, the lovely, the holy!

II. The Prologue

Avalokita, the holy Lord and Bodhisattva, was moving in the deep course of the wisdom which has gone beyond. He looked down from on high, he beheld but five heaps, and he saw that in their own-being they were empty.

III. The Dialectics of Emptiness. First Stage

Here, O Sariputra, form is emptiness, and the very emptiness is form; emptiness does not differ from form, form does not differ from emptiness; whatever is form, that is emptiness, whatever is emptiness, that is form. The same is true of feelings, perceptions, impulses, and consciousness.

IV. The Dialectics of Emptiness. Second Stage

Here, O Sariputra, all dharmas are marked with emptiness; they are not produced or stopped, not defiled or immaculate, not deficient or complete.

V. The Dialectics of Emptiness. Third Stage

Therefore, O Sariputra, in emptiness there is no form, nor feeling, nor perception, nor impulse, nor consciousness; no eye, ear, nose, tongue, body, mind; no forms, sounds, smells, tastes, touchables or objects of mind; no sight-organ-element, and so forth, until we come to: no mind-consciousness-element; there is no ignorance, no extinction of ignorance, and so forth, until we come to: there is no decay and death, no extinction of decay and death; there is no suffering, no origination, no stopping, no path; there is no cognition, no attainment, and no non-attainment.

VI. The Concrete Embodiment and Practical Basis of Emptiness

Therefore, O Sariputra, it is because of his indifference to any kind of personal attainment that a Bodhisattva, through having relied on the perfection of wisdom, dwells without thought-coverings. In the absence of thought-coverings he has not been made to tremble, he has overcome what can upset, and in the end he attains to Nirvana.

VII. Full Emptiness is the Basis also of Buddhahood

All those who appear as Buddhas in the three periods of time fully awake to the utmost, right and perfect enlightenment because they have relied on the perfection of wisdom.

VIII. The Teaching Brought Within Reach of the Comparatively Unenlightened

Therefore one should know the Prajñaparamita as the great spell, the spell of great knowledge, the utmost spell, the unequalled spell, allayer of all suffering, in truth—for what could go wrong? By the Prajñaparamita has this spell been delivered. It runs like this: Gone, Gone, Gone beyond, Gone altogether beyond, O what an awakening, All Hail!

This completes the Heart of Perfect Wisdom.

The Holy Teaching of Vimalakīrti

One Buddhist scripture that elaborates upon the "wisdom" aspect of the eight-fold path is *The Holy Teaching of Vimalakīrti,* a philosophical satire of conventional conceptions of reality that invites the reader to enter a limitless perfect wisdom where ordinary boundaries of space and time collapse. This is the wisdom of inconceivable liberation, a domain where one transcends the apparent dualities of materiality and immateriality and abides in infinity without, however, leaving the finite world behind. In this realm lives the layman Vimalakīrti, who compassionately invites visitors into his "house," the abode of the infinite, and guides them toward inconceivable liberation by means of vision, metaphor, and paradox.

In "Inconceivable Liberation," one chapter from *The Holy Teaching of Vimala-kīrti,* the monk Śāriputra becomes Vimalakīrti's guest. The historical Śāriputra was a direct disciple of Siddhārtha Gautama, and here he is depicted as a disciple of the Buddha who has grasped the outer formulations of the Buddha's teachings but has not comprehended inner transcendent wisdom. He and the other "disciples" are in a sense allegories of the old dispensation of Buddhism taught by Siddhārtha Gautama; Vimalakīrti and the bodhisattvas represent a new interpretation of the old wisdom. Buddhist life for Śāriputra consists of joining the *sangha,* or Buddhist community, and following the Four Noble Truths; to Vimalakīrti, the Four Noble Truths, if understood in only a limited way, are just verbiage. Śāriputra arrives at Vimalakīrti's house seeking a chair (limited understanding) instead of the Dharma (limitless understanding), and Vimalakīrti critiques the monk for objectifying what is beyond conceptualization and for mistaking the Dharma for a chair.

To expand Śāriputra's inner vision and visually demonstrate the limitless possibilities of the Dharma, Vimalakīrti then collaborates with Mañjuśrī, the archetypal embodiment of wisdom, to conjure from another universe a hierophany of chairs, lion thrones of unimaginable numbers and proportions. Vimalakīrti's house magically accommodates them all, for the world is essentially *śūnyatā*, that is, limitless in all directions. While the bodhisattvas are able to sit upon the thrones by virtue of their greater mental flexibility, the disciples, their vision constricted by an unquestioning acceptance of conventional boundaries of space and time, are unable to seat themselves save by the grace of a Tathāgata ("One of Suchness," a Buddha). Vimalakīrti then tries to suggest to Śāriputra a new perspective on the world that accommodates the infinity of the large and the infinity of the small simultaneously. One who has access to that perfectly enlightened perspective, intimated by the term "inconceivable liberation," is able to envision all the stars and planets in the space of a single pore of skin and maintain limitless universes in the mind's eye.

Śāriputra's worldview, however, is still confined to a superficial comprehension of surface appearances when in the chapter "The Goddess" he encounters a female divinity who lives in Vimalakīrti's house. Śāriputra accepts the commonly held belief that women are inferior to men and must first be reborn as males before they can attain spiritual enlightenment, and he asks the goddess why, if she has supernatural powers, she does not transform herself into a man. She replies by switching genders with him, thus drastically disabusing him of any adherence to mundane dualities of male and female, let alone of inferiority and superiority. Yet lest the dissolution of mundane perspectives itself become a limitation, the goddess quizzically concludes that there is perfect enlightenment because there is no perfect enlightenment. Thus toying with gender and language, the goddess instructs Śāriputra in the unknowable possibilities of unlimited understanding.

Little is known of the origins of the *Vimalakīrti* scripture, but it may have appeared in India around the first century B.C.E. or the first century of the common era. Whatever its language of origin, it was translated into Chinese a number of times from the third to the seventh centuries C.E. under such translators as Kumārajīva (floruit ca. 385–409) and Hsüan-tsang (600–664). The scripture strongly influenced the development of Chinese Buddhist philosophy and is frequently depicted in Chinese art and sculpture. The following selections have been translated from a Tibetan text in consultation with Kumārajīva's and Hsüan-tsang's works.

"Inconceivable Liberation"

Thereupon, the venerable Śāriputra had this thought: "There is not even a single chair in this house. Where are these disciples and bodhisattvas going to sit?"

The Licchavi Vimalakīrti read the thought of the venerable Śāriputra and said, "Reverend Śāriputra, did you come here for the sake of the Dharma? Or did you come here for the sake of a chair?"

Śāriputra replied, "I came for the sake of the Dharma, not for the sake of a chair."

Vimalakīrti continued, "Reverend Śāriputra, he who is interested in the Dharma is not interested even in his own body, much less in a chair. Reverend Śāriputra, he who is interested in the Dharma has no interest in matter, sensation, intellect, motivation, or consciousness. He has no interest in these aggregates, or in the elements, or in the sense-media. Interested in the Dharma, he has no interest in the realm of desire, the realm of matter, or the immaterial realm. Interested in the Dharma, he is not interested in attachment to the Buddha, attachment to the Dharma, or attachment to the Saṅgha. Reverend Śāriputra, he who is interested in the Dharma is not interested in recognizing suffering, abandoning its origination, realizing its cessation, or practicing the path. Why? The Dharma is ultimately without formulation and without verbalization. Who verbalizes: 'Suffering should be recognized, origination should be eliminated, cessation should be realized, the path should be practiced,' is not interested in the Dharma but is interested in verbalization.

"Reverend Śāriputra, the Dharma is calm and peaceful. Those who are engaged in production and destruction are not interested in the Dharma, are not interested in solitude, but are interested in production and destruction.

"Furthermore, reverend Śāriputra, the Dharma is without taint and free of defilement. He who is attached to anything, even to liberation, is not interested in the Dharma but is interested in the taint of desire. The Dharma is not an object. He who pursues objects is not interested in the Dharma but is interested in objects. The Dharma is without acceptance or rejection. He who holds on to things or lets go of things is not interested in the Dharma but is interested in holding and letting go. The Dharma is not a secure refuge. He who enjoys a secure refuge is not interested in the Dharma but is interested in a secure refuge. The Dharma is without sign. He whose consciousness pursues signs is not interested in the Dharma but is interested in signs. The Dharma is not a society. He who seeks to associate with the Dharma is not interested in the Dharma but is interested in association. The Dharma is not a sight, a sound, a category, or an idea. He who is involved in sights, sounds, categories, and ideas is not interested in the Dharma but is interested in sights, sounds, categories, and ideas. Reverend Śāriputra, the Dharma is free of compounded things and uncompounded things. He who adheres to compounded things and uncompounded things is not interested in the Dharma but is interested in adhering to compounded things and uncompounded things.

"Thereupon, reverend Śāriputra, if you are interested in the Dharma, you should take no interest in anything."

When Vimalakīrti had spoken this discourse, five hundred gods obtained the purity of the Dharma-eye in viewing all things.

Then, the Licchavi Vimalakīrti said to the crown prince, Mañjuśrī, "Mañjuśrī, you have already been in innumerable hundreds of thousands of buddha-fields throughout the universes of the ten directions. In which buddha-field did you see the best lion-thrones with the finest qualities?"

Mañjuśrī replied, "Noble sir, if one crosses the buddha-fields to the east, which are more numerous than all the grains of sand of thirty-two Ganges rivers, one will discover a universe called Merudhvaja. There dwells a Tathāgata called Merupradīparāja. His body measures eighty-four hundred thousand leagues in height, and the height of his throne is sixty-eight hundred thousand leagues. The bodhisattvas there are forty-two hundred thousand leagues tall and their own thrones are thirty-four hundred thousand leagues high. Noble sir, the finest and most superb thrones exist in that universe Merudhvaja, which is the buddha-field of the Tathāgata Merupradīparāja."

At that moment, the Licchavi Vimalakīrti, having focused himself in concentration, performed a miraculous feat such that the Lord Tathāgata Merupradīparāja, in the universe Merudhvaja, sent to this universe thirty-two hundred thousand thrones. These thrones were so tall, spacious, and beautiful that the bodhisattvas, great disciples, Śakras, Brahmās, Lokapālas, and other gods had never before seen the like. The thrones descended from the sky and came to rest in the house of the Licchavi Vimalakīrti. The thirty-two hundred thousand thrones arranged themselves without crowding and the house seemed to enlarge itself accordingly. The great city of Vaiśālī did not become obscured; neither did the land of Jambudvīpa, nor the world of four continents. Everything else appeared just as it was before.

Then, the Licchavi Vimalakīrti said to the young prince Mañjuśrī, "Mañjuśrī, let the bodhisattvas be seated on these thrones, having transformed their bodies to a suitable size!"

Then, those bodhisattvas who had attained the superknowledges transformed their bodies to a height of forty-two hundred thousand leagues and sat upon the thrones. But the beginner bodhisattvas were not able to transform themselves to sit upon the thrones. Then, the Licchavi Vimalakīrti taught these beginner bodhisattvas a teaching that enabled them to attain the five superknowledges, and, having attained them, they transformed their bodies to a height of forty-two hundred thousand leagues and sat upon the thrones. But still the great disciples were not able to seat themselves upon the thrones.

The Licchavi Vimalakīrti said to the venerable Śāriputra, "Reverend Śāriputra, take your seat upon a throne."

He replied, "Good sir, the thrones are too big and too high, and I cannot sit upon them."

Vimalakīrti said, "Reverend Śāriputra, bow down to the Tathāgata Merupradīparāja, and you will be able to take your seat."

Then, the great disciples bowed down to the Tathāgata Merupradīparāja and they were seated upon the thrones.

Then, the venerable Śāriputra said to the Licchavi Vimalakīrti, "Noble sir, it is astonishing that these thousands of thrones, so big and so high, should fit into such a small house and that the great city of Vaiśālī, the villages, cities, kingdoms, capitals of Jambudvīpa, the other three continents, the abodes of the gods, the nāgas, the yakṣas, the gandharvas, the asuras, the garuḍas, the kiṃnaras, and the mahoragas—that all of these should appear without any obstacle, just as they were before!"

The Licchavi Vimalakīrti replied, "Reverend Śāriputra, for the Tathāgatas and the bodhisattvas, there is a liberation called 'Inconceivable.' The bodhisattva who lives in the inconceivable liberation can put the king of mountains, Sumeru, which is so high, so great, so noble, and so vast, into a mustard seed. He can perform this feat without enlarging the mustard seed and without shrinking Mount Sumeru. And the deities of the assembly of the four Mahārājas and of the Trayastriṃśā heavens do not even know where they are. Only those beings who are destined to be disciplined by miracles see and understand the putting of the king of mountains, Sumeru, into the mustard seed. That, reverend Śāriputra, is an entrance to the domain of the inconceivable liberation of the bodhisattvas.

"Furthermore, reverend Śāriputra, the bodhisattva who lives in the inconceivable liberation can pour into a single pore of his skin all the waters of the four great oceans, without injuring the water-animals such as fish, tortoises, crocodiles, frogs, and other creatures, and without the nāgas, yakṣas, gandharvas, and asuras even being aware of where they are. And the whole operation is visible without any injury or disturbance to any of those living beings.

"Such a bodhisattva can pick up with his right hand this billion-world-galactic universe as if it were a potter's wheel and, spinning it round, throw it beyond universes as numerous as the sands of the Ganges, without the living beings therein knowing their motion or its origin, and he can catch it and put it back in its place, without the living beings suspecting their coming and going; and yet the whole operation is visible.

"Furthermore, reverend Śāriputra, there are beings who become disciplined after an immense period of evolution, and there are also those who are disciplined after a short period of evolution. The bodhisattva who lives in the inconceivable liberation, for the sake of disciplining those living beings who are disciplined through immeasurable periods of evolution, can make the passing of a week seem like the passing of an aeon, and he can make the passing of an aeon seem like the passing of a week for those who are disciplined through a short period of evolution. The living beings who are disciplined through an immeasurable period of evolution actually perceive a week to be the passing of an aeon, and those disciplined by a short period of evolution actually perceive an aeon to be the passing of a week.

"Thus, a bodhisattva who lives in the inconceivable liberation can manifest all the splendors of the virtues of all the buddha-fields within a single buddha-field. Likewise, he can place all living beings in the palm of his right hand and can show them with the supernatural speed of thought all the buddha-fields without ever leaving his own buddha-field. He can display in a single pore all the offerings ever offered to all the Buddhas of the ten directions, and the orbs of all the suns, moons, and stars of the ten directions. He can inhale all the hurricanes of the cosmic wind-atmospheres of the ten directions into his mouth without harming his own body and without letting the forests and the grasses of the buddha-fields be flattened. He can take all the masses of fire of all the supernovas that ultimately consume all the universes of all the buddha-fields into his stomach without interfering with their functions. Having crossed buddha-fields as numerous as the sands of the Ganges downward, and having taken up a buddha-field, he can rise up through buddha-fields as numerous as the sands of the Ganges and place it on high, just as a strong man may pick up a jujube leaf on the point of a needle.

"Thus, a bodhisattva who lives in the inconceivable liberation can magically transform any kind of living being into a universal monarch, a Lokapāla, a Śakra, a Brahmā, a disciple, a solitary sage, a bodhisattva, and even into a Buddha. The bodhisattva can transform miraculously all the cries and noises, superior, mediocre, and inferior, of all living beings of the ten directions, into the voice of the Buddha, with the words of the Buddha, the Dharma, and the Saṅgha, having them proclaim, 'Impermanent! Miserable! Empty! Selfless!' And he can cause them to recite the words and sounds of all the teachings taught by all the Buddhas of the ten directions.

"Reverend Śāriputra, I have shown you only a small part of the entrance into the domain of the bodhisattva who lives in the inconceivable liberation. Reverend Śāriputra, to explain to you the teaching of the full entrance into the domain of the bodhisattva who lives in the inconceivable liberation would require more than an aeon, and even more than that."

Then, the patriarch Mahākāśyapa, having heard this teaching of the inconceivable liberation of the bodhisattvas, was amazed, and he said to the venerable Śāriputra, "Venerable Śāriputra, if one were to show a variety of things to a person blind from birth, he would not be able to see a single thing. Likewise, venerable Śāriputra, when this door of the inconceivable liberation is taught, all the disciples and solitary sages are sightless, like the man blind from birth, and cannot comprehend even a single cause of the inconceivable liberation. Who is there among the wise who, hearing about this inconceivable liberation, does not conceive the spirit of unexcelled, perfect enlightenment? As for us, whose faculties are deteriorated, like a burned and rotten seed, what else can we do if we do not become receptive to this great vehicle? We, all the disciples and solitary sages, upon hearing this teaching of the Dharma, should utter a cry of regret that would shake this billion-world-galactic universe! And as for the bodhisattvas, when they hear this inconceivable liberation they should be as joyful as a young crown prince when he takes the diadem and is anointed, and they should increase to the utmost their devotion to this inconceivable liberation. Indeed, what could the entire host of Māras ever do to one who is devoted to this inconceivable liberation?"

When the patriarch Mahākāśyapa had uttered this discourse, thirty-two thousand gods conceived the spirit of unexcelled, perfect enlightenment.

Then, the Licchavi Vimalakīrti said to the patriarch Mahākāśyapa, "Reverend Mahākāśyapa, the Māras who play the devil in the innumerable universes of the ten directions are all bodhisattvas dwelling in the inconceivable liberation, who are playing the devil in order to develop living beings through their skill in liberative technique. Reverend Mahākāśyapa, all the miserable beggars who come to the bodhisattvas of the innumerable universes of the ten directions to ask for a hand, a foot, an ear, a nose, some blood, muscles, bones, marrow, an eye, a torso, a head, a limb, a member, a throne, a kingdom, a country, a wife, a son, a daughter, a slave, a slave-girl, a horse, an elephant, a chariot, a cart, gold, silver, jewels, pearls, conches, crystal, coral, beryl, treasures, food, drink, elixirs, and clothes—these demanding beggars are usually bodhisattvas living in the inconceivable liberation who, through their skill in liberative technique, wish to test and thus demonstrate the firmness of the high resolve of the bodhisattvas. Why? Reverend Mahākāśyapa, the bodhisattvas demonstrate that firmness by means of terrible austerities. Ordinary persons have no power to be thus demanding of bodhisattvas, unless they are granted the opportunity. They are not capable of killing and depriving in that manner without being freely given the chance.

"Reverend Mahākāśyapa, just as a glowworm cannot eclipse the light of the sun, so, reverend Mahākāśyapa, it is not possible without special allowance that an ordinary person can thus attack and deprive a bodhisattva. Reverend Mahākāśyapa, just as a donkey could not muster an attack on a wild elephant, even so, reverend Mahākāśyapa, one who is not himself a bodhisattva cannot harass a bodhisattva. Only one who is himself a bodhisattva can harass another bodhisattva, and only a bodhisattva can tolerate the harassment of another bodhisattva. Reverend Mahākāśyapa, such is the introduction to the power of the knowledge of liberative technique of the bodhisattvas who live in the inconceivable liberation."

"The Goddess"

Śāriputra: Goddess, what prevents you from transforming yourself out of your female state?

Goddess: Although I have sought my "female state" for these twelve years, I have not yet found it. Reverend Śāriputra, if a magician were to incarnate a woman by magic, would you ask her, "What prevents you from transforming yourself out of your female state?"

Śāriputra: No! Such a woman would not really exist, so what would there be to transform?

Goddess: Just so, reverend Śāriputra, all things do not really exist. Now, would you think, "What prevents one whose nature is that of a magical incarnation from transforming herself out of her female state?"

Thereupon, the goddess employed her magical power to cause the elder Śāriputra to appear in her form and to cause herself to appear in his form. Then the goddess, transformed into Śāriputra, said to Śāriputra, transformed into a goddess, "Reverend Śāriputra, what prevents you from transforming yourself out of your female state?"

And Śāriputra, transformed into the goddess, replied, "I no longer appear in the form of a male! My body has changed into the body of a woman! I do not know what to transform!"

The goddess continued, "If the elder could again change out of the female state, then all women could also change out of their female states. All women appear in the form of women in just the same way as the elder appears in the form of a woman. While they are not women in reality, they appear in the form of women. With this in mind, the Buddha said, 'In all things, there is neither male nor female.' "

Then, the goddess released her magical power and each returned to his ordinary form. She then said to him, "Reverend Śāriputra, what have you done with your female form?"

Śāriputra: I neither made it nor did I change it.

Goddess: Just so, all things are neither made nor changed, and that they are not made and not changed, that is the teaching of the Buddha.

Śāriputra: Goddess, where will you be born when you transmigrate after death?

Goddess: I will be born where all the magical incarnations of the Tathāgata are born.

Śāriputra: But the emanated incarnations of the Tathāgata do not transmigrate nor are they born.

Goddess: All things and living beings are just the same; they do not transmigrate nor are they born!

Śāriputra: Goddess, how soon will you attain the perfect enlightenment of Buddhahood?

Goddess: At such time as you, elder, become endowed once more with the qualities of an ordinary individual, then will I attain the perfect enlightenment of Buddhahood.

Śāriputra: Goddess, it is impossible that I should become endowed once more with the qualities of an ordinary individual.

Goddess: Just so, reverend Śāriputra, it is impossible that I should attain the perfect enlightenment of Buddhahood! Why? Because perfect enlightenment stands upon the impossible. Because it is impossible, no one attains the perfect enlightenment of Buddhahood.

Śāriputra: But the Tathāgata has declared: "The Tathāgatas, who are as numerous as the sands of the Ganges, have attained perfect Buddhahood, are attaining perfect Buddhahood, and will go on attaining perfect Buddhahood."

Goddess: Reverend Śāriputra, the expression, "the Buddhas of the past, present and future," is a conventional expression made up of a certain number of syllables. The Buddhas are neither past, nor present, nor future. Their enlightenment transcends the three times! But tell me, elder, have you attained sainthood?

Śāriputra: It is attained, because there is no attainment.

Goddess: Just so, there is perfect enlightenment because there is no attainment of perfect enlightenment.

Then the Licchavi Vimalakīrti said to the venerable elder Śāriputra, "Reverend Śāriputra, this goddess has already served ninety-two million billion Buddhas. She plays with the super-knowledges. She has truly succeeded in all her vows. She has gained the tolerance of the birthlessness of things. She has actually attained irreversibility. She can live wherever she wishes on the strength of her vow to develop living beings."

Meditations on the Body

Contemplative techniques introduced from India combined with native Chinese practices for developing the forces within the body. The two traditions are combined in unknown proportions in the *Secret Instructions of the Holy Lord on the Scripture of Great Peace (T'ai-p'ing sheng-chün pi-chih),* a work that perhaps contains elements of earlier, now lost, Chinese texts from the late first century B.C.E. Some of the content of the *Instructions* might then predate the arrival of Buddhism, but the extant version of the *Instructions* dates only to the late sixth century and has probably been greatly influenced by the foreign teaching.

Underlying this selection from the *Instructions* is the fundamental belief in the essential continuity between the self and the larger universe, a worldview expressed earlier, for example, in the *Great Learning,* which also emphasized peace. The method for actualizing that continuity in the *Instructions* is somewhat different, however, and involves the cultivation of essences and energy, or vital force *(ch'i),* within the body and advocates the use of chemical and herbal substances to assist in that cultivation. The distribution of energies within the body had been described as early as the *Tso chuan,* when Tzu-ch'an explained the wraith of Po-yu; he did not, however, suggest how one might utilize those energies to enhance long life or develop foreknowledge.

The projection of the *Great Learning* was a stepwise extension from the self to the outer world, but the *Instructions* adopts a numerical correlative perspective that associates the macrocosm of the four seasons and Five Agents, or Five Elements, with the microcosm of the inner body. Communication is effected by "gods" who dwell within the body and travel freely between the self and the outside world. For Confucius, in contrast, communication with the world beyond the body was actualized through the values of humanity and virtue. In the *Instructions,* sacrifices to the spirits of heaven, earth, land and grain, and mountains and rivers, once the prerogative only of the enfeoffed lords of the Chou dynasty, have now become internalized forces that are accessible to anyone from any social class.

Like the *Hsün Tzu* and the "Centrality and Equilibrium," the *Instructions* assumes the possibility of a triadic relationship between human beings, heaven, and earth, but it places much more emphasis on the notion of oneness or wholeness evidenced in the *Tao-te ching;* Hsün Tzu, on the other hand, had insisted on discrete differences between the three. And while Mencius was able to guide his vital energy, the *Instructions* posits a unitary primordial energy that gives rise to things. Reverence toward the ancestors, who are now perceived as mere expressions of the yin force and do not rank with the perfected, is given less priority than the development of the self through inwardly focused contemplative practices. The lights perceived within the body recall the pure brightness of virtue engendered by the focusing of the will in presacrificial vigils of the *Book of Rites,* but those vigils had encouraged eidetic visions; the envisioning of inner lights in the *Instructions,* however, is completely aniconic. The extent to which these envisioning exercises are derived from Buddhism is unclear, but such practices are common to many schools of Buddhist thought.

Selection from the *Secret Instructions of the Holy Lord on the Scripture of Great Peace*

The Holy Lord said:

The three energies together are unified in the One. There is essence, there is spirit, and there is energy. These three are originally one. They are founded in heaven and earth and form the root of all human energy. Human beings receive spirit from heaven, essence from earth, and energy from the middle harmony of heaven and earth. Joined together they are the One. Thus spirit moves by riding along on energy, while essence resides in the middle between them. The three support each other and form an integrated whole.

To pursue long life you must love energy, venerate spirit, and value essence. Human beings originally come from the energy of primordial chaos. This energy brings forth essence, which in turn gives birth to spirit. Spirit brings forth light. People are also based on the energy of yin and yang. As this energy revolves it brings forth essence. Essence in turn revolves and becomes spirit. Spirit revolves and light is born.

To pursue long life you must guard energy and harmonize spirit and essence. Never let them leave your body, but continue to think of them as joined in one. With prolonged practice your perception will become finer and subtler. Quite naturally you will be able to see within your body. The physical body will become gradually lighter, the essence more brilliant, and the light more concentrated. In your mind you will feel greatly restful, delighted and full of joy. You will go along with the energy of Great Peace. By then cultivating yourself, you can turn around and go along with all without. Within there will be perfect longevity; without there will be perfect accordance with the order of the universe. Without the exertion of any muscle you naturally attain Great Peace.

To practice guarding the light of the One, when you have not yet attained concentration, just sit quietly with your eyes closed. There is no light seen in the inner eye.

Practice guarding the One like this for a long time and a brilliant light will arise. In the radiance of this light you can see all the four directions. Following it you can travel far. Using it, you can examine your person and body with penetration. The host of spirits will assemble. Thus you can transform your physical body into pure spirit.

The practice of guarding the light of the One is the root of long life. With it, you can control the myriad spirits and go beyond all through the brilliant gateway of light.

Practice guarding the One and concentrate on the light. It will first arise like fire. Be careful not to let it slip! The light will initially be red; with prolonged practice it will turn white. After another long stretch, it will be green. As you penetrate these lights, they will come nearer and nearer and eventually merge into one brilliance. Nothing is not illumined within; the hundred diseases are driven out. Guard it and never slacken! You will go beyond the world and ascend to heaven!

In guarding the light of the One, you may see a light as bright as the rising sun. This is a brilliance as strong as that of the sun at noon.

In guarding the light of the One, you may see a light entirely green. When this green is pure, it is the light of lesser yang.

In guarding the light of the One, you may see a light entirely red, just like fire. This is a sign of transcendence.

In guarding the light of the One, you may see a light entirely yellow. When this develops a greenish tinge, it is the light of central harmony. This is a potent remedy of the Tao.

In guarding the light of the One, you may see a light entirely white. When this is as clear as flowing water, it is the light of lesser yin.

In guarding the light of the One, you may see a light entirely black. When this shimmers like deep water, it is the light of greater yin.

In guarding the light of the One, you may see your own abdomen pervaded by light while the four directions are utterly in darkness. This is the light of great harmony, the Tao of great accordance.

In guarding the light of the One, you may perceive utter darkness without and total blackness within. There is nothing to hold on to, nothing to see. This is the light of human disease, disorder, and nervousness. Take medicines and drugs to remedy this, then try to see any of the seven lights described above. To do so proceed in the following way:

1. Focus on primordial energy and non-action by meditating on your body without the One. Just imagine your body as pervaded by a white light. When the flourishing energy within is quite shapeless, there is nothing that is not done, nothing that is not known.
2. Practice emptiness, nonbeing, and spontaneity by concentrating on the center of the body. There will be a white radiance both above and below, pure like jade without the smallest flaw. This is the image of primordial energy and non-action.
3. Count and measure in deep meditation all of your body, from top to toe. The distinctions between the five fingers, the exact nature of your physical body within and without— think of them as never constant. This meditation follows emptiness and nonbeing.
4. Meditate on the gods residing in the five orbs and observe how they come and go. Carefully watch their movements. If you can put their activities into words, you can predict your good and bad fortune. This practice follows counting and measuring.
5. The Great God of the Tao: Let the gods emerge from your body and mingle with the five agents and four seasons. The green, yellow, white, and black will thus equally come to be stored within. The gods emerge and enter, come and go freely as divine officials of the five agents and four seasons. Use them to subdue the hundred evil [demons].
6. The Spirits of Sensuous Attractions: Let the gods burrow deep and rout them out from the soil. The God of the Tao urges them all toward positive efforts; still they remain half-evil.
7. The Administration of Earth: These are the deities of heaven and earth, the four seasons, soil and grain, mountains and rivers. Worship and offer sacrifices to them all. They will let you pass through all obstacles. You can traverse wherever you wish. Evil and false [demons] will be destroyed and can never resurface.
8. Foreign Gods: These are strange and alien. Their ways cannot be controlled. They make people talk foolish things. Sometimes they are similar to the perfected; sometimes they are more like evil [demons].
9. The Ancestors: They are of pure yin quality and do not belong among the perfected. They are just ordinary ghosts and spirits.

The Tao of guarding the One applied in antiquity as much as today. There have always been various kinds of people guarding the One. Those of highest wisdom guard it and go beyond the world. Those of medium wisdom guard it and become emperors and kings, faithful servants and virtuous officials. People of lesser talents practice it and are free from joy and anger. Through it, all under heaven is entirely free from bad things.

Alchemical Recipes for Immortality

Longevity was a blessing received by many, but immortality was an achievement available only to the few. Efforts to attain immortality were initiated at least as early as the Ch'in dynasty (221–207 B.C.E.), when the first emperor of that era became obsessed with finding an elixir that, when ingested, would grant him eternal life; he dispatched envoys to the eastern oceans to find the fabled "Isles of the Blessed," islands inhabited by immortals, where such substances could be obtained. Detailed instructions for preparing similar potions are explained in this selection from the chapter "Gold and Cinnabar" from the *Book of the Master Who Embraces Simplicity: Inner Chapters (Pao P'u-tzu nei-p'ien)* by Ko Hung (Ge Hong; 283–343). From an established gentry family in southern China, Ko was successful in seeking political office but opted eventually for the life of a recluse, writing extensively on both political and social topics as well as spiritual endeavors.

Ko's recipes for immortality are based on earlier scriptures such as the *Scripture of the Yellow Emperor's Divine Cinnabar of the Nine Tripods,* which cites the effectiveness of an elixir consumed by the Yellow Emperor himself, a legendary figure associated with various curative powers. Ko's formulas here eschew such practices as breathing exercises, gymnastics, and the ingestion of herbal medicines in favor of concoctions based on the vermilion mineral cinnabar, or mercuric sulfide, the ore from which mercury is extracted. Mercuric sulfides prepared and ingested according to Ko's formulations no doubt often induced death, rather than immortality, within the time limits indicated. To the initiated, this was considered not physical mortality but translation into another realm beyond the understanding of vulgar skeptics. Studying the Tao and consuming elixirs allowed superior practitioners to ascend into heaven, which here is viewed as a bureaucracy of officialdom that mirrors the government on earth.

Selection from the *Book of the Master Who Embraces Simplicity*

The *Scripture of the Yellow Emperor's Divine Cinnabar of the Nine Tripods* states that the Yellow Emperor ingested the cinnabar and ascended as an immortal *(hsien)*. It also says that even though regulating the breath and ingesting herbal medicines may prolong life, death is nonetheless inevitable with such methods; ingesting the divine [*shen,* "spiritlike"] cinnabar, on the other hand, brings longevity of immeasurable duration. It allows one to endure as long as heaven and earth themselves endure, mounting clouds and harnessing them to dragons, roaming high and low throughout the vast empyrean. The Yellow Emperor conveyed the above to Hsüan Tzu, the Master of Profound Mystery, warning him that this Way *(Tao)* is extremely intense and must be communicated only to people worthy of it. This Way may not be told to anyone of lesser caliber, even if one proffers mountains of jade as compensation. Those who are given it must make a pact by tossing a human-shaped gold figurine and a gold fish into a river flowing east; they must make a covenant by smearing their lips with blood. Only those with the bones of the divine immortals themselves may see this Way.

To compound the cinnabar, repair to the uninhabited fastnesses of a great mountain range, accompanied by no more than three people. First maintain a vigil of a hundred days, and bathe and scent yourself until you are purified; keep away from unclean things and avoid common people. Do not let people who do not believe in the Way know what you are doing. If you should desecrate the divine elixir, it cannot be completed; when done, however, not only you but your entire family can become immortal. People nowadays do not compound divine elixirs but on the contrary place their faith in herbal ones. But herbs rot when buried, disintegrate when boiled, and burn up when heated: if such things cannot preserve even the life within themselves, how can they bring life to human beings? The nine cinnabars, however, are essential for

prolonging one's life. But these are not things ordinary people should know about, for the doltish hoi polloi only clamor for wealth and rank. Are not such people just the walking dead? At the time of compounding, one must make sacrificial offerings; sacrifices have their own chapter, with illustrations and formulations.

The first cinnabar is called the Efflorescent Cinnabar. To make it, first prepare "black and yellow," using solutions of orpiment and alum; then prepare ten catties each of mountain salts, salts of alum, rock oyster grit, red stone, soapstone, and lake powder to make a six-to-one paste. Heat this for thirty-six days, and when it is done, you can attain immortality by ingesting it for seven days. Moreover, you can make pills of this cinnabar with dark emollient; heat it over an intense flame, and it will instantaneously turn into gold. You can also take 240 grains of it, mix it with a hundred catties of liquid silver, heat it, and it will also turn into gold. When the gold is done, then so is the elixir. But if the gold is not done, then cover the elixir and heat it for a number of days, as above; this always works.

The second cinnabar is called the Divine Cinnabar or Divine Charm. After ingesting it for a hundred days, you will become immortal and be able to walk through water and fire, for by rubbing it on the bottom of your feet you can walk on water. Ingest three scoops of it, and you can wipe out the three malignancies and nine parasites and overcome the hundred ailments.

The third cinnabar is called the Divine Cinnabar. Ingest one scoop for a hundred days, and you will become immortal; if even domestic animals swallow it, they will not die. It will also fend off weapons. Ingest it for a hundred days, and you will become immortal; moreover, jade maidens and spirits of mountains and rivers will appear in human form to wait on you.

The fourth is the Returning Cinnabar. Ingest one scoop for a hundred days and you will become immortal; red birds and phoenixes will flutter above you, and jade maidens will come to your side. Take one scoop, mix it with one measure of liquid silver, heat it, and it will turn to gold. Rub this cinnabar on money and other things; spend them, and they will return the next day. Writing with this cinnabar over someone's eyes will make all ghosts vanish.

The fifth is the Caked Cinnabar. For immortality, ingest it for thirty days. Ghosts and spirits will come to attend you, and jade maidens will come before you.

The sixth is the Refined Cinnabar. For immortality, ingest it for ten days. Combined with quicksilver and heated, it also turns to gold.

The seventh is the Supple Cinnabar. For immortality, take one scoop for a hundred days. Mixed with the juice of wild raspberries and ingested for ninety days, it can allow even old codgers over ninety to sire children. Mixed with lead and heated, it will turn to gold.

The eighth is the Hidden Cinnabar. Ingest it, and you can become an immortal the next day.

Holding a piece the size of a date pit will ward off all ghosts; writing with the cinnabar over gates and doors keeps away all baneful things and forces as well as robbers, thieves, tigers, and wolves.

The ninth is the Cold Cinnabar. For immortality, take one scoop for a hundred days. Immortal youths and maidens will come to attend you; you will be able to fly and soar lightly without need of feathered wings.

If you attain only one of these nine cinnabars, you can become immortal; you do not have to make all of them, but only the ones you want. But if you ingest the nine cinnabars and want to ascend to heaven, you may do so; you may also remain in the human realm, however, if that is your wish. In any case, you can come and go as you please, without impediments. Nothing will be able to harm you.

SUI
(581-618)
AND T'ANG
(618-907)
DYNASTIES

The Mind-to-Mind Transmission
of the Dharma

In early Indian Buddhism, the term "sutra," or scripture, referred only to the words spoken by the Buddha himself, but the Chinese *Platform Sutra of the Sixth Patriarch* claims scriptural status even though it records teachings propounded not by the Buddha but by a Chinese master. The use of the term "platform" in the title is unknown, but it may refer to a raised structure from which teachers of the Buddhist Dharma gave instruction. The Sixth Patriarch is Hui-neng (638–713), the Sixth Patriarch of the Ch'an (Japanese Zen) Buddhist tradition in China. "Ch'an" is the Chinese term used to transliterate the Sanskrit word *dhyāna,* the meditative states of the eightfold path of early Buddhism. While the various schools of Buddhism in China all espoused some kind of meditation, the tradition that particularly emphasized that practice came to be known as the Ch'an school, and a genealogy of Ch'an masters was created retroactively to trace to the Buddha himself a tradition of direct mind-to-mind transmission of enlightenment.

According to Ch'an tradition, the Buddha's own direct experience of enlightenment was communicated through a series of masters in India and was brought to China by Bodhidharma (floruit ca. 520 C.E.), a figure of legendary proportions who eventually was considered the First Patriarch of Chinese Ch'an Buddhism. The imperative of Ch'an practice was the direct apprehension of one's own "Buddha nature," and to that end Bodhidharma emphasized a direct perception of reality that did not depend on (but did not reject) the written language; for centuries, in contrast, many translators and Buddhist scholars had relied on the scriptural tradition for their understanding of Buddhism.

Hui-neng was the sixth in this line of patriarchal transmission, and this selection from the beginning of his *Platform Sutra of the Sixth Patriarch* relates the essential principles of Ch'an Buddhism. Hui-neng has already become the Sixth Patriarch by the time the sutra begins, and he narrates the story himself in a lecture on the Dharma addressed to a large crowd. Hui-neng's recollection of his impoverished childhood suggests what might be meant by the term Buddha nature: a universal, innate perceptivity that is not defined by culture or education. Hui-neng's illiteracy does not prevent him from instantaneously comprehending the *Diamond Sutra,* a profoundly difficult text of great subtlety. He immediately sets out to find the Fifth Patriarch, who is on the verge of death and is looking for someone to whom he can bequeath the robe, the symbol of authority, and the Dharma, or teaching.

The ensuing poetry contest contrasts the insights of the head monk (associated with the mannered aspects of culture, education, and the authority of tradition) with Hui-neng (associated with the naturalness of direct perception). Drawing upon the metaphor of the Bodhi tree, the tree beneath which the Buddha attained enlightenment, the verse by the head monk still suggests some tendency to perceive Buddha nature as something that needs to be purified. Hui-neng's verse, however, suggests a direct appreciation of the ultimately pure character of the Buddha nature. He has grasped the original nature of his own *prajñā* wisdom, or insight, the requisite to ultimate enlightenment *(bodhi)* that can only be found within oneself.

Selection from the *Platform Sutra of the Sixth Patriarch*

The Master Hui-neng said: "Good friends, purify your minds and concentrate on the Dharma of the Great Perfection of Wisdom."

The Master stopped speaking and quieted his own mind. Then after a good while he said: "Good friends, listen quietly. My father was originally an official at Fan-yang. He was [later] dismissed from his post and banished as a commoner to Hsin-chou in Ling-nan. While I was still a child, my father died and my old mother and I, a solitary child, moved to Nan-hai. We suffered extreme poverty and here I sold firewood in the market place. By chance a certain man bought some firewood and then took me with him to the lodging house for officials. He took the firewood and left. Having received my money and turning towards the front gate, I happened to see another man who was reciting the Diamond Sutra. Upon hearing it my mind became clear and I was awakened.

"I asked him: 'Where do you come from that you have brought this sutra with you?'

"He answered: 'I have made obeisance to the Fifth Patriarch, Hung-jen, at the East Mountain, Feng-mu shan, in Huang-mei hsien in Ch'i-chou. At present there are over a thousand disciples there. While I was there I heard the Master encourage the monks and lay followers, saying that if they recited just the one volume, the Diamond Sutra, they could see into their own natures and with direct apprehension become Buddhas.'

"Hearing what he said, I realized that I was predestined to have heard him. Then I took leave of my mother and went to Feng-mu shan in Huang-mei and made obeisance to the Fifth Patriarch, the priest Hung-jen.

"The priest Hung-jen asked me: 'Where are you from that you come to this mountain to make obeisance to me? Just what is it that you are looking for from me?'

"I replied: 'I am from Ling-nan, a commoner from Hsin-chou. I have come this long distance only to make obeisance to you. I am seeking no particular thing, but only the Buddhadharma.'

"The Master then reproved me, saying: 'If you're from Ling-nan then you're a barbarian. How can you become a Buddha?'

"I replied: 'Although people from the south and people from the north differ, there is no north and south in Buddha nature. Although my barbarian's body and your body are not the same, what difference is there in our Buddha nature?'

"The Master wished to continue his discussion with me; however, seeing that there were other people nearby, he said no more. Then he sent me to work with the assembly. Later a lay disciple had me go to the threshing room where I spent over eight months treading the pestle.

"Unexpectedly one day the Fifth Patriarch called his disciples to come, and when they had assembled, he said: 'Let me preach to you. For people in this world birth and death are vital matters. You disciples make offerings all day long and seek only the field of blessings, but you do not seek to escape from the bitter sea of birth and death. Your own self-nature obscures the gateway to blessings; how can you be saved? All of you return to your rooms and look into yourselves. Men of wisdom will of themselves grasp the original nature of their *prajñā* intuition. Each of you write a verse and bring it to me. I will read your verses, and if there is one who is awakened to the cardinal meaning, I will give him the robe and the Dharma and make him the Sixth Patriarch. Hurry, hurry!'

"The disciples received his instructions and returned, each to his own room. They talked it over among themselves, saying: 'There's no point in our purifying our minds and making efforts to compose a verse to present to the priest. Shen-hsiu, the head monk, is our teacher. After he obtains the Dharma we can rely on him, so let's not compose verses.' They all then gave up trying and did not have the courage to present a verse.

"At that time there was a three-sectioned corridor in front of the Master's hall. On the walls were to be painted pictures of stories from the Laṅkāvatāra Sutra, together with a picture in commemoration of the Fifth Patriarch transmitting the robe and Dharma, in order to disseminate them to later generations and preserve a record of them. The artist, Lu Chen, had examined the walls and was to start work the next day.

"The head monk Shen-hsiu thought: 'The others won't present mind-verses because I am their teacher. If I don't offer a mind-verse, how can the Fifth Patriarch estimate the degree of understanding within my mind? If I offer my mind to the Fifth Patriarch with the intention of gaining the Dharma, it is justifiable; however, if I am seeking the patriarchship, then it cannot be justified. Then it would be like a common man usurping the saintly position. But if I don't offer my mind then I cannot learn the Dharma.' For a long time he thought about it and was very much perplexed.

"At midnight, without letting anyone see him, he went to write his mind-verse on the central section of the south corridor wall, hoping to gain the Dharma. 'If the Fifth Patriarch sees my verse and says that it . . . and there is a weighty obstacle in my past karma, then I cannot gain the Dharma and shall have to give up. The honorable Patriarch's intention is difficult to fathom.'

"Then the head monk Shen-hsiu, at midnight, holding a candle, wrote a verse on the central section of the south corridor, without anyone else knowing about it. The verse read:

The body is the Bodhi tree,
The mind is like a clear mirror.
At all times we must strive to polish it,
And must not let the dust collect.

"After he had finished writing this verse, the head monk Shen-hsiu returned to his room and lay down. No one had seen him.

"At dawn the Fifth Patriarch called the painter Lu to draw illustrations from the Laṅkā-vatāra Sutra on the south corridor wall. The Fifth Patriarch suddenly saw this verse and, having read it, said to the painter Lu: 'I will give you thirty thousand cash. You have come a long distance to do this arduous work, but I have decided not to have the pictures painted after all. It is said in the Diamond Sutra: "All forms everywhere are unreal and false." It would be best to leave this verse here and to have the deluded ones recite it. If they practice in accordance with it they will not fall into the three evil ways. Those who practice by it will gain great benefit.'

"The Master then called all his disciples to come, and burned incense before the verse. The disciples came in to see and all were filled with admiration.

"The Fifth Patriarch said: 'You should all recite this verse so that you will be able to see into your own natures. With this practice you will not fall into the three evil ways.'

"The disciples all recited it, and feeling great admiration, cried out: 'How excellent!'

"The Fifth Patriarch then called the head monk Shen-hsiu inside the hall and asked: 'Did you write this verse or not? If you wrote it you are qualified to attain my Dharma.'

"The head monk Shen-hsiu said: 'I am ashamed to say that I actually did write the verse, but I do not dare to seek the patriarchship. I beg you to be so compassionate as to tell me whether I have even a small amount of wisdom and discernment of the cardinal meaning or not.'

"The Fifth Patriarch said: 'This verse you wrote shows that you still have not reached true understanding. You have merely arrived at the front of the gate but have yet to be able to enter it. If common people practice according to your verse they will not fall. But in seeking the ultimate enlightenment *(bodhi)* one will not succeed with such an understanding. You must enter the gate and see your own original nature. Go and think about it for a day or two and then make another verse and present it to me. If you have been able to enter the gate and see your own original nature, then I will give you the robe and the Dharma.' The head monk Shen-hsiu left, but after several days he was still unable to write a verse.

"One day an acolyte passed by the threshing room reciting this verse. As soon as I heard it I knew that the person who had written it had yet to know his own nature and to discern the cardinal meaning. I asked the boy: 'What's the name of the verse you were reciting just now?'

"The boy answered me, saying: 'Don't you know? The Master said that birth and death are vital matters, and he told his disciples each to write a verse if they wanted to inherit the robe and the Dharma, and to bring it for him to see. He who was awakened to the cardinal meaning would be given the robe and the Dharma and be made the Sixth Patriarch. There is a head monk by the name of Shen-hsiu who happened to write a verse on formlessness on the walls of the south corridor. The Fifth Patriarch had all his disciples recite the verse, [saying] that those who awakened to it would see into their own self-natures, and that those who practiced according to it would attain emancipation.'

"I said: 'I've been treading the pestle for more than eight months, but haven't been to the hall yet. I beg you to take me to the south corridor so that I can see this verse and make obeisance to it. I also want to recite it so that I can establish causation for my next birth and be born in a Buddha-land.'

"The boy took me to the south corridor and I made obeisance before the verse. Because I was uneducated I asked someone to read it to me. As soon as I had heard it I understood the cardinal meaning. I made a verse and asked someone who was able to write to put it on the wall of the west corridor, so that I might offer my own original mind. If you do not know the original mind, studying the Dharma is to no avail. If you know the mind and see its true nature, you then awaken to the cardinal meaning. My verse said:

> Bodhi originally has no tree,
> The mirror also has no stand.
> Buddha nature is always clean and pure;
> Where is there room for dust?

"Another verse said:

> The mind is the Bodhi tree,
> The body is the mirror stand.
> The mirror is originally clean and pure;
> Where can it be stained by dust?

"The followers in the temple were all amazed when they heard my verse. Then I returned to the threshing room. The Fifth Patriarch realized that I had a splendid understanding of the cardinal meaning. Being afraid lest the assembly know this, he said to them: 'This is still not complete understanding.'

"At midnight the Fifth Patriarch called me into the hall and expounded the Diamond Sutra to me. Hearing it but once, I was immediately awakened, and that night I received the Dharma. None of the others knew anything about it. Then he transmitted to me the Dharma of Sudden Enlightenment and the robe, saying: 'I make you the Sixth Patriarch. The robe is the proof and is to be handed down from generation to generation. My Dharma must be transmitted from mind to mind. You must make people awaken to themselves.' "

Nailing a Stick into Empty Space:
Ch'an Master I-hsüan

Kill the Buddha, advises Ch'an master I-hsüan (died 867), known also as Master Lin-chi. I-hsüan was revered as the founding figure of the Lin-chi tradition of Buddhism, a tradition that took its name from Lin-chi Monastery, his residence. His unorthodox teaching methods were acquired from Ch'an master Hsi-yün (died 850), also known as Huang-po, as he lived on Huang-po Mountain. I-hsüan's sayings were recorded by his pupils, and in this selection "the Master" is I-hsüan; the sayings are taken from his *Recorded Conversations of Ch'an Master I-hsüan (Lin-chi Hui-chao Ch'an shih yü-lu)*.

His admonition to kill the Buddha, kill one's parents, and kill the patriarchs is obviously not meant to be taken literally; it is a figurative attack on spiritual and intellectual parasitism. I-hsüan has no use for bodhisattvas or "arhats," those "worthy ones" of history who attained enlightenment. To undermine formalism, he shouts and beats his disciples into awareness and into a self-reliance autonomous of even heaven and earth itself. His statement that no effort is necessary in Buddhism must be tempered by the contrasting urgency of his beatings.

I-hsüan's hallmark is his unconventional teaching technique; he is well known for his *kung-ans*, literally "public cases," an expression better known in English as *koan,* the Japanese pronunciation of that term. Kung-ans are paradoxical stories or sayings, language games intended to unsettle the listener's preconceptions. One of the most famous of all is I-hsüan's dried-excrement stick kung-an, which is a commentary on the universality of the Buddha nature, which is in even the most common things. The fictive Vimalakīrti could resort to magical apparitions and transformations to lead Śāriputra to enlightenment, but in real life, a human Ch'an master must resort to more mundane but equally direct techniques for creating the same effect. Similar to the goddess's statement that ultimately there is no attainment of perfect enlightenment, I-hsüan playfully asserts that there is not really very much in his own master's Buddhism.

Selections from the *Recorded Sayings of Ch'an Master I-hsüan*

1. The Prefect, Policy Advisor Wang, and other officials requested the Master to lecture. The Master ascended the hall and said, "Today it is only because I, a humble monk, reluctantly accommodate human feelings that I sit on this chair. If one is restricted to one's heritage in expounding the fundamental understanding [of salvation], one really cannot say anything and would have nothing to stand on. However, because of the honorable general advisor's strong request today, how can the fundamental doctrines be concealed? Are there any talented men or fighting generals to hurl their banners and unfold their strategy right now? Show it to the group!"

A monk asked, "What is the basic idea of the Law preached by the Buddha?" Thereupon the Master shouted at him. The monk paid reverence. The Master said, "The Master and the monk can argue all right."

Question: "Master, whose tune are you singing? Whose tradition are you perpetuating?"

The Master said, "When I was a disciple of Huang-po, I asked him three times and I was beaten three times."

As the monk hesitated about what to say, the Master shouted at him and then beat him, saying, "Don't nail a stick into empty space."

2. The Master ascended the hall and said, "Over a lump of reddish flesh there sits a pure man who transcends and is no longer attached to any class of Buddhas or sentient beings. He comes in and out of your sense organs all the time. If you are not yet clear about it, look, look!"

At that point a monk came forward and asked, "What is a pure man who does not belong to any class of Buddhas or sentient beings?" The Master came right down from his chair and, taking hold of the monk, exclaimed, "Speak! Speak!" As the monk deliberated what to say, the Master let him go, saying, "What dried human excrement-removing stick is the pure man who does not belong to any class of Buddhas or sentient beings!" Thereupon he returned to his room.

3. The Master ascended the hall. A monk asked, "What is the basic idea of the Law preached by the Buddha?" The Master lifted up his swatter. The monk shouted, and the Master beat him.

[The monk asked again], "What is the basic idea of the Law preached by the Buddha?" The Master again lifted up his swatter. The monk shouted, and the Master shouted also. As the monk hesitated about what to say, the Master beat him.

Thereupon the Master said, "Listen, men. Those who pursue after the Law will not escape from death. I was in my late Master Huang-po's place for twenty years. Three times I asked him about the basic idea of the Law preached by the Buddha and three times he bestowed upon me the staff. I felt I was struck only by a dried stalk. Now I wish to have a real beating. Who can do it to me?"

One monk came out of the group and said, "I can do it."

The Master picked up the staff to give him. As he was about to take it over, the Master beat him.

4. The Master ascended the hall and said, "A man stands on top of a cliff, with no possibility of rising any further. Another man stands at the crossroad, neither facing nor backing anything. Who is in the front and who is in the back? Don't be like Vimalakīrti (who was famous for his purity), and don't be like Great Gentleman Fu (who benefited others). Take care of yourselves."

5. The Master told the congregation: "Seekers of the Way. In Buddhism no effort is necessary. All one has to do is to do nothing, except to move his bowels, urinate, put on his clothing, eat his meals, and lie down if he is tired. The stupid will laugh at him, but the wise one will understand. An ancient person said, 'One who makes effort externally is surely a fool.'"

6. *Question:* "What is meant by the mind's not being different at different times?"

The Master answered, "As you deliberated to ask the question, your mind has already become different. Therefore the nature and character of dharmas have become differentiated. Seekers of the Way, do not make any mistake. All mundane and supramundane dharmas have no nature of their own. Nor have they the nature to be produced [by causes]. They have only the name Emptiness, but even the name is empty. Why do you take this useless name as real? You are greatly mistaken! . . . If you seek after the Buddha, you will be taken over by the devil of the Buddha, and if you seek after the patriarch, you will be taken over by the devil of the patriarch. If you seek after anything, you will always suffer. It is better not to do anything. Some unworthy priests tell their disciples that the Buddha is the ultimate, and that he went through three infinitely long periods, fulfilled his practice, and then achieved Buddhahood. Seekers of the Way, if you say that the Buddha is the ultimate, why did he die lying down sidewise in the forest in Kuśinagara after having lived for eighty years? Where is he now? . . . Those who truly seek after the Law will have no use for the Buddha. They will have no use for the bodhisattvas or arhats. And they will have no use for any excellence in the Three Worlds (of desires, matter, and pure spirit). They will be distinctly free and not bound by material things. Heaven and earth may turn upside down but I shall have no more uncertainty. The Buddhas of the ten cardinal directions may appear before me and I shall not feel happy for a single moment. The three paths (of fire, blood, and swords) to hell may suddenly appear, but I shall not be afraid for a single moment. Why? Because I know that all dharmas are devoid of characters. They exist when there is transformation [in the mind] and cease to exist when there is no transformation. The Three Worlds are but the mind, and all dharmas are consciousness only. Therefore [they are all] dreams, illusions, and flowers in the air. What is the use of grasping and seizing them? . . .

"Seekers of the Way, if you want to achieve the understanding according to the Law, don't be deceived by others and turn to [your thoughts] internally or [objects] externally. Kill anything that you happen on. Kill the Buddha if you happen to meet him. Kill a patriarch or an arhat if you happen to meet him. Kill your parents or relatives if you happen to meet them. Only then can you be free, not bound by material things, and absolutely free and at ease. . . . I have no trick to give people. I merely cure disease and set people free. . . . My views are few. I merely put on clothing and eat meals as usual, and pass my time without doing anything. You people coming from the various directions have all made up your minds to seek the Buddha, seek the Law, seek emancipation, and seek to leave the Three Worlds. Crazy people! If you want to leave the Three Worlds, where can you go? 'Buddha' and 'patriarchs' are terms of praise and also bondage. Do you want to know where the Three Worlds are? They are right in your mind which is now listening to the Law."

7. Ma-ku came to participate in a session. As he arranged his seating cushion, he asked, "Which face of the twelve-face Kuan-yin faces the proper direction?"

The Master got down from the rope chair. With one hand he took away Ma-ku's cushion and with the other he held Ma-ku, saying, "Which direction does the twelve-face Kuan-yin face?"

Ma-ku turned around and was about to sit in the rope chair. The Master picked up the staff and beat him. Ma-ku having grasped the staff, the two dragged each other into the room.

8. The Master asked a monk: "Sometimes a shout is like the sacred sword of the Diamond King. Sometimes a shout is like a golden-haired lion squatting on the ground. Sometimes a shout is like a rod or a piece of grass [used to attract fish]. And sometimes a shout is like one which does not function as a shout at all. How do you know which one to use?"

As the monk was deliberating what to say, the Master shouted.

9. When the Master was among Huang-po's congregation, his conduct was very pure. The senior monk said with a sigh, "Although he is

young, he is different from the rest!" He then asked, "Sir, how long have you been here?"

The Master said, "Three years."

The senior monk said, "Have you ever gone to the head monk (Huang-po) and asked him questions?"

The Master said, "I have not. I wouldn't know what to ask."

The senior monk said, "Why don't you go and ask the head monk what the basic idea of the Law preached by the Buddha clearly is?"

The Master went and asked the question. But before he finished, Huang-po beat him. When he came back, the senior monk asked him how the conversation went. The Master said, "Before I finished my question, he already had beaten me. I don't understand." The senior monk told him to go and ask again.

The Master did and Huang-po beat him again. In this way he asked three times and got beaten three times. . . . Huang-po said, "If you go to Ta-yü's place, he will tell you why."

The Master went to Ta-yü, who asked him, "Where have you come from?"

The Master said, "I am from Huang-po's place."

Ta-yü said, "What did Huang-po have to say?"

The Master said, "I asked three times about the basic idea of the Law preached by the Buddha and I was beaten three times. I don't know if I was mistaken."

Ta-yü said, "Old kindly Huang-po has been so earnest with you and you still came here to ask if you were mistaken!"

As soon as the Master heard this, he understood and said, "After all, there is not much in Huang-po's Buddhism."

The Poetry of Cold Mountain

Cold Mountain is at once a person, a place, and a state of mind. About the first of these three, little is actually known: Han-shan, literally "Cold Mountain," is the literary name of a poet who lived sometime between the sixth and ninth centuries. It is unknown whether the three hundred or so poems attributed to Han-shan were actually composed by one person, and some scholars even question whether anyone named Han-shan ever existed. A T'ang dynasty (618–907) preface to his poetry, which probably recounts local lore rather than historical fact, relates that Han-shan was a poor and somewhat eccentric recluse who lived in the T'ien-t'ai mountains along the coast of central China. He and his equally eccentric friend Shih-te, who worked in the kitchen of a nearby temple and occasionally provided Han-shan food from the temple stores, were believed to be bodhisattvas in disguise.

In Chinese painting, these two idiosyncratic figures were sympathetically depicted as a pair of beggarlike waifs; they had left the world and wisely ridiculed those still enamored of it. The content of Han-shan's poems themselves, however, allows room for much speculation about the personality of their author or authors. Han-shan's poetry has sometimes been associated with Ch'an Buddhism, but few verses suggest any specific connection with that tradition. Many, however, reveal a general Buddhist sense of the transience of the world as well as an awareness of emptiness. The poems selected here describe the imagery of Cold Mountain and are quite typical of much of Han-shan's work.

Cold Mountain, the place and state of mind, is a realm silently animated with Chuang Tzu's piping of heaven. In antiquity, prognosticators had read landslides and other natural phenomena for signs from a hidden world, and Han-shan seems to read the subtler signs of Cold Mountain with a similar intensity. He finds a Way through the mountains precisely the opposite of the path most travelers take: he sits in one place and instead lets the mountain move around him. Sitting still in the hut, it is noon before he realizes the sun has risen; sitting against the cliff, grass grows through his feet. It is perhaps this Way of stillness that never ends; farther away than can be told, it shows no trace of human footsteps and does not reach the world.

Poems of Han-shan

3.

The Way to Cold Mountain is laughable:
Not even a trace of horses or carts!
Just valleys webbed in countless twisting
　　turns,
And mountain ridges ranged unthinkably
　　high.
The dew weeps on every kind of plant,
But the wind soughs only through the
　　pines.
Those times when I lose the path,
My physical form just asks my shadow,
　　"Where to?"

28.

I climb up the Way to Cold Mountain,
But the Cold Mountain road is endless:
Long valleys of boulders stacked stone
　　　　upon stone,
Broad streams thick with dense
　　undergrowth.
The mosses are slippery, though there's
　　been no rain;
Pines cry out, but it's not the wind.
Who can get beyond worldly
　　attachments
And sit with me among the white
　　clouds?

49.

I came once to sit here on Cold
　　　　Mountain,
And I've tarried now for thirty years.
Yesterday I went to visit relatives and
　　friends,
But more than half had gone to the
　　Yellow Springs.
Gradually snuffed out like a burned-
　　down candle,
Long life once flowed in a surging
　　torrent.
This morning I face my lonely reflection
And unconsciously shed streams of
　　　　tears.

154.

Cold Mountain is full of mysterious
　　　　wonders,
And those who climb it are always filled
　　with awe:
When the moon shines, its waters flash
　　and glitter;
When the wind blows, plants whisper
　　and sigh.
Shriveled plums turn snowflakes into
　　blossoms;
Bare trees avail themselves of clouds for
　　leaves.
Falling rains bring forth ethereal rarities
　　seldom seen;
Unless the day is clear, you can't go
　　climbing.

176.

The spots where I stop and linger
Are too deep and secluded to tell.
There's no wind; those vines move by
　　themselves.
No fog, but it's always twilight in the
　　bamboo.
For whom do the stream's waters roll?
Mountain clouds suddenly bunch
　　themselves together.
At the noon hour, sitting in my hut,
I begin to sense the sun rising over my
　　head.

190.

"There is a bodily self" and "There is
　　not a bodily self";
"I am," but then again, "I am not."
Thinking about such things, I weigh all
　　sides,
Whiling away the hours, sitting with my
　　back against a cliff,
Green grass growing up through my
　　feet,
Red dust settling atop my head.
Local folk, seeing me like this,
Set out offerings of wine and fruit as if
　　before a coffin.

226.

I delight in the Way of everyday life,
Here among the mist-veiled vines and
caves of stone.
In the wilds I am footloose and free,
Lounging with my old friends the white
clouds.
There's a road, but it doesn't lead to the
world;
I have "no-mind," so who could bother
me?
On a bed of stone, I sit through the
night alone
As a full moon ascends Cold Mountain.

256.

Nowadays, people search for a road
among the clouds,
But the cloud road is mysterious and
bears no signs.
The mountain heights are steep and
dangerous,
And their wide torrents are virtually
impenetrable;
Dark-green crags before and behind you,
White clouds to the east and west.
You want to know where the cloud road
is?
It lies in vacuity and emptiness.

311.

You have Cold Mountain poems at
home?
Better than reading scrolls of sutras,
Copy them out on a folding screen
And glance over them now and then.

The Writings of Han Yü

Han Yü (768–824) is one of the most noted literary figures in all of Chinese history, and his prose and verse styles influenced the direction of Chinese literature. A celebrated writer even in his own day, he served in various government offices and led a successful if somewhat turbulent political career. Government appointments were the goal of most educated men, who might become career officials only after passing a series of civil service examinations on literary, historical, and political questions. Han Yü passed the highest levels of the examination system in his mid twenties and held various positions in the central and provincial government for the remainder of his life.

Han Yü's writings on what might in the West be considered religious themes reveal the complexity of the interaction of the varied spiritual traditions in China, and several of his essays on such topics are presented here. He is noted particularly for his efforts to reinvigorate the native Chinese classical tradition and composed the essay "An Inquiry on the Way" *(Yüan tao),* not included here, that elevates what he calls the Way of Confucius at the expense of the Way of the Buddhists and Taoists. Confucius's way values humanity and righteousness, principles only destroyed by Lao Tzu; Taoists and Buddhists, he asserts, seek only escape from social obligations and human relationships, while the teachings of the ancient kings in the *Odes, History,* and *Changes,* in contrast, created social norms that brought prosperity and refined culture to all people.

Han Yü's "Memorial on the Bone of Han Yü's Buddha" of 819 reveals that his distaste for Buddhism is informed not necessarily by a knowledge of the Four Noble Truths but by a cultic folk practice that itself bears no resemblance to the teachings of Siddhārtha Gautama: the worship of a relic of the Buddha. Addressing himself directly to the ruler, Hsien-tsung (reign 805–819), Han Yü contrasts the long-lived regimes of the ancient Chinese sage kings, who did not worship the Buddha, with the brief reigns of Han and later rulers who did; his arguments also appeal to a xenophobic distaste of things foreign. Han Yü is moreover concerned that the people will be encouraged by the display of the relic to immolate themselves and present offerings of their own flesh as homage. This practice is probably derived from the self-immolations of the bodhisattva Medicine King in chapter 23 of the *Lotus Sutra,* which claims that those who make offerings of toes and fingers can attain complete and perfect enlightenment. Han Yü asserts that the relic of the Buddha is not a blessing but an article of death; following ancient precedent, it should be treated with the exorcistic deprecations of shamans to drive away its baneful influences. The emperor was not convinced by these arguments, however, and Han Yü escaped execution only by virtue of his political connections.

"The Girl of Mt. Hua," very different in tone, is a rhapsodic praise of a young Taoist woman that borders on the erotic. How should one reconcile Han Yü's critiques of Lao Tzu with his implicit praise of this woman's erudite exposition of the Tao? Her lectures on spiritual truths have emptied rival halls of Buddhist monks and Taoist priests alike, and her ability to turn people back toward native traditions partially coincides with Han Yü's own agenda. The woman has attracted the attentions of the heavenly court itself, and the deliberately ambiguous imagery surrounding the Jade Countenance suggests both a celestial sovereign and his earthly representative. Suggesting that the young men infatuated with her have serious competition from higher powers, Han Yü perhaps intends his descriptions of credulous followers as a satire on unseemly motivated beliefs, but one suspects he protests too much.

As a government official, Han Yü was required to perform the religious functions appropriate to a regional representative in the service of the Son of Heaven, a tradition that had continued from ancient times when enfeoffed lords were responsible for the mountains, rivers, and other natural forces within their domain. The collected writings of many Chinese thinkers include prayers and invocations to various spirits, and "Against the God of the Wind" and "Proclamation to the Crocodile" are works of this type. The adversarial tone of the "God of the Wind" would not have been found in the *Tso chuan,* for example, which understood imbalances in the natural world as cause for human reflection. By T'ang times, however, the imperial court has apparently assumed for itself many of the prerogatives once attributed only to the spirit world, and lesser spirits are becoming viewed as forces less powerful than the emperor himself. By at least late Ch'ing (1644–1911) times this tendency became very clear, and plaques given to a temple and its resident spirit by the imperial court employ the language of a superior (the emperor) granting a boon to an inferior (the spirit). Han Yü suggests that if the God of Wind does not cooperate, he will be punished by the Son of Heaven.

It has been suggested that the "Proclamation to the Crocodile" is written as a satire, and it is possible that the admonitions to reptiles are actually directed at corrupt officials or criminals. Yet it is entirely likely that the invocation was meant to be taken seriously; sacrifices of drowned animals were recorded in the *Rites of Chou,* and Han Yü draws upon the precedent of legendary culture heroes such as Yü (third millennium B.C.E.), who drained swamps and dug canals to create an ordered human realm out of the chaos and wilderness of nature. As populations expanded in the T'ang into territories long unoccupied, government officials responsible for land reclamation perceived themselves as continuing Yü's work.

"Memorial on the Bone of Buddha"

I humbly submit that Buddhism is but one of the religious systems obtaining among the barbarian tribes, that only during the later Han dynasty did it filter into the Middle Kingdom, and that it never existed in the golden age of the past.

In remote times Huang-ti ruled for a hundred years, and lived to the age of a hundred and ten; Shao Hao ruled for eighty years and lived to the age of a hundred; Chuan Hsü ruled for seventy-nine years and lived to the age of ninety-eight; Emperor Ku ruled for seventy years to the age of a hundred and five; Emperor Yao for ninety-eight years to the age of a hundred and eighteen; while both emperors Shun and Yü lived to be a hundred. During this time the empire was in a state of perfect equilibrium and the people lived to ripe old age in peace and prosperity; but as yet the Middle Kingdom did not know of Buddha. After this T'ang of Yin lived to be a hundred. His grandson T'ai Mou ruled for seventy-five years, and Wu Ting for fifty-nine years; and though the histories do not tell us to what age they lived, it cannot in either case be reckoned at less than a hundred. In the Chou dynasty Wen Wang lived to be ninety-seven, and Wu Wang to be ninety-three, whilst Mu Wang was on the throne for a hundred years. As Buddhism had still not penetrated to the Middle Kingdom, this cannot be attributed to the worship of him.

It was not until the reign of Ming-ti of Han that Buddhism first appeared. Ming-ti's reign lasted no longer than eighteen years, and after him disturbance followed upon disturbance, and reigns were all short. From the time of the five dynasties, Sung, Ch'i, Liang, Ch'en and Yüan Wei onwards, as the worship of Buddha slowly increased, dynasties became more short-lived. Wu-ti of Liang alone reigned as long as forty-eight years. During his reign he three times consecrated his life to Buddha, made no animal sacrifices in his ancestral temple, and ate but one meal a day of vegetables and fruit. Yet in the end he was driven out by the rebel Hou Ching and died of starvation in T'ai-ch'eng, and his state was immediately destroyed. By worshipping Buddha he looked for prosperity but found only disaster, a sufficient proof that Buddha is not worthy of worship.

When Kao-tsu succeeded the fallen house of Sui, he determined to eradicate Buddhism. But the ministers of the time were lacking in foresight and ability, they had no real understanding of the way of the ancient kings, nor of the things that are right both for then and now. Thus they were unable to assist the wise resolution of their ruler and save their country from this plague. To my constant regret the attempt stopped short. But you, your majesty, are possessed of a skill in the arts of peace and war, of wisdom and courage the like of which has not been seen for several thousand years. When you first ascended the throne you prohibited recruitment of Buddhist monks and Taoist priests and the foundation of new temples and monasteries; and I firmly believed that the intentions of Kao-tsu would be carried out by your hand, or if this were still impossible, that at least their religions would not be allowed to spread and flourish.

And now, your majesty, I hear that you have ordered all Buddhist monks to escort a bone of the Buddha from Feng-hsiang and that a pavilion be erected from which you will in person watch its entrance into the Imperial Palace. You have further ordered every Buddhist temple to receive this object with due homage. Stupid as I am, I feel convinced that it is not out of regard for Buddha that you, your majesty, are praying for blessings by doing him this honour; but that you are organising this absurd pantomime for the benefit of the people of the capital and for their gratification in this year of plenty and happiness. For a mind so enlightened as your majesty's could never believe such nonsense. The minds of the common people however are as easy to becloud as they are difficult to enlighten. If they see your majesty acting in this way, they will think that you are wholeheartedly worshipping the Buddha, and will say: "His majesty is a great sage, and even he worships the Buddha with all his heart. Who are we that we should any of us grudge our lives in his service?" They will cauterize the crowns of their heads, burn off their fingers, and in bands of tens or hundreds cast off their clothing and scatter their money and from daylight to darkness follow one another in the cold fear of being too late. Young and old in one mad rush will forsake their trades and callings and, unless you issue some prohibition, will flock round the temples, hacking their arms and mutilating their bodies to do him homage. And the laughter that such unseemly and degenerate behaviour will everywhere provoke will be no light matter.

The Buddha was born a barbarian; he was unacquainted with the language of the Middle Kingdom, and his dress was of a different cut. His tongue did not speak nor was his body clothed in the manner prescribed by the kings of old; he knew nothing of the duty of minister to prince or the relationship of son to father. Were he still alive today, were he to come to court at the bidding of his country, your majesty would give him no greater reception than an interview in the Strangers' Hall, a ceremonial banquet, and the gift of a suit of clothes, after which you would have him sent under guard to the frontier to prevent him from misleading your people. There is then all the less reason now that he has been dead so long for allowing this decayed and rotten bone, this filthy and disgusting relic to enter the Forbidden Palace. "I stand in awe of supernatural beings," said Confucius, "but keep them at a distance." And the feudal lords of olden times when making a visit of condolence even within their own state would still not approach without sending a shaman to precede them and drive away all evil influences with a branch of peach-wood. But now and for no given reason your majesty proposes to view in person the reception of this decayed and disgusting object without even sending ahead the shaman with his peach-wood wand; and to my shame and indignation none of your ministers says that this is wrong, none of your censors has exposed the error.

I beg that this bone be handed over to the authorities to throw into water or fire, that Buddhism be destroyed root and branch for ever, that the doubts of your people be settled once and for all and their descendants saved from heresy. For if you make it known to your people that the actions of the true sage surpass ten thousand times ten thousand those of ordinary men, with what wondering joy will you be acclaimed! And if the Buddha should indeed possess the power to bring down evil, let all the bane and punishment fall upon my head, and as heaven is my witness I shall not complain.

In the fullness of my emotion I humbly present this memorial for your attention.

"The Girl of Mt. Hua"

In streets east, streets west, they
    expound the Buddhist canon,
clanging bells, sounding conches, till the
    din invades the palace;
"sin," "blessing," wildly inflated, give
    force to threats and deceptions;
throngs of listeners elbow and shove as
    though through duckweed seas.
Yellow-robed Taoist priests preach their
    sermons too,
but beneath their lecterns, ranks grow
    thinner than stars in the flush
    of dawn.
The girl of Mount Hua, child of a Taoist
    home,
longed to expel the foreign faith, win
    men back to the Immortals;
she washed off her powder, wiped her
    face, put on cap and shawl.
With white throat, crimson cheeks, long
    eyebrows of gray,
she came at last to ascend the chair,
    unfolding the secrets of Truth.
For anyone else the Taoist halls would
    hardly have opened their doors;
I do not know who first whispered the
    word abroad,
but all at once the very earth rocked
    with the roar of thunder.
Buddhist temples were swept clean, no
    trace of a believer,

while elegant teams jammed the lanes
    and ladies' coaches piled up;
Taoist halls were packed with people,
    many sat outside;
for latecomers there was no room, no
    way to get within hearing.
Hairpins, bracelets, girdle stones were
    doffed, undone, snatched off,
till the heaped-up gold, the mounds of
    jade glinted and glowed in the
    sunlight.
Eminent eunuchs from the heavenly
    court came with a summons to
    audience;
ladies of the six palaces longed to see
    the Master's face.
The Jade Countenance nodded approval,
    granting her return;
dragon-drawn, mounting a crane, she
    came through blue-dark skies.
These youths of the great families—what
    do they know of the Tao,
milling about her a hundred deep,
    shifting from foot to foot?
Beyond cloud-barred windows, in misty
    towers, who knows what
    happens there
where kingfisher curtains hang tier on
    tier and golden screens are
    deep?
The immortal's ladder is hard to climb,
    your bonds with this world
    weighty;
vainly you call on the bluebird to deliver
    your passionate pleas!

"Against the God of the Wind"

Of this drought, who is the cause? I know the author: it is the God of the Wind who is to blame. The hills made the clouds to rise, the marshes sent up their vapour. The thunder whipped the chariot, the lightning shook the banner. The rain was promising, ready to fall; but the God of the Wind was angry, and the clouds could not stay still. The Sun Crow in his kindness had pity upon the people. He dimmed his radiance, and sent not his fiery spirit to battle. But you, God of the Wind, instead what did you do?

For you what else could we have done? We looked for a suitable time, we made ready the materials for the sacrifice. The lamb was full fat, the wine was full sweet. There was food enough for repletion, drink enough for drunkenness. The God of the Wind's anger, what brought it about? The clouds were banked thick, you blew and thinned them. The vapour was ready to condense, you blew and scattered it. You melted the vapour so that it could not transform, you froze the clouds so that they could not shed their rain.

You, God of the Wind, should you wish to escape this crime, what further have you to say? Heaven above, which sees all things, has records, has laws. I now present my charge and for this crime who shall pay? The sentence of Heaven will fall upon you; when it does there can be no repentance; and God of the Wind, even if you die, what man will mourn for you?

"Proclamation to the Crocodile"

On the twenty-fourth day of the fourth month of the fourteenth year of Yüan-ho, Han Yü, Governor of Ch'ao-chou, had his officer Ch'in Chi take a sheep and a pig and throw them into the deep waters of Wu creek as food for the crocodile. He then addressed it as follows:

When in ancient times the former kings possessed the land, they set fire to the mountains and the swamp, and with nets, ropes, fish-spears and knives expelled the reptiles and snakes and evil creatures that did harm to the people, and drove them out beyond the four seas. When there came later kings of lesser power who could not hold so wide an empire, even the land between the Chiang and the Han they wholly abandoned and gave up to the Man and the Yi, to Ch'u and to Yüeh: let alone Ch'ao which lies between the five peaks and the sea, some ten thousand li from the capital. Here it was that the crocodiles lurked and bred, and it was truly their rightful place. But now a Son of Heaven has succeeded to the throne of T'ang, who is godlike in his wisdom, merciful in peace and fierce in war. All between the four seas and within the six directions is his to hold and to care for, still more the land trod by the footsteps of Yü and near to Yangchou, administered by governors and prefects, whose soil pays tribute and taxes to supply the sacrifices to Heaven and to Earth, to the ancestral altars and to all the deities. The crocodiles and the governor cannot together share this ground.

The governor has received the command of the Son of Heaven to protect this ground and take charge of its people; but you, crocodile, goggle-eyed, are not content with the deep waters of the creek, but seize your advantage to devour the people and their stock, the bears and boars, stags and deer, to fatten your body and multiply your sons and grandsons. You join issue with the governor and contend with him for the mastery. The governor, though weak and feeble, will not endure to bow his head and humble his heart before a crocodile, nor will he look on timorously and be put to shame before his officers and his people by leading unworthily a borrowed existence in this place. But having received the command of the Son of Heaven to come here as an officer, he cannot but dispute with you, crocodile: and if you have understanding, do you hearken to the governor's words.

To the south of the province of Ch'ao lies the great sea, and in it there is room for creatures as large as the whale or roc, as small as the shrimp or crab, all to find homes in which to live and feed. Crocodile, if you set out in the morning, by the evening you would be there. Now, crocodile, I will make an agreement with you. Within full three days, you will take your ugly brood and remove southwards to the sea, and so give way before the appointed officer of the Son of Heaven. If within three days you cannot, I will go to five days: if within five days you cannot, I will go to seven. If within seven days you cannot, this shall mean either that finally you have refused to remove, and that though I be governor you will not hear and obey my words; or else that you are stupid and without intellect, and that even when a governor speaks you do not hear and understand.

Now those who defy the appointed officers of the Son of Heaven, who do not listen to their words and refuse to make way before them, who from stupidity and lack of intellect do harm to the people and to other creatures, all shall be put to death. The governor will then choose skilful officers and men, who shall take strong bows and poisoned arrows and conclude matters with you, crocodile, nor stop until they have slain you utterly. Do not leave repentance until too late.

In Search of a Woman's Spirit:
The Poetry of Po Chü-i

Imperial Consort Yang, or Yang Kuei-fei (Yang Guifei, died 756), is the great tragic beauty of China whose fame in literature and painting rivals that of Cleopatra in the West. She was the favorite of the many consorts of the emperor Hsüan-tsung (reign 713–756), known also as the Brilliant Emperor because of the cultural efflorescence that marked his reign. In 755, however, a rebellion by General An Lu-shan compelled the court to retreat to Szechuan (the old kingdom of Shu). Collapse of the political order was not attributed to the emperor's or government's own incompetence but to the distracting beauty of Yang Kuei-fei, who was murdered en route by the fleeing entourage. Hsüan-tsung consequently abdicated the throne.

The details of Yang Kuei-fei's life and death are retold and embellished in "A Song of Unending Sorrow" by the celebrated T'ang poet Po Chü-i (Bo Ju'i; 772–846). Serving in various official posts, he was a productive writer and composed nearly three thousand verses; "Unending Sorrow" is one his best-known works. Some years after the imperial consort's death, Po relates, the emperor enjoined a Taoist priest to search for her, as by T'ang times the duties of soul summoning once ascribed to shamans have become assumed by other religious professionals. The priest departs on a spirit journey and finds Yang Kuei-fei on an island in the ocean, the enchanted isles sought by the first emperor of Ch'in. Yang Kuei-fei does not return with the priest and sends only tokens of her continued devotion.

Even individual lines from the "Song of Unending Sorrow" inspired art and drama in later centuries. Paintings of anonymous women stepping from their baths are assumed to depict Yang Kuei-fei; the Peking opera *The Drunken Consort* is a fictional account of her reaction to the emperor's attentions toward another woman. Po Chü-i's poetry became extremely popular in Japan by the twelfth century, and Yang Kuei-fei's story entered the repertoire of Japanese Noh drama some centuries later in the play *Yōhiki*.

"A Song of Unending Sorrow"

China's Emperor, craving beauty that
    might shake an empire,
Was on the throne, for many years,
    searching, never finding,
Till a little child of the Yang clan,
    hardly even grown,
Bred in an inner chamber, with no one
    knowing her,
But with graces granted by heaven and
    not to be concealed,
At last one day was chosen for the
    imperial household.
If she but turned her head and smiled,
    there were cast a hundred
    spells,
And the powder and paint of the Six
    Palaces faded into nothing.
. . . It was early spring. They bathed
    her in the Flower-Pure
    Pool,
Which warmed and smoothed the
    creamy-tinted crystal of her
    skin,
And, because of her languor, a maid
    was lifting her
When first the Emperor noticed her and
    chose her for his bride.
The cloud of her hair, petal of her
    cheek, gold ripples of her
    crown when she moved,
Were sheltered on spring evenings by
    warm hibiscus-curtains;
But nights of spring were short and the
    sun arose too soon,
And the Emperor, from that time forth,
    forsook his early hearings
And lavished all his time on her with
    feasts and revelry,
His mistress of the spring, his despot of
    the night.
There were other ladies in his court,
    three thousand of rare beauty,
But his favors to three thousand were
    concentered in one body.
By the time she was dressed in her
Golden Chamber, it would be
    almost evening;
And when tables were cleared in the
    Tower of Jade, she would
    loiter, slow with wine.
Her sisters and brothers all were given
    titles;
And, because she so illumined and
    glorified her clan,
She brought to every father, every
    mother through the empire,
Happiness when a girl was born rather
    than a boy.
. . . High rose Li Palace, entering blue
    clouds,
And far and wide the breezes carried
    magical notes
Of soft song and slow dance, of string
    and bamboo music.
The Emperor's eyes could never gaze on
    her enough—
Till war-drums, booming from Yü-yang,
    shocked the whole earth
And broke the tunes of "The Rainbow
    Skirt and the Feathered
    Coat."
The Forbidden City, the nine-tiered
    palace, loomed in the dust
From thousands of horses and chariots
    headed southwest.
The imperial flag opened the way, now
    moving and now pausing—
But thirty miles from the capital, beyond
    the western gate,
The men of the army stopped, not one
    of them would stir
Till under their horses' hoofs they might
    trample those moth-
    eyebrows . . .
Flowery hairpins fell to the ground, no
    one picked them up,
And a green and white jade hair-tassel
    and a yellow-gold hair-bird.
The Emperor could not save her, he
    could only cover his face.
And later when he turned to look, the
    place of blood and tears

Was hidden in a yellow dust blown by a
  cold wind.
 . . . At the cleft of the Dagger-Tower
  Trail they crisscrossed through
  a cloud-line
Under O-mei Mountain. The last few
  came.
Flags and banners lost their color in the
  fading sunlight . . .
But as waters of Shu are always green
  and its mountains always blue,
So changeless was his majesty's love
  and deeper than the days.
He stared at the desolate moon from his
  temporary palace,
He heard bell-notes in the evening rain,
  cutting at his breast.
And when heaven and earth resumed
  their round and the dragon-car
  faced home,
The Emperor clung to the spot and
  would not turn away
From the soil along the Ma-wei slope,
  under which was buried
That memory, that anguish. Where was
  her jade-white face?
Ruler and lords, when eyes would meet,
  wept upon their coats
As they rode, with loose rein, slowly
  eastward, back to the capital.
 . . . The pools, the gardens, the palace,
  all were just as before,
The Lake T'ai-yi hibiscus, the Wei-yang
  Palace willows;
But a petal was like her face and a
  willow-leaf her eyebrow—
And what could he do but cry whenever
  he looked at them?
 . . . Peach-trees and plum-trees
  blossomed, in the winds of
  spring;
Lakka-foliage fell to the ground, after
  autumn rains;
The Western and Southern Palaces were
  littered with late grasses,
And the steps were mounded with red
  leaves that no one swept away.

Her Pear-Garden Players became white-
  haired
And the eunuchs thin-eyebrowed in her
  Court of Pepper-Trees;
Over the throne flew fireflies, while he
  brooded in the twilight.
He would lengthen the lamp-wick to its
  end and still could never sleep.
Bell and drum would slowly toll the
  dragging night-hours
And the River of Stars grow sharp in the
  sky, just before dawn,
And the porcelain mandarin-ducks on the
  roof grow thick with morning
  frost
And his covers of kingfisher-blue feel
  lonelier and colder
With the distance between life and death
  year after year;
And yet no beloved spirit ever visited
  his dreams.
 . . . At Ling-ch'ün lived a Taoist priest
  who was a guest of heaven,
Able to summon spirits by his
  concentrated mind.
And people were so moved by the
  Emperor's constant brooding
That they besought the Taoist priest to
  see if he could find her.
He opened his way in space and clove
  the ether like lightning
Up to heaven, under the earth, looking
  everywhere.
Above, he searched the Green Void,
  below, the Yellow Spring;
But he failed, in either place, to find the
  one he looked for.
And then he heard accounts of an
  enchanted isle at sea,
A part of the intangible and incorporeal
  world,
With pavilions and fine towers in the
  five-colored air,
And of exquisite immortals moving to
  and fro,
And of one among them—whom they
  called The Ever True—

With a face of snow and flowers
    resembling hers he sought.
So he went to the West Hall's gate of
    gold and knocked at the jasper
    door
And asked a girl, called Morsel-of-Jade,
    to tell The Doubly-Perfect.
And the lady, at news of an envoy from
    the Emperor of China,
Was startled out of dreams in her nine-
    flowered canopy.
She pushed aside her pillow, dressed,
    shook away sleep,
And opened the pearly shade and then
    the silver screen.
Her cloudy hair-dress hung on one side
    because of her great haste,
And her flower-cap was loose when she
    came along the terrace,
While a light wind filled her cloak and
    fluttered with her motion
As though she danced "The Rainbow
    Skirt and the Feathered Coat."
And the tear-drops drifting down her sad
    white face
Were like a rain in spring on the
    blossom of the pear.
But love glowed deep within her eyes
    when she bade him thank her
    liege,
Whose form and voice had been strange
    to her ever since their
    parting—
Since happiness had ended at the Court
    of the Bright Sun,

And moons and dawns had become long
    in Fairy-Mountain Palace.
But when she turned her face and looked
    down toward the earth
And tried to see the capital, there were
    only fog and dust.
So she took out, with emotion, the
    pledges he had given
And, through his envoy, sent him back a
    shell box and gold hairpin,
But kept one branch of the hairpin, and
    one side of the box,
Breaking the gold of the hairpin,
    breaking the shell of the box;
"Our souls belong together," she said,
    "like this gold and this shell—
Somewhere, sometime, on earth or in
    heaven, we shall surely meet."
And she sent him, by his messenger, a
    sentence reminding him
Of vows which had been known only to
    their two hearts:
"On the seventh day of the Seventh-
    month, in the Palace of Long
    Life,
We told each other secretly in the quiet
    midnight world
That we wished to fly in heaven, two
    birds with the wings of one,
And to grow together on the earth, two
    branches of one tree."
. . . Earth endures, heaven endures;
    sometime both shall end,
While this unending sorrow goes on and
    on for ever.

SUNG
(960-1279)
AND YÜAN
(1279-1368)
DYNASTIES

The Great Ultimate of Chou Tun-i

A popularized idea of the Great Ultimate, or *T'ai-chi,* is perhaps better known in the West through a kind of shadow boxing called *t'ai-chi ch'üan,* or "fist of the Great Ultimate," a kind of gymnastics that accelerates the embodiment of the powers of the cosmos within the human frame. The Sung (960–1279) thinker Chou Tun-i (Zhou Dunyi; 1017–1073), however, considers the notion much more conceptually, and the Great Ultimate constitutes one aspect of his synthetic explanation of the interrelationships between human conduct and universal forces. Chou Tun-i's "An Explanation of the Diagram of the Great Ultimate" is an important landmark in a Sung dynasty trend to create systematic cosmologies from the heterogeneous body of literature transmitted from ancient and medieval times.

Chou Tun-i's "Explanation" envisions a holistic, endlessly transforming system of forces that includes the Great Ultimate *(T'ai chi),* a concept from the *Book of Changes;* the Ultimate of Nonbeing *(Wu chi),* a notion from the *Tao-te ching;* yin and yang, popular ideas from Han cosmology; the Five Agents, mentioned as early as the *Book of History;* heaven and earth; and human moral values, such as those asserted by Mencius to be common to all human beings. The ideal for human beings is neither monk, priest, nor shaman but the sage, whose operative principles are the Mean (centrality), correctness, humanity, and righteousness. Chou also espouses the lessening of desires, a notion derived from the *Tao-te ching,* and tranquillity, which appears in several classical texts. He closes with three quotations from the *Book of Changes,* thus emphasizing the importance of that text. Chou's "Explanation" of course engendered many more issues than it explained, and later scholars continued Chou's trend toward systematization.

According to some accounts, Chou admired Buddhist thought, but no Buddhist influence is evident in this work. Sensitive to the world of nature, he sympathized even with plants and did not cut the grasses and weeds beneath his window. The philosophers Ch'eng Hao (1032–1085) and Ch'eng I (1033–1107) studied with him as teenagers, and Chou's love for things inspired them to stop hunting. Chou held several offices and retired to Mount Lu in Kiangsi Province, a location long known as a retreat for painters and recluses.

"An Explanation of the Diagram of the Great Ultimate"

The Ultimate of Non-being and also the Great Ultimate *(T'ai-chi)!* The Great Ultimate through movement generates yang. When its activity reaches its limit, it becomes tranquil. Through tranquillity the Great Ultimate generates yin. When tranquillity reaches its limit, activity begins again. So movement and tranquillity alternate and become the root of each other, giving rise to the distinction of yin and yang, and the two modes are thus established.

By the transformation of yang and its union with yin, the Five Agents of Water, Fire, Wood, Metal, and Earth arise. When these five material forces *(ch'i)* are distributed in harmonious order, the four seasons run their course.

The Five Agents constitute one system of yin and yang, and yin and yang constitute one Great Ultimate. The Great Ultimate is fundamentally the Non-ultimate. The Five Agents arise, each with its specific nature.

When the reality of the Ultimate of Non-being and the essence of yin, yang, and the Five Agents come into mysterious union, integration ensues. *Ch'ien* (Heaven) constitutes the male element, and *k'un* (Earth) constitutes the female element. The interaction of these two material forces engenders and transforms the myriad things. The myriad things produce and reproduce, resulting in an unending transformation.

It is man alone who receives (the Five Agents) in their highest excellence, and therefore he is most intelligent. His physical form appears, and his spirit develops consciousness. The five moral principles of his nature (humanity or *jen,* righteousness, propriety, wisdom, and faithfulness) are aroused by, and react to, the external world and engage in activity; good and evil are distinguished; and human affairs take place.

The sage settles these affairs by the principles of the Mean, correctness, humanity, and righteousness (for the way of the sage is none other than these four), regarding tranquillity as fundamental. (Having no desire, there will therefore be tranquillity.) Thus he establishes himself as the ultimate standard for man. Hence the character of the sage is "identical with that of Heaven and Earth; his brilliancy is identical with that of the sun and moon; his order is identical with that of the four seasons; and his good and evil fortunes are identical with those of spiritual beings." The superior man cultivates these moral qualities and enjoys good fortune, whereas the inferior man violates them and suffers evil fortune.

Therefore it is said that "yin and yang are established as the way of Heaven, the weak and the strong as the way of Earth, and humanity and righteousness as the way of man." It is also said that "if we investigate the cycle of things we shall understand the concepts of life and death." Great is the *Book of Changes!* Herein lies its excellence!

All People Are Brothers and Sisters: Chang Tsai's *Western Inscription*

A universal cosmology conceived on the model of a human family is developed in Chang Tsai's (Zhang Zai; 1020–1077) *Western Inscription (Hsi ming)*. Originally one chapter from his *Correcting Youthful Ignorance (Cheng meng)*, the *Inscription* was of such great importance in the development of Sung ethical philosophies that it is often treated as an independent work; a very short essay, it is presented here in its entirety. It was so named because it was inscribed on the western wall of his studio.

The *Western Inscription* is considered one of the most important articulations of the notion of humanity, and it suggests a humanity more deeply informed by charity than is characteristic of the Chou philosophers. Ideas of filial piety, of human nature, and of the self, or body, are expanded to embrace the entire universe. In contrast with the *Great Learning*, which moves in a linear progression from managing the family to ordering the state and finally to bringing peace to the realm, the *Western Inscription* in one step enlarges the idea of the family to include even heaven and earth. Chang Tsai's vision has the universal scope of Vimalakīrti's, but it is a vision focused directly on human relationships, particularly family relationships; the last section of the passage admiringly notes historical paragons of filial piety.

Chang Tsai originally studied Buddhism and Taoism but eventually turned toward the learning of Confucian texts. He held various official posts and lectured to the emperor on government. Late in life, he served in the Board of Imperial Sacrifice.

The *Western Inscription*

Heaven is my father and Earth is my mother, and even such a small creature as I finds an intimate place in their midst.

Therefore that which fills the universe I regard as my body and that which directs the universe I consider as my nature.

All people are my brothers and sisters, and all things are my companions.

The great ruler (the emperor) is the eldest son of my parents (Heaven and Earth), and the great ministers are his stewards. Respect the aged—this is the way to treat them as elders should be treated. Show deep love toward the orphaned and the weak—this is the way to treat them as the young should be treated. The sage identifies his character with that of Heaven and Earth, and the worthy is the most outstanding man. Even those who are tired, infirm, crippled, or sick; those who have no brothers or children, wives or husbands, are all my brothers who are in distress and have no one to turn to.

When the time comes, to keep himself from harm—this is the care of a son. To rejoice in Heaven and to have no anxiety—this is filial piety at its purest.

He who disobeys [the Principle of Nature] violates virtue. He who destroys humanity is a robber. He who promotes evil lacks [moral] capacity. But he who puts his moral nature into practice and brings his physical existence into complete fulfillment can match [Heaven and Earth].

One who knows the principles of transformation will skillfully carry forward the undertakings [of Heaven and Earth], and one who penetrates spirit to the highest degree will skillfully carry out their will.

Do nothing shameful in the recesses of your own house and thus bring no dishonor to them. Preserve your mind and nourish your nature and thus (serve them) with untiring effort.

The Great Yü hated pleasant wine but attended to the protection and support of his parents. Border Warden Ying brought up and educated the young and thus extended his love to his own kind.

Shun's merit lay in delighting his parents with unceasing effort, and Shen-sheng's reverence was demonstrated when he awaited punishment without making an attempt to escape.

Tsang Shen received his body from his parents and reverently kept it intact throughout life, while Po-ch'i vigorously obeyed his father's command.

Wealth, honor, blessing, and benefits are meant for the enrichment of my life, while poverty, humble station, and sorrow are meant to help me to fulfillment.

In life I follow and serve [Heaven and Earth]. In death I will be at peace.

The Writings of Chu Hsi

One of the most important thinkers in Chinese history is Chu Hsi (Zhu Xi; 1130–1200), whose influence extended as far as Korea and Japan. In modern Confucian temples his spirit tablet (a plaque bearing the deceased's name that serves as a resting place for the spirit invoked during sacrifices) stands in the central shrine of the temple along with those of Confucius, Mencius, and Yen Hui, Confucius's favorite disciple; no other post-Han philosopher is accorded such an honor.

These selections from his writings relate some of his more philosophical ideas as well as his views on religious themes, such as his attitude toward the spirit of Confucius. The entries on the mind, nature, and the feelings; on principle and material force; and on heaven and earth are from the *Complete Works of Chu Hsi (Chu Tzu ch'üan-shu)*. Following the original arrangement of the text, the order of the entries illustrates Chu Hsi's priorities as they begin first with the cultivation of the individual and only then move to larger cosmogonic theories. Many of his writings, like those of other thinkers, take the form of question-and-answer discussions with pupils recorded by the student. Entries from the *Complete Works* follow that format.

The selection on the mind, the nature, and the feelings describes what might be called an inner cosmology of the human being. Chu Hsi's synthesis within the self of the Great Ultimate, yin and yang, and human values recalls Chou Tun-i's "Explanation of the Diagram of the Great Ultimate," yet Chu Hsi moreover describes the interactions of the mind, the nature, and the feelings within that system. He also gives new emphasis to the idea of principle *(li)*, an old idea that had appeared infrequently in the classics; originally referring to the natural patterns and grains in jade or wood, it later was extended to include the patterns and grains of the universe itself. Human nature, for Chu Hsi, is this principle. His theories of human nature and the mind incorporate the notions of commiseration and humanity from Mencius, the condition before and after the arising of activity from the "Centrality and Equilibrium," and a theory of the mind as master that strongly parallels the ideas of Hsün Tzu. Chu Hsi's conception of the nature as vacuous or empty may also ultimately be derived from Hsün Tzu's conception of the mind, rather than from any Buddhist idea of emptiness, as he was not sympathetic to Buddhist philosophy.

This synthesis, then, draws upon pre-Han values but grounds them in principle, the very stuff of the universe. Chu Hsi further explains the primordial forces of the universe in terms of the interactions of both principle and material force, or vital force *(ch'i)*. Classical scholars of the Chou period, in contrast, had employed analogies from nature to explain human nature, but had not focused on the elemental essences of the natural world for their own sake. Chu Hsi also develops a cosmogony, or notion of the origins of the universe, and a theory of how the first human being was created. This he understands not in terms of a creator deity but in terms of the self-operating circulation and coagulation of such forces as yin and yang and the Five Agents.

On questions concerning the nature of spiritual beings, Chu Hsi emphasizes Confucius's admonition to attend first to human beings and only then to spirits, and to respect spirits, but keep them at a distance. Chu Hsi understands spirits also in terms of the interactions of yin and yang and material force. The clear aspects of material force become the *hun* anima soul and *p'o* corporeal soul, whereas the more turbid aspects become the physical body. At death, material force disintegrates, but only over a long period of time of uncertain duration. During sacrificial offerings, it is this remaining material force *(ch'i)* that allows a resonance between the sacrificer and the spiritual being.

Although his interpretation of spiritual beings might thus sound somewhat scholastic, Chu Hsi himself nevertheless understood some spirits very personally: he offered sacrifices to the spirits of the Confucian sages, as is recorded in his "Sacrificial Report to Confucius on the Completion of the Restorations at the White Deer Hollow Academy" *(Pai-lu-tung ch'eng kao hsien-sheng wen)* of 1180, which is addressed to Confucius, Mencius, and Yen Hui. Confucius had received sacrificial offerings from the imperial court since at least the first century B.C.E., a practice maintained into the Sung and eventually into modern times. Whereas those ceremonies were part of a statewide institutional ritual system, however, Chu Hsi's sacrifices to Confucius reflect a more direct and personal relationship with the sage, and Chu Hsi performed such rites at various milestones in his academic career, as when he completed the restoration of the White Deer Hollow Academy, where he taught.

Besides sacrifices to Confucius, Chu Hsi also presented offerings to the altars of the land and grain and, on a number of occasions, prayed for both rain and clear weather. He wrote extensively on ritual and devised new standards for household rites. In a draft of a memorial of 1189, he warned the ruler of the dangers of becoming deluded by the occult. Mountebanks throughout history had availed themselves of esoteric practices to create social disorder, he cautions, admonishing the ruler to follow historical precedent and adhere to careful study and inquiry (maxims espoused in the "Centrality and Equilibrium") in his dealings with the spirit world.

A native of Fukien Province, Chu Hsi passed the highest level of civil service examinations at the unusually early age of nineteen. Over the course of his life he intermittently served in a number of official positions, but he declined many posts and held various sinecures at temples and devoted his time to writing and teaching.

The Mind, the Nature, and the Feelings

85. The nature is comparable to the Great Ultimate, and the mind to yin and yang. The Great Ultimate exists only in the yin and yang, and cannot be separated from them. In the final analysis, however, the Great Ultimate is the Great Ultimate and yin and yang are yin and yang. So it is with nature and mind. They are one and yet two, two and yet one, so to speak. Philosopher Han Yü (768–824) described nature as humanity, righteousness, propriety, wisdom, and faithfulness and the feelings as pleasure, anger, sorrow, and joy. This is an advance over other philosophers on the problem of human nature. As to his division of human nature into three grades (superior, medium, and inferior), he has only explained material force but not nature.

86. Although nature is a vacuity, it consists of concrete principles. Although the mind is a distinct entity, it is vacuous, and therefore embraces all principles. This truth will be apprehended only when people examine it for themselves.

87. Nature consists of principles embraced in the mind, and the mind is where these principles are united.

88. Nature is principle. The mind is its embracement and reservoir, and issues it forth into operation.

89. Some time ago I read statements by Wu-feng (Hu Hung, 1100–1155) in which he spoke of the mind only in contrast to nature, leaving the feelings unaccounted for. Later when I read Heng-ch'ü's (Chang Tsai's) doctrine that "the mind commands man's nature and feelings," I realized that it was a great contribution. Only then did I find a satisfactory account of the feelings. His doctrine agrees with that of Mencius. In the words of Mencius, "the feeling of commiseration is the beginning of humanity." Now humanity is nature, and commiseration is feeling. In this, the mind can be seen through the feelings. He further said, "Humanity, righteousness, propriety, and wisdom are rooted in the mind." In this, the mind is seen through nature. For the mind embraces both nature and the feelings. Nature is substance and feelings are function.

90. Nature is the state before activity begins, the feelings are the state when activity has started, and the mind includes both of these states. For nature is the mind before it is aroused, while feelings are the mind after it is aroused, as is expressed in [Chang Tsai's] saying, "The mind commands man's nature and feelings." Desire emanates from feelings. The mind is comparable to water, nature is comparable to the tranquillity of still water, feeling is comparable to the flow of water, and desire is comparable to its waves. Just as there are good and bad waves, so there are good desires, such as when "I want humanity," and bad desires which rush out like wild and violent waves. When bad desires are substantial, they will destroy the Principle of Heaven, as water bursts a dam and damages everything. When Mencius said that "feelings enable people to do good," he meant that the correct feelings flowing from our nature are originally all good.

91. The mind means master. It is master whether in the state of activity or in the state of tranquillity. It is not true that in the state of tranquillity there is no need of a master and there is a master only when the state becomes one of activity. By master is meant an all-pervading control and command existing in the mind by itself. The mind unites and apprehends nature and the feelings, but it is not united with them as a vague entity without any distinction.

Principle *(Li)* and Material Force *(Ch'i)*

100. In the universe there has never been any material force without principle or principle without material force.

101. *Question:* Which exists first, principle or material force?

Answer: Principle has never been separated from material force. However, principle "exists before physical form [and is therefore without it]" whereas material force "exists after physical form [and is therefore with it]." Hence when spoken of as being before or after physical form, is there not the difference of priority and posteriority? Principle has no physical form, but material force is coarse and contains impurities.

102. Fundamentally principle and material force cannot be spoken of as prior or posterior. But if we must trace their origin, we are obliged to say that principle is prior. However, principle is not a separate entity. It exists right in material force. Without material force, principle would have nothing to adhere to. As material force, there are the Agents (or Elements) of Metal, Wood, Water, and Fire. As principle, there are humanity, righteousness, propriety, and wisdom.

103. Question about the relation between principle and material force.

Answer: I-ch'uan (Ch'eng I) expressed it very well when he said that principle is one but its manifestations are many. When heaven, earth, and the myriad things are spoken of together, there is only one principle. As applied to man, however, there is in each individual a particular principle.

104. *Question:* What are the evidences that principle is in material force?

Answer: For example, there is order in the complicated interfusion of the yin and the yang and of the Five Agents. Principle is there. If material force does not consolidate and integrate, principle would have nothing to attach itself to.

105. *Question:* May we say that before heaven and earth existed there was first of all principle?

Answer: Before heaven and earth existed, there was after all only principle. As there is this principle, therefore there are heaven and earth. If there were no principle, there would also be no heaven and earth, no man, no things, and, in fact, no containing or sustaining (of things by heaven and earth) to speak of. As there is principle, there is therefore material force to operate everywhere and nourish and develop all things.

Question: Is it principle that nourishes and develops all things?

Answer: As there is this principle, therefore there is this material force operating, nourishing, and developing. Principle itself has neither physical form nor body.

Heaven and Earth

123. In the beginning of the universe there was only material force consisting of yin and yang. This force moved and circulated, turning this way and that. As this movement gained speed, a mass of sediment was compressed (pushed together), and since there is no outlet for this, it consolidated to form the earth in the center of the universe. The clear part of material force formed the sky, the sun, and moon, and the stars and zodiacal spaces. It is only on the outside that the encircling movement perpetually goes on. The earth exists motionless in the center of the system, not at the bottom.

124. In the beginning of the universe, when it was still in a state of undifferentiated chaos, I imagine there were only water and fire. The sediment from water formed the earth. If today we climb the high mountains and look around, we will see ranges of mountains in the shape of waves. This is because the water formed them like this, though we do not know in what period they solidified. The solidification was at first very soft, but in time it became hard.

Question: I imagine it is like the tide rushing upon and making waves in the sand.

Answer: Yes. The most turbid water formed the earth and the purest fire became wind, thunder, lightning, the stars, and the like.

125. *Question:* From the beginning of the universe to this day, it has not yet been ten thousand years. I do not know how things looked before then.

Answer: The past is to be understood in the same way.

Further question: Can the universe be destroyed?

Answer: It is indestructible. But in time man will lose all moral principles and everything will be thrown together in a chaos. Man and things will all die out, and then there will be a new beginning.

Further question: How was the first man created?

Answer: Through the transformation of material force. When the essence of yin and yang and the Five Agents are united, man's physical form is established. This is what the Buddhists call production by transformation. There are many such productions today, such as lice.

126. *Question:* With reference to the mind of Heaven and Earth and the Principle of Heaven and Earth. Principle is moral principle. Is mind the will of a master?

Answer: The mind is the will of a master, it is true, but what is called master is precisely principle itself. It is not true that outside of the mind there is principle, or that outside of principle there is a mind.

127. Heaven and Earth have no other business except to have the mind to produce things. The material force of one origin (the Great Ultimate including principle and material force) revolves and circulates without a moment of rest, doing nothing except creating the myriad things.

Question: Master Ch'eng I said, "Heaven and Earth create and transform without having any mind of their own. The sage has a mind of his own but does not take any [unnatural] action."

Answer: That shows where Heaven and Earth have no mind of their own. It is like this: The four seasons run their course and the various things flourish. When do Heaven and Earth entertain any mind of their own? As to the sage, he only follows principle. What action does he need to take? This is the reason why Ming-tao (Ch'eng Hao) said, "The constant principle of Heaven and Earth is that their mind is in all things and yet they have no mind of their own. The constant principle of the sage is that his feelings are in accord with all creation, and yet

he has no feelings of his own." This is extremely well said.

Question: Does having their mind in all things not mean to pervade all things with their mind without any selfishness?

Answer: Heaven and Earth reach all things with this mind. When man receives it, it then becomes the human mind. When things receive it, it becomes the mind of things (in general). And when grass, trees, birds, animals receive it, it becomes the mind of grass, trees, birds, and animals (in particular). All of these are simply the one mind of Heaven and Earth. Thus we must understand in what sense Heaven and Earth have mind and in what sense they have no mind. We cannot be inflexible.

"Sacrificial Report to Confucius on the Completion of the Restorations at the White Deer Hollow Academy"

Here on the eighteenth day of the third month of the seventh year of the Ch'un-hsi era, I present a sacrificial report to Confucius, the Ancient Sage, the Perfected Sage, the King of Refined Culture. In relating some accounts of this place concerning its national and regional significance, I note that the White Deer Hollow Academy is located some fifteen leagues northeast of the city. In the T'ang dynasty, Li Po lived here as a recluse when he sojourned in the Kiangnan region, and eventually a national academy was built to commemorate him. Emperor T'ai-tsung frequently donated books, and for a number of years instruction at the academy flourished. But eventually no one was to be seen studying there, and as time passed the buildings became completely overgrown with weeds. But I thought back to the academy's previous prosperity, and with a number of other scholars received permission to revive instruction at the academy and supervise it. Had I not done so I fear I would have incurred some reproof, and so I decided to restore this place. Now it prospers again and the construction work is complete, and I am about to lead several like-minded colleagues in learned discussions. I have done all this to provide for the transmission of the teachings of the ancient sages and teachers and to respond to the beneficent guidance of Emperor T'ai-tsung. As the drums sound to herald the beginning of school and the pupils take up their satchels, I lead the guests, teachers, and students in the rites of sacrificial oblations to Confucius, Yen Hui, and Mencius, so that you may draw nigh to partake of these offerings.

Draft Memorial of 1189

The *Book of History* says, "Heaven has a manifest way, and its manifold things are clearly manifest" [*T'ai-shih hsia*], and it says, "To those who do good it will send down manifold blessings; to those who do evil, it will send down manifold misfortunes" [*I-hsün*]. So people's misfortunes or blessings are all brought about by themselves. It is neither possible that someone who has committed evil can pray and obtain blessings, nor is it likely that someone who has not committed evil and has preserved what is morally upright will suffer misfortune.

How much more is this true for a sovereign king who has received heaven's mandate and serves as the ruler of the suburban altars, ancestral temples, altars to the land and grain, spirits, and human beings! If he is able to develop his virtue, implement good government, and look after the welfare of the great masses of the people, then need the elimination of disasters and harms depend on exorcism? Need the advent of blessings and prosperity depend on prayer? If he acts contrary to these principles, then he offends heaven, incurs the enmity of human beings, and angers the spirits. Even though he may try to ward off malevolent ghosts and attract good people to serve in his government, he will do so to no avail.

Such it was with the ancient kings when they formulated rites. Everyone from the Son of Heaven down to the common people had constant standards when they "gave thanks to their origins" [*Book of Rites, Chiao t'e-sheng*] and presented offerings to their parents. The sacrificial animals, ritual objects, the times, and the days that the sacrifices were held all had constant standards. The visible realm had its rites and music, the hidden realm had its ghosts and spirits [*Book of Rites, Yüeh chi*], and one principle penetrated everything, for from the very beginning they were without separation.

Now if a rite is performed that is not recorded in the ritual texts, then spirits will not come to partake of it. This would be an instance of "sacrificing to a spirit that does not belong to one" [*Analects* 2.24], and it would be a wanton sacrifice. "Wanton sacrifices bring no blessings" [*Book of Rites, Ch'ü-li*]. This is clearly written in the classics. It is not that these constant standards are purposely established to prohibit wanton sacrifices, but that the principle is a natural one and cannot be altered. If, in a state of unmindfulness, one seems to see some uncanny thing, this is due to one's mind losing its self-governing qualities, and it will thus erroneously give rise to anxiety and doubts. Then shamans, invocators, and wizards will avail themselves of this opportunity to practice their treacherously deceptive bewitching arts. As soon as their arts are put into practice, misfortune will ensue, and there will be no end to it. Both in ages past and in modern times there have been people who, because of this, have incurred extreme chaos and disorder—how can one count just how many?

The lesson is not far to seek. One must do very concentrated study and inquiry to become clear about the principles of human nature and of the mandate; one's mind will thus comprehend things clearly and be without doubts or confusion. What should be, let there be, and what should not be, let there not be. Otherwise how could one grasp and hold on to ritual, maintain one's standards, and cut off charlatanism and falseness at their source? Under the administration of the ancient kings, those people who held to sinister ways to create chaos in the government or who availed themselves of ghosts and spirits to confuse the masses were punished without fail and were paid no heed. The ancient kings pondered such matters deeply.

It has been stated in the "Annals" that "those who are clear about the nature of heaven and earth cannot be moved by spirit prodigies; those who are clear about the principles of the ten thousand things cannot be deceived by the uncanny" [*Han History*, "Annals of Suburban Sacrifice"]. It is not very difficult to find out where some people have gone wrong.

Ch'en Ch'un's Learning of the Way

One of Chu Hsi's most noted pupils is Ch'en Ch'un (1159–1223), also known by his literary name as Master Pei-hsi, or Master Northern River. Although he did not enjoy great success in the civil service examinations, Ch'en was widely respected as a teacher and received special official appointments directly from the emperor. His major work is his *Explanation of Terms by Master Pei-hsi (Pei-hsi tzu-i)*, a systematic catalogue of the terms common to Sung dynasty discourses on the Confucian Way.

Of similar importance are his lectures at Yen-ling, a place near Hangchow in southern China. His "System of the Learning of the Way" is one of those lectures, which were given at the request of a local prefect who was developing the region's school system. Ch'en Ch'un emphasizes the this-worldliness of the Way, or Tao, which is found in everyday life. Within the multiplicity of human affairs and human values, Ch'en Ch'un apprehends a unitary underlying principle: the Principle of Heaven *(t'ien li)*, which has one source but many varied expressions. The term *t'ien-li* had appeared in the *Book of Rites* but only became an important ontological principle in the twelfth century as developed by the philosophers Ch'eng Hao and Ch'eng I. Alluding extensively to the ancient classics and the writing of Chou philosophers, Ch'en Ch'un asserts that this normative principle is what it should be and is imbued with value; it is obvious and accessible to everyone and moreover is easy to follow. Ch'en Ch'un's Tao, then, is quite different from the vague and elusive Tao of Lao Tzu or from the Way of Chuang Tzu, whose holy man in the clouds is far removed from daily affairs.

"The System of the Learning of the Way"

What the sages and worthies have called the Learning of the Way is not a principle that is too obscure and difficult to investigate or any affair that is too lofty and difficult to practice. It is nothing but ordinary daily human affairs. For while the Way is rooted deeply within the Mandate of Heaven, it actually operates in the midst of daily life. With reference to the mind, its substance consists of the nature of humanity, righteousness, propriety, and wisdom, and its function consists of the feelings of compassion, shame and dislike, deference and yielding, and the sense of right and wrong. With reference to the body, its provision consists in the utility of the ear, the eye, the mouth, the nose, and the four limbs, and the associations consist in the relationship of the ruler and the minister, father and son, husband and wife, brothers, and friends. With reference to human affairs, in private life there are personal cultivation, regulation of the family, responding to affairs and dealing with things; and in going out to serve in the government, there are attending to the office, managing the state, caring for the people, and controlling the multitude. In minor matters, there are rising and resting, speaking and moving, clothes, and food. In major matters, there are rites and music, law and government, finance, and the army. In each of these thousands of details and tens of thousands of threads there is a specific principle that is definite, unchangeable, and what should be. All that is the Principle of Heaven as it naturally is and its operation is perfectly clear. It is not something that man can bring about by force. The one source develops into many variations; that means substance and function come from the same source. The many variations are combined into the one source; that means there is no gap between the manifest and the hidden. This is the goodness bestowed on us by the Lord on High, and this is the normal nature the people keep. Because all people share it and thus their minds are unobstructed, intelligent, and not beclouded, it is called the clear character (*ming-te*). Because it is followed by all without any obstruction, it is called the universal path. The endowment of Yao and Shun and the man in the street is the same, and the natural endowment of Confucius and people in every hamlet of ten families is similar. The sage becomes a sage because he is born with the knowledge (of *ming-te*) and practices it naturally and easily. What the student learns is to probe into it and practice it. Anyone who says his ruler cannot (develop this character) destroys his ruler, and any ruler who says his people cannot do so destroys his people, and anyone who says he himself cannot do so destroys himself. "Hold it fast and you preserve it. Let it go and you lose it." Follow it and there will be fortune. Go against it and there will be misfortune. For it is obvious and easy to know, and wide and smooth and easy to walk on. How can this be anything detached from daily life, standing by itself, too obscure and hard to understand, or too lofty and difficult to practice? If anyone goes beyond it and seeks elsewhere, what he is after will not be the Way that is central and perfectly correct, but something sages and worthies do not talk about.

The Way of the Taoist Tradition
of Perfect Truth

The Way of the Taoist tradition of Perfect Truth *(Ch'üan-chen),* also called Perfect Reality or Complete Clarity, is outlined in these precepts for followers. This tradition looked to Wang Che (1112–1170) as its founder, a man also known by his religious name of Wang Ch'ung-yang, or Master Wang of Developed Yang. From Shensi Province in northern China, Wang studied Confucian texts in his youth and initially aspired to a career in the military; he eventually became a mountain recluse, practiced Buddhism for a time, and finally became a master of the Tao *(tao-shih).* He journeyed eastward to Shantung Province and there gained many disciples; one of them, Ch'iu Ch'ang-ch'un (1148–1227), attracted the notice of Genghis Khan.

Wang's teaching of Perfect Truth was a synthesis of several traditions, and his followers were enjoined to read not only the *Tao-te ching* but also Buddhist literature on the perfection of wisdom *(Prajñāpāramitā* literature), as well as the *Classic of Filial Piety (Hsiao ching),* a Han compilation. That mixture of ideas is reflected in these fifteen precepts. Although the ideas of nature and destiny (the mandate) are from Confucian teachings, the injunction to leave the family for a cloistered life would seem to transgress the Confucian ideal of filial piety, which enjoins people to remain at home and care for their parents until their death. Yet one does not actually leave the mundane world: one leave's only the mundane mind behind on an inner spiritual journey. While the goal of spiritual development is to become a sage, it is to become a sage who is in, but not of, this world. Some of the vocabulary of the precepts is borrowed from Buddhism, for example, the three realms and the middle path of love without attachment. Older ideas of the alchemical transformation of the body have been interpreted figuratively, and the new agent of metamorphosis is meditation.

"Master Ch'ung-yang's Fifteen Precepts for Establishing the Teaching"

On the Cloistered Life

All those who choose to leave their families and homes should join a Taoist monastery, for it is a place where the body may find rest. Where the body rests, the mind also will gradually find peace; the spirit and the vital energy will be harmonized, and entry into the Way *(Tao)* will be attained.

In all action there should be no overexertion, for when there is overexertion, the vital energy is damaged. On the other hand, when there is total inaction, the blood and vital energy become sluggish. Thus a mean should be sought between activity and passivity, for only in this way can one cherish what is permanent and be at ease with one's lot. This is the way to the correct cloistered life.

On Cloud-like Wandering

There are two kinds of wandering. One involves observing the wonders of mountains and waters; lingering over the colors of flowers and trees; admiring the splendor of cities and the architecture of temples; or simply enjoying a visit with relatives and friends. However, in this type of wandering the mind is constantly possessed by things, so this is merely an empty, outward wandering. In fact, one can travel the world over and see the myriad sights, walk millions of miles and exhaust one's body, only in the end to confuse one's mind and weaken one's vital energy without having gained a thing.

In contrast, the other type of wandering, cloud-like wandering, is like a pilgrimage into one's own nature and destiny in search of their darkest, innermost mysteries. To do this one may have to climb fearsome mountain heights to seek instruction from some knowledgeable teacher or cross tumultuous rivers to inquire tirelessly after the Way. Yet if one can find that solitary word which can trigger enlightenment, one will have awakened in oneself perfect illu-

mination; then the great matters of life and death will become magnificent, and one will become a master of the Perfect Truth. This is true cloud-like wandering.

On Book-Learning

In learning from books, one who merely grasps onto the literal sense of words will only confuse his eyes. If one can intuit the true meaning behind the words and bring one's heart into harmony with it, then the books themselves can be discarded. One must therefore first attain an understanding of meanings and locate the principles behind them; then one should discard the principle and internalize the meaning into one's heart. When the meaning is understood, then the mind will withdraw from externals, and in time will naturally become responsive to reality. The light of the mind will overflow, the spirit of wisdom will become active, and no problem will be insolvable.

Thus one should diligently cultivate the inner self, never letting one's mind run wild, lest one lose his Nature and Destiny. If one cannot fully comprehend the true meanings of books, and only tries to read more and more, one will end up merely jabbering away before others, seeking to show off one's meager talent. This will not only be detrimental to one's self-cultivation but it may do harm to one's spirit and vital energy. In short, no matter how many books one reads, they will be of no avail in attaining the Way. To understand fully the deep meaning of books, one must incorporate them into one's mind.

On the Art of Medicine

Herbs are the treasures of the hills and the waters, the essence of the grass and the trees. Among the various herbs there are those which are warm and those which are cold; properly used, they can help in supplying elements to or eliminating them from the body. There are active and less active medicines, those that work externally and internally. Therefore people who know thoroughly the power of herbs can save lives, while those who do not will only do further harm to the body. Therefore the man of the Way must be expert in this art. But if he cannot be, he should not pursue it further because it will be of no use in the attainment of the Way and will even be detrimental to his accumulation of merits. This is because those who pride themselves in such knowledge crave after worldly goods, and do not cultivate the Truth. They will pay for such transgression either in this life or the next. The Perfect Truth Taoist must pay heed to this.

On Residence and Covering

Sleeping in the open air would violate the sun and the moon, therefore some simple thatched covering is necessary. However, it is not the habit of the superior man to live in great halls and lavish palaces, because to cut down the trees that would be necessary for the building of such grand residences would be like cutting the arteries of the earth or cutting the veins of a man. Such deeds would only add to one's superficial external merits while actually damaging one's inner credits. It would be like drawing a picture of a cake to ward off hunger or piling up snow for a meal—much ado and nothing gained. Thus the Perfect Truth Taoist will daily seek out the palace hall within his own body and avoid the mundane mind which seeks to build lavish external residences. The man of wisdom will scrutinize and comprehend this principle.

On Companionship

A Taoist should find true friends who can help each other in times of illness and take care of each other's burials at death. However he must observe the character of a person before making friends with him. Do not commit oneself to friendship and then investigate the person's character. Love makes the heart cling to things and should therefore be avoided. On the other hand, if there is no love, human feelings will be strained. To love and yet not to become attached to love—this is the middle path one should follow.

There are three dimensions of compatibility and three of incompatibility. The three dimen-sions of compatibility are an understanding mind, the possession of wisdom, and an intensity of aspiration. Inability to understand the external world, lack of wisdom accompanied by foolish acts, and lack of high aspiration accompanied by a quarrelsome nature are the three dimensions of incompatibility. The principle of establishing oneself lies in the grand monastic community. The choice of a companion should be motivated by an appreciation of the loftiness of a person's mind and not by mere feelings or external appearance.

On Sitting in Meditation

Sitting in meditation which consists only of the act of closing the eyes and seating oneself in an upright position is only a pretense. The true way of sitting in meditation is to have the mind as immovable as Mount T'ai all the hours of the day, whether walking, resting, sitting, or reclining. The four doors of the eyes, ears, mouth, and nose should be so pacified that no external sight can be let in to intrude upon the inner self. If ever an impure or wandering thought arises, it will no longer be true quiet sitting. For the person who is an accomplished meditator, even though his body may still reside within this dusty world, his name will already be registered in the ranks of the immortals or free spirits *(hsien)* and there will be no need for him to travel to far-off places to seek them out; within his body the nature of the sage and the virtuous man will already be present. Through years of practice, a person by his own efforts can liberate his spirit from the shell of his body and send it soaring to the heights. A single session of meditation, when completed, will allow a person to rove through all the corners of the universe.

On Pacification of the Mind

There are two minds. One is quiet and unmoving, dark and silent, not reflecting on any of the myriad things. It is deep and subtle, makes no distinction between inner and outer, and contains not a single wandering thought. The other mind is that mind which, because it is in contact with external forms, will be dragged into all kinds of thoughts, pushed into seeking out beginnings and ends—a totally restless and confused mind. This confused mind must be eliminated. If one allows it to rule, then the Way and its power will be damaged, and one's Nature and Destiny will come to harm. Hearing, seeing, and conscious thoughts should be eliminated from all activities, from walking, resting, sitting, or reclining.

On Nurturing One's Nature

The art of cultivating one's Nature is like that of playing on the strings of a musical instrument: too great a force can break the string, while too weak a pull will not produce any sound; one must find the perfect mean to produce the perfect note. The art of nurturing one's Nature is also like forging a sword: too much steel will make the sword too brittle while too much tin will make it too malleable. In training one's Nature, this principle must be recognized. When it is properly implemented, one can master one's Nature at will.

On Aligning the Five Primal Energies

The Five Primal Energies are found in the Middle Hall. The Three Primal Energies are located at the top of the head. If the two are harmonized, then, beginning with the Green Dragon and the White Tiger [the supreme Yin-Yang pair], the ten thousand gods in the body will be arranged in perfect harmony. When this is accomplished, then the energy in the hundred veins will flow smoothly. Cinnabar [symbol for Nature] and mercury [symbol for Destiny] will coalesce into a unity. The body of the adept may still be within the realm of men, but the spirit is already roving in the universe.

On the Union of Nature and Destiny

Nature is spirit. Destiny is material energy. When Nature is supported by Destiny it is like a bird buoyed up and carried along by the wind—flying freely with little effort. Whatever one wills to be, one can be. This is the meaning in the line from the *Classic of the Shadowy Talismans:* "The bird is controlled by the air."

The Perfect Truth Taoist must treasure this line and not reveal its message casually to the uninitiated. The gods themselves will chide the person who disobeys this instruction. The search for the hidden meaning of Nature and mind is the basic motif of the art of self-cultivation. This must be remembered at all times.

On the Path of the Sage

In order to enter the path of the sage, one must accumulate patiently, over the course of many years, merit-actions and true practices. Men of high understanding, men of virtue, and men who have attained insight may all become sages. In attaining sagehood, the body of the person may still be in one room, but his nature will already be encompassing the world. The various sages in the various Heavens will protect him, and the free spirits and immortals in the highest realm of the Non-Ultimate will be around him. His name will be registered in the Hall of the Immortals, and he will be ranked among the free spirits. Although his bodily form is in the world of dust, his mind will have transcended all corporal things.

On Transcending the Three Realms

The Three Realms refer to the realms of desire, form, and formlessness. The mind that has freed itself from all impure or random thoughts will have transcended the first realm of desire. The mind that is no longer tied to the perception of objects in the object-realm will have transcended the realm of form. The mind that no longer is fixed upon emptiness will further transcend the realm of formlessness. The spirit of the man who transcends all three of these realms will be in the realm of the immortals. His Nature will abide forever in the realm of Jade-like Purity.

On Cultivating the Body of the Law

The Body of the Law is formless form. It is neither empty nor full. It has neither front nor back and is neither high nor low, long nor short. When it is functioning, there is nothing it does not penetrate. When it is withdrawn into itself, it is obscure and leaves no trace; it must be cultivated in order to attain the true Way. If the cultivation is great, the merit will be great; if the cultivation is small, the merit will be small. One should not wish to return to it, nor should one be attached to this world of things. One must allow Nature to follow its own course.

On Leaving the Mundane World

Leaving the mundane world is not leaving the body; it is leaving behind the mundane mind.

Consider the analogy of the lotus; although rooted in the mud, it blossoms pure and white into the clear air. The man who attains the Way, although corporally abiding in the world, may flourish through his mind in the realm of sages. Those people who presently seek after non-death or escape from the world do not know this true principle and commit the greatest folly.

The words of these fifteen precepts are for our disciples of aspiration. Examine them carefully!

A Woman Adept Attains the Way

The historical Wang Che, or Wang Ch'ung-yang, of the Perfect Truth Taoist tradition had seven particularly developed disciples called the Seven Perfected. Extensive hagiographies of their lives appeared even in the Sung and Yüan (1279–1368) dynasties, and their biographies became the basis of the folk novel *Seven Taoist Masters,* which dates to perhaps the early sixteenth century. The selection from *Seven Taoist Masters* here recounts the spiritual attainments of Sun Pu-erh (1119–1183), the only woman of the Seven Perfected. Her religious name, Pu-erh, means literally "not two," and suggests both a philosophical understanding of the nuances of multiplicity and unity as well as an unwavering, unified focus of purpose. Historical references allude to her skills as a poet, and she purportedly developed many followers in the city of Lo-yang, the ancient capital of China located along the Yellow River. A work titled *The Codified Sayings of the Primordial Goddess Sun Pu-erh (Sun Pu-erh Yüan-chün fa-yü),* a text of uncertain provenance that describes meditation practices for women, may perhaps be the work of her disciples.

In the novel, each of the Seven Perfected has a particular spiritual obstacle, and Sun Pu-erh's is intellectualism. She realizes this in a conversation with her "brother," Ma Tan-yang, who is actually her spouse; upon embarking on a search for the Way, Sun and Ma have renounced sexual desire but still live together in a platonic relationship. Sun goes again to her teacher, Wang Ch'ung-yang, who gives her further instructions on three different options for spiritual development. In the secret vocabulary of internal alchemy, he describes the meditation practices for making the human body a virtual alchemical crucible for generating spiritual powers. When she realizes that the highest path is blocked off to her because of her female nature, she defaces herself, flees her spouse, and heads for Lo-yang. Even sacrificing her physical beauty does not protect her from the advances of Chang San and Li Ssu (fictive names that are the equivalent of "Smith and Jones" in English), which she fends off with magical powers.

The proportions of historical fact and fictional embellishment in this selection from the *Seven Taoist Masters* are unknown; nevertheless, the special problems Sun Pu-erh confronts because she is a woman do not conflict with the universal experiences of women in any culture. Alone of all the Seven Perfected, Sun Pu-erh is the only one who radically immolates herself physically before achieving the Tao, which suggests the unique difficulties women encountered in religious practice.

Selection from *Seven Taoist Masters*

Sun Pu-erh felt as if she had awakened from a bad dream. Everything now seemed clear. She sighed and said to Ma Tan-yang, "Brother, if not for your help I would have remained in the depths of illusion and ruined myself. Usually I am more intelligent in dealing with daily matters, but when it comes to learning Taoist knowledge you surpass me by far." Ma Tan-yang said, "It is not because I grasp the instructions of our teacher better, but because for a long time you closed your mind to learning new things. You thought you had learned all there was to learn. Your intelligence became an obstacle to your training. Learning is limitless. Not many can fully grasp this idea." Sun Pu-erh thanked Ma Tan-yang and said, "From now on I shall be humble and learn whatever there is to learn." Ma Tan-yang returned to his room, happy that Sun Pu-erh had realized her mistakes and was now ready to progress again.

A few days later Ma Tan-yang prepared to attend the birthday celebration of an aunt in a nearby town. He asked Sun Pu-erh to accompany him, but she pleaded sick and said she could not make the journey. So Ma Tan-yang packed the gifts, loaded them on a mule, and set out alone.

Sun Pu-erh sat in her room and thought once more about Ma Tan-yang's words. She especially remembered his saying that she had lost her motivation to learn. Left alone in the mansion, she thought things through. Ma Tan-yang would be away for a few days, and the servants were busy. This would be a good opportunity for her to go to Wang Ch'ung-yang and humbly ask for instructions.

She went to the meditation hall and found Wang Ch'ung-yang sitting quietly in meditation. She knelt at the doorway and said respectfully, "Sir, your student Sun Pu-erh has been stupid and did not appreciate your teachings. Now that Ma Tan-yang has explained everything to me, I am ashamed of myself and what I have done. I would like to ask for forgiveness and hope that you will instruct me again." She bowed low several times. Wang Ch'ung-yang beckoned her in and said, "You may stand up now. I shall describe to you three vehicles of the Taoist path. Listen well and then tell me which vehicle you aspire toward. Those who seek that Tao are nonattached to life and death. The heart is void of form and free from dust. There are no thoughts or feelings that tie one to the material plane. Their being is like the bright moon in a cloudless sky. With the spark of original nature they intuit the mystery of heaven and earth. They understand the principles behind the union of *yin* and *yang,* and, using the methods of internal alchemy, they return to the void and emerge with the Tao. They are at one with the sun and moon, they age with the heaven and earth and achieve the highest rank of immortality in heaven. This is the Great Vehicle. It is the fastest and the most direct path to immortality. Those who cultivate the Middle Vehicle observe the festivals of the gods and immortals with veneration, chant regularly the names of the gods and refrain from meat on designated vegetarian days. By immersing themselves in chanting, they purify the heart and let the original nature shine. In due time their spirit ascends to the heavens, and they become immortals of the middle rank. Those who cultivate the Lower Vehicle do good deeds, and by so doing their original nature is prevented from being tainted. They are contented and are at peace with themselves, living a long and healthy life. In due time, when they have accumulated enough good works, they will ascend to heaven and become immortals of the lower ranks." Wang Ch'ung-yang finished speaking, smiled, and asked Sun Pu-erh, "To which vehicle do you aspire?" Sun Pu-erh replied, "Your student aspires to the Great Vehicle." Wang Ch'ung-yang said, "You have ambitious aspirations, but I don't know whether you have the discipline and perseverance to pursue that path." Sun Pu-erh said, "Sir, my aspirations are not ambitious, but my will is strong. I am willing to sacrifice everything to attain the Great Vehicle."

Wang Ch'ung-yang then said, "Those who cultivate the Tao must find a place that is conducive to training. Certain places are filled with power, and training at these power places will enhance one's progress. There is a power hidden in the city of Loyang, and the gods have ordained that an immortal will emerge from there. One need merely cultivate oneself there for ten to twelve years, and immortality will be attained. Are you willing to go?" Sun Pu-erh said, "I am willing to go anywhere if that is what is required to cultivate the Great Vehicle." Wang Ch'ung-yang looked at Sun Pu-erh and then shook his head. "You cannot go." Sun Pu-erh said, "I am willing to do anything. I am willing to die, if necessary." Wang Ch'ung-yang said, "Dying is a waste if it achieves no purpose. To simply throw your life away is to rob yourself of the chance to become an immortal. Loyang is more than a thousand miles away. You will meet with perils along the way. You will be the target of men who desire your beauty. They will rape you and molest you. And rather than be shamed, you would take your own life before they touch you. Now, is that not wasting your life to no purpose? Not only will you not achieve immortality but you will throw away what was given to you by Heaven. That is why I said you cannot go."

Sun Pu-erh left the meditation hall and went directly to the kitchen. Telling the servants to leave, she filled a wok with cooking oil, heated the oil until it was hot, and then poured in cold water. The oil sizzled, and sparks of hot liquid shot out of the wok. Sun Pu-erh closed her eyes and let the liquid hit her face, burning the skin in numerous places; even after healing, the burns would leave scars and marks all over her face. She then returned to Wang Ch'ung-yang and said, "Look at my ugly face. Now will you allow me to travel to Loyang?" Wang Ch'ung-yang clapped his hands and said, "I have never seen one as determined as you are or willing to sacrifice so much. I did not come to Shantung Province in vain. You shall go to Loyang."

Wang Ch'ung-yang then taught Sun Pu-erh the methods of internal alchemy. He showed her how to immerse fire in water, how to unite *yin* and *yang,* and how to conceive and nourish the spirit. When he was satisfied that Sun Pu-erh remembered and understood the instructions, he said, "Remember, hide your knowledge. Do not let people know you are a seeker of the Tao. After you have finished the Great Alchemical Work, then you may reveal yourself and teach others. In the meantime, let your face heal. Do not even let your servants know of your plans. Leave as soon as you are ready. You need not come to say farewell to me. We shall meet again soon at the celebration of the ripening of the immortal peach."

Sun Pu-erh thanked Wang Ch'ung-yang and left the meditation hall. On her way back to her room, she ran into a servant, who screamed when she saw the lady's face. When the servant recovered her wits, she asked Sun Pu-erh, "Lady, what has happened to your face?" Sun Pu-erh said, "I was cooking a snack for the teacher, and by mistake I added water to the cooking oil. I did not get out of the way in time, and the sizzling liquid shot into my face. It is nothing serious." Sun Pu-erh locked herself in her room for the next few days and reviewed Wang Ch'ung-yang's instructions.

When Ma Tan-yang returned home, the servants at once told him about his wife's accident in the kitchen. Ma Tan-yang went to Sun Pu-erh's room, saw her face, and consoled her. Gently he said, "You should have been more careful. Let the servants do the cooking. The lady of the house should not be working in the kitchen. Now your beautiful face is ruined with scars." Sun Pu-erh stared at Ma Tan-yang and cackled madly. "Are you the messenger of the Empress of Heaven? Have you come to invite me to attend the celebrations in heaven? If so, let's get going!" She opened the window and jumped out. Pretending to slip, she deliberately fell and lay on the ground, groaning. Ma Tan-yang ran out, put his arms around her and helped her up. Sun Pu-erh laughed and cried like a mad woman. Ma Tan-yang escorted her back to her room and then went to Wang Ch'ung-yang.

Seeing his teacher, Ma Tan-yang said, "Sir, my wife has gone mad. She has lost her mind. She is talking nonsense, and she laughs and cries for no reason." Wang Ch'ung-yang said, "If she is not mad, how can she become an immortal?" Ma Tan-yang did not understand Wang Ch'ung-yang's remark. He was about to ask his teacher what it meant when Wang Ch'ung-yang waved his hand and told him to leave. Sadly, Ma Tan-yang went back to his room.

Sun Pu-erh's pretended insanity succeeded in getting Ma Tan-yang and everyone else in the mansion to leave her alone. She reviewed Wang Ch'ung-yang's instructions repeatedly until she could perform them naturally and effortlessly. A month passed, and Sun Pu-erh looked at her face in the mirror. Scars and pockmarks dotted her face. Since she had not combed her hair for a month, she was no longer the beautiful wife of a wealthy merchant. Sun Pu-erh was delighted. She was now ready to make the journey to Loyang. With a piece of charcoal she smeared her face and her clothing. Looking like a mad beggar-woman, she ran out into the living room, laughed wildly, and rushed out the front door. A servant tried to stop her, but she bit the girl in the arm. Yelping in pain, the servant let go of her. The other servants alerted Ma Tan-yang. He hurried to the living room, but was told that the lady had already left the house. Ma Tan-yang and the servants searched the town and the immediate countryside for Sun Pu-erh, but they could not find her.

Knowing that Ma Tan-yang would search for her, Sun Pu-erh had hidden herself inside a haystack on a nearby farm. She heard the voices of the servants and her husband and continued to conceal herself until it was dark. When everything was silent, she quietly slipped out and walked toward Loyang. Along the way, she slept in abandoned temples and caves. She obtained her food from begging, and when people asked who she was, she acted insane and uttered nonsense. In this way, people left her alone, and eventually she arrived safely at Loyang.

In Loyang, Sun Pu-erh found shelter in an abandoned house. Daily she begged in the city. When people tried to communicate with her, she acted insane, and as time went on she be-

came known as the "mad beggar-woman." Because of her ugly face and her madness, the townspeople left her alone and she was able to practice internal alchemy without distraction.

In the city of Loyang there were two wanderers of seedy character called Chang San and Li Ssu. They solicited every woman they saw, and they raped those who refused their company. One day the two men saw Sun Pu-erh begging on a street corner. They noticed that despite her rags and the scars on her face Sun Pu-erh was quite attractive. That night, when Chang San and Li Ssu were returning home from an evening at the brothels, it occurred to Chang San that they might finish their evening of fun with the mad beggar-woman. When he voiced his plan to Li Ssu, the latter said, "We cannot do that. Don't you know the saying 'Those who take advantage of mad people will meet with bad luck all their lives'?" Chang San said, "I don't care about the superstitious sayings of old women. I am not afraid of the gods of Heaven or earth. I am going to have some fun with that woman." Chang San strode ahead toward the abandoned house where Sun Pu-erh was living. Li Ssu followed behind apprehensively.

Just as the abandoned house came into view, ominous storm clouds gathered in the sky. Suddenly there was a flash of lightning and a loud crack of thunder. When Chang San and Li Ssu recovered from the deafening sound, they found that they were being struck by enormous hailstones. Since they were on the outskirts of town, they had to run a good distance before they could find shelter from the balls of ice. As they ran, Li Ssu said to his friend, "You should have listened to me. That was the wrath of Heaven coming down on us." Chang San cursed under his breath and tried to run faster, but he tripped over a pile of logs hidden by the tall grass and fell into a thorny bush. Bruised and bleeding, he got up and staggered toward the gates of the inner city.

By the time Chang San and Li Ssu reached the inner city, the sky had cleared and a bright moon shone. Chang San was bleeding badly. He had been pelted by enormous hailstones and cut by sharp thorns. Li Ssu, on the contrary, had not received a single scratch. It appeared that only the small hailstones had struck him. Chang San finally sighed and said, "I am convinced. That mad woman cannot be touched." Li Ssu replied, "Now you know. I hope that you have learned your lesson well this time and will not try to bother her again." Chang San said, "The lesson was learned well. From now on I will not even walk in the direction of that abandoned house."

The next day Li Ssu related the incident to all his friends, and the story spread around the city. From then on in the town no one made fun of her when she begged or went near the abandoned house she was living in. Thus Sun Pu-erh was left in peace for the twelve years that she lived in Loyang.

Mortal Love and Divine Retribution
in Yüan Drama

From 1279 to 1368, China was ruled by Mongol peoples from the north, whose culture was made known to medieval Europe through the semihistorical travel accounts of Marco Polo (1254–1324). Dramatic arts flourished during the Yüan, and a vast repertoire of dramas on romantic, religious, and historical themes gained widespread popularity. Called *tsa-chü,* "mixed entertainments" or "variety shows," these dramas were narrative plays usually four acts in length; accompanied by music and singing, they were performed on both permanent and temporary stages often constructed near temples.

Chang Boils the Sea is by Li Hao-ku (early thirteenth century), about whom almost nothing is known. Unselfconsciously combining Confucian values, Chinese mythology, and cosmologies from popular Taoist and Buddhist folk belief, the play revolves around the tensions between earthly love and divine retribution. The plot is carried by the Buddhist transmigration of souls from one life to the next. The Taoist Gold Immortal Page and Jade Immortal Maiden fell in love in a previous existence, thus succumbing to the spiritual obstacle of desire and hence accumulating bad karma (volitional deeds or attitudes that are obstacles to liberation). As punishment, they have been reborn into the world of mortals until they repay a "debt of love," after which they may return to their immortal states.

The page, now Chang Yü, is a Confucian scholar who has availed himself of the solitude of the Temple of the Stone Buddha to prepare for the civil service examinations. He is skilled at playing the *ch'in,* or zither, a common scholarly talent. The ancient *Book of Rites* records that rites and music offer a means of communicating with the invisible world of spirits, and thus it is not unusual that he invokes with his playing the woman Ch'ung-lien, the daughter of the Dragon King, particularly as they have karmic connections from previous lives. In contrast to the "Rhyme-Prose on the Goddess of the Lo," the play describes the object of the female gaze in Ch'ung-lien's infatuated description of Chang Yü; unlike the goddess, the dragon maiden readily assents to marriage.

The immortal Taoist priestess Mao-nü appears, the emissary of the immortal Tung Hua, to set Chang Yü back on the correct path but only after first helping him repay his debt of love. The magical implements she gives him might be interpreted as symbolic representations of the agent metal, one of the Five Agents (of metal, water, earth, fire, and wood), and with a fire of wood he boils the water to make the sea dry land. At the critical moment when Chang Yü and Ch'ung-lien are to become man and wife, however, the transcendent realm manifests itself in the form of the immortal Tung Hua, and they ascend again to the desireless realm beyond the earthly world of impermanence and sorrow.

Chang Boils the Sea implies the superiority of Taoist over Buddhist powers, as the Buddhist Abbot is a comic figure who ironically serves as a matchmaker. Moreover, it ultimately claims the superiority of the transcendent Taoist realm of the immortals, but it also implies that this realm can only be reached by directly confronting human desire.

Chang Boils the Sea

CHARACTERS

TUNG HUA, *an immortal*

ABBOT FA YÜN

CHANG YÜ, *a student*

CH'IUNG-LIEN, *daughter to the Divine Dragon King of the Eastern Sea*

MEI-HSIANG, *maid to Ch'iung-lien*

MAO-NÜ, *an immortal*

DIVINE DRAGON KING OF THE EASTERN SEA

A RUNNER, *a* SERVANT BOY *and* SEA-WARRIORS

ACT ONE

Enter TUNG HUA.

TUNG HUA: I am Tung Hua, an immortal of the Upper Rank. Once upon a time a Gold Immortal Page and a Jade Immortal Maiden fell in love with each other during the Festival of the Green Jasper Pool. Both were banished as a punishment to be born into the World of Mortals. The Gold Page was born a boy into a Chang family in Chao-chou. He is widely read in the Confucian classics and has become quite a scholar. The Jade Maiden was born a girl in the house of the Divine Dragon King of the Eastern Sea. Not until they have repaid this ancient debt of love shall I bring them to their senses and lead them back to the Path of Immortality. *Exit.*

Enter ABBOT FA YÜN *with his* RUNNER.

ABBOT FA YÜN: I am Fa Yün, Abbot of the Temple of the Stone Buddha. This ancient temple of ours is situated on the shore of the Eastern Sea. Often the Dragon King and his sea-warriors come here for their amusement. Go out to the gate, runner, and send me word if you see any visitor coming.

RUNNER: Yes, your reverence.

Enter CHANG YÜ *and his* SERVANT BOY.

CHANG YÜ: I am Chang Yü. My parents died long ago. From my childhood I have studied the classics quite diligently, and yet I don't know why, I have never been able to pass the imperial examination. Today I have nothing to do, so I have come to while away the time by the seashore. Look, an ancient temple, and a runner standing at the gate. Has this temple got a name, my man?

RUNNER: Got a name! A mountain without a name would be very confusing; a temple without a name would be too vulgar for words. This is the Temple of the Stone Buddha.

CHANG YÜ: Go and tell the abbot that a young student is here and wishes to pay his respects to him.

RUNNER: There's a young student at the gate. He wishes to pay his respects to you, master.

ABBOT: Ask him to come in. [*The* ABBOT *sees* CHANG YÜ.] Where do you come from, may I ask, master scholar?

CHANG YÜ: I am a native of Chao-chou. I saw what a quiet place your ancient temple was, and I hoped your reverence would let me have a room where I could revise my studies.

ABBOT: We have plenty of rooms in the temple. Runner, prepare a room in a quiet place somewhere in the south-east quarter so that the scholar can study.

CHANG YÜ: I've nothing else to offer your reverence but two taels of silver. Please accept it as a donation to the temple.

ABBOT: Since you so wish, I accept it. Get the room ready, runner, and prepare the scholar a meal. *Exeunt.*

Enter the RUNNER, CHANG YÜ *and his* SERVANT BOY.

RUNNER: We've given you this quiet room. Here you can turn somersaults, play football, dance a devil-dance, do any silly thing you can think of. Just please yourself, enjoy yourself! I'm off to the Hall of Meditation to wait on my master. *Exit.*

CHANG YÜ: The life the monks lead is peaceful and civilized; and no idlers about for ever making a noise. What a wonderful opportu-

nity for me to study! It's getting dark. Bring
the *ch'in*, boy. I'll play a tune or two to
amuse myself. [*The* SERVANT BOY *places
the* ch'in *on the table.*] Light the lamp and
burn a joss-stick. [*The* SERVANT BOY *lights
the lamp and burns a joss-stick.*]
I hope I shall not play in vain on themes
    of running streams and lofty
    peaks;
With Chung Chi gone, how few are left
    of music's connoisseurs!
Tonight beside the lamp I'll play a strain
    or two,
Perhaps a wandering fish may come out
    to listen.

Enter CH'IUNG-LIEN, *daughter to the*
DRAGON KING, *with her maid,*
MEI-HSIANG.

CH'IUNG-LIEN: I am Ch'iung-lien, the third
daughter of the Divine Dragon King of the
Eastern Sea. With my maid Mei-hsiang I
have come to while away the evening walk-
ing on the seashore.
MEI-HSIANG: Look at the vast sea, how calm
and clear it is! And the same colour as the
great sweep of the sky. What a beautiful
scene!
CH'IUNG-LIEN:
Look, rising from the sea, ten thousand
    brightly coloured clouds,
And a wheel of bright moon glints
    among the waves.
MEI-HSIANG: Are the sights and scenes in
the sea not the same as those in the world
of mortals?
CH'IUNG-LIEN:
Look at the noblest palaces of the world
    of mortals,
How can they be compared with the
    Dragon Palaces of the Watery
    Realm,
So clear, so deep!
Heavenly caves and happy abodes where
    to live as we please,
So blue, so vast!

Never disturbed by babbling ducks or
    clamour of geese in flight.
MEI-HSIANG: I am sure between Heaven and
Earth there can be hardly any comparison.
CH'IUNG-LIEN:
They are not to be compared; one sweep
    and the glories of the world of
    men are gone,
Like autumn grass in a whirl of dust.
Spring passes, summer comes; autumn,
    then winter again.
They hear now the crow of the
    dawn-heralding cock,
Now the tick of the night-measuring
    clock,
Never thinking it is their lives that they
    fritter away.

CHANG YÜ *plays the* ch'in; MEI-HSIANG
listens.

MEI-HSIANG: Where does that sound come
from?
CH'IUNG-LIEN:
Listen, the evening breeze stirring,
A wind descending on ten thousand
    pines,
The splash of river rushing,
Water falling down a sheer gorge.
It is not the lotus-gathering girls plying
    their oars,
Nor the fisherman beating a plank at the
    stern,
It would arouse the night sleeper from
    heavy-eyed sleep.
MEI-HSIANG: The sound is quite unlike any
other.
CH'IUNG-LIEN:
It is not the dangling jade trinkets'
Rhythmic tinkling,
Nor the jostling iron horses
Jangling in the eaves,
Nor from priest's temple cell
Beating of stone *ch'ing* or bell.
Each note disturbs me, sets my heart
    trembling.
Why, it is the sound of strings!
Who can be playing the *ch'in?*

CHANG YÜ *plays on.*

MEI-HSIANG: It must be someone in the temple making the noise.
CH'IUNG-LIEN: It's someone playing the *ch'in.*
MEI-HSIANG: Listen!
CH'IUNG-LIEN:
There is endless emotion in phrase after
    phrase;
Note after note the tune goes on and on,
Like trembling gold chrysanthemums the
    autumn wind stirs,
Like the fragrance of *kuei* the autumn
    wind carries,
Like emerald bamboo swaying where the
    autumn wind dallies.
I, ya, ya!
Like gold-thread shuttle travelling the
    loom of brocade,
Ti, lu, lu!
Like pearls slipping from a woman's
    hand dancing and sparkling.

MEI-HSIANG *steals a glance at* CHANG YÜ.

MEI-HSIANG: It's a student playing the *ch'in*
here. What a splendid young man!
CH'IUNG-LIEN:
The strings express his inmost thoughts,
His fingers his dexterity.
More than *p'i pa,* slowly plucking,
    softly sweeping
It speaks of his true nature and his
    outward grace,
His face a Taoist's, his bearing like a
    god's.
Despite myself it stirs my deepest
    feelings.
MEI-HSIANG: You who understand music are
bound to be moved. Even I find the strains
of his music very pleasant on the ear. Certainly he plays well.
CH'IUNG-LIEN:
Truly he is gifted,
Nay, his art is near divine,
Expressing sadness like a singing swan,
Intensity like a winter cricket,

Delicacy like a flower's face,
Majesty like the thunder's roll—
Music to dispel ten thousand forms of
    idle sorrow!
A scholar so excellent in this one thing
Must excel in a hundred more.
I have tiptoed here, stealing each step.
He moves from mood to mood.
How much more their power over me
    than the poems of P'an-pan
    over Huang T'ing-chien!
Like a wonderful night upon one pillow
    wandering one immortal
    dream.

A string snaps.

CHANG YÜ: Why has the string suddenly
snapped? There must be someone listening
secretly. I shall go out and look.

CH'IUNG-LIEN *draws back.*

CH'IUNG-LIEN: What a handsome young
man!

CHANG YÜ *sees her.*

CHANG YÜ: What a lovely young woman!
May I ask, lady, what family you are from
and why you are wandering abroad in the
night?
CH'IUNG-LIEN:
My home is in realms of azure cloud
And in the midst of green waves,
Attended by those who wear scales and
    horns.
Deep in the rich Palace of Crystals I
    live,
Daughter of a sea-dweller, one Dragon
    by name,
Surpassing even the immortal maid Hsü
    Fei-ch'iung.
Do all stars not gather in homage round
    the North Star?
Do all rivers not pay their tribute to the
    Eastern Sea?
CHANG YÜ: Your name is Dragon. I remember there's such a name in the Book of
Surnames. So, gentle lady, you have a sur-

name. Have you no other? What brings you here?

CH'IUNG-LIEN: I am the third daughter of Mr Dragon and my name is Ch'iung-lien. I heard you playing the *ch'in* so I came to listen.

CHANG YÜ: If you come to listen to the *ch'in* you must love and understand music very well. Why not come into my study and I will play a piece for you? Will you?

CH'IUNG-LIEN: Willingly. [CH'IUNG-LIEN *enters the study*.] May I ask you your name, sir?

CHANG YÜ: My name is Chang Yü, I am a native of Chao-chou. My parents died when I was young. I've studied very hard at the classics but somehow I've never been able to pass the imperial examination. In the course of studying and travelling I've arrived here. I have no wife.

MEI-HSIANG: What impudence this scholar has! Who asked whether you had a wife or not?

SERVANT BOY: It's not only my master who hasn't a wife; I haven't got a wife either.

CHANG YÜ: If you don't mind being poor, will you become my wife?

CH'IUNG-LIEN: You are gifted and clever, handsome and wise. With all my heart I will become your wife. But I have parents and I must ask them. On the fifteenth day of the eighth month, at the Mid-autumn Festival, come to our home and they will receive you formally as their son-in-law.

CHANG YÜ: Since you consent, surely it would be best if we were married tonight. How wonderful that would be! How can I wait until the Mid-autumn Festival?

SERVANT BOY: That's true! I can't wait either.

MEI-HSIANG: You can't wait! That's easily settled.

CH'IUNG-LIEN: The proverb has it, "Time is nothing where love is concerned." Why can't you wait?

CHANG YÜ: May I ask where is your home?

CH'IUNG-LIEN:
Only thirty thousand fathoms beneath the
    blue sea,
And as perilous as the Twelve Peaks of
    Mount Wu.

CHANG YÜ: If you keep your word I'll be faithful and true.

CH'IUNG-LIEN:
With sweet words you play with me,
    play with me,
With smiling face you flatter me, flatter
    me.
Watch for August's icy wheel to rise
    from east of the sea,
Then the mists will withdraw, the skies
    be clear,
Breezes waft through the bamboo screen;
Then shall be the harmony of cloud and
    rain.
Smiling you and I shall follow each
    other,
Nor shall it be for only half a year.

CHANG YÜ: Since you've promised to be my wife, will you leave me something as a pledge?

CH'IUNG-LIEN: I have here a handkerchief woven from the silk of the ice silkworm. I've nothing better as a pledge of my love. Water will not wet it nor will it burn in fire.

CHANG YÜ: How can I thank you, dear lady!

SERVANT BOY: What will you give me as a pledge, Mei-hsiang?

MEI-HSIANG: I'll give you a broken rush-leaf fan. Take that home to fan your fire.

SERVANT BOY: Where will I find you?

MEI-HSIANG: Go to Brick Pagoda Street, at the corner of the Sheep Market, outside the entrance to the police station. Look for me there.

CH'IUNG-LIEN:
Do you not know what it is when two
    hearts are one?
Only a foolish heart would understand.
I am not a demon devouring men,
Don't be alarmed or dismayed.
The destiny of our former lives shall be
    fulfilled in this,

At the Mid-autumn Festival our happi-
ness shall be complete.
Rest assured!
Cast aside the ten thousand miles of mist
and doubt,
Where I am all is tranquil,
With none of the cares of the World of
Dust.

CHANG YÜ: I will come. [*Exeunt* CH'IUNG-
LIEN *and* MEI-HSIANG.] This woman's
beauty has bewitched me. There is none to
compare with her in all the world. She tells
me I must look for her by the seashore. I
cannot wait till the Mid-autumn Festival.
Look after my sword, my *ch'in* and my box
of books, boy. With this handkerchief I am
ready to dare anything. I'm going to the
seashore to look for her. *Exit.*

SERVANT BOY: What a fool my master is! For
all we know she might be a demon or a
monster. He believes the first thing she says,
and off he goes chasing after her. I'll tell the
abbot and his runner and we'll catch him up.
Exit.

ACT TWO

Enter CHANG YÜ.

CHANG YÜ: Where has she gone? I can see
nothing but green hills and blue water, cypresses and pine-trees. I can't go any further,
and I can't go back. O what misery! I'll rest
awhile on that rock over there. [*Withdraws.*]

Enter MAO-NÜ.

MAO-NÜ:
The mulberry field is now field, now
sea.
In a glance a hundred years go by.
Turn your mind to higher things,
And who will not gain immortality?
I was formerly a maidservant in the Palace
of Ch'in. One day I went into a mountain to
gather herbs, and ever after that I ate only
uncooked food. Gradually my body became
lighter and lighter, and so I attained the
Great Way. I am known to the world as the
immortal Mao-nü. Wandering at will today I
chanced to come to this place, the eastern
shore of the sea. What a great expanse of
water!
The bright brimming ice moon rises
from the edge of the sea,
The bright beaming red sun turns the
mountain ridge.
The sun and moon come and go,
Only the mountains and the sea remain.
Whatever the river, great or small,
All that is water
Returns to the sea.

CHANG YÜ: [*comes forward*]: What place can
this be? Oh, what luck! Here is a woman
coming this way—a Taoist priestess. I will
ask her. What is this place, may I ask,
mother?

MAO-NÜ:
Since you so ask,
First tell me your reason.

CHANG YÜ: I have come here to look for my
love. I don't know where she has gone.

MAO-NÜ: Who are you, young man, and
where are you from?

CHANG YÜ: I am a native of Chao-chou. I
have been travelling and studying. At the
moment I am staying at the Temple of the
Stone Buddha. Last night while I was playing
the *ch'in* a woman and her maid came to
listen. She told me she was the daughter of
a certain Mr Dragon and that her name was
Ch'iung-lien. And she promised to meet me
on the seashore on the day of the Mid-autumn
Festival. After she was gone I made my way
to this place and suddenly I found myself
lost. I thought her the most bewitching creature; there is not another like her in all the
world.

MAO-NÜ: If she said her name was Dragon,
had you no misgivings?
Don't you know the women of the
Dragon Palace are enchant-
resses?
And are you willing to risk the remain-
der of your life
All to incur a debt of love?

The Dragon is a green-eyed god, is
    given to suspicion;
His evil nature knows no bounds,
In his malice he can work all forms of
    harm.
CHANG YÜ: Is he as wicked as that?
MAO-NÜ:

Ah,
When he shows his teeth and spreads his
    claws,
And lightly lifts his horned head,
In an instant he raises waves and
    billows,
In another shakes the hills and moun-
    tains,
In another rolls up the Yangtze and Huai
    rivers.
When he grows large,
The universe is not large enough,
When small,
He can hide in a mustard seed.
He displays his strength,
Reveals his supernatural power,
Unleashes his venom at will.

CHANG YÜ: It is the woman's surname that
is Dragon. Why do you start speaking of
dragons, mother?
MAO-NÜ: Don't you know that the Dragon is
not to be trifled with, young man?
He can raise clouds and mists,
In a trice they come,
Move winds and rain;
Stir storms of dust.
I fear a sudden cruel fright will lose you
    life and limb.
Do not keep your promise to love the
    Dragon's daughter,
And throw away your talents and your
    chance of fame and honour.

CHANG YÜ: Now I begin to understand. She
is a daughter from the palace of a Dragon
king, and her father is nothing but evil. How
could he be willing to give his daughter to
be my wife? The marriage is certainly out of
the question. But Ch'iung-lien, what made
you come and listen to my playing of the
ch'in? [*downcast*]

MAO-NÜ: I am not an ordinary mortal. I have
been sent by Tung Hua, an immortal of the
Upper Rank, and commanded to bring you
back to the Path of the True Way. He will
not have you led astray.

CHANG YÜ *bows to* MAO-NÜ.

CHANG YÜ: My eyes are only mortal eyes and
I did not recognize my counsellor for an
immortal. I beg you to forgive me.
MAO-NÜ: That woman who came to listen to
you playing the *ch'in* is the third daughter of
the Dragon King of the Eastern Sea, and her
name is Ch'iung-lien. She lives hidden in the
Dragon Palace deep within the sea. How can
you hope to find her?
CHANG YÜ: I believe that this daughter of the
Dragon and I are destined to love each other.
MAO-NÜ: What makes you think this?
CHANG YÜ: If we were not destined to love
each other how could she have been willing
to ask me to go to her home on the night
of the Mid-autumn Festival, and there be
received as a son-in-law? What is more, she
gave me this handkerchief as a pledge of
her love.
MAO-NÜ: This handkerchief is certainly from
the Dragon Palace. It is true then that the girl
has fallen in love with you. But the Divine
Dragon King is ill-tempered and violent.
How will he be so ready to give his beloved
daughter to be your wife? I will make the
marriage possible for you by giving you three
magic treasures. They will subdue him, sure
enough. Then you need have no fear that he
won't give his daughter to be married to you.

CHANG YÜ *kneels to* MAO-NÜ.

CHANG YÜ: I long to see your magic treasures,
O immortal.
MAO-NÜ: Here I give you one silver pan, one
gold coin, and one iron ladle.

CHANG YÜ *takes them from her*.

CHANG YÜ: I beg you, teach me how to use
them best.

MAO-NÜ: Take this ladle and fill the pan with water out of the sea; into the water put the gold coin. Then boil the water down one tenth of an inch and the sea will drop one hundred feet; boil it down two tenths of an inch and the sea will drop two hundred feet; boil it till the pan is dry and there before you will be the bottom of the sea. How will the Divine Dragon King be able to go on living there then? He is bound to send someone to invite you to be his son-in-law.

CHANG YÜ: Thank you for your guidance, great immortal. But I don't know how far the seashore is from here.

MAO-NÜ: Go straight on some score of miles from here, and there you will come to the shore of the Island of the Gate of Sands. These treasures,

From Purple Mansion and Jade Terrace
    they come, in realms of Purity
    and Light,
From the vast blue sphere of Heaven.
No matter how you carry out your task,
No matter what schemes you may
    devise,
Your heart's desires shall be fulfilled,
Its every passion gratified.
These treasures do not beg for favours,
Nor do they admit of bribes;
They will be your matchmakers,
And see you made a son-in-law,
Entwine you as branches of two different
    trees,
Unfold you as two flowers from a single
    stem,
Unite you as the twin phoenixes
In the harmony of fish in stream.
Boil the vast sea dry!   *Exuent.*

ACT THREE

Enter the RUNNER.

RUNNER: Last night when our scholar was playing the *ch'in* he was bewitched and carried off by a spirit. His servant boy hurried off to look for him, and my master, without any thought for what he was doing, sent me

out to look for him too. The forest was deep and the mountain path dangerous. Where was I to find him? Suddenly I came face to face with a tiger. He bared his teeth and waved his claws, then went for me. Quick as a flash I picked up a stone the size of a goose egg and threw it at him. I don't know how my aim could have been so steady, but the stone went right into his throat. I watched the animal struggle and collapse, and then in one breath I ran two hundred miles, and that's how I got away with my life and arrived here.

One life's already bewitched and gone,
But why should I die without good
    reason?
Much better to follow the scholar and
    die
An amorous ghost beneath a peony. *Exit.*

Enter CHANG YÜ *with his* SERVANT BOY.

CHANG YÜ: Here we are already at the seashore. Strike your flint and start the fire. Collect a few stones together to make a tripod and put the pan on it. [*The* SERVANT BOY *places the pan on the stones.*] Now take the ladle and fetch some seawater. [*The* SERVANT BOY *ladles out water.*] When the pan is full put the gold coin in. Keep the fire burning, it must be a good fire to make the water boil quickly.

SERVANT BOY: Why didn't you say so before? I could easily have brought with me the rush-leaf fan that the woman's maid gave me. What am I going to fan the fire with? [*The* SERVANT BOY *fans the fire with his coat sleeve.*] Look, the water is boiling.

CHANG YÜ: The water's boiling! Let me look what's happening to the sea. [CHANG YÜ *looks in surprise.*] Extraordinary! It's true, the whole sea is bubbling and boiling, seething and steaming. The magic works!

SERVANT BOY: When the water boils here, the water in the sea boils too. How can it be that the sea does the same as the water in the pan?

Enter the ABBOT *in a panic.*

ABBOT: While I was meditating on my couch the Dragon King of the Eastern Sea sent someone to tell me that a young man had set the sea boiling, he didn't know how! The Dragon King is at his wits' end and doesn't know where to hide himself. He has begged me to persuade the youth to stop the fire at once. Why, it's none other than the student who came yesterday and took a room in my temple, the master scholar Chang Yü. My Temple of the Stone Buddha is close by the Eastern Sea. Now the Dragon is in danger, how can I stand by and do nothing to save him!

I see bloody vapour from the Palace of
　　　Crystals pouring to the sky,
I cannot breathe for the parching smoke
　　　that chokes my nose and
　　　mouth.
I do not know what tricks he employs,
He merely wishes to show off his
　　　power.
Even if there were thunder and rain,
Not even that would relieve the alarm.
See the brocade-scaled fish leap and
　　　pierce the hearts of waves,
And the silver-footed crabs scramble
　　　sideways up the shore to hide.

The ABBOT *approaches* CHANG YÜ.

You, master scholar, what are you boiling here?

CHANG YÜ: I am boiling the sea.

ABBOT: Why?

CHANG YÜ: I will tell you, your reverence. Last night while I was playing the *ch'in* in the temple a young woman came to listen. Later she told me she was the third daughter of a certain Mr Dragon and her name was Ch'iung-lien, and she promised to meet me on the day of the Mid-autumn Festival. I don't see her coming so I am boiling the sea here, and I am determined to boil it until she comes out.

ABBOT:
The student is unable to enjoy his love,
So he turns the sea into a scented bath!

A scholar should be gentle and gracious
　　　in his ways,
And practise the arts of peace and
　　　courtesy.
How can you resort to such a hot-headed
　　　trick?

CHANG YÜ: Don't interfere, your reverence. Go and beg your alms elsewhere.

ABBOT:
I do not come to beg for alms,
Nor do I seek your charity.
I come only to visit you.

CHANG YÜ: Visit me? I am a poor student, I have nothing to give.

ABBOT:
I am after all a Buddhist priest,
I do no wrong if I beg for alms.

CHANG YÜ: If I could find that woman and be accepted as a son-in-law, then I would have something to give you.

ABBOT:
Merely because of a beautiful girl
Not making a son-in-law of a fine fellow
　　　like you,
You call down this calamity from
　　　Heaven!
If you are poor, be poor!
And don't match yourself against her il-
　　　lustrious family.
Where did you get this boiling lead, this
　　　mercury and volcanic fire?
Where did you find this remedy for love-
　　　sickness?

CHANG YÜ: I shall be plain with your reverence. As long as the girl who came to me last night does not come out I shall go on boiling the sea.

ABBOT: Master scholar, listen to me! The Divine Dragon King of the Eastern Sea has appointed me his matchmaker to come and make you his son-in-law. What do you say to that?

CHANG YÜ: Don't make fun of me, your reverence. Look at the sea, one huge expanse of misty water. I am only a mortal, how am I to enter that?

SERVANT BOY: Don't worry, master. Simply

follow the abbot. If he doesn't get drowned it's not likely that you will!

ABBOT [*aside*]:

I am very anxious to get to the bottom
of this.
Take your time and consider well.
Point your finger at the water and it will
turn to land,
Divide it and it will become firm beneath your feet,
As firm as if it were a path among the
wild grass of the plain.

CHANG YÜ: Won't it be dark going to the bottom of the sea?

ABBOT:

On the contrary, as bright as the sun
coming out of his mansion.

CHANG YÜ: No matter what you say, I am still only a mortal. How dare I go into the sea?

ABBOT:

Though the great sea is named the Eastern Ocean,
You are not to stand on ceremony.
Go! the Dragon King waits to receive
you as his son-in-law.

CHANG YÜ: I've heard that the fairy Isle of Phoenixes and Unicorns in the middle of the Western Sea is surrounded by a ring of thin water three thousand feet deep where even a feather would sink. How then am I to go?

ABBOT:

Say nothing of rings of thin water three
thousand feet deep.
This is a land of shimmering brocade, a
watery kingdom of abundant
riches.

CHANG YÜ *looks about.*

CHANG YÜ: The ocean seems so vast to me. It has no edge, no shore. It looks just as if it is joined to the sky. How terrifying!

ABBOT:

You say it seems as vast and boundless
as the sky;
The more it shows how boundless is his
magnanimity.

CHANG YÜ: Well, let me pack up my trea-

sures. If only your reverence could ensure my affair were a success!

SERVANT BOY: That woman has a maid with her and she better be mine, otherwise I'll go on burning this fire!

ABBOT:

Come, away, away!
To orchid pavilions
And painted halls.
Believe me, believe me,
Not a word I say
Shall prove a lie.

CHANG YÜ: You are sure?

ABBOT:

You,
Your thoughts are always petty and
mean.
She,
Already she is richly dressed and
adorned,
Soon,
Soon to be married to you.
Come, away, away!
To the sleep of lovebirds beneath a
golden net.

CHANG YÜ: I shall follow your reverence. If only we could come together soon like the moon at its full, and not break the promises we made!

ABBOT:

You, beauty and her scholar, are so in-
tent on love
You have thrown her parents into con-
sternation.
You with your handsome bearing and no-
ble talents,
She with her jadelike body and flower-
like scents,
Both of you of one heart and mind,
Yours is a fitting marriage—
A husband and wife beyond compare!

Let us go. *Exeunt the* ABBOT *and* CHANG
YÜ.

SERVANT BOY: My master has hurried off quite happily into the sea with his reverence and left me alone on the shore to look after these blessed treasures. If he really gets married I suppose it'll be a month before he comes out. I'll pack up all these things and go straight back to the temple, and see if I can't find the runner and have some fun with him. *Exit.*

ACT FOUR

Enter the DRAGON KING *and his* SEA-WARRIORS.

DRAGON KING: Ask the student and my daughter to come here.

Enter CHANG YÜ *and* CH'IUNG-LIEN.

CH'IUNG-LIEN: Go into the hall and meet my father.

CHANG YÜ: I am ready.

CH'IUNG-LIEN: When we bid each other good-bye that night, who would have thought we should see such a day!

Waves and billows stood between us,
    making strangers of friends.
I was afraid that in endless darkness we
    would each take separate ways.
I suffered in a living hell,
I tried hard to endure it all,
That from the farthest corners of the sea
    and sky
One day again we may be brought to-
    gether.

CHANG YÜ *and* CH'IUNG-LIEN *make obeisance to the* DRAGON KING.

DRAGON KING: Where did the two of you meet?

CH'IUNG-LIEN:
I took advantage of a green sea and clear
    ripples,
A pleasant hour and lovely scene,
A light cloud and a slender mist,
A cool air encircling the crystal jar,
The jade dews trickling,
The gold wind rustling,
The season of the Mid-autumn Festival,
The time when all was solitude,

All voices hushed, the first watch of the
    night.

DRAGON KING: You had never met the student before! And it was the first watch and all was quiet! How did it happen that you promised to marry him? Tell me.

CH'IUNG-LIEN:
I went to him by the moon's brightness,
    mounting the steps,
Listening to the *ch'in,* a music out of
    this world,
Just like the call of a crane beyond the
    clouds,
Wild geese chanting at the edge of the
    sky,
The song of a bird on the branch of a
    tree.
He was longing to find a bride,
And I fearing to be left a maid.
Who could say if it were wise or foolish
Whether we chose to be lovers or not:
At once our thoughts and hearts were
    one,
Before we knew we were like fish in
    stream.

DRAGON KING: Who gave you those magic treasures, master scholar?

CHANG YÜ: I am a poor student. I couldn't hope to own any such treasures myself. But when I was in pursuit of your daughter I came to the seashore and there I chanced to meet a priestess, an immortal. She gave them to me.

DRAGON KING: You nearly burnt me to death, master scholar. I suppose my daughter is the cause of all this.

Enter TUNG HUA.

TUNG HUA: Listen to my command, Divine Dragon.

The DRAGON KING, CHANG YÜ *and* CH'IUNG-LIEN *fall to their knees.*

TUNG HUA: Chang Yü is not your son-in-law, Divine Dragon, nor is Ch'iung-lien your daughter. In their former lives they were a Gold Page and Jade Maiden living in the World of Immortals. Because there they fell in love with each other they were sent down to the lower world as a punishment. Now they have repaid their debt of love I have come to summon them from your watery kingdom to return again to the Jasper Pool and become immortal once more.

CH'IUNG-LIEN:

Together hand in hand today we mount
    to Heaven again,
This handkerchief as a pledge of love
    has not been kept in vain.
Idly we shall watch the Peaches of Im-
    mortality redden on the trees,
For we have cast off this World of Dust
    and its Boundless Bitter Sea.

MING

DYNASTY

(1368-1644)

The Writings of Wang Yang-ming

The "Great Learning," the short chapter from the *Book of Rites* that Chu Hsi had promoted as an independent text, became the focus of numerous commentaries by Confucian, Buddhist, Taoist, and even Chinese Muslim scholars. One of the best known of these interpretations is the *Inquiry on the Great Learning* by the Ming (1368–1644) dynasty scholar, official, and military strategist Wang Shou-jen. He is known better as Wang Yang-ming (1472–1529) after the name of his retreat in the Yang-ming valley in Chekiang Province. Wang was one of the most influential thinkers of the Ming period; his teachings were widely promulgated in Japan through the nineteenth century and remained popular with many Chinese reformers and political thinkers into the twentieth. The *Inquiry* is one of his most important works.

Wang in his early twenties became interested in the investigation of things, one of the steps of the "Great Learning," but his attempt to investigate bamboo by contemplating it directly over a period of days only resulted in mental debilitation. He eventually developed the idea that the investigation of things was an internal process of looking within, in the mind, and not an external process of apprehending things from outside the self. Rejecting Chu Hsi's rearrangement of the "Great Learning" that placed investigating things before making the thoughts sincere, Wang insisted that knowing comes from within and not from without, and from this developed his idea of the innate knowing of the good.

These beginning passages from his *Inquiry,* which are phrased as a series of questions and answers, first recall the three main principles of the "Great Learning": manifesting the clear character (bright virtue), loving the people, and abiding in the highest good. But these three are only platforms for Wang's own ideas of the forming of one body with all things and the innate knowing of the good. His vision of regarding all things as one body entails extending the principle of humanity to all things, even animals, plants, and inanimate objects. He begins with Mencius's idea of the mind that cannot bear to see the suffering of others, but enlarges it to include even the suffering of broken bricks and tiles. Like Mencius, he believes that people are inherently good, and moreover emphasizes that if people genuinely realize the inherent innate knowing of the good, they will be able to overcome selfish desires and abide in the great learning.

Wang Yang-ming also spoke to themes more specifically related to the spirit world, issues addressed in some of his philosophical letters, two of which are presented here. His letter to Prefect T'ung on prayers for rain, dated 1503, reflects his view that prayers should be performed as acts of self-reflection and unselfish concern for others. Cautioning that the magic and charms performed by latter-day sorcerers are in and of themselves ineffective, he nonetheless assures Prefect T'ung that prayers performed by someone of inner integrity will evoke a sympathetic response from heaven.

His letter on spirits and immortals, dated 1508, suggests that Wang, like most thinkers, could find no easy explanation for such matters. He acknowledges that people such as Kuang-ch'eng-tzu, an immortal mentioned in the *Chuang Tzu,* and Li Po-yang (Lao Tzu) lived to unusual ages, but adds that harmony with the Way is related to a natural endowment from heaven, not to magical arts such as those practiced by the Taoist Shang-yang-tzu (Ch'en Chih-hsü, floruit 1330s). As early as the Chou dynasty, he adds, the philosopher Yin-wen-tzu (born 380 B.C.E.?) had decried occult practices. The Confucian idea of immortality, Wang implies, is the immortality of ideas and values, in the sense that Yen-tzu (Yen Hui), the favorite disciple of Confucius, has never passed away.

Selection from *Inquiry on the Great Learning*

Question: The *Great Learning* was considered by a former scholar [Chu Hsi] as the learning of the great man. I venture to ask why the learning of the great man should consist in "manifesting the clear character"?

Master Wang said: The great man regards Heaven and Earth and the myriad things as one body. He regards the world as one family and the country as one person. As to those who make a cleavage between objects and distinguish between the self and others, they are small men. That the great man can regard Heaven, Earth, and the myriad things as one body is not because he deliberately wants to do so, but because it is natural to the humane nature of his mind that he do so. Forming one body with Heaven, Earth, and the myriad things is not only true of the great man. Even the mind of the small man is no different. Only he himself makes it small. Therefore when he sees a child about to fall into a well, he cannot help a feeling of alarm and commiseration. This shows that his humanity *(jen)* forms one body with the child. It may be objected that the child belongs to the same species. Again, when he observes the pitiful cries and frightened appearance of birds and animals about to be slaughtered, he cannot help feeling an "inability to bear" their suffering. This shows that his humanity forms one body with birds and animals. It may be objected that birds and animals are sentient beings as he is. But when he sees plants broken and destroyed, he cannot help a feeling of pity. This shows that his humanity forms one body with plants. It may be said that plants are living things as he is. Yet even when he sees tiles and stones shattered and crushed, he cannot help a feeling of regret. This shows that his humanity forms one body with tiles and stones. This means that even the mind of the small man necessarily has the humanity that forms one body with all. Such a mind is rooted in his Heaven-endowed nature, and is naturally intelligent, clear, and not beclouded.

For this reason it is called the "clear character." Although the mind of the small man is divided and narrow, yet his humanity that forms one body can remain free from darkness to this degree. This is due to the fact that his mind has not yet been aroused by desires and obscured by selfishness. When it is aroused by desires and obscured by selfishness, compelled by greed for gain and fear of harm, and stirred by anger, he will destroy things, kill members of his own species, and will do everything. In extreme cases he will even slaughter his own brothers, and the humanity that forms one body will disappear completely. Hence, if it is not obscured by selfish desires, even the mind of the small man has the humanity that forms one body with all as does the mind of the great man. As soon as it is obscured by selfish desires, even the mind of the great man will be divided and narrow like that of the small man. Thus the learning of the great man consists entirely in getting rid of the obscuration of selfish desires in order by his own efforts to make manifest his clear character, so as to restore the condition of forming one body with Heaven, Earth, and the myriad things, a condition that is originally so, that is all. It is not that outside of the original substance something can be added.

Question: Why, then, does the learning of the great man consist in loving the people?

Answer: To manifest the clear character is to bring about the substance of the state of forming one body with Heaven, Earth, and the myriad things, whereas loving the people is to put into universal operation the function of the state of forming one body. Hence manifesting the clear character consists in loving the people, and loving the people is the way to manifest the clear character. Therefore, only when I love my father, the fathers of others, and the fathers of all men can my humanity really form one body with my father, the fathers of others, and the fathers of all men. When it truly forms one body with them, then the clear character of filial piety will be manifested. Only when I love my brother, the brothers of others, and the brothers of all men can my humanity really form one body with my brother, the brothers of others, and the brothers of all men. When it truly forms one body with them, then the clear character of brotherly respect will be manifested. Everything from ruler, minister, husband, wife, and friends to mountains, rivers, spiritual beings, birds, animals, and plants should be truly loved in order to realize my humanity that forms one body with them, and then my clear character will be completely manifested, and I will really form one body with Heaven, Earth, and the myriad things. This is what is meant by "manifesting the clear character throughout the empire." This is what is meant by "regulation of the family," "ordering the state," and "bringing peace to the world." This is what is meant by "full development of one's nature."

Question: Then why does the learning of the great man consist in "abiding in the highest good"?

Answer: The highest good is the ultimate principle of manifesting character and loving people. The nature endowed in us by Heaven is pure and perfect. The fact that it is intelligent, clear, and not beclouded is evidence of the emanation and revelation of the highest good. It is the original substance of the clear character which is called innate knowledge of the good. As the highest good emanates and reveals itself, we will consider right as right and wrong as wrong. Things of greater or less importance and situations of grave or light character will be responded to as they act upon us. In all our changes and movements, we will stick to no particular point, but possess in ourselves the Mean that is perfectly natural. This is the ultimate of the normal nature of man and the principle of things. There can be no consideration of adding to or subtracting from it. If there is any, it means selfish ideas and shallow cunning, and cannot be said to be the highest good. Naturally, how can anyone who does not watch over himself carefully when alone, and who has no refinement and singleness of mind, attain to such a state of perfection? Later generations fail to realize that the highest good is inherent in their own minds, but exercise their selfish ideas and cunning and grope for it outside their minds, believing that every event and every object has its own peculiar definite principle. For this reason the law of right and wrong is obscured; the mind becomes concerned with fragmentary and isolated details and broken pieces; the selfish desires of man become rampant and the Principle of Nature is at an end. And thus the learning of manifesting character and loving people is everywhere thrown into confusion. In the past there have, of course, been people who wanted to manifest their clear character. But simply because they did not know how to abide in the highest good, but instead drove their own minds toward something too lofty, they thereby lost them in illusions, emptiness, and quietness, having nothing to do with the work of the family, the state, and the world. Such are the followers of Buddhism and Taoism. There have, of course, been those who wanted to love their people. Yet simply because they did not know how to abide in the highest good, but instead sank their own minds in base and trifling things, they thereby lost them in scheming strategy and cunning techniques, having neither the sincerity of humanity nor that of commiseration. Such are the followers of the Five Despots and the pursuers of success and profit. All of these defects are due to a failure to know how to abide in the highest good. Therefore abiding in the highest good is to manifesting character and loving people as the carpenter's square and compass are to the square and the circle, or rule and measure to length, or balances and scales to weight. If the square and the circle do not abide by the compass and the carpenter's square, their standard will be wrong; if length does not abide by the rule and measure, its adjustment will be lost; if weight does not abide by the balances, its exactness will be gone; and if manifesting clear character and loving people do not abide by the highest good, their foundation will disappear. Therefore, abiding in the highest good so as to love people and manifest the clear character is what is meant by the learning of the great man.

"To Prefect T'ung, On Asking for Rain"

Yesterday, your two subordinates, Yang and Lee, came with your letter, and inquired about the art of making rain.

. . . The Way of Heaven is hidden and distant. How can an ordinary mortal probe and understand it? However, your concern for the welfare of the people, and your diligence on their behalf, are so sincere, that I must not neglect sending you a word of reply.

Confucius once said, "I have already been praying for a long time." The prayer of a gentleman is not limited to the moments spent in formal prayer for Yüeh, but refers especially to daily conduct. You have been governor in Yüeh for several years already. All that pertains to removing evils for the people, promoting their welfare and benefit, can be called "prevenient" prayer, and need not wait until today. But the summer drought is still with us, and the rain has not yet come. Is there perhaps some reason for this? In the ancient times, during periods of drought, the ruler would eat less and refrain from enjoying music, re-examine judicial cases, and decrease taxation. He would pay special attention to sacrifices, to inquiring about the sufferings of the people, and take the blame for the drought on himself—distributing alms, and praying for the people to the spirits of the mountains, rivers, of earth and harvest. That was why there were sacrifices begging Heaven for rain, and proclamations of self-criticism and examination, and vows for self-reform. What historical records referred to by saying, "King T'ang [d. 1753 B.C.?] blamed himself for six things," what the *Book of Rites* said: "During the great summer sacrifice for rain to God, all the instruments of music are employed," what the *Spring-Autumn Annals* recorded: "In autumn, during the ninth month, there was a great sacrifice for rain"—all belong to this category. I had heard of these ancient practices, but never of magic or

charms for obtaining rain. Only later magicians practised these from time to time. When these were men of integrity and perseverance, then, even if their actions were not always in accordance with the Mean, but differed from the ordinary, they were still able to obtain rain. All such reports, however, come to us from miscellaneous accounts of minor importance and not from the Classics. The gentleman tends to consider these happenings as coincidences. As to our present-day priests and sorcerers, many of these are little different from the loafers and ruffians of the market places. How can we therefore expect them to rebuke the thunder, to call forth wind and rain?

I would rather advise you to come out and contemplate yourself at the official hall, to stop whatever business is not urgent, open the door for the reform of self, to set aright cases of injustice, forbid luxury and sophistication, strengthen your sincerity and purify your mind, reproaching yourself, and praying on behalf of the people of the eight counties [of Yüeh], the spirits of the mountains, rivers, of the earth and grain. And, if the people wish to employ the service of priests to pray for them, let them do so without interference, but also without your sponsorship, and without your relying on them. For, with your style of conduct, you have certainly nothing to be ashamed of in front of the spirits. And if, facing such events, you examine yourself even more, leading your subordinates to beg sincerely for rain, then, even though Heaven sends us drought, there will be no harm. If only human affairs can be regulated, some response from Heaven ought to come within ten days. And, on my part, though I am no different from the common people, if I did know the art of obtaining rain, how would I dare to sit back and watch the people suffer without doing anything about it? . . . In one or two days, I too shall pray at Nan-chen, to help your fervour. If only you beg with your whole heart for the people, without allowing yourself to be deceived by false teachings, and without anxiety to obtain a better reputation, then, although the way of

Heaven is distant, it has never failed to respond to a case of such fervour.

"In Reply to Questions About Spirits and Immortals"

You asked me whether spirits and immortals exist. Thrice you have written and I have not replied, not because I do not wish to reply, but because I did not know what to say! Yesterday, your younger brother came, and desired very much to get an answer. Actually, ever since the age of eight I have been interested in such matters. More than thirty years have passed since then. My teeth are becoming unsteady, several of my hairs have turned white, my eyes cannot see beyond a foot's distance, and my ears cannot hear beyond the distance of ten feet. Moreover, I am often bedridden with sickness for entire months. My need of medicine as well as my capacity for it is growing. These are all the results of my interest in spirits and immortals. But people who know me still say glibly that I can yet attain this Way of Immortality, and you too, having heard such talk and believing it readily, have asked me about it! Since there is no way out for me, I shall say a few foolish words to you about it.

In ancient times, there were perfect men, of genuine virtue and mature *tao*, who lived in harmony with *yin* and *yang* and the four seasons, away from the world and its vanities. Concentrating their sperm [*ching*] and their energies, they moved between Heaven and Earth, seeing and hearing things which were beyond the scope of ordinary experience. Such were Kuang-ch'eng-tzu who lived to the age of one thousand five hundred years without weakening his powers, Li Po-yang who lived through the dynasties of Shang and Chou, and who went west through the Han-ku Pass. These men really existed. To deny that would be to deceive you. However, to correspond to the *tao* in our breathing and movements, to keep our energy and bones intact, refer to a natural endowment received at the beginning of our existence. This is the work of Heaven, not what human force can compass.

Stories concerning men of later generations who could ascend with their families into the air, transform objects, borrow corpses and return to life again, refer to deceptive and strange things belonging to the realm of secret magic and ingenious arts—what Yin-wen-tzu called illusion, what the Buddhists call heterodoxy. If such actions are called real, you would be equally deceived. After all, words cannot describe what lies between existence and non-existence. One can understand after long reflections and deep self-cultivation. Before having reached the proper state, it is not possible to force such knowledge.

However, we Confucians also have our own doctrine of immortality. Yen-tzu died at the age of thirty-two, and yet still lives today. Can you believe this? Men of later generations such as Shang-yang-tzu possessed certain skills, which could not be called the real *tao*. As to Bodhidharma [fl. 460–534?] and Hui-neng [638–713], they would be closer to the *tao*. But we can still not be sure of this. If you wish to hear more about this doctrine, you need to retire into the mountains or forests for thirty years, perfect your ears and eyes, unify your mind and ambition, keep your breast free from the least particle of dust. And then you can discuss this Way. But at present, you are still far from the Way of Immortality.—Please forgive my bold words!

Poetry of the Spirit

Poetry sometimes suggests the realities of Chinese spirituality that doctrine glosses over: otherwise, how would one know that the Taoist Huang had died of alcoholism? Poets unintentionally recorded the actual religious practices of both rich and poor, and as they moved in the same intellectual circles as educated monks, their verses provide incidental insights into the lives of religious practitioners.

"Ballad of the Neighborhood Shaman" by the poet Kao Ch'i (1336–1374) describes the services performed by the local shaman, who expels sickness and prolongs life, just as did his Chou dynasty counterparts. Wang Yang-ming might have decried such practices, but the shaman's ministrations are appreciated by his customers. How the shaman brings the god at night is unclear; perhaps he leads a costumed or masked accomplice, or perhaps he invokes the god only in imagination. The paper money is most likely specially produced imitation paper currency like that still used today as offerings and bribes to ghosts and spirits. Kao Ch'i is one of the most eminent poets of the Ming period; he was executed by Ming T'ai-tsu (reign 1368–1398), the first emperor of the Ming, whose political purges resulted in the deaths of thousands of literati.

"The Taoist Huang Has Died of Alcoholism" is by the celebrated painter Shen Chou (1427–1509), who was also an accomplished poet. Intoxication, lust, desire for wealth, and bad temper were cardinal vices of some Taoist sects, and the fate of the two men described here indicates that not all Taoist masters attained perfection. Hsü Wei (1521–1593), the author of "A Buddhist Monk Cut and Burned His Flesh to Make the Rains Stop," is likewise better known as a painter than a poet; his subtle facility for evoking solid forms with unstudied washes inspired a new style of brush technique. He studied with a disciple of Wang Yang-ming. Of a somewhat erratic personality, Hsü wrote plays extolling the achievements of women but beat his third wife to death and spent part of his life in prison. But he also, as this poem shows, was in contact with Buddhist monks. Over the centuries, Buddhism in China appropriated and transformed many of the rites of classical antiquity, such as the ancient prayer for rain, which was performed in the event of floods as well as droughts. In Chou times, such rites were usually rendered effective by the internalized principle of sincerity; the *Tso chuan* in the twenty-first year of the reign of Duke Hsi, however, also records that the duke wanted to cremate the shaman who unsuccessfully danced the rain sacrifice, perhaps as punishment or perhaps to render the rite efficacious. The accounts of the bodhisattva Medicine King in chapter 23 of the *Lotus Sutra* also extol the virtues of self-immolation by burning. Both the *Tso* and *Lotus* traditions may have influenced the monk's belief that burning himself with incense would stop the rains. The poet associates the monk with Hsi Ho, the charioteer of Chinese myth who drives the sun across the heavens, and with the immortal Chang, probably Chang Tao-ling (died between 157 and 178), a historical figure who purportedly discovered an elixir of life and ascended into heaven. King Aśoka (reign ca. 268–239 B.C.E.) was the Indian patron of Buddhism attributed with its diffusion and propagation throughout the subcontinent; the Inspector of Fields may refer to a human official or the image of a tutelary deity of husbandry.

Mo Shih-lung (ca. 1539–1587), the author of the remaining poems and also a painter, was well connected in the art and intellectual circles of Shanghai. Several important treatises on painting are attributed to him, such as the *Discourse on Painting (Hua shuo)*, which some believe to be the work of Mo's student Tung Ch'i-ch'ang (1555–1636), one of the most prominent calligraphers and painters of the Ming period. Mo's poems illustrate the connections and friendships between the literati and hermits, monks, and nuns. "Saying Good-bye to Feng the Hermit" relates the wandering mountain pilgrimages of nonsectarian hermits whose existence is only faintly recorded in most religious literature. Mo's "I Went to Gold Mountain to Visit a Ch'an Master But He Was Not at Home" suggests that he made mountain pilgrimages himself to visit a Ch'an master in whom he sees a modern-day Hui-yüan (344–416), a broadly learned master of *dhyāna* practices, monastic discipline, and scriptural teachings. He also associates the master with the historical Buddha himself, who died while resting between two śāla trees, and with Bodhidharma, the First Patriarch of Chinese Ch'an, who was reportedly seen on a mountaintop after his death, holding a sandal.

"Saying Good-bye to a Singing Girl Who Has Decided to Become a Nun" suggests that Mo is acquainted both with the "azure towers," the realm of the courtesan, as well as the nunnery. Frequenting courtesans was an acceptable literati pastime in the Ming in many circles; some of the women, who were probably sold into prostitution as young girls, were well educated in poetry, painting, and literature and became established artists in their own right. Depending on their level in the social and economic hierarchy of the demimonde, the women might have some choice in their partners and become virtual kept mistresses, but leaving their establishments usually required the payment of large sums of money. How this singing-girl managed to leave is unknown. The "True Vehicle" is Buddhism; the yak-tail whisk, the Ch'an master's scepter of authority. Mo's optimistism about the woman's future suggests the opportunities monastic life might provide her.

For all his interest in spiritual matters, however, Mo's "Drinking Wine" suggests he is skeptical of ever becoming a Buddha or immortal, and he instead places his faith in more worldly pastimes. He nevertheless admires the abilities of those who aspire to higher spiritual planes, such as the monk in deep trance in "The Meditation Rock." The verse juxtaposes the solidity of the rock (and, by association, the mental firmness of determination of the meditating monk) with the ephemerality of blossoming flowers. Meditation is often considered a practice performed in temple halls, but Siddhārtha Gautama attained enlightenment meditating in the forest, and his example is emulated by the monk here. "To the Monk Wu-hsia on the Occasion of His Editing the Lotus Sutra" contrasts the specificity of the written scriptural word with the nonverbal mind-to-mind transmission of direct experience advocated by Bodhidharma.

"Ballad of the Neighborhood Shaman"

If people in this neighborhood get sick,
    they'll never take a drug;
as soon as His Lordship God arrives
    the demon of sickness leaves.
They run to welcome the old shaman
    who brings the god at night,
when white sheep and red carp in
        profusion
    are offered up to him.
A man and woman earnestly
    bow before the altar:
"Our family is poor and has no meat,
    oh god, please take no offense!"
The old shaman beats the drum,
    dances now and sings;
paper money swishing, swishing
    in burgeoning dark wind.
The shaman proclaims,
    "Originally, your life was to run out
        here,
but the god, mindful of your devotion,
    has postponed your death!"
The shaman escorts the god to his horse,
    and walks out of the door;
the family climb up on the roof,
    and cry to the soul to return.

"The Taoist Huang Has Died of Alcoholism"

Your master died from drinking too
    much;
now you have followed in his steps.
A mound of dregs will be your grave,
your tombstone inscribed with the "Ode
    in Praise of Wine."
Unsteady on your feet, you tripped and
    stumbled,
your face flushed, your liver wasted.
Now you are gone, not even your
    shadow remains;
there is only your portrait, drawn in my
    poem.

"A Buddhist Monk Cut and Burned His Own Flesh to Make the Rains Stop—A Man from His Native Place Asked Me to Write a Poem to Send to Him"

The sky extends upwards for ninety
    thousand miles.
When it wants to be clear it is clear,
    when it wants to rain it rains.
For the rain god and the sun god
    it's as easy as herding sheep:
they receive their orders and carry them
    out;
    who would presume to complain?
So what kind of man is this Buddhist
    monk,
daring to set up an altar with banners
    and drums?
With his cracking whip he stands up to
    Heaven
and cries out to Hsi-ho to bring back the
    chariot of the sun!
The immortal Chang in broad daylight
    flew up into the sky—
now this monk has a chance to do even
    better than that!
All he does is to burn a bit of incense
    on an inch of his flesh
and the ocean calls the clouds back to
    the kingdom of water.
The local alchemists are all impressed by
    what the monk has done,
and the magistrate gives him a piece of
    red silk.
But still, this man, virtuous as King
    Ashoka,
    must bear the pain with his own
        body
while the farmers all bow down to the
    Inspector of Fields.

"Saying Good-bye to Feng the Hermit"

Where will your strange pilgrimage take
    you next?

How far will you travel
    through southern trees, southern
        clouds?
Your boat winds its way
    past nine bends of the river
where Incense Burner Peak juts into the
    sky.
I know you will seek out all the famous
    mountains—
don't disappoint the immortals, they are
    waiting for you!
This may be the trip—you will
    experience wonders
and command flying dragons
    at the Cliff of Purple Sky.

"I Went to Gold Mountain to Visit a Ch'an Master but He Was Not at Home"

A Buddhist monastery across a stone
    bridge—
here I would sweep away the dust of
    confusion
        and call upon the Hui-yüan of our
        day.
His home is between two śāla trees,
    among the cold clouds,
while he walks deep in the mountains,
    holding one sandal in his hands.
The roar of a waterfall
    sounds like pure Sanskrit chanting;
evening wind sings in pine trees
    beyond the courtyard.
Why cling to Causality and insist
    on seeing him face to face?
One reading of the poem he has left
    behind
    and my inner self
        returns to the Void.

"Saying Good-bye to a Singing Girl Who Has Decided to Become a Nun"

You have called at the gate of the True
    Vehicle,
    your worldly self is no more.

You have said farewell forever
    to the golden chambers,
        the wind and the dust.
Lightly you wield the yak-tail whisk;
    your singing fan lies on the floor.
You learn to adjust your meditation
    cushion,
        and laugh at the dancer's mat.
No more resentment when rouge fades
    like red flowers;
no longer will the feathered hairdo
        appear in your mirror.
Mist, light, water—quiet Zen mind:
I know a new springtime
    will bloom
        in the Realm of Emptiness.

"Drinking Wine"

I don't believe in becoming a Buddha,
    reborn in Paradise;
and talk of Immortals flying off in broad
        daylight
    is nonsense.
All I'll do is swim my way through a
    lifetime of wine—
a much better plan than struggling to
    live for a thousand years!

"The Meditation Rock"

Gnawed at by lichens,
    covered by moss—
        a rock, old in centuries.
When was it
    that the monk sat here
        to meditate in the silent woods?
Let the flowers
    beside this rock
        scatter petals like rain—
they cannot distract
    the mind of the monk
        who has entered deep trance.

"To the Monk Wu-hsia on the Occasion of His Editing the Lotus Sutra"

You have edited a thousand pages of
    palm-leaf manuscripts;

for years now, your mind has been
devoted
to the Buddhist canon.
I ask you the true meaning

of Bodhidharma's trip to China:
no written word has ever explained this
mystery.

Monkey's Journey to the West

The true story of the T'ang dynasty translator Hsüan-tsang (600–664), who traveled to India to bring Buddhist scriptures to China, inspired popular drama and literature for centuries. Drawing upon the body of folktales that had developed around the monk's journey through Central Asia into the Ganges River region of northern India, the writer Wu Ch'eng-en (ca. 1500–1582) created *The Journey to the West (Hsi-yu chi),* a novel that can be read at many different levels as popular entertainment, spiritual pilgrimage, and religious satire. The narrative relates the travels of Hsüan-tsang (known here as Tripitaka after the name given to the Buddhist canon) and several unlikely companions in the Dharma: a white horse, and three farcical demonlike characters called Monkey, Pigsy, and Sandy. Working together they overcome the perils and obstacles of the pilgrimage and attain the wisdom of the Buddha's teaching when they arrive in India.

At one level, the novel may be understood as an allegory of the self on a journey to enlightenment, and the characters may be interpreted as symbolizing different aspects of that self. From an unenlightened perspective, those aspects are hindrances to development; from an enlightened perspective, however, they are the very means of spiritual development. Tripitaka, ever anxious and doubtful, has both the strengths and weaknesses of intellectualism and conceptualization. Monkey, generated from the adamantine essence of the universe, represents the mind that is at once grasping and flighty but powerfully perceptive. Pigsy is desire, concupiscence, and sloth; Sandy is capable but relatively inert. The characters in some ways parallel the "five aggregates": the white horse might be interpreted as the material form that carries the others along; Sandy, as elemental sensation; Monkey, as perception; Pigsy, as volitional action, or karma; and Tripitaka as consciousness. Each requires the facilities of the other four. Perhaps the author never intended such a parallel, but the analogy does suggest the allegorical possibilities of the narrative. Not only inspired by Buddhism, however, the *Journey to the West* also incorporates teachings from Taoism and Chinese folklore.

This chapter from the novel finds the travelers at the end of their journey in India just as they are entering the land of the Buddha; they are at the foot of the mountain of Vulture Peak, where the Buddha, Śākyamuni, resides. The "Bodhisattva" they refer to is Kuan-yin, who throughout the novel reveals a wiliness unbecoming of her status as archetype of compassion and mercy. Confronting a body of water, they must find a bridge for crossing to the other shore, an allusion to the perfection of wisdom that allows one to cross over to another realm of understanding. This wisdom is symbolized by the bottomless boat that ferries souls to salvation, conveying only those who have cast off their coarser selves. Meeting the Buddha, they are handed the scriptures by Ānanda and Kāśyapa, historical figures who were the disciples of Siddhārtha Gautama but here are depicted as venal Chinese bureaucrats. At first, most believe that the blank scriptures given the pilgrims are a swindle perpetrated by the unremunerated Ānanda and Kāśyapa, but the Buddha finally reveals that the blank scriptures actually are the ones that contain the highest truth. To appease the spiritual needs of those of lesser understanding, however, he gives the pilgrims scrolls with writing on them, claiming that they are the source of the "three religions" of Confucianism, Taoism, and Buddhism. The journey does not end here, however, for more perils await them before they eventually return successfully to China.

Selection from *Monkey:*
Folk Novel of China

They travelled westward for many months, and at last began to be aware that the country through which they were now passing was different from any that they had seen. Everywhere they came across gem-like flowers and magical grasses, with many ancient cypresses and hoary pines. In the villages through which they passed every family seemed to devote itself to the entertainment of priests and other pious works. On every hill were hermits practising austerities, in every wood pilgrims chanting holy writ. Finding hospitality each night and starting again at dawn, they journeyed for many days, till they came at last within sudden sight of a cluster of high eaves and towers. "Monkey, that's a fine place," said Tripitaka, pointing to it with his whip. "Considering," said Monkey, "how often you have insisted upon prostrating yourself at the sight of false magicians' palaces and arch impostors' lairs, it is strange that when at last you see before you Buddha's true citadel, you should not even dismount from your horse." At this Tripitaka in great excitement sprang from his saddle, and walking beside the horse was soon at the gates of the high building. A young Taoist came out to meet them. "Aren't you the people who have come from the east to fetch scriptures?" he asked. Tripitaka hastily tidied his clothes and looking up saw that the boy was clad in gorgeous brocades and carried a bowl of jade dust in his hand. Monkey knew him at once. "This," he said to Tripitaka, "is the Golden Crested Great Immortal of the Jade Truth Temple at the foot of the Holy Mountain." Tripitaka at once advanced bowing. "Well, here you are at last!" said the Immortal. "The Bodhisattva misinformed me. Ten years ago she was told by Buddha to go to China and find someone who would fetch scriptures from India. She told me she had found someone who would arrive here in two or three years. Year after year I waited, but never a sign! This meeting is indeed a surprise." "I cannot thank you enough, Great Immortal, for your patience," said Tripitaka.

Then they all went into the temple and were shown round by the Immortal; tea and refreshments were served, and perfumed hot water was brought for Tripitaka to wash in. Soon they all turned in for the night. Early next day Tripitaka changed into his brocaded cassock and jewelled cap, and staff in hand presented himself to the Immortal in the hall of the temple, to take his leave. "That's better!" said the Immortal. "Yesterday you were looking a bit shabby; but now you look a true child of Buddha!" Tripitaka was just going when the Immortal stopped him, saying, "You must let me see you off." "It's really not necessary," said Tripitaka. "Monkey knows the way." "He only knows the way by air," said the Immortal. "You have got to go on the ground." "That's true enough," said Monkey. "We will trouble you just to set us on the right way. My Master is pining to get into the presence of the Buddha, and it would be a pity if there were any delay." Taking Tripitaka by the hand he led him right through the temple and out at the back. For the road did not go from the front gate, but traversed the courtyards and led on to the hill behind. "You see that highest point, wreathed in magic rainbow mists," said the Immortal, pointing to the mountain. "That is the Vulture Peak, the sacred precinct of the Buddha." Tripitaka at once began kowtowing. "Master," said Monkey, "you had better keep that for later on. If you are going to kowtow all the way up to the top, there won't be much left of your head by the time we get there. It's still a long way off." "You stand already on Blessed Ground," said the Immortal. "The Holy Mountain is before you. I shall now turn back."

Monkey led them up the hill at a leisurely pace. They had not gone more than five or six leagues when they came to a great water about eight leagues wide. It was exceedingly swift and rough. No one was to be seen in any direction. "I don't think this can be the right way," said Tripitaka. "Do you think the Immortal can possibly have been mistaken. This water is so wide and so rough that we cannot possibly get across." "This is the way all right," said Monkey. "Look! Just over there is a bridge. That's the right way to Salvation." Presently Tripitaka came to a notice-board on which was written Cloud Reach Bridge. But it proved, when they came up to it, that the bridge consisted simply of slim tree trunks laid end on end, and was hardly wider than the palm of a man's hand. "Monkey," protested Tripitaka in great alarm, "it's not humanly possible to balance on such a bridge as that. We must find some other way to get across." "This is the right way," said Monkey, grinning. "It may be the right way," said Pigsy, "but it's so narrow and slippery that no one would ever dare set foot on it. And think how far there is to go, and what it's like underneath." "All wait where you are, and watch while I show you how," cried Monkey. Dear Monkey! He strode up to the bridge, leapt lightly on to it and had soon slipped across. "I'm over!" he shouted, waving from the other side. Tripitaka showed no sign of following him, and Pigsy and Sandy bit their fingers murmuring, "Can't be done! Can't be done!" Monkey sprang back again and pulled at Pigsy, saying, "Fool, follow me across." But Pigsy lay on the ground and would not budge. "It's much too slippery," he said. "Let me off. Why can't I have a wind to carry me!" "What would be the good of that?" said Monkey. "Unless you go by the bridge you won't turn into a Buddha." "Buddha or no Buddha," said Pigsy, "I'm not going on to that bridge." The quarrel was at its height, when Sandy ran between them and at last succeeded in making peace. Suddenly Tripitaka saw someone punting a boat towards the shore and crying, "Ferry, ferry!" "Stop your quarrelling, disciples," said Tripitaka. "A boat is coming." They all gazed with one accord at the spot to which he pointed. A boat was coming indeed; but when it was a little nearer they saw to their consternation that it had no bottom. Monkey with his sharp eyes had already recognized the ferryman as the Conductor of Souls, also called Light of the Banner. But he did not tell the others, merely crying "Ahoy, ferry, ahoy!" When the boat was along shore, the ferryman again cried "Ferry, ferry!" "Your boat is broken

and bottomless," said Tripitaka, much perturbed. "How can you take people across?" "You may well think," said the ferryman, "that in a bottomless boat such a river as this could never be crossed. But since the beginning of time I have carried countless souls to their Salvation." "Get on board, Master," said Monkey. "You will find that this boat, although it has no bottom, is remarkably steady, however rough the waters may be." Seeing Tripitaka still hesitate, Monkey took him by the scruff of the neck and pushed him on board. There was nothing for Tripitaka's feet to rest on, and he went straight into the water. The ferryman caught at him and dragged him up to the side of the boat. Sitting miserably here, he wrung out his clothes, shook out his shoes, and grumbled at Monkey for having got him into this scrape. But Monkey, taking no notice, put Pigsy and Sandy, horse and baggage, all on board, ensconcing them as best he could in the gunwale. The ferryman punted them dexterously out from shore. Suddenly they saw a body in the water, drifting rapidly down stream. Tripitaka stared at it in consternation. Monkey laughed. "Don't be frightened, Master," he said. "That's you." And Pigsy said, "It's you, it's you." Sandy clapped his hands. "It's you, it's you," he cried. The ferryman too joined in the chorus. "There *you* go!" he cried. "My best congratulations." He went on punting, and in a very short while they were all safe and sound at the other side. Tripitaka stepped lightly ashore. He had discarded his earthly body; he was cleansed from the corruption of the senses, from the fleshly inheritance of those bygone years. His was now the transcendent wisdom that leads to the Further Shore, the mastery that knows no bounds.

When they were at the top of the bank, they turned round and found to their astonishment that boat and ferryman had both vanished. Only then did Monkey tell them who the ferryman was. Tripitaka began thanking his disciples for all they had done for him. "Every one of us," said Monkey, "is equally indebted to the other. If the Master had not received our vows and accepted us as his disciples we should not have had the chance to do good works and win salvation. If we had not protected the Master and mounted guard over him, he would never have got rid of his mortal body. Look, Master, at this realm of flowers and happy creatures—of phoenixes, cranes and deer. Is it not a better place indeed than the haunted deserts through which you and I have passed?" Tripitaka still murmured his thanks, and with a strange feeling of lightness and exhilaration they all set off up the Holy Mountain and were soon in sight of the Temple of the Thunder Clap, with its mighty towers brushing the firmament, its giant foundations rooted in the seams of the Hill of Life.

Near the top of the hill they came upon a party of Upasakas filing through the green pinewoods, and under a clump of emerald cedars they saw bands of the Blessed. Tripitaka hastened to bow down to them. Worshippers male and female, monks and nuns pressed together the palms of their hands, crying, "Holy priest, it is not to us that your homage should be addressed. Wait till you have seen Śākyamuni, and afterwards come and greet us each according to his rank." "He's always in too much of a hurry," laughed Monkey. "Come along at once and let us pay our respects to the people at the top." Twitching with excitement Tripitaka followed Monkey to the gates of the Temple. Here they were met by the Vajrapani of the Four Elements. "So your Reverence has at last arrived!" he exclaimed. "Your disciple Hsüan Tsang has indeed arrived," said Tripitaka, bowing. "I must trouble you to wait here a moment, till your arrival has been announced," said the Vajrapani. He then gave instructions to the porter at the outer gate to tell the porter at the second gate that the Vajrapani wished to report that the priest from China had arrived. The porter at the second gate sent word to the porter at the third gate. At this gate were holy priests with direct access to the Powers Above. They hurried to the Great Hall and informed the Tathāgata, the Most Honoured One, even Śākyamuni Buddha himself that the priest from the Court of China had arrived at the Mountain to fetch scriptures.

Father Buddha was delighted. He ordered the Bodhisattva, Vajrapanis, Arhats, Protectors, Planets and Temple Guardians to form up in two lines. Then he gave orders that the priest of T'ang was to be shown in. Again the word was passed along from gate to gate: "The priest of T'ang is to be shown in." Tripitaka, Monkey, Pigsy and Sandy, carefully following the rules of etiquette prescribed to them, all went forward, horse and baggage following. When they reached the Great Hall they first prostrated themselves before the Tathāgata and then bowed to right and left. This they repeated three times, and then knelt before the Buddha and presented their passports. He looked through them one by one and handed them back to Tripitaka, who bent his head in acknowledgment, saying, "The disciple Hsüan Tsang has come by order of the Emperor of the great land of T'ang, all the way to this Holy Mountain, to fetch the true scriptures which are to be the salvation of all mankind. May the Lord Buddha accord this favour and grant me a quick return to my native land."

Hereupon the Tathāgata opened the mouth of compassion and gave vent to the mercy of his heart: "In all the vast and populous bounds of your Eastern Land, greed, slaughter, lust and lying have long prevailed. There is no respect for Buddha's teaching, no striving towards good works. So full and abundant is the measure of the people's sins that they go down forever into the darkness of Hell, where some are pounded in mortars, some take on animal form, furry and horned. In which guise they are done by as they did on earth, their flesh becoming men's food. Confucius stood by their side teaching them all the virtues, king after king in vain corrected them with fresh penalties and pains. No law could curb their reckless debauches, no ray of wisdom penetrate their blindness.

"But I have three Baskets of Scripture that can save mankind from its torments and afflictions. One contains the Law, which tells of Heaven, one contains the Discourses, which speak of Earth, one contains the Scriptures, which save the dead. They are divided into thirty-five sections and are written upon fifteen thousand one hundred and forty-four scrolls. They are the path to Perfection, the gate that leads to True Good. In them may be learnt all the motions of the stars and divisions of earth, all that appertains to man, bird, beast, flower, tree and implement of use; in short; all that concerns mankind is found therein. In consideration of the fact that you have come so far, I would give you them all to take back. But the people of China are foolish and boisterous; they would mock at my mysteries and would not understand the hidden meaning of our Order . . . Ānanda, Kāśyapa," he cried, "take these four to the room under the tower, and when they have refreshed themselves, open the doors of the Treasury, and select from each of the thirty-five sections a few scrolls for these priests to take back to the East, to be a boon there forever."

In the lower room they saw countless rarities and treasures, and were still gazing upon them in wonder when spirits ministrant began to spread the feast. The foods were all fairy fruits and dainties unknown in the common world. Master and disciples bowed acknowledgment of Buddha's favour and set to with a good will. This time it was Pigsy who was in luck and Sandy who scored; for Buddha had provided for their fare such viands as confer long life and health and magically transform the substance of common flesh and bone. When Ānanda and Kāśyapa had seen to it that the four had all they wanted, they went into the Treasury. The moment the door was opened, beams of magic light shot forth, filling the whole air far around. On chests and jewelled boxes were struck red labels, on which were written the names of the holy books. The two disciples of Buddha led Tripitaka up to the place where the scriptures lay, and inviting him to study the titles said, "Having come here from China you have no doubt brought a few little gifts for us. If you will kindly hand them over, you shall have your scriptures at once." "During all my long journey," said Tripitaka, "I have never once found it necessary to lay in anything of the kind." "Splendid," said the disciples. "So we're

to spend our days handing over scriptures gratis! Not a very bright outlook for our heirs!" Thinking by their sarcastic tone that they had no intention of parting with the scriptures, Monkey could not refrain from shouting angrily, "Come along, Master! We'll tell Buddha about this and make him come and give us the scriptures himself." "Don't shout," said Ānanda. "There's nothing in the situation that demands all this bullying and blustering. Come here and fetch your scriptures." Pigsy and Sandy, mastering their rage and managing to restrain Monkey, came across to take the books. Scroll by scroll was packed away into the bundle, which was hoisted on to the horse's back. Then the two luggage packs were tied up and given to Pigsy and Sandy to carry. They first went and kowtowed their thanks to Buddha and then made for the gates. To every lesser Buddha that they met they bowed twice; to every Bodhisattva once. Then leaving the great outer gates they paid their respects to the groups of monks and nuns and, saying farewell, went back down the mountain as fast as they could.

Now in an upper room that looked on to the Treasury there happened to be sitting Dīpankara, the Buddha of the Past. He overheard the whole conversation about the handing over of the scriptures, and had a notion that if they were given no gratuity, Ānanda and Kāśyapa would revenge themselves by substituting scriptures with nothing in them. "The poor fools," he said to himself, "certainly have no idea of the trick that is being played on them, and will discover too late that their whole journey has been wasted." "Is there anyone here that could take a message for me?" he asked. The White Heroic Bodhisattva stepped forward, "I want you to put forth all your magic powers," said Dīpankara, "catch up Tripitaka, get those scriptures away from him and bring him back to get proper ones."

The White Heroic Bodhisattva sat astride a whirlwind and made off as fast as his magic powers would carry him. The wind he rode on had a strange perfume, which Tripitaka, when he first perceived it, thought merely to be one of the portents of Paradise. But a moment later, a great rushing sound was heard, and a hand suddenly stretched out from space, seized the scriptures and bore them away. Tripitaka beat his breast and groaned, Pigsy rolled off in pursuit, while Sandy clutched at the empty pannier. Monkey leapt into the air; but the White Heroic Bodhisattva, seeing him draw near, feared that he might strike out blindly with his cudgel before any explanation could be given. So he tore open the scripture-parcel and threw it to the ground.

Monkey, when he saw the parcel fall and its contents scattered by the scented gale, lowered his cloud and went to see in what condition the scrolls were. He was soon joined by Pigsy, who had given up the pursuit, and they both began collecting the scrolls and bringing them to where Tripitaka was waiting. He was weeping bitterly. "Little did I think," he sobbed, "that even in Paradise we should be thus molested by savage demons!" Sandy now opened one of the scrolls that he had brought. It was snowy white; there was not a trace of so much as half a letter upon it. "Master," he said, handing it to Tripitaka, "This scroll has got no writing in it." Monkey then opened a scroll; it too was blank. Pigsy did the same; only to make the same discovery. "We had better look at them all," said Tripitaka. They did so, and found that all were blank. "I must say it's hard luck on the people of China," sobbed Tripitaka. "What is the use of taking to them these blank books? How shall I dare face the Emperor of T'ang? He will say I am playing a joke on him and have me executed on the spot."

Monkey had by now guessed what had happened. "Master," he said, "I know what's at the bottom of this. It is all because we refused to give Ānanda and Kāśyapa their commission. This is how they have revenged themselves on us. The only thing to do is to go straight to Buddha and charge them with fraudulent withholding of delivery." They all agreed, and were soon back at the temple gates. "They've come back to change their scriptures," said the bands of the blessed, laughing. This time they were allowed to go straight in. "Listen to this!" shouted Monkey. "After all the trouble we had getting here from China, and after you specially ordered that we were to be given the scriptures, Ānanda and Kāśyapa made a fraudulent delivery of goods. They gave us blank copies to take away; I ask you, what is the good of that to us?" "You needn't shout," said Buddha smiling. "I quite expected that those two would ask for their commission. As a matter of fact, scriptures ought not to be given on too easy terms or received gratis. On one occasion some of my monks went down the mountain to Srāvastī with some scriptures and let Chao, the Man of Substance, read them out loud. The result was that all the live members of his household were protected from all calamity and the dead were saved from perdition. For this they only charged gold to the weight of three pecks and three pints of rice. I told them they had sold far too cheap. No wonder they gave you blank copies when they saw you did not intend to make any payment at all. As a matter of fact, it is such blank scrolls as these that are the true scriptures. But I quite see that the people of China are too foolish and ignorant to believe this, so there is nothing for it but to give them copies with some writing on." Then he called for Ānanda and Kāśyapa, and told them to choose a few scrolls with writing, out of each of the thirty-five divisions of the scriptures, hand them over to the pilgrims, and then inform him of the exact titles and numbers.

The two disciples accordingly took the pilgrims once more to the Treasury, where they again asked Tripitaka for a little present. He could think of nothing to give them except his golden begging bowl. He told Sandy to find it, and holding it up before him in both hands, he said to the two disciples, "I am a poor man and have been travelling for a long time. I fear I have nothing with me that is suitable as a present; but perhaps you would accept this bowl which the Emperor of China gave me with his own hand, that I might use it to beg with on the road. If you will put up with so small a trifle, I am sure that when I return to China and report upon my mission, you may count upon being suitably rewarded. I hope on these terms you will this time give me scriptures with writing on them, or I fear his Majesty will be disappointed and think that all my efforts have been wasted." Ānanda took the bowl with a faint smile. But all the divinities in attendance—down to the last kitchen-boy god—clapped one another on the back and roared with laughter, saying, "Well, of all the shameless . . . ! They've made the scripture seekers pay them a commission!" The two disciples looked somewhat embarrassed, but Ānanda continued to clutch tightly at the bowl. Kāśyapa meanwhile began looking out the scriptures and handing them over to Tripitaka. "Disciples," said he, "keep a sharp look out, to see that the same thing doesn't happen again." Five thousand and forty-eight scrolls were duly handed over. All of them had writing. Then they were properly arranged and loaded on the horse's back, and a few that were over were made into a packet and given to Pigsy to carry. The other luggage was carried by Sandy, while Monkey led the horse. Tripitaka carried his priest's staff and wore his jewelled cap and brocaded cassock. In this guise they all once more presented themselves before Buddha.

Seated on his Lotus Throne, the Blessed One ordered the two Great Arhats to beat on their cloud gongs and summon to the Throne the three thousand Buddhas, the eight Vajrapanis, the four Bodhisattvas, the five hundred Arhats, the eight hundred monks and all the congregation of the faithful. Those that were entitled to be seated were ordered to sit upon their jewelled thrones, and those that were to stand were ranged in two files on either hand. Soon heavenly music was heard from afar, a magic radiance filled the air. When the whole company was duly assembled, Buddha asked his two disciples for an exact account of the scriptures that they had handed over. Ānanda and Kāśyapa then read over the list, beginning with the Book of the Great Decease, and ending with the Kośa Śāstra. "These books," said Ānanda, "written on five thousand and forty-eight scrolls, have all been given to the priest of China to keep forever in their land. They are all now securely packed on their horse's back or in parcels to be carried by hand, and the pilgrims are here to thank you."

Tripitaka and the disciples tethered the horse, put down the burdens and bowed with the palms of their hands pressed together. "The efficacy of these scriptures is boundless," said Buddha. "They are not only the mirror of our Faith, but also the source and origin of all three religions. When you return to the world and show them to common mortals, they must not be lightly handled. No scroll must be opened save by one who has fasted and bathed. Treasure them, value them! For in them is secreted the mystic lore of Immortality, in them is revealed the wondrous receipt for ten thousand transformations."

Tripitaka kowtowed his thanks, doing leal homage, and prostrating himself three times, as he had done before. When they reached the outer gates, they paid their respects to the bands of the faithful, and went on their way.

After dismissing the pilgrims, Buddha broke up the assembly. Presently the Bodhisattva Kuan-yin appeared before the throne, saying, "Long ago I was instructed by you to find someone in China who would come here to fetch scriptures. He has now achieved this task, which has taken him five thousand and forty days. The number of the scrolls delivered to him is five thousand and forty-eight. I suggest that it would be appropriate if he were given eight days in which to complete his mission, so that the two figures may concord." "A very good idea," said Buddha. "You may have that put into effect." He then sent for the eight Vajrapanis and said to them, "You are to exert your magic powers and carry back Tripitaka to the East. When he has deposited the scriptures, you are to bring him back here. All this must be done in eight days, that the number of days taken by the journey may concord with the number of scrolls allotted to him." The Vajrapanis at once went after Tripitaka, caught him up and said to him, "Scripture-taker, follow us." A sudden lightness and agility possessed the pilgrims and they were borne aloft upon a magic cloud.

CH'ING DYNASTY

DYNASTY

(1644-1911)

Tales of the Supernatural

Doctrinal and philosophical formulations of spiritual beliefs, whether Confucian, Taoist, or Buddhist, are but one aspect of the Chinese tradition, which also includes folk beliefs expressed in tales of the supernatural. Confucius did not speak of the preternatural and the fantastic, but tales of the bizarre nonetheless attracted a wide following of both credulous readers as well as those who read the stories as entertainment. Such accounts reveal popular beliefs not likely to be described in more formal expositions of religious tenets. One of the best-known collections of stories of the supernatural is Pu Songling's (P'u Sung-ling; 1640–1715) *Strange Tales from Make-Do Studio (Liao-chai chih-i)*. Pu collected many of the tales from popular culture, rewriting and supplementing them with his own additions and comments as "Chronicler of the Tales"; some stories, however, are entirely his own invention. Four selections from his *Strange Tales* are included here.

"The Mural" describes what can happen when Chu Hsi's warnings about becoming deluded by spiritual beings are not heeded. While visiting a Ch'an monastery, a scholar receives from an unexpected quarter a teaching on lust, one of the "three poisons" of Buddhism, along with greed and hatred. Tales of the supernatural allow their characters, both male and female, a freedom of sexual expression scarcely encouraged by the ideals of conventional society.

"Monk Jin" hints at the realities, if not the ideals, of Ch'ing dynasty (1644–1911) Buddhism; "Jin" is a surname that literally means "money." A model of the satire of exaggeration, the tale's closely observed details nonetheless indicate some basis in historical fact, and its descriptions of monasticism and funeral preparations are convincing depictions of everyday life.

The gruesomeness of "Painted Skin" is characteristic of many tales of the bizarre. Scholar Wang receives a lesson on the illusoriness of superficial appearances that nearly costs him his life, for the demon he encounters is looking for a victim to take its place in death so that it may return to the world of the living. It preys on Wang's weakness of lust. The Taoist master is able to control these forces with the symbols of his power: the fly whisk and the bottle gourd. Such gourds, bulbous at both ends but pinched in the middle, bear a wide range of associations, and suggest womblike or stomachlike labyrinths, self-contained miniature universes, and powers of longevity. Here it indicates the power of delimitation and containment. In this tale the life of the Confucian scholar is entirely in the hands of his wife, the Taoist, and the madman, people who in the conventional scheme of contemporary social relationships would be considered his inferiors. Here that order of power is reversed, and the elite are forced to absorb what is conveyed to them from below.

"Ghost-Girl Xiaoxie" reveals the permeability of the barriers between the realms of ghosts and human beings and describes the role of Taoist masters in facilitating that interaction. Ghost women and female fox-spirits appear frequently in tales of the supernatural, often as sexually aggressive, or at least sexually available, women who represent the obverse of the ideals of chaste womanhood prescribed by society. Physical contact with such uncanny forces was believed to cause inevitable death. The skeptical scholar Tao, however, patiently overcomes the uninhibited Qiurong and Xiaoxie and gradually encourages them to conform to standards of wifely behavior.

Tao is aided by the ghosts against the injustices of the human world, and his encounter with the legal system reflects how the bureaucracies of the human and spirit world mirror one another in Ch'ing popular belief. While Tao is imprisoned by a human judge, Qiurong is abducted by one of the judges of the underworld, which is supervised by the spirit of the city god. Justice eventually prevails in both realms, but only because Tao and the two ghost-girls help one another; earthly justice frees Tao, and divine retribution takes its course as Xiaoxie's brother is rewarded by being reborn in another realm. The powers of the Taoist priest allow the two realms to conjoin; Tao, now happily situated with a demure wife and concubine, fulfills the Confucian dream of earning official rank through the examination system.

"The Mural"

While staying in the capital, Meng Longtan of Jiangxi and Master of Letters Zhu once happened upon a monastery. Neither the shrine-hall nor the meditation room was very spacious, and only one old monk was found putting up within. Seeing the guests enter, the monk straightened up his clothes, went to greet them and showed them around the place. An image of Zen Master Baozhi stood in the shrine-hall. On either side wall were painted fine murals with lifelike human figures. The east wall depicted the Buddhist legend of "Heavenly Maidens Scattering Flowers." Among the figures was a young girl with flowing hair with a flower in her hand and a faint smile on her face. Her cherry-red lips were on the verge of moving, and the liquid pools of her eyes seemed to stir with wavelike glances. After gazing intently for some time, Zhu's self-possession began to waver and his thoughts grew so abstracted that he fell into a trance. His body went adrift as if floating on mist; suddenly he was inside the mural. Peak upon peak of palaces and pavilions made him feel as if he was beyond this earth. An old monk was preaching the *Dharma* on a dais, around which stood a large crowd of viewers in robes with their right shoulders bared out of respect. Zhu mingled in among them.

Before long, he felt someone tugging furtively at his sleeve. He turned to look, and there was the girl with flowing hair giving him a dazzling smile. She tripped abruptly away, and he lost no time following her along a winding walkway into a small chamber. Once there, he hesitated to approach any farther. When she turned her head and raised the flower with a beckoning motion, he went across to her in the quiet, deserted chamber. Swiftly he embraced her and, as she did not put up much resistance, they grew intimate. When it was over she told him not to make a sound and left, closing the door behind her. That night she came again. After two days of this, the girl's companions realized what was happening and searched together until they found the scholar.

"A little gentleman is already growing in your belly, but still you wear those flowing tresses, pretending to be a maiden," they said teasingly. Holding out hairpins and earrings, they pressured her to put her hair up in the coiled knot of a married woman, which she did in silent embarrassment. One of the girls said, "Sisters, let's not out-stay our welcome." At this the group left in a titter.

Looking at the soft, cloudlike chignon piled atop her head and her phoenix ringlets curved low before her ears, the scholar was more struck by her charms than when she had worn her hair long. Seeing that no one was around, he began to make free with her. His heart throbbed at her musky fragrance but, before they had quite finished their pleasure, the heavy tread of leather boots was heard. A clanking of chains and manacles was followed by clamorous, arguing voices. The girl got up in alarm. Peering out, they saw an officer dressed in armor, his face black as lacquer, with chains in one hand and a mace in the other. Standing around him were all the maidens. "Is this all of you?" asked the officer. "We're all here," they answered. "Report if any of you are concealing a man from the lower world. Don't bring trouble on yourselves." "We aren't," said the maidens in unison. The officer turned around and looked malevolently in the direction of the chamber, giving every appearance of an intention to search it. The girl's face turned pale as ashes in fear. "Quick, hide under the bed," she told Zhu in panic. She opened a little door in the wall and was gone in an instant. Zhu lay prostrate, hardly daring to take a little breath. Soon he heard the sound of boots stumping into, then back out of the room. Before long, the din of voices gradually receded. He regained some composure, though the sound of passers-by discussing the matter could be heard frequently outside the door. After cringing there for quite some time, he heard ringing in his ears and felt a burning ache in his eyes. Though the intensity of these sensations threatened to overwhelm him, there was no choice but to listen quietly for the girl's return. He was reduced to the point that he no longer recalled where he had been before coming here.

Just then his friend Meng Longtan, who had been standing in the shrine-hall, found that Zhu had disappeared in the blink of an eye. Perplexed, he asked the monk what had happened. "He has gone to hear a sermon on the *Dharma*," said the monk laughingly. "Where?" asked Meng. "Not far" was the answer. After a moment, the monk tapped on the wall with his finger and called, "Why do you tarry so long, my good patron?" Presently there appeared on the wall an image of Zhu standing motionless with his head cocked to one side as if listening to something. "You have kept your travelling companion waiting a long time," called the monk again." Thereupon he drifted out of the mural and down to the floor. He stood woodenly, his mind like burned-out ashes, with eyes staring straight ahead and legs wobbling. Meng was terribly frightened, but in time calmed down enough to ask what had happened. It turned out that Zhu had been hiding under the bed when he heard a thunderous knocking, so he came out of the room to listen for the source of the sound.

They looked at the girl holding the flower and saw, instead of flowing hair, a high coiled chignon on her head. Zhu bowed down to the old monk in amazement and asked the reason for this. "Illusion is born in the mind. How can a poor mendicant like myself explain it?" laughed the monk. Zhu was dispirited and cast down; Meng was shaken and confused. Together they walked down the shrine-hall steps and left.

The Chronicler of the Tales comments: " 'Illusion is born in the mind.' These sound like the words of one who has found the truth. A wanton mind gives rise to visions of lustfulness. The mind dominated by lust gives rise to a state of fear. The Bodhisattva made it possible for the ignorant persons to attain realization for themselves. All the myriad transformations of illusion are nothing but the movements of the human mind itself. The old monk spoke in earnest solicitude, but regrettably there is no sign that the youth found enlightenment in his

words and entered the mountains with hair unbound to seek the truth."

"Monk Jin"

Monk Jin came from Zhucheng district. His father was a shiftless idler who sold him for a few hundred coppers to Five-Lotus-Mountain Monastery. As a boy he was too slow a learner to practice the "pure livelihood" of sutra reading, meditation, and the like. Instead, he drove pigs to market like an indentured servant. In time Monk Jin's master died, leaving behind a small amount of money. Jin absconded from the monastery with as much of the money as he could lay hands on and went off to be a peddler. He was skillful at getting the better of people with tricks like bloating his sheep with water or monopolizing commodities at market fairs. Within a few years he made a quick fortune and bought land and buildings in Waterslope Ward. His disciples, lined up in bristling rows, numbered a thousand at daily roll call. He had over a thousand *mu* of rich land around the ward, and within it he built several dozen houses. The residents were monks, not laypersons. Even such laypersons as were there were poor men with no means of livelihood, who had brought their wives and children to live in rented rooms and work the land as tenants. Within every gate were quadrangles of dormitories where such people lived. The monk's residence was situated in the center of these dwellings and fronted by a reception parlor. Pillars, beams, and roof supports glittered with designs in gold leaf and enamel. The tables and folding screens at the head of the hall shone with such crystalline brilliance they could have been used as mirrors. Behind this was the sleeping chamber, with bead curtains and embroidered canopies. A dense odor of orchid and musk invaded the visitor's nostrils. The bed was of carved sandalwood inlaid with mother-of-pearl. The brocaded quilts on the bed were layered a foot and some inches thick. The walls were all but covered with landscapes and portraits of beautiful women by famous painters.

At a single drawn-out call, dozens of men

outside the door rumbled in thunderous response. Men with tiny tassels on their caps and leather boots on their feet would flock in like crows and stand with their necks stretched out like swans. They took orders with their mouths pressed shut and their ears pricked up. Guests showed on a moment's notice; a banquet for ten or more tables was arranged at a shouted command. Rich meats, full-bodied wines, steamed dishes and smoked delectables were laid out in disorderly profusion.

Though he did not dare to keep singing girls, he had ten or more budding boys, all irresistibly charming. They wrapped their heads in bandanas of black gauze, sang seductive songs and were by no means unpleasant to hear and see. If Jin went out, he was escorted by thirty or forty horsemen whose waist-mounted bows and arrows touched and rattled against each other. Servants addressed him as "Sir." Even the common people of the district "Grandfather"-ed and "Uncle"-ed him. They never called him "Master" or "Abbot" or used his *dharma* name. His disciples were not quite as conspicuous as he when they went out, but even they were the equals of young noblemen with their horses' manes tossing in the wind and their cloud-patterned trappings. Jin also went in for social connections in a big way: the very breath he drew had an effect over thousands of *li*. This gave him leverage over local officials, who feared what would happen if they ever got on his bad side.

As for Jin's character, he was crude and illiterate. From crown to toes he did not have a refined bone in his body. Never in his life did he take up a sutra or hold a mantra in mind, nor did his feet ever leave their traces in monasteries and abbeys, nor did he keep a chanting bell or drum in his room. Such things were never seen or heard by his disciples.

Among his renters were loose, attractive women who looked as if they belonged in the capital. Their rouge and face powder were provided by the monks, who were never frugal with their money. Consequently, the ward had hundreds of residents who, in a manner of speak-ing, were farmers without farming. Occasionally a murderous tenant would chop off a monk's head and bury it under his bed. Later he would be sent away without much of an investigation. These were some of the things that went on there.

Jin also bought a child with a family name different from his own and made the boy his own son. He hired a tutor to teach him examination writing. The boy was intelligent and good at composition, so Jin had him admitted to the district academy. Soon he rose by predictable steps to the rank of Grand Academy scholar. Before long he travelled to Shuntian prefectual examinations and won the title of master of letters. From then on Jin was widely known as the Grand Sire. People who had once called him "Great" now prefaced that with "Great," and those who had knelt on mats before him now kept their hands at their sides and bowed to him like sons and grandsons.

Not long afterward the Grand Sire expired. The master of letters put on hempen mourning clothes, slept on a straw mat with a clod pillow, and faced north, toward the soul of the departed, as he bewailed his orphan's lot. The beggars' staffs of Jin's disciples covered a whole bed. Of course the delicate sobbing from behind the mourning curtain was made by the master of letter's wife and no one else. The wives of high-ranking officials came, all done up in their best finery, to part the curtain and offer their condolences. So the roads were congested with officials' carriages and horses. On the day of burial, awnings and pavilions merged into a cloud of colors. Pennants and banners blocked out the sun. Lifelike straw figures wrapped in gold foil and silk accompanied the deceased to his grave. The burial objects included several dozen canopied carriages with mounted escorts, a thousand horses, and one hundred beautiful women. They built a gigantic spirit guard and guide to the underworld out of papier maché, and outfitted them with black turbans and metal armor. They were supported by inner wooden frames and borne along by men inside. Each was provided with a mechanism that, when turned, caused the giants' beards and eyebrows to wave in the air. The flashing light of their eyes made them look as if they were about to bellow with rage. Those who looked upon them were dumbstruck, and small children who saw them from a distance ran away squealing. The paper mansion that was to be sent to the underworld had the grandeur of a palace. It was a complex of adjoining towers, pavilions, chambers, and galleries that covered several dozen *mu*. If anyone could have entered one of its thousands of gates and doors he would never have found his way out. The offerings and representational objects were too numerous to mention one by one. The canopies of the mourners' carriages rubbed against each other in the road. No one from the provincial officials—who approached with bent backs and bowed as if at the emperor's morning audience—down to senior licentiates, collegians of the Imperial Academy of Learning and office clerks—who lowered their hands to the ground and followed them with their foreheads—dared to do anything to the young master or the deceased's disciples.

By now the whole district had turned out to view the spectacle. Men and women sweated and panted against one another in the street. There were husbands leading wives, mothers carrying babies and brothers calling their sisters. Blaring music, booming drums and the clanging of a hundred street operas mingled with their cries to make a bubbling cauldron of noise that drowned all human speech. Nothing of the onlookers could be seen below their shoulders: there were only thousands of milling heads. A pregnant woman was stricken with labor pains. Her friends fanned out about her and spread their skirts to make a curtain. As soon as the baby's squalling was heard it was wrapped up in a torn-off dress without anyone bothering to see if it were a boy or girl, and taken off in someone's arms. With some friends holding her up and some pulling her along, the mother managed to hobble away. What a sight!

After the burial, the money and property left by Jin were divided into two parts, one of which went to his son and one to his disciples. The

master of letters got half and, in all four directions around his residence were none but the brotherhood of the cloth. The monks went on addressing each other as brothers, and it is said they went on looking out for one another's interests.

The Chronicler of the Tales comments: "This is a sect which was never included in the Northern or Southern schools of Buddhism and which did not come down from the Sixth Patriarch. One can say that this sect developed its own unique dharma. I have also heard that the man who knows the emptiness of the five aggregates and stays undefiled by the six dusts is called a monk, or follower of higher things. When a man speaks the dharma with his mouth and meditates on his cushion he is called a follower of posturings. One whose shoes are perfumed by the flowers of Chu and who has worn his umbrella hat beneath the sky of Wu is a man of many wanderings. One who noisily chimes bells of different sizes is called a chanter of songs, and one who grovels at other people's feet like a dog or buzzes like a carrion-fly around gamblers on a binge is called a follower of hellish wrongs. Now which was it in Jin's case? Was it "higher things," "posturings," "wanderings," "songs," or "hellish wrongs?"

"Painted Skin"

Scholar Wang of Taiyuan went out for a morning walk and came upon a lone young woman with a bundle in her arms, hurrying along and faltering at every step. Running up behind, he found her to be in the bloom of youthful beauty, and his heart loved and delighted in her.

"Why are you walking all by yourself before the break of day?" he asked.

The girl answered, "Why should a passerby who can do nothing for my misery bother to ask?"

"What is your misery?" asked the scholar. "If there is anything I can do to help, I won't refuse."

The girl answered moodily: "My parents sold me to a rich family as a concubine, thinking of nothing but the marriage gift they would receive.

The wife was terribly jealous: mornings she reviled me and evenings she insulted me with beatings. It was too much for me to bear. I must escape to some place far away."

"Where will you go?" he asked.

"A fugitive does not choose a destination."

"My house is not far. Can I trouble you to pay me a visit?"

The girl followed him, delighted. The scholar picked up her bundle of possessions and showed her the way home. Seeing that the house was empty, she asked, "Why isn't anyone in your family here?"

"It's only my studio," was the answer.

"This is a wonderful place. If you pity me and wish to save me, my presence here must be a well-guarded secret." Having agreed to this, the scholar took her to bed with him.

He concealed her in a secret room, and several days passed without anyone being the wiser. The scholar revealed something of this to his wife Chen, who suspected that she was a dowry-maid or concubine from some important family and urged him to send her away. The scholar did not listen.

One day he went to the market, where he came upon a Taoist who turned and looked at him in astonishment, asking: "What have you come up against?"

"Nothing," he answered.

"An aura of evil surrounds you," said the Taoist. "Why do you say *nothing?*" The scholar denied this vigorously, whereupon the Taoist walked away muttering: "Such delusion! It only goes to show there are people in this world who don't even wake up when death is around the corner." The strangeness of these words stirred suspicion of the girl in the scholar's mind. But then he wondered how such an obviously beautiful girl could be a monster. He concluded that the Taoist probably made use of exorcism to make a living.

Soon he came to his studio gate, but it was blocked from inside and he could not enter. Suspicious that something had gone wrong, he leapt over a place where the wall had crumbled. The studio door would not open either. He tiptoed to a window and peeped in to see a frightful demon with green face and jagged, sawlike teeth. It spread a human skin on the bed, and painted the skin with color-dipped brushes. That done, the demon threw the brushes aside, lifted the skin and shook the wrinkles out as if it were a piece of clothing. The demon pulled the skin over its body and changed instantly into a young woman.

The scholar slunk away from the studio on all fours, greatly frightened at what he had seen. He ran to see the Taoist, who was nowhere to be found. He went searching everywhere and finally came upon him in a field. There he knelt upright and begged to be saved.

The Taoist said: "With your leave I will drive the monster away. But it has to suffer greatly before it can find someone to take its place. I really can't bear to kill it." With this he handed the scholar a fly-whisk, instructing him to hang it above the door to his bedroom. Before parting, they arranged to meet at the Blue Emperor Temple.

When he returned, the scholar did not dare to enter the studio, so he slept in an inner chamber and hung the whisk over the door. A short time into the second watch of the night, muted sounds could be heard outside. Not daring to look himself, the scholar had his wife Chen peek out. She saw the girl come toward the door and then stop short at the sight of the whisk. She stood there grinding her teeth for quite some time and then left. In a short while she returned and stormed: "That Taoist is trying to scare me off. But don't tell me I should spit out what has come into my mouth!"

She pulled down the whisk and tore it to pieces, battered down the door and came into the room. Jumping right onto the scholar's bed, she tore a gash into his chest, ripped out his heart and ran away with it. Chen wailed. A maid came in and held up a candle: the scholar was already dead. Blood from his chest cavity was splattered everywhere. Chen sniveled in terror, not daring to sob out loud. The next day she had the scholar's second brother run to tell the Taoist.

The Taoist exploded: "I took pity on that ghost, but still it had the gall to do such a thing!" He followed the scholar's brother home, but the girl had disappeared. The Taoist lifted his head and looked upwards in all directions. "Luckily she isn't hiding far from here," he exclaimed, and then asked, "Whose house is that in the south courtyard?"

"I live there," said the second brother.

"She's in your place now," said the Taoist.

This startled the second brother, but he was not convinced.

The Taoist asked, "Has anyone you don't know been here?"

"I went to the Blue Emperor Temple this morning, so I have no idea. I'll go back and ask." The young man left and returned in a short while to say: "There was someone. An old woman came this morning asking for work as a household servant. My wife discouraged her, but she is still there."

"It's her all right," said the Taoist. He and the second brother went to the latter's house. He stood in the middle of the courtyard holding a wooden sword and cried, "Pay me back for my whisk, you hideous fiend!" The old woman's face blanched with panic when she heard his voice. She ran through the gate, trying to escape. The Taoist caught up with her and struck. The old woman fell flat, her human skin peeled away, and she changed into a fearsome demon that lay there bellowing like a pig. The Taoist dealt a death blow, skewered its head with his wooden sword and held it up in the air. The body changed into dense vapor that whirled into a single mass on the ground. The Taoist brought out his bottle gourd, uncorked it, and placed it in the smoke. There was the sound of a mouth sucking in breath, and in the wink of an eye the smoke was gone. The Taoist corked the gourd and put it in his pouch. Everyone stared at the human skin, which was complete with arms, legs and finely detailed eyes. The Taoist rolled it up with a sound like rolling up a scroll painting, then put it too into his pouch, after which he said good-bye and started to leave. The scholar's wife Chen bowed before him at the gate, beg-

ging in tears for a spell that would bring her husband to life. The Taoist apologized that it was beyond him. She was even more stricken and laid on the ground, refusing to get up. The Taoist pondered this and said, "My powers are insufficient to raise the dead. But I will recommend a man who may be able to. Go and ask him, and maybe things will work out."

"Who is he?"

"There is a madman in the market who often lies on piles of refuse. Try asking his advice and imploring his help. Do not be angry if he insults you in his madness." The second brother, too, had heard of the madman. Thereupon he took leave of the Taoist and went to the market with his sister-in-law. They found the beggar singing loonily in the street. Snot dangled in a long string from his nose, and he was unapproachably filthy. Chen approached him on her knees.

The beggar laughed: "So the beauty loves me, does she?" Chen told him what had happened. He howled again with laughter, saying: "Any man could be your husband. Why bring *him* to life?" Chen would not give up her entreaties. "How strange! Her man dies, and she begs *me* to give back his life. Am I Yama, king of the underworld?" In a fit of anger he struck Chen with his staff. Chen steeled herself against the pain and took the beating. The crowd in the street gathered round so closely that the two were walled in. The beggar hacked up phlegm until it filled his cupped hand, then held it up to Chen's face, saying: "Eat it."

Chen's face flushed and grimaced with reluctance, but thinking of the Taoist's instructions, she forced it down. As it entered her throat, it felt hard like compacted fuzz. It slid slowly down into her chest and clotted firm.

The beggar howled with laughter: "Oh, the beauty loves me!" He rose and walked away without looking back. She trailed him till he went into a temple and went right in after him, but could not see where he had gone. Though she searched everywhere in the gloom, there was no sign of him. There was nothing to do but walk through the crowd in embarrassment and return home. Grieving at her husband's horrible death and burning with the humiliation of eating phlegm, she was racked by such sobs of misery she wanted to die then and there.

The time came to drain the blood and put the corpse in its coffin. The servants looked on stock still, not daring to approach. Chen embraced the corpse and put its vitals back into the abdomen, wailing as she got them tidy. When her wails reached their highest pitch her voice gave way: suddenly she felt like vomiting. The clotted thing that had settled on her diaphragm churned suddenly upwards and out. Before she could turn her head it had landed in the corpse's chest cavity. There before her amazed eyes was a human heart, jumping with rhythmic beats and giving off a warm, steamy vapor. She was awestruck. She quickly closed the cavity with her hands and squeezed the body with all her strength. When she relaxed her embrace slightly, a breath of warmth issued from the opening. At this she tore plain silk into strips and hastily wrapped them around the torso. The corpse gradually became warm to the touch of her caressing hand. She put a cover over it. In the middle of the night she lifted the cover for a look: breath was coming from her husband's nostrils. In the morning he came to life.

"I was senseless, as if in a dream," he told them. "All I could feel was a burning pain in my chest." They looked for the gash but saw only a coin-sized scab. Even this soon healed.

The Chronicler of the Tales comments: "How foolish are the people of this world! That which is clearly bewitching they think beautiful. How deluded are the fools of this world! What is clearly trustworthy they think absurd. And as for those who net the beauties they adore, their wives must bear the shame of eating what others have disgorged. The way of heaven is reciprocity, but foolish, deluded people do not wake up. Is this not a pity?!"

"Ghost-Girl Xiaoxie"

The mansion of Ministry Secretary Jiang in Weinan was haunted by a large number of supernatural beings that misled people. Because of this the Jiang family moved away, leaving an old man to watch the gate. This man died, as did several others that were sent to take his place, so the house was deserted. In the same neighborhood lived a scholar named Tao Wangsan, a carefree, self-assured sort, who enjoyed the companionship of courtesans but always left them when the drinking was over. Some friends had a courtesan follow him to his place. He let her in with a smile but did not lay a hand on her all night. Once while staying overnight at the secretary's mansion, he earned a high place in his host's estimation by firmly refusing the advances of a maid who went to him at night.

Tao lived in dire poverty. Moreover, he had just been bereaved of his wife, and his tiny thatched hut was unbearably hot in sweltering summer. For these reasons he asked the secretary if he might make use of the vacant mansion. The secretary refused because of the hauntings. This inspired the scholar to write an essay entitled "Further Arguments on the Non-Existence of Ghosts" and present it to the secretary with the comment: "What can a ghost do to me?"

At last the secretary gave in to his determined requests, and the scholar went there to clean up and move into one of the rooms. At dusk he set down a book and went out to bring in some other things. When he came back the book was gone. Baffled by this turn of events, he lay quietly on his bed looking at the ceiling and waiting for what would happen next. After the duration of a meal he heard footsteps. Looking out of the corner of his eyes, he saw two young women coming from an inner chamber and replacing the missing book on the desk. One was about twenty and the other seventeen or eighteen. Both of them were beautiful. They walked hesitantly to the side of his bed and exchanged grins. The scholar kept quiet and did not stir. The older girl raised her foot and planted it on the scholar's belly: the younger one covered her mouth with her hand to stifle a giggle. The scholar felt himself wavering: he made a sober effort to straighten his thoughts and succeeded in turning his eyes away. The girl came closer and stroked his whiskers with her left hand as she patted his cheek with her right, which caused the younger to laugh all the more. The scholar leapt up and shouted, "How dare you ghosts behave this way?"

The two girls ran off in fright. The scholar feared they would bother him at night and wanted to move back home, but he felt ashamed not to back up his words with deeds, so he lit a lamp and stayed up reading. Spectral forms flitted about in the dark, but he did not ever glance at them. When it was almost the middle of the night, he went to bed with a candle burning. The minute his eyelids shut he felt someone poking a fine object into his nose. The exceedingly itching sensation was too much for him: he let loose with a mighty sneeze, which was answered by muffled laughter from a dark corner. Saying nothing, he pretended to be asleep and waited for them to try again. Soon he saw the younger girl roll a slip of paper into the shape of a toothpick and then come toward him, placing each foot carefully like a crane and crouching like an egret. He leapt up and railed at her. She floated into hiding. Again he lay down, and this time she stuck something in his ear. He had to put up with these torments the whole night.

At cockcrow the sounds finally died down, and the scholar slept soundly. He saw and heard nothing of the girls all day, but at sundown they were there before he knew it. That night he started a cooking fire, intending to stay up until morning. The older girl gradually approached, leaned her forearm against the table and watched him read. Without warning she reached over and closed his book. He grabbed angrily at her, but she had already floated out of reach. A little while passed, and again she flipped it shut, so he pressed down on the book with his hands as he read. Before long the younger girl stole up behind him, put her hands over his eyes, darted away and stood at a distance giggling.

The scholar shook his finger at her and scolded, "You little imp! It will be all over for you when I catch you."

This did nothing to deter them, so he said playfully: "I don't know the first thing about riding young fillies in bed, so what's the use of pestering me?" The two girls grinned and turned toward the stove, where they set to work splitting firewood, rinsing rice and doing the cooking for him. He looked up and praised them: "Now isn't this better than the idiotic way you were acting?"

Soon the rice gruel was done, and they raced to set chopsticks, a spoon and earthenware bowl on the desk. "How can I show my gratitude for your helpfulness?"

"No need. We mixed arsenic and essence of falcon feathers with your rice."

"There has never been any ill-will between us," he said. "I don't think you would do that to me?" When his bowl was empty, they filled it again: they ran back and forth trying to outdo one another in helpfulness. He enjoyed their attentions and grew accustomed to them. As time passed they became more familiar, until one day he invited them to sit down for a talk and asked their names.

"My name is Qiurong and my surname is Qiao: she is Xiaoxie of the Ruan family," said the older.

When he inquired into their backgrounds, Xiaoxie said laughingly: "Silly man. Why should you ask about our families when you haven't shown your true feelings toward us. Are you thinking about marriage?"

"Do you think I am so unfeeling as to be unmoved by your beauty?" he asked earnestly. "But any man who is touched by dark, supernatural forces must die. If you don't like living with me, you can leave. If you like living with me, it's all right to stay. If you don't care for me, why should two nice girls like you lower yourselves? If you do have love in your heart, why would you wish to cause the death of a book-crazed scholar?"

Visibly moved, the two girls exchanged glances. From then on they were less forward in their playfulness. Still they sometimes slipped their hands under his shirt or pulled down his pants, but he did not let it bother him. One day he got up from a book he was in the middle of copying and went out. On his return he found

Xiaoxie hunched over the desk, writing brush in hand, copying for him. Seeing him, she threw down the brush and laughed, looking at him with sidelong glances. He took a close look: her characters were too ill-formed to be called calligraphy, but the lines were evenly spaced.

"You are a woman of refinement," he praised her. "If you enjoy this, I'll teach you." He took her on his lap and guided her hand to show her how to make the strokes. When Qiurong came into the room her face fell abruptly, obviously out of jealousy.

Xiaoxie laughed and said, "I learned calligraphy from my father when I was little, but I haven't practiced for ages, so it feels like it's coming back to me in a dream." Qiurong said nothing. The scholar sensed what she felt but, pretending not to notice, he set her on his lap, handed her a brush and said, "Let me see if you can do it."

She wrote several characters and got up. "Miss Qiurong wields a mighty pen!" was his comment, which brightened Qiurong's face.

The scholar thereupon folded a piece of paper, tore it into halves and wrote model characters on each one for them to copy while he went to read under another lamp, secretly relieved that they would stop bothering him now they had something to keep them busy. When they were done copying, they stood respectfully before the desk waiting for his comments. Qiurong had never learned to recognize characters, and her scribbling was undecipherable. When he finished making a few offhand corrections, a humiliated look came over her face as she realized she was not Xiaoxie's rival, but the scholar's praise and reassurance finally cleared the clouds on her brow.

From then on the two girls treated the scholar as their teacher. When he sat they scratched his back; when he lay down they massaged his thighs. Far from affronting him, they vied to please. After a month Xiaoxie was writing in an unexpectedly neat and elegant hand, for which he occasionally praised her. Qiurong was sorely abashed: her rouge and mascara were streaked with trickling tears that would not stop until the scholar went to great lengths to reassure her. To make her feel better, he taught her to read and found her to possess remarkable powers of comprehension. Once he had pointed something out, she never needed to ask a second time. Often she stayed up all night trying to outread the scholar.

Xiaoxie also brought her third brother to bow before the scholar and become his student. He was fifteen or sixteen years old and well-favored in face and bearing. His gift to his teacher was an as-you-will sceptre of gold. The scholar assigned him the same classic that Qiurong was studying. Soon the hall was filled with reciting voices: the scholar had founded a private school for ghosts. The ministry secretary was delighted by the news of this and began to pay him a regular salary. After several months Qiurong and third brother were accomplished in poetry and frequently presented poems to each other. Xiaoxie secretly told the scholar not to teach Qiurong: he agreed not to. When Qiurong told him to stop teaching Xiaoxie, he assented to her too.

The day came when the scholar left to take part in an examination. The girls sniffed and tears ran down their cheeks as they said their farewells.

"Maybe you should ask to be excused from this examination on grounds of illness," said third brother. "Otherwise, I'm afraid you will land in an unfortunate predicament."

The scholar considered it degrading to ask for leave on account of illness, so he went anyway. Prior to this the scholar, who was fond of writing topical poems in a satirical vein, had offended a nobleman in the district, who brooded daily over how he could retaliate. He secretly bribed the civil examiner to have Tao thrown in prison on a trumped-up charge of misconduct. The scholar ran out of pocket money and was forced to beg for food from other prisoners. He had already resigned himself to death when suddenly a person appeared out of nowhere in his cell. It was Qiurong. She set dishes of food before him, gave him a long sorrowful look and quavered: "Third brother's fear that you would come to harm was well-founded. He and I came together: now he is going to the governor's *yamen* to lodge an appeal." She slipped out unnoticed after speaking only these few words.

The next day when the governor went out, third brother stopped him in the street crying "Injustice!" The governor agreed to read his appeal.

After appearing in the prison to let the scholar know of third brother's plan, Qiurong had gone back to watch the outcome. Three days went by without her showing up again. For the scholar, helplessness and the misery of hunger made each day pass like a year. Suddenly Xiaoxie appeared in his cell in great anguish and said, "On her way back Qiurong passed through the shrine to the City-God. The Black Judge of the Western Corridor abducted her and tried to force her to be his chambermaid, but she would not give in, so now she too is in captivity. I ran the hundred *li* here so fast I nearly dropped. When I reached the northern wall the sole of my foot was punctured by a nasty thorn. The pain went right through to the marrow of my bones. I'm afraid I won't be able to come again." She showed him her foot covered with crimson blood, then pulled out three taels of gold, hobbled away, and disappeared.

Meanwhile the governor, having ascertained that third brother lacked even a tenuous relationship with the accused and was making an appeal for no good reason, ordered his men to beat him with staffs only to see him dive to the ground and disappear. The amazed governor read the written appeal which the strange visitant had just given him and was touched by the content and the manner of writing. He had the scholar brought out for questioning and asked "Who is this third brother?" The scholar pretended not to know. The governor realized the injustice of the sentence and released him.

The whole evening of the scholar's return passed without anyone coming. It was late in the night before Xiaoxie finally came and reported gloomily: "Third brother was seized by a corridor spirit in the governor's *yamen* and taken to the underworld court. The king of the underworld sent him to be reborn into a rich family in consideration of his commendable deeds. I submitted a statement to the city god speaking out against Qiurong's undue detainment, but the case was pigeonholed and I was not given an audience. Now what can I do?"

The scholar flew into a rage and spluttered, "Who does that black fiend think he is, taking liberties like this? Tomorrow I'm going to knock his image over and grind it to mud under my feet. While I'm at it I'll give that city god a piece of my mind for letting his underlings get out of hand like this. Is he off in some drunken dream or what?"

The two of them sat there sharing their indignation and sorrow. Before they knew it the fourth watch was nearly at an end. Suddenly Qiurong appeared out of thin air. When they had gotten over their joyful surprise, they pressed her to tell them all that had happened.

Tears ran down Qiurong's face as she said, "I suffered terribly because of you! The judge threatened me with knives and clubs every day, but today he suddenly let me go. He said, 'I only behaved as I did out of my tender feelings for you. But you were unwilling, and anyway I did not molest you. Please convey that fact to Tao, who is foreordained to be minister of punishments, and ask him not to reproach me.' "

The scholar was elated by this and found himself wishing he could sleep with her. "Today I want to die in your arms," he said.

The two women answered glumly: "Now that you have opened our eyes for us, we know a little something about right and wrong. We could not bear it if what we did to show our love caused you to die."

They persisted in refusing, but they submissively bowed their heads with wifelike tenderness. The difficulties they had gone through had completely done away with their feelings of jealousy.

One day as the scholar walked along the road he met a Taoist priest who turned to him and said, "You are giving off a ghost aura." Because the Taoist's manner of speaking was so extraordinary, the scholar told him everything. The Taoist said, "These ghosts are too good to let down."

With this he wrote out two paper charms and gave them to the scholar, saying: "When you get home give one to each ghost, and let fate decide who will be the lucky one. The moment you hear a funeral procession for a young woman outside your gate, have the ghosts swallow the charms and run out. The one who gets there first will come to life."

The scholar took the charms with a bow, returned home and relayed the instructions to the girls. Sure enough, a little more than a month later they heard the sound of people mourning the death of a young woman in their family. The two girls raced to the spot. Xiaoxie was so flustered that she forgot to swallow her charm. As the hearse passed by, Qiurong ran straight to it, jumped into the coffin and disappeared. Xiaoxie, who was unable to find a way in, sobbed miserably and turned back. The scholar went out for a look and found that it was a funeral procession for a daughter of the wealthy Hao family. Everyone present had seen a girl jump through the top of the coffin and disappear. Now, while they gaped in bewilderment, a voice was heard from within the coffin. The bearers took the coffin off their shoulders and opened it for a look. The girl had come back to life. They put her down outside the scholar's studio and formed a circle around her. The girl opened her eyes with a start and asked for the scholar. In response to Mr. Hao's questions she answered, "I am not your daughter."

Then she told him the truth, but this was not enough to convince Hao, who wanted to have her carried back to his house. The girl refused to go: instead, she darted into the scholar's studio, lay down, and would not rise. Whereupon Hao acknowledged the scholar as his son-in-law and left. The scholar went to her and took a good look: her features were different, but this face was no less radiantly beautiful than Qiurong's own. This was a joyful blessing beyond his expectations. He was making an earnest declaration of his everlasting affection

when they were interrupted by a muffled ghostly sobbing—it was Xiaoxie crying in a dark corner. Pitying her from the depths of his heart he picked up the lamp, walked over to her and spoke eloquent words of consolation. Still the sleeves and front of her blouse were soaked with tears, and nothing he said could relieve her misery. She did not leave until near dawn. At daybreak Hao, every bit the new father-in-law, sent maids and serving women with dowry chests. That night when the scholar walked through the bedroom curtain, Xiaoxie started crying again. This went on every night for a week. Husband and wife were so affected by her dismal presence that they could not consummate their marriage. The scholar worried over the matter, but he could not come up with a solution.

"That Taoist priest is surely an immortal," said Qiurong. "If you go and plead with him, he might take pity on her and save her."

This seemed sensible to the scholar. He trailed the Taoist to where he was staying, kowtowed to him and stated his reason for coming. The Taoist protested that he had "no magical abilities," but the scholar would not give up his distraught pleading.

"This foolheaded scholar won't give a person a moment's peace. I suppose there is a bond of fate between us. All right, I'll do whatever lies within my power."

He went home with the scholar, asked for a quiet room and warned that he was not to be disturbed. Then he closed the door behind him and assumed a sitting position. For over ten days he did not eat or drink. Peeking in on him, they saw that he was deep in a trance. One morning as they were getting up a young woman parted the curtains and entered. The radiance of her bright eyes and gleaming teeth shone into their eyes.

"I've been trudging the whole night through," she said with a little laugh, "and now I am utterly worn out! You would not leave me alone, so I had to run myself ragged: I was a hundred *li* from here before I found a nice bodily dwelling. She is coming with the Taoist. When she shows up, he will turn her over to you."

As dusk closed in that evening, Xiaoxie appeared. The strange girl jumped up and ran to embrace her. Their outlines overlapped and then merged into a single body which fell stiffly on the floor. The Taoist came out of his room, joined his hands before his chest, and turned to leave. The scholar bowed to him and saw him off. When he came back in, the girl had regained consciousness. He helped her onto the bed. As she rested the circulation of vital energy through her body was gradually restored, but she clutched at her legs and moaned of sharp muscular pain in her feet and thighs. Several days passed before she was on her feet.

Later the scholar went up for examinations and won a place on the roster of prospective officials. A fellow examinee named Cai Zijing visited him on some matter or other and stayed several days. When Cai caught sight of Xiaoxie returning from next door, he ran over to her and practically trod on her heels. Xiaoxie turned away and ran from the room, seething inwardly at his rashness. Cai turned and unburdened himself to the scholar: "There is something on my mind which could be a shock to people who hear of it. Can I confide in you?"

The scholar questioned him until he let it out: "Three years ago my little sister died young. Two nights later her body disappeared. To this day this remains a mystery to me. I saw your wife just now, and I wonder how she came to bear such a startling resemblance to my sister?"

The scholar answered jokingly, "My wife is homely, how can she compare with your sister? But since you are my fellow candidate and my close friend, there could not be any harm in introducing my wife to you."

With this he entered the inner chamber and had Xiaoxie dress in her burial clothes to greet the guest.

"She really is my sister," Cai exclaimed in great astonishment. Tears began to run down his face. The scholar then told him the whole story. Cai howled gleefully: "My sister is still alive! I must hurry home and give my parents the comfort of knowing she is alive." And so he left. After a few days the whole family came, and afterward they exchanged visits with the scholar just as the Hao family did.

The Chronicler of the Tales comments: "To find one matchless beauty is no easy matter, not to speak of two at once! This is something that only happens once every few thousand years, and then only to a man who can keep himself from running off with whatever woman is available. Was the Taoist priest an immortal? What made his magic so powerful? With the right magic, hideous ghouls can be worth befriending."

Confessions of a Ghost

According to Confucius's pupils, the master did not discuss strange marvels, the use of force, chaos and disorder, or spirits (*Analects* 7.20). While Confucius nonetheless spoke of spirits in the context of ritual, he never indulged in ghost stories such as those included in Yüan Mei's (1716–1798) *What the Master Did Not Discuss (Tzu pu yü)*. A distinguished writer, poet, and literary critic, Yüan is also well known for this collection of tales of the unnatural and the uncanny. The anecdotes of this compilation, although perhaps reworked in Yüan's own style, are purportedly based on actual incidents he heard personally from friends or gathered from contemporary literature. Yüan was from an educated family, and two of his sisters were also accomplished poets; he himself supported the education of women poets and helped publish their works. His garden park in Nanking, which he claimed was the prototype of Prospect Garden in Ts'ao Hsüeh-ch'in's (1715–1763) *The Story of the Stone*, became a center of literary activity in that southern city.

"Ch'ang-ko Complains of a Grievance," a selection from Yüan Mei's *What the Master Did Not Discuss*, is purportedly based on an actual criminal legal case recorded in the Peking Gazette *(T'ang-pao)*. The Gazette is not a specific periodical; it is a general term for a kind of informational news literature of official and imperial documents and rescripts compiled in the capital of Peking and distributed to officials in the provinces. They were printed by government sources and were also reprinted by private presses, who profited from the sales of these documents to a local market of both government personnel and private individuals. Yüan Mei claims to have learned of the Ch'ang-ko incident from this type of source; in terms of style the story resembles actual legal cases, and it is not unlikely that Yüan's claim is true. Even if it were based only on hearsay, however, the case nevertheless reveals popularly accepted beliefs in the power of the dead to manifest themselves in the realm of the living.

The case begins with the theft of antiques from one of the pavilions in Ching Shan, or Red Hill, an imperial garden park in the capital also known as Coal Hill, or Mei Shan. When called in for questioning, the suspect Chao Erh "confesses": that is, the spirit of Ch'ang-ko, the murdered boy, possesses Chao Erh and speaks through him. Ch'ang-ko's family was Manchu, for he states that he belonged to the Plain Yellow Banner, one of the eight main groups of Manchu society, which was organized under banner colors. The Manchu were a Jürchen people of the northeast who ruled China throughout the Ch'ing period (1644–1911).

As was usual in homicides meriting the death penalty, the case is reported by the Board of Punishments to the emperor with the board's recommendations for appropriate punishment. In applying the letter of the law to a case not specifically included in the vast range of rules and regulations of the Ch'ing dynasty legal codes, the board was required to support its judgments according to the closest possible regulations and precedents, and here it considers both the articles on homicide and on voluntary surrender. Many cases of homicide resulted in death by strangulation or decapitation, but penalties could be reduced by certain mitigating circumstances, one of which was voluntary surrender: if culpable persons voluntarily surrendered themselves to the authorities and confessed, they might be granted a more lenient sentence. The board initially considers reducing Chao Erh's punishment because he confessed to the crime, but then decides that it was not a voluntary confession by the culprit at all but was a plaint presented by the ghost of the murdered boy. The board's legal decisions are thus informed by beliefs articulated as early as the *Tso chuan*, which claimed that wraiths of persons who have been the victims of violence will linger about human beings and cause their deaths.

"Ch'ang-ko Complains
of a Grievance"

On the third day of the eighth month of the sixteenth year of Ch'ien-lung [September 21, 1751], I read in the Peking Gazette about the disappearance of several antiques from Ching Shan. The officials of the Imperial Household suspected that dirt carriers had stolen the articles, so they called in several tens of workers and had them stand for questioning. During the questioning, one of the workers suddenly knelt and said: "My name is Ch'ang-ko. I am a bannerman of the Plain Yellow Banner. I am twelve years old. One day when I went to the market to shop, a worker by the name of Chao Erh tried to force me to commit sodomy. When I refused, he killed me with a knife and buried me in a charcoal yard outside the Hou-tsai Gate. My parents still do not know what has happened to me. Master, please dig out my corpse, examine it, and help me to right the wrong."

Upon finishing the above utterance, the worker fell prostrate on the ground. But after a short while he again leaped to his feet and said: "I am Chao Erh. It is I who killed Ch'ang-ko."

Observing his behavior, the officials of the Imperial Household realized that some injustice had taken place, so they transferred Chao Erh to the custody of the Board of Punishments. The corpse was subsequently exhumed and the examination revealed that the alleged wounds were clearly present. The Board of Punishments' officials then paid a visit to the parents of Ch'ang-ko. They said that their son had indeed been missing for one month and they did not know that he had died. The officials from the Board of Punishments then arrested and tried Chao Erh, who gave a true and complete account of the homicide.

The Board of Punishments presented a palace memorial to the emperor, saying that the offender, Chao Erh, had himself revealed the details of the offense. The board pointed out that the facts of Chao's case are close to the factual situation that would constitute voluntary surrender, so that according to the precedents he should be granted a reduction in punishment. The board, however, went on to say that since Chao's confession was actually forced from him by the suffering ghost, it would be improper to adhere to such precedents. The board therefore recommended that Chao be punished with immediate decapitation. An imperial rescript was subsequently received ordering that the case be handled as recommended by the Board of Punishments.

The Story of the Stone

Generally acknowledged as the most philosophically profound of China's novels, *The Story of the Stone* recounts the declining fortunes of a fabulously wealthy aristocratic clan, the house of Jia (Chia). Virtually the entire narrative takes place within the confines of the walled space of the family villas and their adjoining park, Prospect Garden. The wider scope of the narrative, however, is expressed through a dialectical progression between reality and unreality that leads to eventual disenchantment and enlightenment: the surname Jia is itself a homophone for the character meaning "unreal." Created by Ts'ao Hsüeh-ch'in (Cao Xueqin, 1715–1763), himself from an affluent family whose prosperity was dissolved by political misfortune, the novel is considered to be somewhat autobiographical in nature.

The main character of the novel is a stone of jade that has been given human life and is now the young scion of the Jia family named Bao-yu (Pao-yü), or "Precious Jade." He is unlikely to enhance the family fortunes by succeeding in the civil service examinations, for he rejects the by-now mannered Confucian educational curriculum in favor of poetry contests in Prospect Garden. The park and its small pavilions and cottages serve as a residence for Bao-yu and his female cousins and maidservants, and he prefers eating their lipstick to studying the works of Mencius. Sexually androgynous, Bao-yu is an emotionally sensitive free spirit entirely unsuited to the task of becoming the future family patriarch and is incapable of emulating the cruelty and insensitivity of his forebears. Like Chuang Tzu's Hun-tun, who dies when others try to bore the norms of conformity into him, Bao-yu eventually "dies," at least in spirit, under his family's attempts to make him conform to social expectations: when he reaches adulthood, they deceive him into marrying a woman who is a paragon of Confucian virtues. Bao-yu, not unexpectedly, goes mad.

The *Story of the Stone* records the day-to-day lives of the Jia family and its servants, and it thus provides insights into the values held by both rich and poor. These two selections from the novel reveal the multiplicity of religious beliefs and attitudes that the various members of the household express toward one particular event: the death of Bao-yu's beloved maid Skybright, which occurs while Bao-yu is yet an adolescent. Because of some improprieties Skybright allegedly committed with Bao-yu, the family elders unjustly eject her from their employ and return her to her callous cousins, her only known relatives, knowing she will die of consumption within a few days. Skybright does die, but a little maid, wanting to console Bao-yu, has falsely told him that Skybright on her deathbed said she was not actually dying but was assuming a post in heaven as a flower official in charge of hibiscus blossoms.

All too ready to believe the maid, Bao-yu composes an elegy and performs a small ceremony in Skybright's memory to invoke her spirit, and the first selection from the novel records his invocation to Skybright, now addressed as the Hibiscus Fairy. Considerably more artful than Chu Hsi's prayer to Confucius and Mencius, Bao-yu's elegy characteristically turns social norms upside down: the hierarchy of master and servant is reversed as the noble son of a powerful family makes obeisance to the spirit of a poor serving maid. Implicitly critical of his mother and father, Bao-yu's text reveals no filial piety. The elegy contains hints of a curse that Skybright's angry spirit, like the wraith of Po-yu from the *Tso chuan,* will return to the family to avenge her unjust expulsion from the Jia house. At the conclusion of the rite, the little maid who attended Skybright at her deathbed falls for her own story and fears the Hibiscus Fairy has actually appeared; it turns out only to be Bao-yu's cousin and love, Dai-yu (Tai-yü).

The second selection relates the exorcism of the Hibiscus Fairy from Prospect Garden and takes place some time later. By now the family fortunes have begun to decline at the adjoining family villas, the Ning-guo and Rong-guo mansions. The Imperial Concubine, a woman of the family who had been one of the emperor's consorts, has passed away and thus left the family bereft of a valuable political connection. Bao-yu is married to the Confucian paragon Bao-chai (Pao-ch'ai) and is no longer in command of his senses; the other occupants of Prospect Garden have grown up and no longer frequent the place as before. When a member of the family becomes ill after walking through the grounds, spirit-possession is diagnosed as the cause of her malaise.

The ensuing consultation with Half-Immortal Mao reveals how the *Book of Changes* was used for divination; Mao's arcane prognostications are initially received rather skeptically but the diviner gradually convinces his audience. The belief that Skybright has become a flower sprite takes on greater and greater credence, and Prospect Garden is locked shut. Shortly before her death, Skybright had been seriously mistreated by her cousin Wu Gui, and when Wu Gui dies unexpectedly, the Jia family fears Skybright's avenging spirit. Jia She, Baoyu's uncle, calls for an exorcism, an exercise considered laughable by some members of the family. While not everyone believes in the efficacy of the Taoist rite, however, few doubt the sprite's power, and the garden remains uninhabited. The reactions of even the scholarly patriarchs of the family, who react to the hauntings with both disdain and fear, reveal the ambiguities and uncertainties inherent in people's attitudes toward the spirit world.

The Invocation of the
Hibiscus Fairy

But Bao-yu was still grieving for Skybright. The sight of the hibiscus by the lake reminded him of what the little maid had told him about her. As he stood gazing sorrowfully at the bushes, an idea suddenly came to him.

"Since I wasn't able to see her in her coffin, why don't I pay my last respects to her here, in the presence of her flowers?"

He was on the point of kneeling down in front of them when another thought occurred to him.

"That's all very well, but I can't do it just anyhow. In order to show proper respect I must first make sure that I am dressed correctly. And I must prepare a little ceremony and make her some sort of offering."

This led to further cogitation.

"It says somewhere in the classics, 'Where there is faith enough and goodwill, duckweed boiled in puddle-water is an offering acceptable to the gods and a dish fit to be set before princes.' Proper respect evidently has nothing to do with the value of the offering. And I could always write something to read out before I made it."

He began to plan what he would write. "An elegy" it would be called. It would be a bit like one of those long Chu poems—*Li sao* or *The Summons of the Soul*—but with elements of other things as well. And of course a lot of it would be original. He sat down and began writing it as soon as he got back to his apartment. As it was to please himself, he could be as wild and extravagant as he liked and compose as quickly as his imagination would let him. Soon the draft was finished, and he took a piece of white material of the kind they call "mermaid silk," which he knew Skybright had been fond of, and after first writing the title on it in large characters:

THE SPIRIT OF THE HIBISCUS:
AN ELEGY AND INVOCATION

he copied out the text in a neat *kai-shu* hand and carried it with him into the Garden. The little maid who had told him about Skybright's transformation had to follow him with some things for the offering on a tray: a cup of tea, some autumn flowers in a vase of water, and some charcoal in a little burner for starting a fire with. When his solemn bowings and kneelings were over, he hung the silk up on the branches of a hibiscus and began tearfully to read out the words:

The year being one in the era of Immutable Peace, the month that in which the sweet odours of hibiscus and cassia compete, the day, a heavy and doleful day, I, most wretched and disconsolate JADE of the House of Green Delights, having with due reverence prepared and got together buds of flowers, silk of mermaids, water of the Drenched Blossoms stream and Fung Loo tea (all things of little value in themselves, yet sufficient to attest the devotion of a true believer) do here offer them up in sacrifice to her that has now, in the Palace of the White God, become SPIRIT OF THE HIBISCUS, having power and dominion over the flowers of autumn.

It is now sixteen years since the BLEST SPIRIT descended into the world of men. As to her native place and the lineage in which she was born, they were long since forgotten; but for five years and eight months of that time she was, in my rising up and lying down, in my washings and combings, in my rest and play, my constant close companion and helpmate.

It is to be recorded of her that in estimation she was more precious than gold or jade, in nature more pure than ice or snow, in wit more brilliant than the sun or stars, in complexion more beautiful than the moon or than flowers. Who of the maidens did not admire her accomplishments? Who among the matrons did not marvel at her sagacity?

But if baleful scritch-owls that hate the heights can cause the kingly eagle to be taken in a net, and rank and stinking weeds, envious of another's fragrance, can cause the sweet herb of grace to be uprooted, it is not to be thought that a shrinking flower could withstand the whirlwind's blast, or a tender willow-tree be proof against the buffetings of the tempest. When the envenomed tongue of slander was wagged against her, she pined inwardly with a wasting sickness: the red of her cherry lips faded and only sad and plaintive sounds issued out of them; the bloom of her apricot cheeks withered and none but lean and haggard looks were to be seen upon them.

Slanders and slights crept from behind every curtain; thorns and thistles choked up the doors and windows of her chamber. Yet truly she had done no infamous thing. She entered a silent victim into the eternal, a wronged innocent into the everlasting: a more notable martyr (though but a mere girl) to the envy of excellence than he who was drowned at Long Sands; a more pitiable sufferer from the peril of plain dealing than he that was slain upon Feather Mountain.

Yet since she stored up her bitterness in silence, none recognized the treasure that was lost in her, cut off so young. The fair cloud dispersed, leaving no means to trace the beauteous outline of its former shape. It were a hard thing to hunt out the Isle of the Blest from among the multitudinous islands of the ocean and bring back the immortal herb that should restore her: the raft is lost that went to look for it.

It was but yesterday that I painted those delicate smoke-black eyebrows; and who is there today to warm the cold jade rings for her fingers? The medicine she drank stands yet upon the stove; the tears are still wet on the garment she once wore. The phoenix has flown and MUSK'S vanity-box has burst apart for sorrow; the dragon has departed, and RIPPLE'S comb has broken its teeth for grief. The magpie has forsaken my chamber: it is in vain for the maidens to hang up their needles on Seventh Night and pray for nimble fingers. My buckle with the love-ducks is broken: the seamstress is no more who could repair the silk-work of its girdle.

And this being the season of autumn when the power of metal predominates and the White God is master of the earth, the signs themselves are melancholy. I wake from dreams of her on a lonely couch and in an empty room. As the moon veils herself behind the trees of the garden, the moonlight and the sweet form I dreamed of are in the same moment extinguished; as the perfume fades from the hangings of my bedchamber, the laboured breath and whispered words I strove to catch at the same time fall silent. Dew pearls the pavement's moss; the launderer's beat is borne in unceasingly through my casement. Rain wets the wall-fig; a flute's complaint carries uncertainly from a near-by courtyard.

Her sweet name is not extinguished, for the parrot in his cage under the eaves ceases not to repeat it; and the crabtree in my courtyard whose half-withering was a foretokening of her fate stands yet her memorial. But no more shall the sound of her lotus feet betray her at hide-and-seek behind the screen; no more will her fingers cull budding orchids for the game of match-my-flower in the garden. The embroidery silks are thrown aside in a tangle: never again will she cut them with her silver scissors. The sheeny silk lies creased and crumpled: never again shall her hot-iron smooth out its perfumed folds.

In her last hour, when I might else have gone to her, I was called in haste from the Garden by a Father's summons; when, grieving, I sought to take leave of her abandoned body, I could not see it because it had been removed by a Mother's command; and when I was told that her corpse had been consumed, I repented of my jesting vow that we should share the same grave-hole together, for that were now impossible, and that our ashes should commingle, for ash she is already become.

In the burning-ground by the old temple, green ghost-fires flicker when the west wind blows. On its derelict mounds, scattered bones gleam whitely in the setting sun. The wind sighs in the tall trees and rustles in the dried-up grasses below. Gibbons call sadly from tombs that are hidden in the mist, and ghosts flit weeping down the alley-ways between the tombs. At such times must the young man in his crimson-curtained bed seem most cruelly afflicted; at such times must the maiden beneath the yellow earth seem most cruelly ill-fated.

The tears of Ru-nan fall in bloody drops upon the wind, and the complaint of Golden Valley is made to the moon in silence. Vengeance is for demons and baleful bogles; the gentle spirits of maidens are not wont to be jealous, though wronged. Natheless shall the backbiters not lightly escape her; their mouths shall be squeezed in vices; the hearts of those cruel harridans shall be ripped: for her anger is kindled against them.

Though the bond between us was a slight one, yet can it not easily be broken; and because she was ever close to me in my thoughts, I could not forbear to make earnest inquiry concerning her. Thus it was revealed to me that the God had sent down the banner of his authority and summoned her to his Palace of Flowers, to the end that she who in life was like a flower should in death have dominion over the hibiscus. At first when I heard the words of the little maid touching this appointment, I thought them fantastical; but now that I have pondered them in my heart, I know them to be worthy of perfect credence. How so?

Did not Ye Fa-shan compel Li Yong's sleeping spirit to compose an epitaph? And was not the soul of Li He summoned in order that he might write a memorial in heaven? The circumstances may differ, but the principle is the same. God chooses his ministers according to their capabilities, else how could they discharge the duties that are required of them? And who more fit and meet than her to be given this charge that has been laid upon her? Truly, here at last she has a work that is worthy of her.

And because I would have her descend here in this place, I have composed these verses to invoke her with, fearing that the common speech of mortals might be offensive to her immortal ear. . . .

My mind is in a turmoil, uncertain whether I wake or dream. I gaze at the sky with sighs of disappointment; I wait in uncertainty with weeping eyes. My speech grows silent: only the music of the wind in the grove of bamboos is to be heard, and the wing-beats of birds as they fly off startled, and the plopping sounds of fish as they nibble at the surface of the water.

Blest Spirit, may my lament go up to thee; may my rite be acceptable to thee.

Wuhu aizai! Receive this offering!

When he had finished reading, he made a little flame with the burner and set fire to the silk. Then he poured the tea out on the ground as a libation, scattered the flowers, and emptied the water out of the vase. He continued to linger there after he had finished, as though unable to tear himself away, and the little maid had to remind him several times that they ought to be getting back. He had just started to go when a laughing voice called out "Stop a minute!" and the maid, turning to look behind her, saw with terror that a female form was stepping out of the bushes.

"Help!" she cried. "It's a ghost! Skybright's spirit really has come back!"

Bao-yu looked back too.

The Exorcism of the Garden

Prospect Garden, once home to such a distinguished little society of young ladies, had since the death of the Imperial Concubine been left to fall into gradual ruin. With Bao-yu's marriage, Dai-yu's death and the departure of Xiang-yun and Bao-qin, the number of residents was already sadly depleted. Then, when the cold weather set in, Li Wan, her cousins Li Qi and Li Wen, Xi-chun and Tan-chun had all moved out to their previous abodes and had only ever gathered together in the Garden to enjoy themselves on particularly fine days or moonlit nights. With Tan-chun no longer at home and Bao-yu still convalescing and confined indoors, there was scarcely anyone left to enjoy the Garden's delights. It became a desolate place, its paths frequented only by the handful of caretakers whom duty still obliged to live there.

On the day of Tan-chun's departure, You-shi had come across to Rong-guo House to see her off. It was getting late by the time she left for home, and she decided to save herself the trouble of taking a carriage by returning through the Garden, using the side gate that communicated with Ning-guo House. As she walked through the grounds she was forcibly struck by the aura of desolation that pervaded the place. The buildings were unchanged, but she noticed that a strip of land along the inside of the Garden wall had already been converted into some sort of vegetable plot. A deep sense of melancholy oppressed her spirit. When she reached home she immediately developed a fever, and though she fought it off for a couple of days eventually she had to retire to bed. During the daytime the fever was not unduly severe, but at night it became almost insupportable and she grew delirious and started babbling to herself. Cousin Zhen sent for a doctor at once, who pronounced that she had caught a chill, which had developed complications and had entered into the *yang-ming* stomach meridian. This accounted for her delirious babbling and hallucinations. She would recover once she had opened her bowels.

You-shi took two doses of the medicine the doctor prescribed, but showed no sign of improvement. If anything she became more deranged than before. Cousin Zhen was now seriously concerned and sent for Jia Rong:

"Get hold of the names of some good doctors in town and send for one immediately. We must have a second opinion."

"But the doctor who came the other day is extremely well thought of," objected Jia Rong. "It seems to me that in Mother's case medicine is of little use."

"How can you talk like that!" exclaimed Cousin Zhen. "If we don't give her medicine, what are we supposed to do? Just let her fade away?"

"I didn't say she couldn't be cured," said Jia Rong. "What was going through my mind was this: when Mother went over to Rong-guo House the other day, she came back through the Garden. And the fever began as soon as she reached home. It could be that she encountered some evil spirit on the way and is now possessed. I happen to know of an excellent fortune-teller in town, by the name of Half-Immortal Mao. He hails from the South, and is something of a specialist in *The Book of Changes*. I think we should ask him for a consultation first. See if he can shed any light on the matter. If that gets us nowhere, then let's by all means look for another doctor."

Cousin Zhen agreed, and they sent for the fortune-teller at once. When he arrived, he and Jia Rong sat down together in the study and after drinking his tea Half-Immortal Mao began the consultation proper:

"On what matter does my esteemed client wish me to consult the *Changes*?"

"It concerns my mother," said Jia Rong. "She has fallen ill. Could you please seek some illumination from the *Changes* on her behalf?"

"Very well," replied Mao. "First I shall require some clean water with which to wash my hands. Then, will you be so good as to light some incense, and to set up a small altar? And I shall proceed with the divination."

The servants carried out these instructions, and Mao extracted the divining cylinder from within his gown, approached the altar, and after making a profound reverence began shaking the cylinder, intoning the following prayer:

"In the name of the Supreme Ultimate, of the Yin and of the Yang, and of the Generative Powers of the Cosmos; in the name of the Holy Signs made manifest in the Great River, which embody the Myriad Transformations of the Universe, and of the Saints who in their wisdom leave no sincere request unheeded: here, in good faith, Mr Jia, on the occasion of his mother's illness, devoutly beseeches the Four Sages, Fu Xi, King Wen, the Duke of Zhou and Confucius, to look down from above and vouchsafe an efficacious response to this his earnest supplication. If evil lies hidden, then bring the evil to light; if good, then show the good. First we ask to be told the Three Lines of the Lower Trigram."

He turned the cylinder upside down and the coins fell onto the tray.

"Ah! Most efficacious: for the Prime we have a Moving Yin."

The second throw gave a Yang At Rest, the third another Moving Yin. $\frac{-X-}{-X-}$. Picking up the coins, Half-Immortal Mao said:

"The Lower Trigram has been communicated. Now let us ask to receive the Three Lines of the Upper Trigram, and thus complete the Hexagram."

These fell as follows: Yang At Rest, Yin At Rest, Yang At Rest. ⚏. Half-Immortal Mao replaced the cylinder and coins inside his gown, and sat down.

"Pray be seated," he said. "Let us consider

this in greater detail. We have here the sixty-

fourth Hexagram, 'Before Completion': ☲ ·

The Line of most significance to you and to your generation is the Tertian, with Fire at the Seventh Branch *Wu,* and the Signature 'Ruin.' This certainly indicates that Dire Misfortune lies in store. You have asked me to consult the *Changes* concerning your mother's illness, and great attention should therefore be paid to the parental Prime, which contains the Signature 'Spectre,' as does the Quintal. It would seem that your mother is indeed seriously afflicted. But all will still be for the best. The present misfortune is concatenated with Water at the First Branch *Zi* and at the Twelfth Branch *Hai;* but when this element wanes, with the Third Branch *Yin* comes Wood and thence Fire. The Signature 'Offspring' at the Tertian also counter-acts the Spectral influence, and with the regener-ative effect of the continuing revolution of both the solar and lunar bodies, in two days the 'Spectre' originally concatenated with Water at the First Branch *Zi* should be rendered void, and by the day *Xu* all will be well. But I see that the parental Prime contains further Spectral per-mutations. I fear your father may himself be afflicted. And your own personal Line has a severe concentration of 'Ruin.' When Water reaches its zenith and Earth its nadir, be prepared for misfortune to strike."

Mao sat back, thrusting his beard forward, as if to emphasize the authenticity of his prognosis.

At the beginning of this rigmarole it was all Jia Rong could do to keep a straight face. But gradually Mao impressed him as a man who knew what he was talking about, and when he went on to predict misfortune for Cousin Zhen, Jia Rong began to take him rather more seri-ously.

"Your exposition is certainly very learned," he commented. "But could you, I wonder, be more precise as to the nature of the illness that is afflicting my mother?"

"In the Hexagram," replied Mao, "Fire at the Seventh Branch *Wu* in the Prime changes to

Water and is thus controlled. This would indi-cate some inner congestion in which both cold and heat are combined. But I am afraid a precise diagnosis lies beyond the limitations of even a more elaborate milfoil reading of the *Changes.* For that, you would have to cast a Six Cardinal horoscope."

"Is that branch of divination one with which you are also conversant?" asked Jia Rong.

"To a certain extent," replied Mao.

Jia Rong asked him to cast the horoscope, and wrote down the relevant Stems and Branches. Mao proceeded to adjust his Diviner's Compass, setting the co-ordinates for the Heav-enly Generals. The reading obtained was: "White Tiger" at the Eleventh Branch *Xu.*

"This Configuration," said Mao, "is known as 'Dissolution of the Soul.' The 'White Tiger' is inauspicious, but is contained and prevented from doing injury when it occurs at a zenith of fortune. In this case, however, it is enveloped in a Mephitic Aura, and occurs at a seasonal passage where Confinement and Death predomi-nate; it is therefore a hungry tiger and sure to do harm. The effect is similar to the spiritual dispersion consequent upon extreme shock. Hence the name of the configuration, which represents a state of acute physical and mental alarm, of profound melancholy; in illness it foresees death, in litigation misfortune. The Ti-ger is seen approaching at sunset, which means the illness must have been contracted in the evening. The wording reads: 'In this configura-tion, a Tiger lies hidden in some old building, making mischief, or manifests itself in some more palpable way.'

"You are enquiring specifically about your parents. In a Yang or daylight environment, the Tiger afflicts the male, while in a Yin or night-time environment it afflicts the female. This configuration therefore bodes ill for both of your parents."

Jia Rong was stunned by this, and turned ashen pale.

"It all sounds very convincing," he said, before Mao could continue. "But it doesn't ex-actly tally with the Hexagram in *The Book of*

Changes. How dangerous is the situation, do you think?"

"Do not panic," said Mao. "Let me look into this a little more carefully."

He lowered his head in thought and mumbled to himself for a few moments. Then:

"All is well! We are saved! My Compass reveals a 'Delivering Spirit' at the Sixth Branch *Si*. In other words, what we have here is a 'Dissolution of the Soul' leading to a 'Restoration of the Spirit,' or Sorrow turning to Joy. There is therefore no real cause for concern. You should just exercise a little caution."

Jia Rong handed him his fee and saw him off the premises, before returning to report to his father:

"The fortune-teller says that Mother's illness was contracted towards evening in an old building, and was caused by an encounter with a White Tiger spirit emanating from a corpse."

"Didn't you say that she came back through the Garden the other evening?" said Cousin Zhen. "It must have been there that she ran into this thing. And didn't your aunt Feng go walking in the Garden too, and fall ill afterwards? She denied having encountered anything out of the ordinary, but the maids and serving-women all told a different story. They said she'd seen a hairy monster up on a hill, with eyes as big as lanterns, and that she'd even heard it talk. It gave your aunt Feng such a fright that she went running home, and immediately fell ill and took to her bed."

"Of course!" exclaimed Jia Rong. "I remember! And I heard Bao-yu's boy Tealeaf say that Skybright had turned into a Hibiscus Fairy. So she must be haunting the Garden, for a start. And when Cousin Lin died, music was heard in the air, so *she's* probably there somewhere too, looking after some other flower. Ugh! It makes your flesh creep, to think of all the sprites and fairies there must be cooped up in there! It used to be perfectly safe when there were plenty of people living there and the place had a feeling of life about it. But now it's so dashed lonely! When Mother went through, she probably trod on one of the flowers, or bumped into one of the fairies. It sounds as if Mao's Hexagram was on the mark all right."

"Did he talk of any real danger?" asked Cousin Zhen.

"According to him, by the day *Xu* all will be well. I must say, though, I hope his calculations don't turn out to be too accurate . . ."

"What do you mean?" asked Cousin Zhen.

"Well, if he's right, then there could be some trouble in store for you too, Father."

As they were talking, there came a cry from one of the serving-women in the inner apartments:

"Mrs Zhen insists on getting up and going to the Garden! The maids can't hold her down!"

Cousin Zhen and Jia Rong went in to pacify You-shi.

"The one in red is coming to get me!" she screamed deliriously. "The one in green is after me!"

The servants found her behaviour at once funny and frightening. Cousin Zhen despatched one of them to buy paper money, and burn it in the Garden. That night You-shi came out in a sweat and calmed down considerably, and by the day *Xu* she gradually started to recover.

Word soon spread that Prospect Garden was haunted, and the caretakers became too frightened to carry out their duties. Plants were left untended, trees unpruned, and all the flower-beds unwatered. No one dared walk around after dark, and as a result the resident wildlife began to make it their own domain. Things eventually got so bad that even in broad daylight the servants would enter the Garden only accompanied and armed with cudgels.

After a few days, Cousin Zhen fell ill as predicted. He did not send for a doctor. Whenever the illness permitted, he went to the Garden to pray and burn paper money; whenever it became severe, he uttered feverish prayers in his chamber. He recovered, and then it was Jia Rong's turn to go down; and after Jia Rong, the others, one by one. This continued for several months, and both households lived in constant fear. Even the slightest rustle or cry of a bird was suspect, and every plant or tree was feared to harbour a malicious spirit. Now that the Garden was abandoned and no longer productive, extra funds were needed again for the various apartments of the household, and this added to the already crushing deficit of Rong-guo House. The Garden's caretakers saw nothing to be gained by staying. They all wanted to leave the place, and invented a whole series of incidents to substantiate the presence of diabolical tree-imps and flower sprites. Eventually they achieved their goal: they were all evacuated, the garden gate was securely locked, and no one dared go in at all. Fine halls, lofty pavilions, elegant rooms and terraces became nothing more than nesting-places for birds and lairs for wild beasts.

Skybright's cousin, Wu Gui, lived, it will be remembered, opposite the rear gate-house of the Garden. It had reached the ears of Wu Gui's wife that Skybright, after her death, had become a flower fairy, and from then on she took the precaution of staying indoors every evening. One day Wu Gui went shopping and stayed out later than usual. His wife had caught a slight cold and during the day took the wrong medicine, with the result that when Wu Gui returned that evening he found her lying dead on the kang. Because of her reputation for promiscuity, other members of the household staff concluded that a sprite must have climbed over the Garden wall, enjoyed her at inordinate length, and finally "sucked the sap" out of her.

This incident put Grandmother Jia in a great tizzy. She increased the guard around Bao-yu's apartment and had it constantly watched and patrolled. Some of the younger maids subsequently claimed to have seen weird red-faced creatures lurking in the vicinity, while others testified to the presence of a strange female apparition of great beauty. Such rumours soon multiplied, and Bao-yu lived in mortal terror. Bao-chai was less easily taken in, and warned the maids that any more fear-mongering would bring them a good hiding. Although this quietened things down a bit, there was still an atmo-

sphere of great apprehension throughout both mansions, and more watchmen were taken on, which was an additional expense.

Jia She was the only one not to believe a word of it.

"There's nothing the matter with the Garden, for heaven's sake! Haunted! What an absurd notion!"

He waited for a warm day when there was a mild breeze, and went to inspect the Garden himself, accompanied by a large number of armed servants. They all advised him against going, but he would not listen. When they entered the Garden, the atmosphere was so dark and sinister, so oppressively Yin, that they could almost touch it. Jia She refused to turn back, and his servants reluctantly followed him in, with many a furtive and shrinking sideways glance. One young lad among them, already scared to death, heard a sudden "whoosh!" and turning to look saw something brightly coloured go flashing past. He uttered a terrified *"Aiyo!"* went instantly weak at the knees and collapsed on the ground. When Jia She looked back and stopped to question him, he replied breathlessly:

"I saw it with my own eyes! I did! A monster with a yellow face and a red beard, all dressed in green! It went up there, into that grotto behind those trees!"

Jia She was somewhat shaken himself.

"Did anyone else see this thing?"

Some of the servants decided to take advantage of the situation and replied:

"Clear as daylight, sir. You were up in front and we didn't want to alarm you, sir. So we tried to keep a grip on ourselves, and act as if nothing had happened."

Jia She now lacked the courage to go any further. He turned back and went home as quickly as possible, telling the boys who had accompanied him not to say anything about what had happened, but merely to let it be known that they had had an uneventful tour of the Garden. He himself needed no further convincing that the Garden was haunted, and began to think it might be advisable to apply to the Taoist

Pontificate for priests to perform an exorcism. His servants, meanwhile, who were by nature fond of making trouble, saw how frightened their master was, and far from concealing the episode, retailed it with a great deal of gusto and embellishment, creating quite a sensation and eliciting a good deal of open-mouthed astonishment.

In the end Jia She decided that there was no other recourse than to go ahead and hold a formal ceremony of exorcism. A suitable day in the almanac was chosen, and an altar was constructed in the Garden, on a dais in the main hall of the Reunion Palace. Images of the Three Pure Ones were set up, flanked by figures of the spirits presiding over each of the Twenty-Eight Constellations, and of the Four Great Commanders—Ma, Zhao, Wen and Zhou. Further down the hall, the sacred precinct was made complete with a diagrammatic representation of the Thirty-Six Heavenly Generals. The air was heavy with flowers and incense, the hall blazed with lanterns and candles. Bells, drums, liturgical instruments and other paraphernalia were arrayed along both sides of the hall, and emblematic banners were hoisted at each of the Five Cardinal Points (the Four Corners and the Centre). The Taoist Pontiff had delegated Forty-Nine Deacons for the ceremony, and they began by spending a whole day purifying the altar. Then three priests went the rounds of the hall, waving smoking bundles of joss-sticks and sprinkling holy water, and when this was done the great Drum of the Dharma thundered forth. The priests now donned their Seven Star Mitres and robed themselves in their chasubles emblazoned with the Nine Heavenly Mansions and the Eight Trigrams. Wearing Cloud-Mounting Pattens on their feet and holding ivory tablets in their hands, they addressed themselves in reverent supplication to the sages. For a full day they chanted the *Arcanum Primordii*, a text renowned for its efficacy in the dispelling of misfortune, the exorcizing of evil spirits and the general enhancement of propitious vibrations. Then they produced the Spirit Roll, which called on the

Heavenly Generals to be present. It was inscribed with the following large characters:

A SUMMONS
IN THE NAME
OF THE
THREE REALMS,
THE ULTIMATE, THE PRIMORDIAL, AND THE PURE;
IN THE NAME
OF THE
SUPREME PONTIFF
AND THE
TALISMANIC POWER VESTED IN HIM;
ALL BENEVOLENT SPIRITS OF THE REGION
ARE HEREBY CALLED TO THIS ALTAR
TO DO SERVICE

The menfolk of both Rong-guo and Ning-guo House had taken courage from the presence of the priests, and were gathered in the Garden to watch the demon-hunt.

"Most impressive!" they all agreed. "All those benevolent spirits and powers are bound to strike fear into the heart of even the most obdurate demon!"

They crowded in front of the altar to watch the rest of the proceedings. The young banner-bearing Deacons took up their positions in the hall, one group at each of the Five Cardinal Points, North, East, South, West and Centre, and awaited their orders. The three priests stood on the lower steps of the altar: one held the Magic Sword and the Holy Water, one the black Seven Star Banner, and one the peach-wood Demon Whip. The music ceased. The gong sounded thrice, the monks intoned a prayer, and the cohorts of banner-bearers began performing circular gyrations. The priests then descended from the altar and instructed the Jia menfolk to conduct them to every storeyed building, studio, hall, pavilion, chamber, cottage or covered walk, every hillside and water's edge in the Garden. In each place they sprinkled the Holy Water and brandished the Magic Sword. On their return, the gong rang out again, the Seven Star Banner was raised aloft and consecrated, and as it descended the Deacons formed a phalanx around it with their lesser banners, and the Demon Whip was cracked three times in the air.

This, thought the Jias, must be the climactic moment; now at last the entire company of evil spirits would be routed and captured. They thronged forward to be in at the finish. But nothing seemed to happen. No apparition, no sound; only the voice of one of the priests, ordering the Deacons to "bring on the jars." These receptacles were duly "brought on," and in them the priests proceeded to "confine" the invisible spirits, sealing them afterwards with official seals. The Abbot inscribed some magical characters in vermilion, and put the jars to one side, giving orders that they should be taken back to the temple. There they were to be placed beneath a pagoda, whose geomantic location would ensure that they and their contents were safely "contained." The temporary altar was dismantled and thanks given to the Heavenly Powers. Jia She made a solemn kowtow of gratitude to the Abbot.

Afterwards Jia Rong and the younger men of the family had a good laugh about it all in private:

"All that pantomime to catch the evil spirits! They might at least have let us have a look! What a farce! They probably didn't manage to catch a single one!"

"Fools!" snapped Cousin Zhen, when he heard this. "Evil spirits don't behave like that at all. At certain times they condense into crude matter, at others they dissolve into the ether. With so many benevolent spirits present of course they wouldn't dare take on material form. It's their etheric form that's in question here. *That* is what Their Holinesses have taken hold of; by so doing they have rendered the spirits harmless. *That* is how the magic works."

The younger generation were only half-convinced, and reserved their judgment until such time as they could observe a more visible diminution in demonic activity; the servants, who were told quite firmly that the spirits had now been caught, became less apprehensive as a result, and no further incidents or sightings were reported; while Cousin Zhen and the other invalids made a complete recovery (which *they* had no hesitation in attributing to the efficacy of the monks' spells).

There was, however, one page-boy who continued to find the whole episode highly amusing, and who shared his amusement with the others:

"I don't know what the earlier business was about, but that day we were in the Garden with Sir She, it was nothing more than a big pheasant that took off out of the undergrowth and went flying past us. Old Ropey got the fright of his life and thought he'd seen a ghost or something. He made a great song and dance about it afterwards. Most of the others believed him and backed him up, and Sir She swallowed the whole thing. Oh well, at least they put on a nice bit of mumbo-jumbo for us!"

But no one was convinced by his version of the story. And certainly no one was willing to live in the Garden again.

MODERN

ERA

(1911-)

Lu Hsün's Critique of Tradition

In short stories, essays, and novels, many writers of the early twentieth century conveyed implicit critiques of Chinese culture and called into question the limiting mores of the scholarly elite as well as the folk practices of popular religious belief. These themes are evident in Lu Hsün's (Lu Xun, 1881–1936) short story "The New-Year Sacrifice," a chronicle of the gradual disintegration of a woman's identity eroded by traditional religious and social values. Lu Hsün wrote the story in 1924, well after the imperial dynastic system had been dismantled by the 1911 revolution that established China as a republic, giving it the intentionally ironic title *Chu fu,* or "invocations for blessings," translated here as "The New-Year Sacrifice."

Perhaps the most prominent writer and social critic of the twentieth century, Lu Hsün is noted for his satiric depictions of a literally cannibalistic social and political order that consumes the lives of individual human beings. He started several literary journals and was an influential voice in the intellectual and political controversies of the twenties and thirties, a time marked by civil disorder, warlordism, and economic chaos. Lu was well acquainted with Western science and European literature and met George Bernard Shaw when the latter visited China in 1933.

"The New-Year Sacrifice" critiques the values of the old patriarchal order, represented here by the sacrifices to paternal ancestors performed at the Chinese lunar New Year. A movable feast that falls sometime in January or February, the Chinese New Year is the most important festival of the calendar, and its observance lasts nearly a week; the events that occur over those few days are thought to portend the family's fortunes for the coming year, and hence taboos are observed on the subjects of death, illness, and financial loss. People traditionally return to their native place at the New Year, and hence the narrator, an urbane man from the city who is acquainted with the larger world, returns to

281

the rural village of Luzhen and lodges at the home of Fourth Uncle, a distant paternal relative. Politically and intellectually conservative, Fourth Uncle is a vestige of the imperial examination system that ended around 1906; his attack on the reformer Kang Youwei (K'ang Yu-wei, 1858–1927) offends the narrator, whom one then knows to be a liberal nontraditionalist, probably tainted with the Western learning of logic, reason, and science. Appalled to see the works of the Sung dynasty Confucian scholars, which by the twentieth century are perceived by many as the source of China's political and economic weakness, the narrator decides to leave his uncle's house as soon as possible. The narrator's identity is never stated, but the tenor of his beliefs suggests Lu Hsün's own voice.

The narrator's encounter with the woman who goes by the name of Xianglin's Wife reveals that tradition offers no convincing explanation of the nature of ghosts or of the afterlife; neither, however, does the new Western learning represented by the narrator. The family patriarch callously acknowledges the death of Xianglin's Wife, a former servant, concerned only that the inauspicious timing of her death would affect the family's own fate. Fourth Uncle had read the Sung philosophers' disquisitions on ghosts and spirits that described them as nothing but the manifestations of the dual forces of yin and yang, but he still believes in the baneful influences carried by people associated with death; the mere fact that Xianglin's Wife is a widow thus makes her a harbinger of misfortune in his eyes.

Xianglin's Wife has no name or identity of her own, and she is known only by her relationship to her first husband, who was a boy ten years her junior. In some parts of China, young women of poor families were betrothed to infant boys; the women then resided with the spouse's family and became virtual indentured servants until the boy came of age and the marriage could be consummated. Xianglin's Wife's first marriage had apparently been of this type. Even upon the death of a husband, however, a woman still resides with her in-laws and remains subject to them for the remainder of her life. Xianglin's Wife, widowed by her first spouse, opts instead to run away from her deceased husband's family and find work as a servant in the Lu household. Her mother-in-law tracks her down and forcibly reclaims her, as the woman is a valuable commodity and can be sold off again in marriage in exchange for a dowry. Poor families could not afford the luxury of chaste widowhood, a custom that encouraged women to marry but once and remain faithful to one husband until death.

Married a second time, this time to a rustic, Xianglin's Wife attempts suicide at the wedding ceremony. For a time her life takes a turn for the better, but the deaths of her second spouse and their son Amao drive her again to the Lu household.

Now, however, she is so spiritually contaminated by the air of death that she may no longer assist in the preparations for the ancestral New Year sacrifices. Amah Liu, a superstitious elderly woman servant who is deeply credulous of Buddhist folk beliefs and popular religious folklore, convinces Xianglin's wife of the terrors of the afterlife, asserting that at death her soul will be cut in two and divided between her former spouses. Xianglin's Wife's attempts to purify herself by buying a threshold at a local temple are not recognized by the family, who do not adhere to such folk beliefs and still forbid her assistance at the sacrifices. Misplaced faith in folk religious beliefs, as well as the superstitious beliefs of even the scholarly Lu household, completely alienate Xianglin's Wife from both the living and the dead, and she never recovers her sanity; her later death during the "invocations of blessings" at the New Year is a silent curse on the family and its traditions.

The New-Year Sacrifice

The end of the year by the old calendar does really seem a more natural end to the year for, to say nothing of the villages and towns, the very sky seems to proclaim the New Year's approach. Intermittent flashes from pallid, lowering evening clouds are followed by the rumble of crackers bidding farewell to the Hearth God and, before the deafening reports of the bigger bangs close at hand have died away, the air is filled with faint whiffs of gunpowder. On one such night I returned to Luzhen, my home town. I call it my home town, but as I had not made my home there for some time I put up at the house of a certain Fourth Mr. Lu, whom I am obliged to address as Fourth Uncle since he belongs to the generation before mine in our clan. A former Imperial Academy licentiate who believes in Neo-Confucianism, he seemed very little changed, just slightly older, but without any beard as yet. Having exchanged some polite remarks upon meeting he observed that I was fatter, and having observed that I was fatter launched into a violent attack on the reformists. I did not take this personally, however, as the object of his attack was Kang Youwei. Still, conversation proved so difficult that I shortly found myself alone in the study.

I rose late the next day and went out after lunch to see relatives and friends, spending the following day in the same way. They were all very little changed, just slightly older; but every family was busy preparing for the New-Year sacrifice. This is the great end-of-year ceremony in Luzhen, during which a reverent and splendid welcome is given to the God of Fortune so that he will send good luck for the coming year. Chickens and geese are killed, pork is bought, and everything is scrubbed and scoured until all the women's arms—some still in twisted silver bracelets—turn red in the water. After the meat is cooked chopsticks are thrust into it at random, and when this "offering" is set out at dawn, incense and candles are lit and the God of Fortune is respectfully invited to come and partake of it. The worshippers are confined to men and, of course, after worshipping they go on letting off firecrackers as before. This is done every year, in every household—so long as it can afford the offering and crackers—and naturally this year was no exception.

The sky became overcast and in the afternoon it was filled with a flurry of snowflakes, some as large as plum-blossom petals, which merged with the smoke and the bustling atmosphere to make the small town a welter of confusion. By the time I had returned to my uncle's study, the roof of the house was already white with snow which made the room brighter than usual, highlighting the red stone rubbing that hung on the wall of the big character "Longevity" as written by the Taoist saint Chen Tuan. One of the pair of scrolls flanking it had fallen down and was lying loosely rolled up on the long table. The other, still in its place, bore the inscription "Understanding of principles brings peace of mind." Idly, I strolled over to the desk beneath the window to turn over the pile of books on it, but only found an apparently incomplete set of *The Kang Xi Dictionary,* the *Selected Writings of Neo-Confucian Philosophers,* and *Commentaries on the Four Books.* At all events I must leave the next day, I decided.

Besides, the thought of my meeting with Xianglin's Wife the previous day was preying on my mind. It had happened in the afternoon. On my way back from calling on a friend in the eastern part of the town, I had met her by the river and knew from the fixed look in her eyes that she was going to accost me. Of all the people I had seen during this visit to Luzhen, none had changed so much as she had. Her hair, streaked with grey five years before, was now completely white, making her appear much older than one around forty. Her sallow, dark-tinged face that looked as if it had been carved out of wood was fearfully wasted and had lost the grief-stricken expression it had borne before. The only sign of life about her was the occasional flicker of her eyes. In one hand she had a bamboo basket containing a chipped, empty bowl; in the other, a bamboo pole, taller than herself, that was split at the bottom. She had clearly become a beggar pure and simple.

I stopped, waiting for her to come and ask for money.

"So you're back?" were her first words.

"Yes."

"That's good. You are a scholar who's travelled and seen the world. There's something I want to ask you." A sudden gleam lit up her lacklustre eyes.

This was so unexpected that surprise rooted me to the spot.

"It's this." She drew two paces nearer and lowered her voice, as if letting me into a secret. "Do dead people turn into ghosts or not?"

My flesh crept. The way she had fixed me with her eyes made a shiver run down my spine, and I felt far more nervous than when a surprise test is sprung on you at school and the teacher insists on standing over you. Personally, I had never bothered myself in the least about whether spirits existed or not; but what was the best answer to give her now? I hesitated for a moment, reflecting that the people here still believed in spirits, but she seemed to have her doubts, or rather hopes—she hoped for life after death and dreaded it at the same time. Why increase the sufferings of someone with a wretched life? For her sake, I thought, I'd better say there was.

"Quite possibly, I'd say," I told her falteringly.

"That means there must be a hell too?"

"What, hell?" I faltered, very taken aback. "Hell? Logically speaking, there should be too— but not neccessarily. Who cares anyway?"

"Then will all the members of a family meet again after death?"

"Well, as to whether they'll meet again or not . . ." I realized now what an utter fool I was. All my hesitation and manoeuvring had been no match for her three questions. Promptly taking fright, I decided to recant. "In that case . . . actually, I'm not sure. . . . In fact, I'm not sure whether there are ghosts or not either."

To avoid being pressed by any further questions I walked off, then beat a hasty retreat to my uncle's house, feeling thoroughly disconcerted. I may have given her a dangerous answer, I was thinking. Of course, she may just be feeling lonely because everybody else is celebrating now, but could she have had something else in mind? Some premonition? If she had had some other idea, and something happens as a result, then my answer should indeed be partly responsible. . . . Then I laughed at myself for brooding so much over a chance meeting when it could have no serious significance. No wonder certain educationists called me neurotic. Besides, I had distinctly declared, "I'm not sure," contradicting the whole of my answer. This meant that even if something did happen, it would have nothing at all to do with me.

"I'm not sure" is a most useful phrase.

Bold inexperienced youngsters often take it upon themselves to solve problems or choose doctors for other people, and if by any chance things turn out badly they may well be held to blame; but by concluding their advice with this evasive expression they achieve blissful immunity from reproach. The necessity for such a phrase was brought home to me still more forcibly now, since it was indispensable even in speaking with a beggar woman.

However, I remained uneasy, and even after a night's rest my mind dwelt on it with a certain sense of foreboding. The oppressive snowy weather and the gloomy study increased my uneasiness. I had better leave the next day and go back to the city. A large dish of plain shark's fin stew at the Fu Xing Restaurant used to cost only a dollar. I wondered if this cheap delicacy had risen in price or not. Though my good companions of the old days had scattered; that shark's fin must still be sampled even if I were on my own. Whatever happened I would leave the next day, I decided.

Since, in my experience, things I hoped would not happen and felt should not happen invariably did occur all the same, I was much afraid this would prove another such case. And, sure enough, the situation soon took a strange turn. Towards evening I heard what sounded like a discussion in the inner room, but the conversation ended before long and my uncle walked away observing loudly, "What a moment to choose! Now of all times! Isn't that proof enough she was a bad lot?"

My initial astonishment gave way to a deep uneasiness; I felt that this had something to do with me. I looked out of the door, but no one was there. I waited impatiently till their servant came in before dinner to brew tea. Then at last I had a chance to make some inquiries.

"Who was Mr. Lu so angry with just now?" I asked.

"Why, Xianglin's Wife, of course," was the curt reply.

"Xianglin's Wife? Why?" I pressed.

"She's gone."

"Dead?" My heart missed a beat. I started and must have changed colour. But since the servant kept his head lowered, all this escaped him. I pulled myself together enough to ask.

"When did she die?"

"When? Last night or today—I'm not sure."

"How did she die?"

"How? Of poverty of course." After this stolid answer he withdrew, still without having raised his head to look at me.

My agitation was only short-lived, however. For now that my premonition had come to pass, I no longer had to seek comfort in my own "I'm not sure," or his "dying of poverty," and my heart was growing lighter. Only from time to time did I still feel a little guilty. Dinner was served, and my uncle impressively kept me company. Tempted as I was to ask about Xianglin's Wife, I knew that, although he had read that "ghosts and spirits are manifestations of the dual forces of Nature," he was still so superstitious that on the eve of the New-Year sacrifice it would be unthinkable to mention anything like death or illness. In case of necessity one should use veiled allusions, but since this was unfortunately beyond me I had to bite back the questions which kept rising to the tip of my tongue. And my uncle's solemn expression suddenly made me suspect that he looked on me too as a bad lot who had chosen this moment, now of all times, to come and trouble him. To set his mind at rest as quickly as I could, I told him at once of my plan to leave Luzhen the next day and go back to the city. He did not press me to stay, and at last the uncomfortably quiet meal came to an end.

Winter days are short, and because it was snowing darkness had already enveloped the whole town. All was stir and commotion in the lighted houses, but outside was remarkably quiet. And the snowflakes hissing down on the thick snowdrifts intensified one's sense of loneliness. Seated alone in the amber light of the vegetable-oil lamp I reflected that this wretched and forlorn woman, abandoned in the dust like a worn-out toy of which its owners have tired, had once left her own imprint in the dust, and those who enjoyed life must have wondered at her for wishing to live on; but now at last she had been swept away by death. Whether spirits existed or not I did not know; but in this world of ours the end of a futile existence, the removal of someone whom others are tired of seeing, was just as well both for them and for the individual concerned. Occupied with these reflections, I listened quietly to the hissing of the snow outside, until little by little I felt more relaxed.

But the fragments of her life that I had seen or heard about before combined now to form a whole.

She was not from Luzhen. Early one winter, when my uncle's family wanted a new maid, Old Mrs. Wei the go-between brought her along. She had a white mourning band round her hair and was wearing a black skirt, blue jacket, and pale green bodice. Her age was about twenty-six, and though her face was sallow her cheeks were red. Old Mrs. Wei introduced her as Xianglin's Wife, a neighbour of her mother's family, who wanted to go out to work now that her husband had died. My uncle frowned at this, and my aunt knew that he disapproved of taking on a widow. She looked just the person for them, though, with her big strong hands and feet; and, judging by her downcast eyes and silence, she was a good worker who would know her place. So my aunt ignored my uncle's frown and kept her. During her trial period she worked from morning till night as if she found resting irksome, and proved strong enough to do the work of a man; so on the third day she was taken on for five hundred cash a month.

Everybody called her Xianglin's Wife and no one asked her own name, but since she had been introduced by someone from Wei Village as a neighbour, her surname was presumably also Wei. She said little, only answering briefly when asked a question. Thus it took them a dozen days or so to find out bit by bit that she had a strict mother-in-law at home and a brother-in-law of ten or so, old enough to cut wood. Her husband, who had died that spring, had been a woodcutter too, and had been ten years younger than she was. This little was all they could learn.

Time passed quickly. She went on working as hard as ever, not caring what she ate, never sparing herself. It was generally agreed that the Lu family's maid actually got through more work than a hard-working man. At the end of the year, she swept and mopped the floors, killed the chickens and geese, and sat up to boil the sacrificial meat, all single-handed, so that they did not need to hire extra help. And she for her part was quite contented. Little by little the trace of a smile appeared at the corners of her mouth, while her face became whiter and plumper.

Just after the New Year she came back from washing rice by the river most upset because in the distance she had seen a man, pacing up and down on the opposite bank, who looked like her husband's elder cousin—very likely he had come in search of her. When my aunt in alarm pressed her for more information, she said nothing. As soon as my uncle knew of this he frowned.

"That's bad," he observed. "She must have run away."

Before very long this inference was confirmed.

About a fortnight later, just as this incident was beginning to be forgotten, Old Mrs. Wei suddenly brought along a woman in her thirties whom she introduced as Xianglin's mother. Although this woman looked like the hill-dweller she was, she behaved with great self-possession and had a ready tongue in her head. After the usual civilities she apologized for coming to take her daughter-in-law back, explaining that early spring was a busy time and they were short-handed at home with only old people and children around.

"If her mother-in-law wants her back, there's nothing more to be said," was my uncle's comment.

Thereupon her wages were reckoned up. They came to 1,750 cash, all of which she had left in the keeping of her mistress without spending any of it. My aunt gave the entire sum to Xianglin's mother, who took her daughter-in-law's clothes as well, expressed her thanks, and left. By this time it was noon.

"Oh, the rice! Didn't Xianglin's Wife go to wash the rice?" exclaimed my aunt some time later. It was probably hunger that reminded her of lunch.

A general search started then for the rice-washing basket. My aunt searched the kitchen, then the hall, then the bedroom; but not a sign of the basket was to be seen. My uncle could not find it outside either, until he went right down to the riverside. Then he saw it set down fair and square on the bank, some vegetables beside it.

Some people on the bank told him that a boat with a white awning had moored there that morning but, since the awning covered the boat completely, they had no idea who was inside and had paid no special attention to begin with. But when Xianglin's Wife had arrived and was kneeling down to wash rice, two men who looked as if they came from the hills had jumped off the boat and seized her. Between them they dragged her on board. She wept and shouted at first but soon fell silent, probably because she was gagged. Then along came two women, a stranger and Old Mrs. Wei. It was difficult to see clearly into the boat, but the victim seemed to be lying, tied up, on the planking.

"Disgraceful! Still . . ." said my uncle.

That day my aunt cooked the midday meal herself, and their son Aniu lit the fire.

After lunch Old Mrs. Wei came back.

"Disgraceful!" said my uncle.

"What's the meaning of this? How dare you show your face here again?" My aunt, who was washing up, started fuming as soon as she saw her. "First you recommended her, then help them carry her off, causing such a shocking commotion. What will people think? Are you trying to make fools of our family?"

"*Aiya*, I was completely taken in! I've come specially to clear this up. How was I to know she'd left home without permission from her mother-in-law when she asked me to find her work? I'm sorry, Mr. Lu. I'm sorry, Mrs. Lu. I'm growing so stupid and careless in my old age, I've let my patrons down. It's lucky for me you're such kind, generous people, never hard on those below you. I promise to make it up to you by finding someone good this time."

"Still . . ." said my uncle.

That concluded the affair of Xianglin's Wife, and before long it was forgotten.

My aunt was the only one who still spoke of Xianglin's Wife. This was because most of the maids taken on afterwards turned out to be lazy or greedy, or both, none of them giving satisfaction. At such times she would invariably say to herself, "I wonder what's become of her now?"—implying that she would like to have her back. But by the next New Year she too had given up hope.

The first month was nearing its end when Old Mrs. Wei called on my aunt to wish her a happy New Year. Already tipsy, she explained that the reason for her coming so late was that she had been visiting her family in Wei Village in the hills for a few days. The conversation, naturally, soon touched on Xianglin's Wife.

"Xianglin's Wife?" cried Old Mrs. Wei cheerfully. "She's in luck now. When her mother-in-law dragged her home, she'd promised her to the sixth son of the Ho family in Ho Glen. So a few days after her return they put her in the bridal chair and sent her off."

"Gracious! What a mother-in-law!" exclaimed my aunt.

"Ah, madam, you really talk like a great lady! This is nothing to poor folk like us who live up in the hills. That young brother-in-law of hers still had no wife. If they didn't marry her off, where would the money have come from to get him one? Her mother-in-law is a clever, capable woman, a fine manager; so she married her off into the mountains. If she'd betrothed her to a family in the same village, she wouldn't have made so much; but as very few girls are willing to take a husband deep in the mountains at the back of beyond, she got eighty thousand cash. Now the second son has a wife, who cost only fifty thousand; and after paying the wedding expenses she's still over ten thousand in hand. Wouldn't you call her a fine manager?"

"But was Xianglin's Wife willing?"

"It wasn't a question of willing or not. Of course any woman would make a row about it. All they had to do was tie her up, shove her into the chair, carry her to the man's house, force on her the bridal headdress, make her bow in the ceremonial hall, lock the two of them into their room—and that was that. But Xianglin's Wife is quite a character. I heard that she made a terrible scene. It was working for a scholar's family, everyone said, that made her different from other people. We go-betweens see life, madam. Some widows sob and shout when they remarry; some threaten to kill themselves; some refuse to go through the ceremony of bowing to heaven and earth after they've been carried to the man's house; some even smash the wedding candlesticks. But Xianglin's Wife was really extraordinary. They said she screamed and cursed all the way to Ho Glen, so that she was completely hoarse by the time they got there. When they dragged her out of the chair, no matter how the two chair-bearers and her brother-in-law held her, they couldn't make her go through the ceremony. The moment they were off guard and had loosened their grip— gracious Buddha!—she bashed her head on a corner of the altar, gashing it so badly that the blood spurted out. Even though they smeared on two handfuls of incense ashes and tied it up with two pieces of red cloth, they couldn't stop the bleeding. It took quite a few of them to shut her up finally with the man in the bridal chamber, but even then she went on cursing. Oh, it was really . . ." Shaking her head, she lowered her eyes and fell silent.

"And what then?" asked my aunt.

"They said that the next day she didn't get up." Old Mrs. Wei raised her eyes.

"And after?"

"After? She got up. At the end of the year she had a baby, a boy, who was reckoned as two this New Year. These few days when I was at home, some people back from a visit to Ho Glen said they'd seen her and her son, and both mother and child are plump. There's no mother-in-law over her, her man is a strong fellow who can earn a living, and the house belongs to them. Oh, yes, she's in luck all right."

After this event my aunt gave up talking of Xianglin's Wife.

But one autumn, after two New Years had passed since this good news of Xianglin's Wife, she once more crossed the threshold of my uncle's house, placing her round bulb-shaped basket on the table and her small bedding-roll under the eaves. As before, she had a white mourning band round her hair and was wearing a black skirt, blue jacket, and pale green bodice. Her face was sallow, her cheeks no longer red; and her downcast eyes, stained with tears, had lost their brightness. Just as before, it was Old Mrs. Wei who brought her to my aunt.

"It was really a bolt from the blue," she explained compassionately. "Her husband was a strong young fellow; who'd have thought that typhoid fever would carry him off? He'd taken a turn for the better, but then he ate some cold rice and got worse again. Luckily she had the boy and she can work—she's able to gather firewood, pick tea, or raise silkworms—so she could have managed on her own. But who'd have thought that the child, too, would be carried off by a wolf? It was nearly the end of spring, yet a wolf came to the glen—who could

have guessed that? Now she's all on her own. Her husband's elder brother has taken over the house and turned her out. So she's no way to turn for help except to her former mistress. Luckily this time there's nobody to stop her and you happen to be needing someone, madam. That's why I've brought her here. I think someone used to your ways is much better than a new hand. . . ."

"I was really too stupid, really . . ." put in Xianglin's Wife, raising her lacklustre eyes. "All I knew was that when it snowed and wild beasts up in the hills had nothing to eat, they might come to the villages. I didn't know that in spring they might come too. I got up at dawn and opened the door, filled a small basket with beans and told our Amao to sit on the doorstep and shell them. He was such a good boy; he always did as he was told, and out he went. Then I went to the back to chop wood and wash the rice, and when the rice was in the pan I wanted to steam the beans. I called Amao, but there was no answer. When I went out to look there were beans all over the ground but no Amao. He never went to the neighbours' houses to play; and, sure enough, though I asked everywhere he wasn't there. I got so worried, I begged people to help me find him. Not until that afternoon, after searching high and low, did they try the gully. There they saw one of his little shoes caught on a bramble. 'That's bad,' they said. 'A wolf must have got him.' And sure enough, further on, there he was lying in the wolf's den, all his innards eaten away, still clutching that little basket tight in his hand. . . ." At this point she broke down and could not go on.

My aunt had been undecided at first, but the rims of her eyes were rather red by the time Xianglin's Wife broke off. After a moment's thought she told her to take her things to the servants' quarters. Old Mrs. Wei heaved a sigh, as if a great weight had been lifted from her mind; and Xianglin's Wife, looking more relaxed than when first she came, went off quietly to put away her bedding without having to be told the way. So she started work again as a maid in Luzhen.

She was still known as Xianglin's Wife.

But now she was a very different woman. She had not worked there more than two or three days before her mistress realized that she was not as quick as before. Her memory was much worse too, while her face, like a death mask, never showed the least trace of a smile. Already my aunt was expressing herself as not too satisfied. Though my uncle had frowned as before when she first arrived, they always had such trouble finding servants that he raised no serious objections, simply warning his wife on the quiet that while such people might seem very pathetic they exerted a bad moral influence. She could work for them but must have nothing to do with ancestral sacrifices. They would have to prepare all the dishes themselves. Otherwise they would be unclean and the ancestors would not accept them.

The most important events in my uncle's household were ancestral sacrifices, and formerly these had kept Xianglin's wife especially busy, but now she had virtually nothing to do. As soon as the table had been placed in the centre of the hall and a front curtain fastened around its legs, she started setting out the wine-cups and chopsticks in the way she still remembered.

"Put those down, Xianglin's Wife," cried my aunt hastily. "Leave that to me."

She drew back sheepishly then and went for the candlesticks.

"Put those down, Xianglin's Wife," cried my aunt again in haste. "I'll fetch them."

After walking round in the hall several times without finding anything to do, she moved doubtfully away. All she could do that day was to sit by the stove and feed the fire.

The townspeople still called her Xianglin's Wife, but in quite a different tone from before; and although they still talked to her, their manner was colder. Quite impervious to this, staring straight in front of her, she would tell everybody the story which night or day was never out of her mind:

"I was really too stupid, really," she would say. "All I knew was that when it snowed and the wild beasts up in the hills had nothing to eat, they might come to the villages. I didn't know that in spring they might come too. I got up at dawn and opened the door, filled a small basket with beans and told our Amao to sit on the doorstep and shell them. He was such a good boy; he always did as he was told, and out he went. Then I went to the back to chop wood and wash the rice, and when the rice was in the pan I wanted to steam the beans. I called Amao, but there was no answer. When I went out to look, there were beans all over the ground but no Amao. He never went to the neighbours' houses to play; and, sure enough, though I asked everywhere he wasn't there. I got so worried, I begged people to help me find him. Not until that afternoon, after searching high and low, did they try the gully. There they saw one of his little shoes caught on a bramble. 'That's bad,' they said. 'A wolf must have got him.' And sure enough, further on, there he was lying in the wolf's den, all his innards eaten away, still clutching that little basket tight in his hand. . . ." At this point her voice would be choked with tears.

This story was so effective that men hearing it often stopped smiling and walked blankly away, while the women not only seemed to forgive her but wiped the contemptuous expression off their faces and added their tears to hers. Indeed, some old women who had not heard her in the street sought her out specially to hear her sad tale. And when she broke down, they too shed the tears which had gathered in their eyes, after which they sighed and went away satisfied, exchanging eager comments.

As for her, she asked nothing better than to tell her sad story over and over again, often gathering three or four hearers around her. But before long everybody knew it so well that no trace of a tear could be seen even in the eyes of the most kindly, Buddha-invoking old ladies. In the end, practically the whole town could recite it by heart and were bored and exasperated to hear it repeated.

"I was really too stupid, really," she would begin.

"Yes. All you knew was that in snowy

weather, when the wild beasts in the mountains had nothing to eat, they might come down to the villages." Cutting short her recital abruptly, they walked away.

She would stand there open-mouthed, staring after them stupidly, and then wander off as if she too were bored by the story. But she still tried hopefully to lead up from other topics such as small baskets, and other people's children to the story of her Amao. At the sight of a child of two or three she would say, "Ah, if my Amao were alive he'd be just that size. . . ."

Children would take fright at the look in her eyes and clutch the hem of their mothers' clothes to tug them away. Left by herself again, she would eventually walk blankly away. In the end everybody knew what she was like. If a child were present they would ask with a spurious smile, "If your Amao were alive, Xianglin's Wife, wouldn't he be just that size?"

She may not have realized that her tragedy, after being generally savoured for so many days, had long since grown so stale that it now aroused only revulsion and disgust. But she seemed to sense the cold mockery in their smiles, and the fact that there was no need for her to say any more. So she would simply look at them in silence.

New-Year preparations always start in Lu-zhen on the twentieth day of the twelfth lunar month. That year my uncle's household had to take on a temporary man-servant. And since there was more than he could do they asked Amah Liu to help by killing the chickens and geese; but being a devout vegetarian who would not kill living creatures, she would only wash the sacrificial vessels. Xianglin's Wife, with nothing to do but feed the fire, sat there at a loose end watching Amah Liu as she worked. A light snow began to fall.

"Ah, I was really too stupid," said Xianglin's Wife as if to herself, looking at the sky and sighing.

"There you go again, Xianglin's Wife." Amah Liu glanced with irritation at her face. "Tell me, wasn't that when you got that scar on your forehead?"

All the reply she received was a vague murmur.

"Tell me this: What made you willing after all?"

"Willing?"

"Yes. Seems to me you must have been willing. Otherwise . . ."

"Oh, you don't know how strong he was."

"I don't believe it. I don't believe he was so strong that you with your strength couldn't have kept him off. You must have ended up willing. That talk of his being so strong is just an excuse."

"Why . . . just try for yourself and see." She smiled.

Amah Liu's lined face broke into a smile too, wrinkling up like a walnut-shell. Her small beady eyes swept the other woman's forehead, then fastened on her eyes. At once Xianglin's Wife stopped smiling, as if embarrassed, and turned her eyes away to watch the snow.

"That was really a bad bargain you struck, Xianglin's Wife," said Amah Liu mysteriously. "If you'd held out longer or knocked yourself to death outright, that would have been better. As it is, you're guilty of a great sin though you lived less than two years with your second husband. Just think: when you go down to the lower world, the ghosts of both men will start fighting over you. Which ought to have you? The King of Hell will have to saw you into two and divide you between them. I feel it really is. . . ."

Xianglin's Wife's face registered terror then. This was something no one had told her up in the mountains.

"Better guard against that in good time, I say. Go to the Temple of the Tutelary God and buy a threshold to be trampled on instead of you by thousands of people. If you atone for your sins in this life you'll escape torment after death."

Xianglin's Wife said nothing at the time, but she must have taken this advice to heart, for when she got up the next morning there were dark rims round her eyes. After breakfast she went to the Temple of the Tutelary God at the west end of the town and asked to buy a threshold as an offering. At first the priest refused, only giving a grudging consent after she was reduced to tears of desperation. The price charged was twelve thousand cash.

She had long since given up talking to people after their contemptuous reception of Amao's story; but as word of her conversation with Amah Liu spread, many of the townsfolk took a fresh interest in her and came once more to provoke her into talking. The topic, of course, had changed to the scar on her forehead.

"Tell me, Xianglin's Wife, what made you willing in the end?" one would ask.

"What a waste, to have bashed yourself like that for nothing," another would chime in, looking at her scar.

She must have known from their smiles and tone of voice that they were mocking her, for she simply stared at them without a word and finally did not even turn her head. All day long she kept her lips tightly closed, bearing on her head the scar considered by everyone as a badge of shame, while she shopped, swept the floor, washed the vegetables and prepared the rice in silence. Nearly a year went by before she took her accumulated wages from my aunt, changed them for twelve silver dollars, and asked for leave to go to the west end of the town. In less time than it takes for a meal she was back again, looking much comforted. With an unaccustomed light in her eyes, she told my aunt contentedly that she had now offered up a threshold in the Temple of the Tutelary God.

When the time came for the ancestral sacrifice at the winter solstice she worked harder than ever, and as soon as my aunt took out the sacrificial vessels and helped Aniu to carry the table into the middle of the hall, she went confidently to fetch the winecups and chopsticks.

"Put those down, Xianglin's Wife!" my aunt called hastily.

She withdrew her hand as if scorched, her face turned ashen grey, and instead of fetching the candlesticks she just stood there in a daze until my uncle came in to burn some incense and told her to go away. This time the change in her was phenomenal: the next day her eyes were sunken, her spirit seemed broken. She took fright very easily too, afraid not only of the dark and of shadows, but of meeting anyone. Even the sight of her own master or mistress set her trembling like a mouse that had strayed out of its hole in broad daylight. The rest of the time she would sit stupidly as if carved out of wood. In less than half a year her hair had turned grey, and her memory had deteriorated so much that she often forgot to go and wash the rice.

"What's come over Xianglin's Wife? We should never have taken her on again," my aunt would sometimes say in front of her, as if to warn her.

But there was no change in her, no sign that she would ever recover her wits. So they decided to get rid of her and tell her to go back to Old Mrs. Wei. That was what they were saying, at least, while I was there; and, judging by subsequent developments, this is evidently what they must have done. But whether she started begging as soon as she left my uncle's house, or whether she went first to Old Mrs. Wei and later became a beggar, I do not know.

I was woken up by the noisy explosion of crackers close at hand and, from the faint glow shed by the yellow oil lamp and the bangs of fireworks as my uncle's household celebrated the sacrifice, I knew that it must be nearly dawn. Listening drowsily I heard vaguely the ceaseless explosion of crackers in the distance. It seemed to me that the whole town was enveloped by the dense cloud of noise in the sky, mingling with the whirling snowflakes. Enveloped in this medley of sound I relaxed; the doubt which had preyed on my mind from dawn till night was swept clean away by the festive atmosphere, and I felt only that the saints of heaven and earth had accepted the sacrifice and incense and were reeling with intoxication in the sky, preparing to give Luzhen's people boundless good fortune.

The Hypocrisy
of Modern Confucianism

The Chinese title of "The Bulwark," *Ti-chu,* alludes to a pillar of rock in the Yellow River that stands solid and unmoving in the torrent known as "China's Sorrow," a flood of water that occasionally sweeps away entire villages and inhabited regions. This epithet refers satirically to the fictional Huang Yi-an, a self-styled bastion of Confucian morality who stands firm against the forces of modernization moving across China in the early twentieth century. Huang is the type of person Confucius must have had in mind when he said "I have never seen a man who loved virtue as much as he loved the attractions of women" (*Analects* 9.17). Huang's character offers many opportunities for comparison between the realities of Confucian scholarly life in the thirties and the ideals of the Confucian philosophers of pre-Han times.

Like the opening verse of the Confucian *Analects,* which remarks on the delights of reading, the first line of "The Bulwark" describes Huang Yi-an engaged in a book; his attention span with the written word, however, never lasts more than a few seconds. He has emulated the external forms of the scholarly Confucian tradition and is a *hsiu-ts'ai,* someone who has passed the preliminary levels of the civil service examination system that by 1936, the year "The Bulwark" was written, had been defunct for thirty years. Huang's purported scholarly abilities notwithstanding, the author suggests that he is not a human at all, but a marine creature: his grey eyes are like those of a "dead fish"; he grunts like a "frog caged in an urn"; his posture is that of a "dried-up shrimp."

Continually quoting from the *Book of Rites* and other ancient texts on propriety and decorum, Huang is nevertheless such an inept communicator and has such limited concentration that he is barely able to impart even a few coherent sentences on womanly virtues to his young marriageable daughter, who seems completely oblivious to the realities of the conjugal responsibilities she must soon accept. He is accompanying his daughter on a boat trip to facilitate a marriage for her that is arranged primarily to benefit his own self-interest. He plans to wed her to Commissioner Yi, whose brothers Yi Lao-erh and Yi Lao-wu, it turns out, are friends of President Hsiao of the Confucian Classics Study Society. Commissioner Yi's high rank suggests he is many years older than his potential bride, and in terms of character one fears he resembles his siblings' friend, President Hsiao. But while Huang Yi-an would delimit his own daughter's freedom with an arranged marriage and with ritual strictures now well over two thousand years old, the women he desires for himself are not the types likely to have read Pan Chao's *Lessons for Women*. Chang T'ien-i's description of the opium-smoking pornographers of the Confucian association is a universal testimony against hypocrisy in any culture. He depicts Huang, the bulwark of traditional values, as a figure less steadfast than stagnant, a quality indicated physically by Huang's obsession with his athlete's foot. The type of Confucian learning that Huang embodies, he seems to suggest, is a tenacious eczema that grows by sacrificing the lives of young women such as Mei-tzu.

Chang T'ien-i (born 1906) was from a well-known scholarly family and became interested in Marxism and other new learnings from the West. He joined the League of Left-Wing Writers, an association formed around the early 1930s that attracted the most distinguished of China's writers, including Lu Hsün.

Chang T'ien-i's "The Bulwark"

Lying sideways on the bed in his cabin, the venerable Mr. Huang Yi-an was reading a book. His right leg was on top of his left, the toes spread wide apart. His left hand was rubbing at the athlete's foot between his toes.

The characters in the book were rippling like shadows in water.

"Why isn't she back yet? That stupid girl!"

Over the rims of his reading glasses he stared at the cabin door. The first-class deck was noisy; a few waiters were shouting excitedly: "Gentlemen, watch out, watch out."

Somewhere people were laughing boisterously and talking about women, and from time to time the *tzu, tzu, tzu* sounds of opium smoking could be heard. The opium combined with the fishy stench of the ship produced a peculiar odor. "Damn it all," he cursed.

He sniffed at the fingers of his left hand, then drew on his socks and walked to the door on his "Double Bridge" brand slippers.

This time he must call Mei-tzu back in! A decent man couldn't let his young daughter run wild. How would it look to others?

Impatiently he pulled open his cabin door about half a foot. With the look of a man facing a duel to the death, he thrust his long face out to appraise the situation. His gray eyes, like those of a dead fish, peered into the lobby around the rims of his glasses.

His daughter was chatting with a fat woman, in exactly the same position as before. Her blouse still unbuttoned, the fat woman was nonchalantly feeding her baby with a fleshy breast. Her face wore a tiny smile as if her ample breasts were a legitimate source of pride.

The old man by the door now knew the woman had switched from one breast to the other. He had taken a peep twice before but seen only her right breast. So they were both equally fair!

A few men were laughing and muttering to one another, occasionally eyeing the women; a young man sitting on a bunk never took his eyes off the woman. His mouth was wide open, as if he wanted a mouthful from the nursing woman.

The only exception was a middle-aged man lying on a bed. He was holding a little book to read in one hand and, legs crossed, scratching his crotch with the other.

"The guy must have jock itch," Huang Yi-an thought to himself. "Huh. The swine! And that shameless fat woman should be arrested by the police!"

He closed the door, sucked in his stomach, and returned to his bunk.

The ship splashed through the water. Below, the engine room was making such thumping noises that a person felt as if his heart were being pounded on.

Someone laughed loudly; the noise seemed to have come from the next room, and was followed by more *tzu, tzu, tzu* sounds.

The old man suddenly thought of the guy with the jock itch. What had he been reading? Why was he so absorbed in his reading? No doubt about it, must be pornography. Even the cover looked like it.

With renewed misgivings he pulled the door open. Scowling, he stuck his head out through the crack between the half-open door and the door-post, looking like a prisoner with his head locked in a cangue.

When his daughter accidentally met his eyes, he immediately signaled with his chin to return her to the cabin.

His face long, he asked her: "Who was the woman you were talking to?"

"A schoolmate's sister-in-law."

"Don't talk to her! Do you understand? She can't be a good woman. One must be careful in one's associations. One must! Don't you see?"

Mei-tzu shot a glance at him and sighed.

He sat on the bunk and removed his shoes. Thrusting out his lower lip, he intoned: "It's not that I enjoy criticizing you. As your father, naturally I want my daughter to be good, above criticism by others. You see, if that woman had any sense of decency, how could she unbutton her blouse in front of all those men? If no distinction is drawn between men and women, are they not like animals? However the world changes, 'propriety' must be observed. And that's the way it should be."

He took off his socks. His right middle finger rubbed between his toes and then he smelled his finger. "For example, even in the privacy of one's own room one still must behave properly, not to speak of . . ."

A loud voice from the next room interrupted him. "Oh, yeah, that woman's called 'Three Open Gates.' Her mouth is good . . ." A fit of giggles seeped through the thin wall.

A tremor went through Huang Yi-an. Holding his chest high, he pretended not to have heard anything. He cleared his throat, pulled a long face, and resumed his talk. From the corners of his eyes he watched his daughter closely as if guarding a treasure. He felt all those degenerates should be locked up! "That's it. I should submit a proposal to the provincial governor. I'm sure it would be accepted," he thought to himself.

The young lady sat quietly, with her right elbow resting on her leg while her hand supported her chin. She stared at the porthole as if lost in thought or reverie.

In contrast with the river, which resembled rice-flour in color, the paddy-fields on the shore were so temptingly green that one might wish nothing better than to take a nap there. In the sky the floating white clouds had blended into one mass with the distant hills. One could almost touch them merely by stretching out a hand.

Inside the ship, however, only Huang Yi-an's deep, hoarse voice could be heard, sometimes mixed with a noise of sniffing.

He was talking about himself. Whenever he lectured his children, he used himself as an example. He put down his well-rubbed left foot and began to rub his right. After kneading his fingers for a while he rattled on. The reason he had recognition in his home town was not because he was rich, not because his family received annually three hundred piculs of grain as rental, not because he was a *hsiu-ts'ai* and had studied law; it was because his moral conduct was different from others'. "Humph! The new

trend, the new trend! Fortunately they have finally come to realize their folly and understand that managing a family, running a nation, and bringing peace to the world are greatly dependent upon traditional learning. Even Magistrate Yao wants me to lecture on the classics. You can see from that, can't you? I only want you to take after me a little bit; if only you wouldn't be influenced by fads, then I'd be content. I don't want you to become a sage. I just . . ."

The rest of his words were drowned out by laughter from the next room. He knit his eyebrows. With his finger suspended in the air halfway to his nose, he continued: "Mei-tzu, did you hear what I just said?"

Startled, Mei-tzu turned toward him, as if just realizing that her father had been speaking to her.

The old man heaved a sigh and shook his head. "It's best not to say anything; there's no one listening anyway. Of late, officials seem to be treading the right path; they even invited me to give lectures on morals. But my own flesh and blood simply ignores me."

He sniffed his finger again. With his eyes closed, he drew a deep breath as if he wanted to enjoy to the full the pleasure of the moment, so that he wouldn't be troubled by unpleasant thoughts. A moment later, unable to remain quiet, he continued: "You're sixteen already, and you don't seem to know a thing. All you have to do is ask your mother. She and I have been together for more than thirty years, and we have never had one flippant conversation. Come to think of it, your mother has never appeared before strange men. Propriety is the basis of human conduct, and this is especially true for women. Do you understand?"

Exhaling, he leaned against the wall and picked up his book. "Pour me a cup of tea." Without lifting his eyes, he moistened his fingertips and leisurely turned the pages. As he took the cup from her, he looked at her face and felt a ticklish sensation in his heart. His child, after all, was quite pretty; he was certain that the wedding plans he had in mind for her would work out and that thenceforward he would be a relative of Commissioner Yi. Like a connoisseur he sipped his tea and smacked his lips. In a much softened tone he said to her: "Mei-tzu, let me tell you something. I don't mean to ask you to inherit all my morals. Yet one must . . . Oh, yes, one must . . . if only . . ."

He stopped for a moment. Inching his body forward a bit, he then told his daughter confidently that if she could pay attention to proper behavior, even generals and ministers would be interested in her and ask for her hand in marriage.

After saying all this, he felt somewhat relieved and leaned back more comfortably against the wall. Though his eyes were fixed on his book, he could not concentrate. His thoughts drifted to the good days ahead of him and he felt buoyant with expectations.

The girl was still sitting quietly, casting her gaze at the sky outside the window as if she were determined to seek illumination from the outside world.

"Didn't you bring any books with you?" he asked.

She raised a guilt-ridden face and shook her head. Then, apparently wanting to prove that she also had some serious work to do, she picked an unfinished sweater from a small basket and began to knit. From time to time she seemed to be in a trance. She stared straight ahead, as if listening to the engine and to the splashing of the water, while at the same time she appeared equally attentive to the din of human noises.

Huang Yi-an cleared his throat and swallowed. His hands scratched frantically between his toes; he let the book lie on his stomach. The wrinkle on his left cheek pulled his mouth sideways, and a glistening drop of saliva hung on his lower lip.

The noises from the next room became increasingly louder, as if they were deliberately meant to be heard by the people in this room. "Then you must be greater than Hsiao Chiang-ping!" "What? What? I only said . . ." After moments of babbling, there was a loud laugh.

The old man in Cabin Number Seven pulled a long face and quit rubbing his toes. "Damn it," he said to himself. "Who are those ruffians? Huh, 'Hsiao Chiang-ping' indeed!" He stiffened his neck and assumed a dignified pose. He didn't stir except to watch his daughter from the corners of his eyes. Thank God, she was ignorant of what they were saying.

Somewhere a mosquito hummed with a quivering rhythm. Meanwhile, the *gung, gung, gung* sounds from the ship were keeping time with the vibration of the mosquito's hum.

Precisely at that moment, someone uttered "Oooh" in the next room. It seemed to be a woman's scream, soon followed by giggles, as if a woman's laughter had been muffled.

Huang Yi-an tensed, feeling as if a soft hairbrush were brushing his insides. He straightened his legs, then bent them again. He sighed and sucked in a breath between his flushed cheeks, while eyeing his daughter.

The sixteen-year-old concentrated on knitting her sweater. Her hands moved deftly, showing no interest in the strange chatter of the next room. Apparently she had neither heard nor seen that type of thing in school.

"Yet that woman is something else . . ." He again thought of those thick nipples and imagined what it would be like to touch them, how they would swell to his touch. Now he was unsure whether he should report her to the police, although he was entitled to do so.

He still had the book and pretended to concentrate, moistening his fingertips with saliva and flipping the pages. But the long characters in the Sung calligraphic style all looked ugly to him, and none made any sense at all.

A current of warmth flowed through his body and his toes itched. He stole a glance at his daughter and, after clearing his throat, looked at her again.

This time the father's and daughter's glances met. He said sullenly: "If you're knitting, then put your heart in it. Why look around?"

Outside a waiter was yelling something at the top of his lungs, almost drowning out other human noises. Someone in a thin voice was humming a tune, inviting one to visualize the seductive way the singer must be twisting her body. But in a moment this sexy tune was cut short by a coarse voice. Apparently there was quarrel over there. Maybe it was a squabble over women. Oh, what a God-forsaken place! Never a moment of peace on the ship.

No sooner had the quarrel ended than the ship's whistle blew, interminably. The blast seemed to be an outburst of long-suppressed lust suddenly coming into the open. The noise entered his head and ran through his body, making him shake all over. His ears rang with the noise long afterward.

His eyes half closed, and feeling vexed, he grunted like a frog caged in an urn. With his mind distracted, he became all the more sensitive to the rocking of the ship. From next door came more *tzu, tzu, tzu* sounds of opium smoking. And the noises came in such intensity that one couldn't help suspecting that someone was gasping for breath while being held down.

Casually, he glanced at his daughter out of the corner of his eye. Maybe this young girl knew everything; perhaps it was only because she was in the presence of her father that she seemed so innocent. There was a sudden tightening in his chest. He glared at her unrelentingly.

The noises from the next room increased in volume. Certainly the people in the room must be worldly wise, with some social standing; they must also have liked certain books. A while back they had talked about a "monk" who could be large and small at will and made references to a dildo made of precious metal. Then the man with the hoarse voice spoke in a carefree tone: "This book really has much to offer. It represents experience. No mistake about it. The woman I met was an expert at 'blowing the flute.' " Another man in a deep voice corrected the first speaker's use of the technical term and said it was not called "blowing the flute." Then an argument ensued.

On this side Huang Yi-an pursed his lips. "Bullshit! They haven't even read the book. What nonsense!" he muttered to himself. "But that woman must be the one they called 'Three Open Gates.' "

After gazing at the wall for a second or so, he looked again at Mei-tzu. Since she was sitting by the porthole, what he saw was a bent silhouette, yet he imagined that her face was flushing, her eyes glistening and moist.

"Huh-hnnh," he coughed loudly, deliberately pulling a long face. Mei-tzu was so startled by the noise that her body trembled. From what he had observed of his daughter, the old man deduced that she must be guilty. Feeling suddenly sick to his stomach, breathing unevenly, his eyes nearly popping out, and glaring at Mei-tzu with mounting rage, he decided to give her a thorough lecture and a good scolding. Yet he was tongue-tied.

"Mei-tzu! . . . You! *Hmm,* damn it all. This, this . . . I'm telling you . . . Don't you remember? A person, a person . . ."

He opened and shut his mouth, his sparse moustache twitching a few times, and after he coughed once, the words burst forth from his throat: "A person shouldn't listen to things that aren't proper."

The daughter gaped at him, her eyes wide open.

"Don't just look at me!" The old man forced these words out from between his teeth. "A person must constantly search his soul and see if he has done anything improper. If he listens to the improper, he himself will become improper. Don't you see?"

Mei-tzu was speechless with amazement: "What? What did I listen to?"

"What did you listen to? The next room, the next room. I think you . . ."

The father stared at his daughter for a while before heaving a long, despairing sigh. He then looked at his own feet, at the ceiling and, in spite of himself, at her again.

She was still staring at him. As if he had been offended, he said fretfully: "If you didn't, you didn't. If you have faults, you must correct them; if you don't, you should try to be better. Why don't you resume your work?"

Mei-tzu dropped her eyelids, and he seriously attempted to read his book. He moistened his fingers with lots of saliva and noisily leafed through the pages. His fingers were shaky and tasted of salt.

The ribald chatter, however, continued to penetrate the gray wall of his cabin undiluted. A man whose voice resembled a martial character's in the Peking opera began to extol the "virtues" of a certain middle-aged woman, but he was soon interrupted by laughter.

Huang Yi-an scowled. Damn it! Who is that woman, and what happens to her later? he wondered.

He lowered his book just enough to glance at his daughter's face. The light outside the window reflecting on her hair made it shine like silver threads.

The men in the next room became more explicit in their descriptions of women, although their expressions, compared with the crude ones of field hands, were more restrained. The talk captivated him, in spite of himself.

"Damnation!" Huang Yi-an's upper lip quivered. Those people were obviously well educated, for their conversational art was so clever that it made such racy talk irresistible.

Sometimes the words came haltingly, like broken threads, and other times in rapid succession like cricket sounds. Once in a while a word or two had him spellbound. Meanwhile he sighed and glared at his daughter. He was warm and sweating. He raised his book high to cover his face, worried that his flushed cheeks might reveal his impropriety to his daughter.

The middle-aged woman they had just referred to—what had happened to her later? he wondered. How could they have the story without an ending? Those idiots should be shot! Why must all this happen when he was traveling with his daughter?

He had thought the second-class section might be too unruly, with people from all quarters of life; yet, he found the first-class section equally disorderly. Maybe the people were just making up tall tales. Otherwise, why wouldn't there be conclusions to their stories?

He hadn't finished a single page; he was shaking. Biting his lower lip, he tried hard not to drool. He was seriously thinking of jumping

out of his bunk, to run a few steps, skip a few times, and roll on the floor. Then he mused that if he were going to roll on the floor, he might as well do it on the bunk. "Ai, even if sages Chu Hsi and Ch'eng Yi were alive today, they too would, ai, feel like this."

Angrily he threw his book aside. Wrinkles to the left of his chin twitched, as he chewed at his lip. His legs bent and his hands rubbed between his toes frantically, as if rushing to finish some task. He worked so hard that he didn't have time to sniff his fingers.

Saliva fell from his lips. He glared at his daughter protectively, afraid that the dropping saliva might give her improper or indecent thoughts. Unconsciously he hummed a tune; a spicy feeling in his throat made him feel good. The young girl cast a glance at him. It was apparent that his excitement had aroused her attention. Then, as if wanting to avoid his stern gaze, she turned to look at the wall.

Suddenly Huang Yi-an ceased his hand movements. "Ridiculous! This is simply ridiculous! All right, I'll just go and take a look." Very quickly he removed his glasses, put on his socks, and felt for his shoes on the floor, legs dangling.

As he opened the door, he assumed a dignified manner and walked with measured steps. His protruding stomach and his hunched back formed his body into an S shape. His tightly shut mouth gave him an air of great determination. He decided to barge into Cabin Number Six with a stern look to stop that immoral chatter. Those idiots should be hanged, couldn't they see he had his sixteen-year-old daughter in the next room? If they had some education, they ought to have heard the name of Huang Yi-an— a Neo-Confucianist, a bulwark in a period of tumult, a relative of Commissioner Yi.

He walked with a limp, pain jabbing him between the toes.

"If they don't heed my warning," he thought, gritting his teeth, "then I can't afford to be polite. I have to report them to the police, charge them with the corruption of morals. And that's a serious offense!"

He concentrated all his strength on his right hand, wanting to pull open the door to Number Six with force. His eyes were sparkling. One could tell at a glance from the deep horizontal creases on his forehead that he had inherited the moralist tradition of the sages of the Southern Sung period.

A waiter with a load on his back walked toward him, muttering: "Gentlemen, watch out, watch out." But Huang stood by the door of Cabin Number Six in a dignified pose and did not stir. The waiter's load brushed against him and knocked his head against the wall, thus straightening his S shaped body. "Hey, you, you!" Huang stared at the waiter's back and suddenly shivered. The crude waiter made him think of these low-class morons—as if a newly healed wound had been torn open. Now everything seemed to be on the right track, except that lowly herd, he thought. He had always guarded himself against them, wary of them. Gritting his teeth, he yelled: "I'll have you hanged!"

He felt that was the cleanest way to handle the likes of him. They did not deserve his edification; only the educated class was worthy of his attention. He watched the waiter disappear around a corner; he then resumed his original dignified posture, thrusting his stomach out.

Gently he touched his forehead and knit his eyebrows. It seemed as if he were on his way to his disciples to recount to them how these scoundrels had mistreated him.

The door creaked. Presently he removed his hand from his forehead and cleared his throat, apparently having decided that since the educated class were easier to deal with, he might as well vent his full indignation on them. "You must all be severely penalized! I'll send you to a magistrate's court and you'll get a flogging. Humph, what do you think you are?" he told himself silently.

Suddenly the door opened and a dark shadow leered at him from the crack. Startled, Huang Yi-an moved his left leg back, so that his two feet were positioned like a capital V. A strong opium smell penetrated his nostrils, sending him into a dream-like state. His body seemed to be floating in the clouds. The merry noises seemed amplified. As he stepped inside the door, the noises subsided, as if swept away by a mild breeze.

Sunlight filtered through the porthole into the smoke-filled room, which reflected a streak of white light. None of the faces was distinguishable except for the one standing by the door facing the light, glaring at him with bloodshot eyes.

On the table were displayed some wine cups and a mound of cooked food wrapped in lotus leaves. A fanciful thought flashed through his mind—he was almost sure that there must be an ox organ cooked in cassia bark somewhere.

On the bunk to the right a bald man was smoking opium, and reclining beside him was a big fellow watching listlessly. Amid the opium smoke the two stared at Huang spitefully. Their eyebrows were knit tight, as if they resented the glare of the opium lamp.

Huang Yi-an raised his head and surveyed the room. Nonchalantly he pursed his lips, cleared his throat, and then slowly opened his mouth.

The big fellow sat up on his bunk. Suddenly he raised his eyebrows in excitement and called out happily: "So, it's you, Yi-weng!"

After a moment of silence, the one standing by the door gently closed it, but it produced a loud noise nonetheless.

Huang Yi-an was stupefied. He narrowed his eyes and then opened them wide in order to size up the occupants of this room. He felt his insides sinking and his skin itching. He did not know whether he was pleased or disappointed at this sudden turn of events.

"What?" he murmured, "Oh, it's President Hsiao of the Society."

"Ha, ha, what a coincidence, what a happy coincidence indeed!"

President Hsiao's large frame glided off the bunk; the light of the opium lamp flickered. With studied casualness he greeted his friend before loudly introducing him to everyone in the room.

It turned out that all those characters were members of the Confucian Classics Study Society. In the manner of a shopkeeper boasting of his wares to customers, the president, with a radiant look and choosing his words carefully, proceeded to introduce Huang to his members: "He too is a classics expert, very well known in his home town." Almost immediately after he broke into somewhat mystifying laughter.

Huang stared at the wall for a moment, licked his lips, and wanted to tell them that District Magistrate Yao had invited him to interpret the classics, and that the provincial governor was also an admirer of his. Moreover, he thought he would tell them these things in a loud voice. He cleared his throat. But just then his friend made him sit down and said: "Since we all have similar interests, we should feel free to say whatever strikes our fancy. Ha, ha, ha, but, by the way, how did you know I was here?"

After scanning the people in the room, Huang forced a smile on his face. Sitting on the edge of a chair and obsequiously inclining his body toward Hsiao, he stammered: "I . . . well, originally I didn't know President Hsiao was here."

"Wonderful, wonderful. Really, it's been more than a year since I saw you," the president said, and cackled like a hen.

The rest of the people seemed to know that the newcomer was not too important, for they soon resumed sipping their wine. One loudly smacked his lips, as if to arouse the others' appetite for the wine. They continued their chit-chat without paying attention to Yi-weng.

In a friendly and yet distant tone President Hsiao asked Huang how he had been, and if anything new had happened in his home town. At the same time he was as much concerned with what the others were saying. From time to time he cut into their conversation, laughing freely.

"Oh, that's right," he said, his eyebrows raised, "Yi Lao-erh told me that you're going to be a relative of Yi Lao-wu."

Blushing, Huang replied, "Yes, yes. As a matter of fact, I'm taking my daughter to him to let him have a look. In the next room . . ."

"What a coincidence . . . What? You heard about the whore who continued to receive customers at sixty? Ha, ha, ha, oooh, very nice. You heard what we said? Is that how you knew I was here? Right?"

"I . . ." Huang lowered his voice, looking at the wall again. "My daughter is on the other side. I'm afraid that she might overhear. This is, well, a little inconvenient."

Unexpectedly President Hsiao burst out laughing. He slapped Huang on the shoulder and the latter almost fell at the impact. "Ai-ya, Yi-weng, you're too much!" He was laughing hard, almost breathless. Rubbing his eyes, he said: "We're all friends. Why such worries? Really, my friend, you've no need to worry. To give you an example, the magicians' public performances are really for the benefit of the audience; they don't play the same tricks on their own partners, do they? So why play games among ourselves? Am I right? Ha, ha, ha."

Huang joined in the laughter. Mouth twitching and looking at the wall, he wondered what his daughter was doing. He tried hard to make himself look as natural and as carefree as possible. Still, he couldn't help feeling sorry for himself for having brought Mei-tzu along on the trip.

Hsiao turned toward the others and, with the approval of his roommates, he stood before Huang. Holding in his stomach, he declared: "I'm always a blunt person and I like to tell it like it is. That year—" he turned in another direction: "What? Oh, that's right. Everyone called her 'pisspool.' Oh, oh, that type, that type is . . ." He made a funny face, patted Huang's shoulder with his right hand, and continued: "That type—ah, Yi-weng is the expert among us. Ha, ha, ha."

Huang was embarrassed, sweat visible on the tip of his nose. He stammered: "I—It's not true."

"Come, don't be polite. Let's have it. You're the expert in this area. I know you, you've tried all the exotic kinds. Ha, ha."

After this endorsement by the president, members clamored to hear about Huang's most exciting sexual escapades and his special amatory talents. They offered him a drink in ritual acceptance of him as a friend. One man announced that since they had similar interests they should be friends immediately.

Their president laughed heartily in agreement and clapped his hands hysterically.

As if someone were tickling him, Huang Yi-an tittered, his eyes forming two slits, his face compressed, and his body bent forward in the shape of a big dried-up shrimp.

He played coy for ten seconds or so. Giving President Hsiao a knowing look, he nodded a few times and whispered: "All right, all right, I'll tell you all." Then he looked around the room and wiped the saliva off his chin. His upper lip twitching, unsteadily he walked on his toes to the door. Then turning his head around, shrugging his shoulder, eyes slanting, he again whispered with a smile: "Wait for me a minute. Be patient."

Once outside the door, he thrust out his stomach. A limp feeling pervaded him; he felt he was floating in the clouds. His excitement was akin to that of an explorer finding some lost treasure. Lifting his head high he glared at the waiters milling around in the lobby and uttered a contemptuous "Humph." Vaguely, he felt he had become more resourceful and had much greater confidence in his ability to handle these low-class morons.

With a steady hand he pulled open the door to Cabin Number Seven. His face long, his eyebrows knitted, he said to his daughter: "Mei-

tzu, go to your schoolmate's—Go to the woman and spend some time with her."

The girl looked at him in surprise. She seemed to be debating whether to take her knitting with her. A moment later she sighed and left the room empty handed.

His gaze followed her motion, and stood to watch her for a while. After taking one angry look at a waiter, he turned his eyes on the middle-aged man lying on the bed. That man was still holding a book with one hand and scratching his crotch with the other. Finally, he glanced sideways at the bosom of the fat woman. The woman had buttoned up her blouse and was playing with her child. When she saw Mei-tzu, she greeted her with a smile. On one of her ample cheeks a dimple emerged.

Huang Yi-an felt he had lost something; then he said to himself calmly: "*Mm*, it's better this way, otherwise it would be . . ."

A smile flashed on his face. He was certain that woman was a lush, since she had a flushed face, bloodshot eyes, and a sleepy look.

A military policeman walked by him. He quickly put on a stern countenance and smacked his lips. With square steps he walked toward Cabin Number Six. His chin raised high, he looked at the end of the passageway.

Then he gently pushed open the cabin door. Human noises welled up; then the door was shut.

After two minutes a tittering laughter burst out.

Mao Tse-tung Overthrows Religious Authority

Dissatisfaction toward tradition, expressed through the written word in such works as Chang T'ien-i's "The Bulwark," was expressed in direct political action under the forces led by Mao Tse-tung (Mao Zedong, 1893–1976). In the twenties and thirties, Mao and his associates launched ideological assaults on several systems of traditional authority: political authority, clan authority, religious authority, and the domination of women by men. This address, "Overthrowing the Clan Authority of the Ancestral Temples and Clan Elders, the Religious Authority of Town and Village Gods, and the Masculine Authority of Husbands," is excerpted from his famous March 1927 "Report on an Investigation of the Peasant Movement in Hunan." It describes his efforts to organize the poorer elements of society into peasant associations to confront political and economic oppression. Religious beliefs are described here not as spiritual paths toward transcendent truths but as vulgar superstitions propounded by local tyrants for their own selfish ends.

Some of Mao's admonitions to the peasants are not entirely new, and in fact the very notion that a ruler promulgate announcements to encourage the instruction of the people dates to such texts as "The Announcement on Alcohol" from the *Book of History*. Mao's appeal to rely on human effort and not on supernatural forces, while due in part to the propagation of scientific learning imported from the West, also recalls Hsün Tzu's similar admonitions to distinguish what belongs to heaven and what belongs to human effort. Hsün Tzu did not, however, seek to eliminate a belief in heaven altogether. Chu Hsi in his memorial of 1189 had earlier warned of the dangers of charlatans who availed themselves of religious beliefs to promote their own interests, but his memorial was a direct appeal to imperial authority; it did not, however, question that authority. He appealed to the authority of careful study and inquiry but did not extol political organization as a remedy against mountebanks.

Mao decries social practices that were particularly disadvantageous to women. "Temples to the martyred virgins" are probably the temples built to honor women who never "remarried" even when their fiancés, to whom they might have been betrothed since childhood, died before marriage. Stone memorial arches commemorated women who never married a second time, even though they may have been very young at the time of their first husband's death. Mao does not, however, suggest that his political party, the Chinese Communist party, should pull down the temples and arches or destroy religious idols themselves, but instead advocates that the party instruct the people so that they will demolish them on their own. He also attacks beliefs in the Eight Characters, a kind of fortune telling based on the creation of a horoscope, as well as the belief that the location and position of ancestors' bones and grave sites will directly influence a family's material fortunes.

His arguments against gods and superstitions are not theological disquisitions but are based primarily on efficaciousness: his new methods of political organization are right because they are effective, and the gods are not. This was an argument that had been employed in religious debates for centuries. In premodern times, a ruler given a choice between Taoism or Buddhism, for example, might choose a tradition not necessarily on its spiritual merits but on the ability of its adepts to produce rain effectively.

This document dates to March 1927, just before the Communist party, led by Mao, and the Nationalist party (Kuomintang or Guomintang), led by Chiang K'ai-shek (died 1975), became enemies. A civil war between these two parties and several military warlord factions lasted until 1949, when Mao's forces established the People's Republic of China on the mainland. Under the People's Republic, concerted efforts to eliminate "feudal superstition" were continued until well after the founding of the state. The Nationalist party established the Republic of China on the island of Taiwan, however, and there many traditional religious practices continued unabated and still flourish despite increasing modernization.

"Overthrowing the Clan Authority of the Ancestral Temples and Clan Elders, the Religious Authority of Town and Village Gods, and the Masculine Authority of Husbands"

A man in China is usually subjected to the domination of three systems of authority: (1) the state system (political authority), ranging from the national, provincial and county government down to that of the township; (2) the clan system (clan authority), ranging from the central ancestral temple and its branch temples down to the head of the household; and (3) the supernatural system (religious authority), ranging from the King of Hell down to the town and village gods belonging to the nether world, and from the Emperor of Heaven down to all the various gods and spirits belonging to the celestial world. As for women, in addition to being dominated by these three systems of authority, they are also dominated by the men (the authority of the husband). These four authorities—political, clan, religious and masculine—are the embodiment of the whole feudal-patriarchal system and ideology, and are the four thick ropes binding the Chinese people, particularly the peasants. How the peasants have overthrown the political authority of the landlords in the countryside has been described above. The political authority of the landlords is the backbone of all the other systems of authority. With that overturned, the clan authority, the religious authority and the authority of the husband all begin to totter. Where the peasant association is powerful, the clan elders and administrators of temple funds no longer dare oppress those lower in the clan hierarchy or embezzle clan funds. The worst clan elders and administrators, being local tyrants, have been thrown out. No one any longer dares to practise the cruel corporal and capital punishments that used to be inflicted in the ancestral temples, such as flogging, drowning and burying alive. The old rule barring women and poor people from the banquets in the ancestral temples has also been broken. The women of Paikuo in Hengshan County gathered in force and swarmed into their ancestral temple, firmly planted their backsides in the seats and joined in the eating and drinking, while the venerable clan bigwigs had willy-nilly to let them do as they pleased. At another place, where poor peasants had been excluded from temple banquets, a group of them flocked in and ate and drank their fill, while the local tyrants and evil gentry and other long-gowned gentlemen all took to their heels in fright. Everywhere religious authority totters as the peasant movement develops. In many places the peasant associations have taken over the temples of the gods as their offices. Everywhere they advocate the appropriation of temple property in order to start peasant schools and to defray the expenses of the associations, calling it "public revenue from superstition." In Liling County, prohibiting superstitious practices and smashing idols have become quite the vogue. In its northern districts the peasants have prohibited the incense-burning processions to propitiate the god of pestilence. There were many idols in the Taoist temple at Fupoling in Lukou, but when extra room was needed for the district headquarters of the Kuomintang, they were all piled up in a corner, big and small together, and no peasant raised any objection. Since then, sacrifices to the gods, the performance of religious rites and the offering of sacred lamps have rarely been practised when a death occurs in a family. Because the initiative in this matter was taken by the chairman of the peasant association, Sun Hsiao-shan, he is hated by the local Taoist priests. In the Lungfeng Nunnery in the North Third District, the peasants and primary school teachers chopped up the wooden idols and actually used the wood to cook meat. More than thirty idols in the Tungfu Monastery in the Southern District were burned by the students and peasants together, and only two small images of Lord Pao were snatched up by an old peasant who said, "Don't commit a sin!" In places where the power of the peasants is predominant, only the older peasants and the women still believe in the gods, the younger peasants no longer doing so. Since the latter control the associations, the overthrow of religious authority and the eradication of superstition are going on everywhere. As to the authority of the husband, this has always been weaker among the poor peasants because, out of economic necessity, their womenfolk have to do more manual labour than the women of the richer classes and therefore have more say and greater power of decision in family matters. With the increasing bankruptcy of the rural economy in recent years, the basis for men's domination over women has already been weakened. With the rise of the peasant movement, the women in many places have now begun to organize rural women's associations; the opportunity has come for them to lift up their heads, and the authority of the husband is getting shakier every day. In a word, the whole feudal-patriarchal system and ideology is tottering with the growth of the peasants' power. At the present time, however, the peasants are concentrating on destroying the landlords' political authority. Wherever it has been wholly destroyed, they are beginning to press their attack in the three other spheres of the clan, the gods and male domination. But such attacks have only just begun, and there can be no thorough overthrow of all three until the peasants have won complete victory in the economic struggle. Therefore, our present task is to lead the peasants to put their greatest efforts into the political struggle, so that the landlords' authority is entirely overthrown. The economic struggle should follow immediately, so that the land problem and the other economic problems of the poor peasants may be fundamentally solved. As for the clan system, superstition, and inequality between men and women, their abolition will follow as a natural consequence of victory in the political and economic struggles. If too much of an effort is made, arbitrarily and prematurely, to abolish these things, the local tyrants and evil gentry will seize the pretext to put about such counter-revolutionary propaganda as "the peasant association has no piety

towards ancestors," "the peasant association is blasphemous and is destroying religion" and "the peasant association stands for the communization of wives," all for the purpose of undermining the peasant movement. A case in point is the recent events at Hsianghsiang in Hunan and Yanghsin in Hupeh, where the landlords exploited the opposition of some peasants to smashing idols. It is the peasants who made the idols, and when the time comes they will cast the idols aside with their own hands; there is no need for anyone else to do it for them prematurely. The Communist Party's propaganda policy in such matters should be, "Draw the bow without shooting, just indicate the motions." It is for the peasants themselves to cast aside the idols, pull down the temples to the martyred virgins and the arches to the chaste and faithful widows; it is wrong for anybody else to do it for them.

While I was in the countryside, I did some propaganda against superstition among the peasants. I said:

"If you believe in the Eight Characters, you hope for good luck; if you believe in geomancy, you hope to benefit from the location of your ancestral graves. This year within the space of a few months the local tyrants, evil gentry and corrupt officials have all toppled from their pedestals. Is it possible that until a few months ago they all had good luck and enjoyed the benefit of well-sited ancestral graves, while suddenly in the last few months their luck has turned and their ancestral graves have ceased to exert a beneficial influence? The local tyrants and evil gentry jeer at your peasant association and say, 'How odd! Today, the world is a world of committeemen. Look, you can't even go to pass water without bumping into a committeeman!' Quite true, the towns and the villages, the trade unions and the peasant associations, the Kuomintang and the Communist Party, all without exception have their executive committee members—it is indeed a world of committeemen. But is this due to the Eight Characters and the location of the ancestral graves? How strange! The Eight Characters of all the poor wretches in the countryside have suddenly turned auspicious! And their ancestral graves have suddenly started exerting beneficial influences! The gods? Worship them by all means. But if you had only Lord Kuan and the Goddess of Mercy and no peasant association, could you have overthrown the local tyrants and evil gentry? The gods and goddesses are indeed miserable objects. You have worshipped them for centuries, and they have not overthrown a single one of the local tyrants or evil gentry for you! Now you want to have your rent reduced. Let me ask, how will you go about it? Will you believe in the gods or in the peasant association?"

My words made the peasants roar with laughter.

The Cult of Mao

Despite his injunctions to destroy religious idols and unseat popular gods in his address to the Hunan peasants in 1927, Mao Tse-tung ironically set out to deify himself in the 1960s. By the mid sixties he had enjoyed nearly fifteen years as the leader of the People's Republic of China, but he suspected that his power was being undermined by some of his political colleagues. His popularity had not been enhanced by the widespread famine a few years earlier that killed an estimated twenty million people; the starvation was due to the measures of the "Great Leap Forward" of the late fifties that advocated increased collectivization of agricultural resources and encouraged deforestation to fuel the furnaces of industrialization. To renew his hold on authority, Mao encouraged a virtual cult of his own personality. As in Shang and early Chou times, the religious and the political realms became virtually indistinguishable.

This selection from *Wild Swans: Three Daughters of China,* the memoirs of the writer Jung Chang (born 1952), describes the cult of Mao from the point of view of a woman who experienced it directly when she was a young girl. Her firsthand account reveals the almost religious devotion the cult instilled in its young followers. It had its own saint in the fictive character of Lei Feng, its own scriptures in the writings of Mao, and its own religious practices of serving the people, continuing class struggle, and devoting oneself to Chairman Mao, a mysterious withdrawn divinity. The new cult rearranged the old idea of the "five relationships," and the filial love once directed toward parents was now saved for Mao. The roles of devotee and protector divinity were reversed, and instead of calling upon a deity such as Kuan-yin to save one from danger, the devotee now braved fires and knives and sacrificed oneself to the deity of Mao. Temples were converted to more secular uses: Jung Chang's school in Chengdu (Ch'eng-tu), the capital of Sichuan (Szechuan) Province, was once a temple to Confucius but is converted into a table-tennis room.

Jung Chang's own biography parallels the turbulent lives of many of her generation in China who lived through the chaos of the Cultural Revolution (1966–1976). She labored as a peasant, a steelworker, and an electrician in the late sixties and early seventies; in 1973 she enrolled at Sichuan University and received a scholarship to study in Britain, where she became a resident.

" 'Father Is Close, Mother is Close, but Neither Is as Close as Chairman Mao' "—The Cult of Mao (1964–1965)

"Chairman Mao," as we always called him, began to impinge directly on my life in 1964, when I was twelve. Having been in retreat for some time after the famine, he was starting his comeback, and in March of the previous year he had issued a call to the whole country, particularly the young, to "learn from Lei Feng."

Lei Feng was a soldier who, we were told, had died at the age of twenty-two in 1962. He had done an awful lot of good deeds—going out of his way to help the elderly, the sick, and the needy. He had donated his savings to disaster relief funds and given up his food rations to comrades in the hospital.

Lei Feng soon began to dominate my life. Every afternoon we left school to "do good deeds like Lei Feng." We went down to the railway station to try to help old ladies with their luggage, as Lei Feng had done. We sometimes had to grab their bundles from them forcibly because some countrywomen thought we were thieves. On rainy days, I stood on the street with an umbrella, anxiously hoping that an old lady would pass by and give me an opportunity to escort her home—as Lei Feng had done. If I saw someone carrying water buckets on a shoulder pole—old houses still did not have running water—I would try unsuccessfully to summon up the courage to offer my help, although I had no idea how heavy a load of water was.

Gradually, during the course of 1964, the emphasis began to shift from boy scoutish good deeds to the cult of Mao. The essence of Lei Feng, the teachers told us, was his "boundless love and devotion to Chairman Mao." Before he took any action, Lei Feng always thought of some words of Mao's. His diary was published and became our moral textbook. On almost every page there was a pledge like: "I must study Chairman Mao's works, heed Chairman Mao's words, follow Chairman Mao's instructions, and be a good soldier of Chairman Mao's." We vowed to follow Lei Feng, and be ready to "go up mountains of knives and down seas of flames," to "have our bodies smashed to powder and our bones crushed to smithereens," to "submit ourselves unquestioningly to the control of the Great Leader"—Mao. The cult of Mao and the cult of Lei Feng were two sides of the same coin: one was the cult of personality; the other, its essential corollary, was the cult of impersonality.

I read my first article by Mao in 1964, at a time when two slogans of Mao's—"Serve the People" and "Never Forget Class Struggle"— dominated our lives. The essence of these two complementary slogans was illustrated in Lei Feng's poem "The Four Seasons," which we all learned by heart:

> Like spring, I treat my comrades
> warmly.
> Like summer, I am full of ardor for my
> revolutionary work.
> I eliminate my individualism as an
> autumn gale sweeps away
> fallen leaves,
> And to the class enemy, I am cruel and
> ruthless like harsh winter.

In line with this, our teacher said we had to be careful whom we helped on our do-good errands. We must not help "class enemies." But I did not understand who they were, and when I asked, neither the teachers nor my parents were keen to elaborate. One common answer was: "like the baddies in the movies." But I could not see anyone around me who looked like the highly stylized enemy characters in the movies. This posed a big problem. I no longer felt sure about seizing bags from old ladies. I could not possibly ask, "Are you a class enemy?"

We sometimes went to clean the houses in an alley next to our school. In one house there was a young man who used to lounge on a bamboo chair watching us with a cynical smile as we toiled away on his windows. Not only did he not offer to help, he even wheeled his bicycle out of the shed and suggested we clean that for him as well. "What a pity," he once said, "that you are not the real Lei Feng, and that there are no photographers on hand to take your pictures for the newspapers." (Lei Feng's good deeds were miraculously recorded by an official photographer.) We all hated the lounger with the dirty bicycle. Could he be a class enemy? But we knew he worked at a machinery factory, and workers, we had been repeatedly told, were the best, the leading class in our revolution. I was confused. . . .

The cult of Mao went hand in hand with the manipulation of people's unhappy memories of their past. Class enemies were presented as vicious malefactors who wanted to drag China back to the days of the Kuomintang, which would mean that we children would lose our schools, our winter shoes, and our food. That was why we had to smash these enemies, we were told. Chiang Kai-shek was said to have launched assaults on the mainland and tried to stage a comeback in 1962 during the "difficult period"—the regime's euphemism for the famine.

In spite of all this talk and activity, class enemies for me, and for much of my generation, remained abstract, unreal shadows. They were a thing of the past, too far away. Mao had not been able to give them an everyday material form. One reason, paradoxically, was that he had smashed the past so thoroughly. However, the expectation of an enemy figure was planted in us.

At the same time, Mao was sowing the seeds for his own deification, and my contemporaries and I were immersed in this crude yet effective indoctrination. It worked partly because Mao adroitly occupied the moral high ground: just as harshness to class enemies was presented as loyalty to the people, so total submission to him was cloaked in a deceptive appeal to be selfless. It was very hard to get behind the rhetoric, particularly when there was no alternative viewpoint from the adult population. In fact, the adults positively colluded in enhancing Mao's cult.

For two thousand years China had an emperor figure who was state power and spiritual authority rolled into one. The religious feelings which people in other parts of the world have toward a god have in China always been directed toward the emperor. My parents, like hundreds of millions of Chinese, were influenced by this tradition.

Mao made himself more godlike by shrouding himself in mystery. He always appeared remote, beyond human approach. He eschewed radio, and there was no television. Few people, except his court staff, ever had any contact with him. Even his colleagues at the very top only met him in a sort of formal audience. After Yan'an, my father only set eyes on him a few times, and then only at large-scale meetings. My mother only ever saw him once, when he came to Chengdu in 1958 and summoned all officials above Grade 18 to have a group photo taken with him. After the fiasco of the Great Leap Forward, he had disappeared almost completely.

Mao, the emperor, fitted one of the patterns of Chinese history: the leader of a nationwide peasant uprising who swept away a rotten dynasty and became a wise new emperor exercising absolute authority. And, in a sense, Mao could be said to have earned his god-emperor status. He *was* responsible for ending the civil war and bringing peace and stability, which the Chinese always yearned for—so much that they said "It's better to be a dog in peacetime than a human being in war." It was under Mao that China became a power to be reckoned with in the world, and many Chinese stopped feeling ashamed and humiliated at being Chinese, which meant a tremendous amount to them. In reality, Mao turned China back to the days of the Middle Kingdom and, with the help of the United States, to isolation from the world. He enabled the Chinese to feel great and superior again, by blinding them to the world outside. Nonetheless, national pride was so important to the Chinese that much of the population was genuinely grateful to Mao, and did not find the cult of his personality offensive, certainly not at first. The near total lack of access to information and the systematic feeding of disinformation meant that most Chinese had no way to discriminate between Mao's successes and his failures, or to identify the relative role of Mao and other leaders in the Communists' achievements.

Fear was never absent in the building up of Mao's cult. Many people had been reduced to a state where they did not dare even to think, in case their thoughts came out involuntarily. Even if they did entertain unorthodox ideas, few mentioned them to their children, as they might blurt out something to other children, which could bring disaster to themselves as well as their parents. In the learn-from-Lei Feng years it was hammered into children that our first and only loyalty should be to Mao. A popular song went: "Father is close, Mother is close, but neither is as close as Chairman Mao." We were drilled to think that anyone, including our parents, who was not totally for Mao was our enemy. Many parents encouraged their children to grow up as conformists, as this would be safest for their future.

Self-censorship covered even basic information. I never heard of Yu-lin, or my grandmother's other relatives. Nor was I told about my mother's detention in 1955, or about the famine—in fact, anything that might sow a grain of doubt in me about the regime, or Mao. My parents, like virtually every parent in China, never said anything unorthodox to their children.

In 1965, my New Year resolution was "I will obey my grandmother"—a traditional Chinese way of promising to behave well. My father shook his head: "You should not say that. You should only say 'I obey Chairman Mao.' " On my thirteenth birthday, in March that year, my father's present was not his usual books of science fiction, but a volume containing the four philosophical works of Mao.

Only one adult ever said anything to me which conflicted with the official propaganda, and that was the stepmother of Deng Xiaoping, who lived some of the time in the apartment block next to ours, with her daughter, who worked in the provincial government. She liked children, and I was constantly in and out of her apartment. When my friends and I stole pickles from the canteen, or picked melon flowers and herbs from the compound garden, we did not dare to take them home for fear of being scolded, so we used to go to her apartment, where she would wash and fry them for us. This was all the more exciting because we were eating something illicit. She was about seventy then, but looked much younger, with tiny feet and a gentle, smooth, but strong face. She always wore a gray cotton jacket and black cotton shoes, which she made herself. She was very relaxed and treated us like equals. I liked sitting in her kitchen chatting with her. On one occasion, when I was about thirteen, I went to see her straight after an emotional "speak-bitterness" session. I was bursting with compassion for anyone who had had to live under the Kuomintang, and I said: "Grandma Deng, how you must have suffered under the evil Kuomintang! How the soldiers must have looted you! And the blood-sucking landlords! What did they do to you?" "Well," she answered, "they didn't always loot . . . and they were not always evil . . . ." Her words hit me like a bombshell. I was so shocked that I never told anyone what she had said. . . .

Politics invaded my life more and more after went to middle school in the autumn of 1964 On our first day we were told we should than Chairman Mao for being there, because hi "class line" had been applied to our year's en rollment. Mao had accused schools and universi ties of having been "occupied by the bourgeoi sie." Now, he had instructed, they should b returned to the working class. Priority should b given to sons and daughters of "good back grounds" *(chu-shen hao)*. This meant havin; workers, peasants, soldiers, or Party officials as parents, particularly as fathers. The application of this "class-line" criterion to the whole society meant that one's lot was more than ever determined by one's family and the accident of birth.

However, the status of a family was often ambiguous: a worker might once have been employed in a Kuomintang office; a clerk did not belong to any category; an intellectual was an "undesirable," but what if he was a Party member? How should the children of such parents be classified? Many enrollment officers decided to play it safe, which meant giving preference to children whose parents were Party officials. They constituted half the pupils in my class.

My new school, the Number Four Middle School, was the leading key school for the whole province and took students with the highest marks in the all-Sichuan entrance exams. In previous years, entrance had been decided solely on the basis of exam results. In my year, exam marks and family background were equally important. . . .

I loved the school from the moment I walked in. It had an imposing gate with a broad roof of blue tiles and carved eaves. A flight of stone stairs led up to it, and the loggia was supported by six red-timber columns. Symmetrical rows of dark-green cypresses enhanced the atmosphere of solemnity leading into the interior.

The school had been founded in 141 B.C. It was the first school set up by a local government in China. At its center was a magnificent temple, formerly dedicated to Confucius. It was well preserved, but was not functioning as a temple any longer. Inside were half a dozen Ping-Pong tables, separated by the massive columns. In front of the carved doors, down a long flight of stairs, lay extensive grounds designed to provide a majestic approach to the temple. A two-story teaching block had been erected, which cut off the grounds from a brook crossed by three little arched bridges, with sculptures of miniature lions and other animals sitting on their sandstone edges. Beyond the bridges was a beautiful garden surrounded by peaches and plane trees. Two giant bronze incense burners were set at the bottom of the stairs in front of the temple, although there was no longer any blue smoke curling up and lingering in the air above them. The grounds on the sides of the temple had been converted into basketball and volleyball courts. Farther along were two lawns where we used to

sit or lie in spring and enjoy the sun during lunch breaks. Behind the temple was another lawn, beyond which lay a big orchard at the foot of a small hill covered with trees, vines, and herbs. . . .

But more and more political indoctrination was creeping into school life. Gradually, morning assembly became devoted to Mao's teachings, and special sessions were instituted in which we read Party documents. Our Chinese-language textbook now contained more propaganda and less classical literature, and politics, which mainly consisted of works by Mao, became part of the curriculum.

Almost every activity became politicized. One day at morning assembly the headmaster told us we were going to do eye exercises. He said Chairman Mao had observed that there were too many schoolchildren wearing spectacles, a sign that they had hurt their eyes by working too hard. He had ordered something to be done about it. We were all terribly moved by his concern. Some of us wept in gratitude. We started doing eye exercises for fifteen minutes every morning. A set of movements had been devised by doctors and set to music. After rubbing various points around our eyes, we all stared intently at the rows of poplars and willows outside the window. Green was supposed to be a restful color. As I enjoyed the comfort the exercises and the leaves brought me, I thought of Mao and repledged my loyalty to him. . . .

At this time Mao had called on the country to go from learning from Lei Feng to learning from the army. Under the defense minister, Lin Biao, who had succeeded Marshal Peng Dehuai in 1959, the army had become the trailblazer for the cult of Mao. Mao also wanted to regimentalize the nation even more. He had just written a well-publicized poem exhorting women to "doff femininity and don military attire." We were told that the Americans were waiting for a chance to invade and reinstate the Kuomintang, and that in order to defeat an invasion by them Lei Feng had trained day and night to overcome his weak physique and become a champion hand-grenade thrower.

Physical training suddenly assumed vital importance. There was compulsory running, swimming, high jumping, working out on parallel bars, shot-putting, and throwing wooden hand grenades. In addition to the two hours of sports per week, forty-five minutes of after-school sports now became obligatory.

I had always been hopeless at sports, and hated them, except tennis. Previously this had not mattered, but now it took on a political connotation, with slogans like: "Build up a strong physique to defend our motherland." Unfortunately, my aversion to sports was increased by this pressure. When I tried to swim, I always had a mental picture of being pursued by invading Americans to the bank of a surging river. As I could not swim, my only choice was between being drowned or being captured and tortured by the Americans. Fear gave me frequent cramps in the water, and once I thought I was drowning in the swimming pool. In spite of compulsory swimming every week during the summer, I never managed to learn to swim all the time I lived in China.

Hand-grenade throwing was also regarded as very important, for obvious reasons. I was always at the bottom of the class. I could only throw the wooden hand grenades we practiced with a couple of yards. I felt that my classmates were questioning my resolve to fight the U.S. imperialists. Once at our weekly political meeting somebody commented on my persistent failure at hand-grenade throwing. I could feel the eyes of the class boring into me like needles, as if to say: "You are a lackey of the Americans!" The next morning I went and stood in a corner of the sports field, with my arms held out in front of me and a couple of bricks in each hand. In Lei Feng's diary, which I had learned by heart, I had read that this was how he had toughened up his muscles to throw hand grenades. After a few days, by which time my upper arms were red and swollen, I gave up, and whenever I was handed the wooden chunk, I became so nervous that my hands shook uncontrollably.

One day in 1965, we were suddenly told to go out and start removing all the grass from the lawns. Mao had instructed that grass, flowers, and pets were bourgeois habits and were to be eliminated. The grass in the lawns at our school was of a type I have not seen anywhere outside China. Its name in Chinese means "bound to the ground." It crawls all over the hard surface of the earth and spreads thousands of roots which drill down into the soil like claws of steel. Underground they open up and produce further roots which shoot out in every direction. In no time there are two networks, one aboveground and one belowground, which intertwine and cling to the earth, like knotted metal wires that have been nailed into the ground. Often the only casualties were my fingers, which always ended up with deep, long cuts. It was only when they were attacked with hoes and spades that some of the root systems went, reluctantly. But any fragment left behind would make a triumphant comeback after even a slight rise in temperature or a gentle drizzle, and we would have to go into battle all over again.

Flowers were much easier to deal with, but they went with even more difficulty, because no one wanted to remove them. Mao had attacked flowers and grass several times before, saying that they should be replaced by cabbages and cotton. But only now was he able to generate enough pressure to get his order implemented— but only up to a point. People loved their plants, and some flowerbeds survived Mao's campaign.

I was extremely sad to see the lovely plants go. But I did not resent Mao. On the contrary, I hated myself for feeling miserable. By then I had grown into the habit of "self-criticism" and automatically blamed myself for any instincts that went against Mao's instructions. In fact, such feelings frightened me. It was out of the question to discuss them with anyone. Instead, I tried to suppress them and acquire the correct way of thinking. I lived in a state of constant self-accusation.

Such self-examination and self-criticism were a feature of Mao's China. You would become a new and better person, we were told. But all this introspection was really designed to serve no other purpose than to create a people who had no thoughts of their own.

The religious aspect of the Mao cult would not have been possible in a traditionally secular society like China had there not been impressive economic achievements. The country had made a stunning recovery from the famine, and the standard of living was improving dramatically. n Chengdu, although rice was still rationed, here was plenty of meat, poultry, and vegeta-les. Winter melons, turnips, and eggplants /ere piled up on the pavements outside the hops because there was not enough space to tore them. They were left outside overnight, nd almost nobody took them; the shops were iving them away for a pittance. Eggs, once so recious, sat rotting in large baskets—there were oo many of them. Only a few years before it lad been hard to find a single peach—now peach ating was being promoted as "patriotic," and fficials went around to people's homes and ried to persuade them to take peaches for next to nothing.

There were a number of success stories which boosted the nation's pride. In October 1964 China exploded its first atomic bomb. This was given huge publicity and touted as a demonstration of the country's scientific and industrial achievement, particularly in relation to "standing up to imperialist bullies." The explosion of the atomic bomb coincided with the ousting of Khrushchev, which was presented as proof that Mao was right again. In 1964 France recognized China at full ambassadorial level, the first leading Western nation to do so. This was received with rapture inside China as a major victory over the United States, which was refusing to acknowledge China's rightful place in the world.

In addition, there was no general political persecution, and people were relatively content. All the credit was given to Mao. Although the very top leaders knew what Mao's real contribution was, the people were kept completely in the dark. Over the years I composed passionate eulogies thanking Mao for all his achievements and pledging my undying loyalty to him.

I was thirteen in 1965. On the evening of 1 October that year, the sixteenth anniversary of the founding of the People's Republic, there was a big fireworks display on the square in the center of Chengdu. To the north of the square was the gate to an ancient imperial palace, which had recently been restored to its third-century grandeur, when Chengdu was the capital of a kingdom and a prosperous walled city. The gate was very similar to the Gate of Heavenly Peace in Peking, now the entrance to the Forbidden City, except for its color: it had sweeping green-tiled roofs and gray walls. Under the glazed roof of the pavilion stood enormous dark-red pillars. The balustrades were made of white marble. I was standing behind them with my family and the Sichuan dignitaries on a reviewing stand enjoying the festival atmosphere and waiting for the fireworks to begin. Below in the square 50,000 people were singing and dancing. *Bang! Bang!* The signals for the fireworks went off a few yards from where I stood. In an instant, the sky was a garden of spectacular shapes and colors, a sea of wave after wave of brilliance. The music and noise rose from below the imperial gate to join in the sumptuousness. After a while, the sky was clear for a few seconds. Then a sudden explosion brought out a gorgeous blossom, followed by the unfurling of a long, vast, silky hanging. It stretched itself in the middle of the sky, swaying gently in the autumn breeze. In the light over the square, the characters on the hanging were shining: "Long Live Our Great Leader Chairman Mao!" Tears sprang to my eyes. "How lucky, how incredibly lucky I am to be living in the great era of Mao Zedong!" I kept saying to myself. "How can children in the capitalist world go on living without being near Chairman Mao, and without the hope of ever seeing him in person?" I wanted to do something for them, to rescue them from their plight. I made a pledge to myself there and then to work hard to build a stronger China, in order to support a world revolution. I needed to work hard to be entitled to see Chairman Mao, too. That was the purpose of my life.

The Revival
of the Spiritual Tradition:
The God of Theater

Despite the destruction in mainland China of temples and works of religious art during the Cultural Revolution in the sixties and seventies, in the late eighties many ancient traditions began to resurface. The ritual performance of several kinds of dramatic arts, such as marionette theater and exorcistic drama, reappeared after an interruption of over forty years. These dramatic art forms, some of which suggest continuities with the religious practices of antiquity, were virtually unknown outside of China until very recently.

In south China, the performance arts have various protector deities, one of which is T'ien Tu-yüan-shuai, or Marshal T'ien, also known by the honorific title of Hsiang Kung, or "Young Master." Revered in some regions as the god of theater and dramatic arts, according to one local legend he was a famous musician of the T'ang dynasty. One version of this legend told by marionettists in Ch'üan-chou, Fukien Province, claims that the god is also surnamed Su. In this tale the events of the god's conception and infancy bear marked parallels to the tale of Chiang Yüan and her son Hou Chi recorded in the ancient *Book of Odes*. As a young man, the god's talents as a musician and dancer enable him to realize on earth the realm envisioned in the emperor's dream of a celestial journey; he choreographs with his own body a concert once heard in the heavens. What others believe to be the measurements for a magical ritual palace, or cosmogram of the universe, are interpreted by the god as a musical score. He enacts the cadences of the score with the dramaturgy of sacred dance, and he creates dimensions of space with movement and gesture.

These themes are also reflected in *The Great Showing of Su*, one of the most important plays from the repertoire of marionette theater in Ch'üan-chou. In the *Great Showing*, as in the legend, the god both entertains his spectators and serves as an intermediary for them with higher spiritual powers. His "showing," or performance, is not only theatrical amusement but is a ritual invocation of blessings and prosperity from heaven on behalf of the local community. Marionette theater is conducted in a religious context; it is performed on temporary bamboo stages constructed at temples, often in conjunction with rites conducted simultaneously by the priest of the temple. Sponsored by the temple's constituency, theater may be performed on the occasion of the birthday of the temple's main deity, be it Kuan-ti, the god of war and justice, for example, or a Wang-yeh, one of the gods of pestilence. Performances usually take place between the hours of midnight and dawn; the marionettes are quite large and stand over three feet in height. The stage, like the ritual palace of the legend, is a cosmo-gram of the universe, for it is built in the shape of the *Book of Change*'s eight basic hexagrams, which are thought to express the underlying structure of the cosmos.

Although the performance is in part secular comic entertainment, the stage actions of the Invoker and of the god detail a serious ritual liturgy. In the *Great Showing,* the god of theater is first himself invoked with libations of wine, and he in turn presents a memorial to even higher divine authorities requesting boons similar to those recorded on Shang and Chou bronzes thousands of years earlier: longevity, offspring, and prosperity. The memorial documents the relationship between the human and spiritual realms. With vows, fasts, and votive offerings, human beings express gratitude and thanksgiving to powers from which they expect favorable responses and tangible rewards. The god's earnest supplications for spiritual assistance are nevertheless a parody of the very seriousness that such an undertaking requires. After invoking such solemn divinities as Yama, the ruler of the underworld, and Kuan-yin, the bodhisattva of compassion, he regales them with stories of incense, flowers, lamps, and candles. The veiled sexual innuendos of these anecdotes would not have been lost on the popular audience: when the scholar Liu Hsi goes to the temple to burn his stick of "incense," for example, the Maiden of Mount Hua becomes pregnant. The god then recounts his own life in verse form before sending the invited divinities back to their respective homes; he closes with a blessing for writers and performers and for the community at large. At yet another level of interpretation, however, the god's great performance mimes the choreography of shamanic celestial journeys as he traces with his feet the cosmological dance steps of "Pacing the Mainstays of Heaven" and "Treading the Dipper." As his body shape-shifts into the characters for the Five Agents, he incarnates the essential forces of the universe.

Dramatic and religious practices also overlap in another kind of performance, the ritual exorcistic dance called Nuo that has recently reappeared in south China. In the Chiang-k'ou area of Fukien Province, Marshal T'ien is one of the protector deities of the young men who train to become spirit mediums of the Nuo exorcism; possessed by various gods, they perform a kind of line dance within the community to dispel baneful influences and noxious spiritual forces. The reemergence of this ritual dance suggests the continuity of ancient traditions within the modern era, for Confucius himself had stood on the steps of his ancestral temple and watched a Nuo exorcism performed.

The Legend of the God

In the reign of emperor T'ang Ming-huang [reign 712–756] there was a woman of the Su family who lived near the Iron-plate Bridge in Hang-chou. Once when on a walk with her maid she stopped by a rice paddy to pick a kernel of rice. It tasted sweet and she swallowed it, becoming pregnant. When she gave birth, her father had the maid take the baby away. The maid set it in the same rice paddy where her mistress had picked the rice kernel, but a few days later, at the bidding of the mother, she returned and found crabs feeding the baby by dribbling spittle into its mouth. She brought the infant home. The child was named T'ien, meaning "field," after the place of his origin; he also kept his mother's surname, Su. The boy initially could not speak, but he was brilliant at his studies and eventually won top honors in the imperial examinations.

At the age of eighteen he was brought to the court of the emperor, where he excelled in music and dance. On one occasion the emperor dreamed of a voyage to the moon and of attending a beautiful concert there; shortly thereafter, a strange book was presented to the court. No one could decipher it, although some suggested it might contain the measurements for the construction of a magical ritual palace (ming-t'ang). When T'ien saw it, he suddenly laughed aloud and said, "That's a musical score." Then he set up some musicians and danced to the music, and the performance was just as the emperor had dreamed. The emperor gave T'ien three cups of wine, but his face turned red, and he collapsed outside on the jade steps. The emperor commanded maidens from the Inner Palace to help him back inside, where they laid him on the emperor's bed. The empress saw him there and, fearing that he would come to a bad end, wrote the numbers "eight" and "ten" above him on the bed, intending to ensure that he live to be eighty. But when he awoke he misread the numbers as eighteen, and he died.

The Great Showing of Su

CAST

INVOKER
THE GOD OF THEATER, or MARSHAL T'IEN, *also known as the* YOUNG MASTER, *here also surnamed* SU
CHORUS OF MUSICIANS AND MARIONETTISTS

[*To an opening drum roll and the sound of gongs, musicians begin a medley of nine tunes, including "Biting lice leaping," "Chickens scratching for grain," "Noise fills the mountains," and "Subduing the Five Killer Specters." The invocation of* THE GOD OF THEATER *begins as the* INVOKER, *holding in his hands a talismanic cone of paper for ritually animating the marionette figures, first bows to the god puppet and then to the stage. The* INVOKER *pours from a bottle a libation of three glasses of wine, cries "Ho ts'ai-a!" and recites the following "hidden spell."*]

INVOKER:
    One stick of fine incense burns on the
        gold altar,
    Silver candles shine red as the sun.
    Golden flowers are arranged in silver
        vases,
    Fine wine is poured into golden cups.
[*The* INVOKER *again makes libations.*] I invoke and worshipfully invite to the altar the Great King of the Jade Sound of the Hall of Music, Commander in Chief T'ien of the Bureau of Wind and Fire of the Ninefold Heavens. I invoke him together with the Elder Lad, the Second Lad, the Judge Who Leads the Tune, the Flute-playing Lad, the Lad Who Brings Good Fortune, the General Whose Dance Dazzles, and the Thirty-six Officials, Generals, and Gods. I offer wine once, twice, and again a third time. Worshipfully I invoke the tutelary god before the stage. A sheaf of spirit money burns, reddening the entire stage! [*The* INVOKER *lights the paper cone and draws Chinese characters in the air with*

it, letting the ashes fall on the four corners of the stage. Sprinkling wine about the stage, the INVOKER *recites the following spell, sprinkling wine on the musical instruments as he names them.*]

INVOKER:

Red bird ascend to heaven,
White phoenix descend to earth.
To the left the green dragon,
To the right the white tiger.
Excellent stage! Excellent backdrop!
Excellent big drum! Excellent small
      drum!
Excellent gong! Excellent cymbal!
Excellent thin clacker!
Ho ts'ai-a!

[Making another libation, he raises a cup and offers it to the god.]

Young Master, please have a drink of wine.
All you gods, please have a drink of wine.
Ho ts'ai-a!

[He dips his finger into the wine and writes eighteen talismans in the palm of his left hand.]

The Eighteen Unions are here. The Eighteen Unions are complete. My disciples, sing high! Ho ts'ai-a!

[He claps three times. The CHORUS OF MUSICIANS AND MARIONETTISTS *sings the song "Luo-li-lian," a tune of alliterative incantatory syllables. The* INVOKER *makes one more libation before tapping the toe of his right foot to signal the musicians to stop; he solemnly sings "Luo-li-lian" before pouring the wine offering back into the bottle. As the drummer plays the "Stage Entrance" and "Official" drum roll, one of the marionettists twists the body of the god, the "Young Master," into the shape of the Chinese character "metal," and he signals with his foot to stop the music. The* GOD *calls out the following verses in* kuan-hua, *the local version of official Mandarin Chinese.*]

YOUNG MASTER: Ho ts'ai-a! One invitation, a second invitation, three ritual invitations!

CHORUS: Three ritual invitations!

YOUNG MASTER: His heaven-born countenance is clear and lovely.

CHORUS: Clear and lovely!

YOUNG MASTER: At eighteen, he sang and laughed "Ha ha."

CHORUS: Laughed "Ha ha!"

YOUNG MASTER: Let me ask you, who made marionettes?

CHORUS: Who made them?

YOUNG MASTER: Master Ch'en P'ing made them.

CHORUS: He made them.

YOUNG MASTER: Now listen here.

CHORUS: We are listening.

YOUNG MASTER: Your Young Master has come here today. Who have you arranged to sing?

CHORUS: Thirty-six flower girls and forty-eight handsome lads.

YOUNG MASTER: Excellent! Your Young Master should dance and sing.

CHORUS: Dance and sing well!

YOUNG MASTER: Thirty-six flower girls and forty-eight handsome lads have been arranged up above on stage. Your Young Master has come up here and should dance and sing. Dance and sing, singing "Li-luo-li-lian." [*Singing "Luo-li-lian," Su T'ien shifts his body alternately into the shapes of the Chinese characters "metal," "wood," "water," "fire," and "earth" as he performs the steps of the ancient ritual dances "Pacing the Mainstays of Heaven" and "Treading the Dipper." He bows to center, left, and right before returning to stage center.*]

YOUNG MASTER:

Listen to the gong and drum sound "ting
      tang,"
The very same play in how many
      different forms.
On my head I wear a headpiece of
      flowers;
On my body, embroidered red cloth.

Where do I not go, where do I not
        come?
Had the god not been invoked, who
        would dare act frivolously?
        [*He kneels.*]
I worshipfully invite the High Perfected
        of the three Realms.
I worshipfully invite the High Perfected
        of the Upper Realm.
I worshipfully invite the High Perfected
        of the Middle Realm.
I worshipfully invite the High Perfected
        of the Lower Realm.

[*Alternately kowtowing and kneeling, he moves
forward on his knees and prostrates himself
before delivering the following memorial to the
spirits on behalf of the patrons of the play.*]

YOUNG MASTER: Today, the insignificant,
antlike persons [*here he recites the names
and place of residence of the patrons*] of
Ch'üan-chou prefecture of Fukien province,
burn incense with sincere feelings, worship,
and make a request. Let it be known that
Heaven is nine levels high and takes sincerity
as its standard. The spirits who dwell three
feet above one's head shine due to goodness;
their universal merit led to their transformation. Greatly they spread forth the luster of
their benevolence. We recite the names of
these antlike persons [*he recites the dates
and times of nativity of the patrons.*] The
destiny of all the above persons depends
upon the radiance of the Stellar Gods of
the Northern Dipper. The gratitude of these
persons toward heaven and earth, which carry
them with profound mercy, moves the Three
Lights of the Sun, Moon, and Stars to shine
down their virtue. These persons themselves
know to take refuge in the Tao and to respond
to unborn karma. The Master of the Lamps,
So-and-so, last year made fine vows and
indeed received divine responses. So today
these people have sincerely prepared lamps,
gold, a sweet pig, a grass-fed goat, and a
marionette theater, and they perform Li-yüan
theater to express their thanks. These fore-

sightful men and women all made fine vows
at various times, and they have not forgotten
what they thought at those times. Moreover,
all these believers have made further vows
and requests and have fasted. They have
sincerely prepared lamps and gold to perform
expiations and express thanks. On this humbly auspicious day, we have set up an altar
of lamps, and we perform marionette theater
and play music. Above, we pray to the Heavenly Perfected. Here we make offerings to
the divine and merciful. Below, we express
our thanks to the divine protector of the
precinct. Happily fulfilling our fine vows,
gathering auspiciousness, we pray for good
fortune and divine protection. Once again
preserve our peace. We prostrate ourselves
before you in the hope that you will let fall
your mercy. Bequeath us the shining good
fortune of the peace and well-being of the
Nine Kings. Let the ten thousand spirits together witness and record longevity for us
lasting for hundreds of thousands of years.
Here is our request and here are our thanks;
soon there will be peace and happiness. The
Ritual of the Lamps has been conducted, the
gate and the courtyard are purified, and our
homes are radiant. Male sons will be born
and wealth increase, raising high the fame of
our families. The five good fortunes will arise
together, the three abundances will reflect
each other, and there will be no disasters
throughout the four seasons. The eight subdivisions of the year will bring good tidings.
We will propagate like spreading melon
vines, resplendent for a hundred generations.
Reverently we make this memorial, in hope
of being heard. [*He recites the current date
and year.*] Memorialized. [*The* GOD *stands
and bows.*] I worshipfully invite Emperor
Yama of the Eastern Sacred Mountain, the
two Lords of the prefectural and city god
temples, the Kuan-yin of this dwelling, the
stove god, the tutelary god, the gods pro-
tecting the doors, and the gods worshiped
with the incense burner of this dwelling.
Young Su fears that he has not made an ex-

haustive invitation and that the preparations will be incomplete. Therefore, I beseech the local tutelary divinity to invite them again. [*He taps his right foot behind his back to stop the music.*] You have been invited! [*The* MU-SICIANS *play the "Victory" melody. Now speaking in the local Ch'üan-chou Hokkien dialect, the* YOUNG MASTER *continues.*]

YOUNG MASTER: Disciples!

CHORUS: Yes!

YOUNG MASTER: Your Young Master has clearly invoked the gods. I must sing of incense, flowers, lamps, and candles, and do reverence to the High Perfected of the Three Realms. How about that?

CHORUS: Excellent!

YOUNG MASTER: Your Young Master will sing badly, and you disciples will harmonize badly.

CHORUS: Young Master will sing well, but we disciples will harmonize badly.

YOUNG MASTER: It is said that incense has a story.

CHORUS: What is the story of incense?

YOUNG MASTER:
Listen, disciples.
Good incense grows on trees.

CHORUS: Grows on trees!

YOUNG MASTER:
Use incense to worship the gods of the
    Three Realms.
Liu Hsi the scholar entered a temple to
    burn incense.
Together with that Third Maiden of
    Mount Hua
They had a child.
The child's name is Aloeswood Lad.
Lian li luo-luo li lian. . . .
After incense comes the story of flowers.

CHORUS: What is the story of flowers?

YOUNG MASTER:
Listen, disciples.
Fair flowers are born on the earth.

CHORUS: Fair flowers are born on the earth!

YOUNG MASTER:
An immortal maiden in heaven loved
    flowers.

She descended to the common realm.
Huang Ch'iu-kung, that fellow,
Went into the garden to admire flowers.
Together with that Magnolia Maiden,
They entwined in love.
Lian li luo-luo li lian. . . .
After flowers comes the story of
    lanterns.

CHORUS: What is the story of lanterns?

YOUNG MASTER:
Listen, disciples.
Light lanterns in the darkness
On the night of the Lantern Festival.
A daughter of the Wang family, that
    woman,
Saw the lanterns fill the town.
Ts'ao Kuo-hua, that fellow,
Went out to trim the lantern wicks
And became fast friends
With the Tou Wen-ch'ing maiden.
Lian li luo-luo li lian. . . .
After lanterns comes the story of
    candles.

CHORUS: What is the story of candles?

YOUNG MASTER:
Listen, disciples.
Fine candles have a perfumed wax.

CHORUS: Fine candles have a perfumed wax!

YOUNG MASTER:
Light them and it fills the hall.
Shining brightly a true light glows.
Kuan Fu-tzu escorted his sister-in-law
Over Five Passes,
Holding a candle until dawn
To carry through his loyalty.
He has left a name through all the ages.
Lian li luo-luo li lian. . . .

[*The* GOD *recites a hidden spell.*] Your Young Master has already invoked the gods. I retire behind the screen and command my disciples to perform a play, reverently worshiping the High Perfected of the Three Realms and all the gods distant and close by. [*To the gods.*] You have been invited! [*Singing "Luo-li-lian," he retires while short sections of traditional plays are performed. He then returns to the stage.*] My surname was Su.

CHORUS: His surname was Su!

YOUNG MASTER:

My home is in Hang-chou
At the head of Iron-plate Bridge,
Three miles from town.

CHORUS: Three miles from town!

YOUNG MASTER:

The Emperor of T'ang noticed
I was deeply poetic.

CHORUS: Deeply poetic!

YOUNG MASTER:

He ordered me to roam the world over.

CHORUS: Roam the world over!

YOUNG MASTER:

Righting wrongs and
Bringing peoples' wishes before
Heavenly Officers.
Suddenly I heard

CHORUS: Suddenly I heard

YOUNG MASTER:

Behind the painted screen
A fine big drum.

CHORUS: A fine big drum!

YOUNG MASTER:

And then I heard
Behind the painted screen
A fine small drum.
The big drum led the small drum
And the small drum led the big drum
Beating ting-tang hsiang ting-tang.

CHORUS: Ting-tang hsiang ting-tang!

YOUNG MASTER:

I, by nature,
By nature love to dance.
I'll dance a "line of geese" dance.

CHORUS: A "line of geese" dance!

YOUNG MASTER:

And then I pace,
Pace a fancy step.

CHORUS: A fancy step!

YOUNG MASTER:

And sing a song of Great Peace.

CHORUS: Great Peace!

YOUNG MASTER:

One verse of Lian-li-luo,
Lian li lian-lian li luo. . . .
Purple clothes, purple clothes

And a golden belt.
In my hand I hold a peony

CHORUS: A peony!

YOUNG MASTER:

On golden steps supported by jade
maidens.

CHORUS: Jade maidens!

YOUNG MASTER:

I collapse drunk, collapse drunk.
Now that is something to boast about.
Luo li-luo luo-luo-li-luo lian. . . .
When I was young I carefully read my
books.
I made a name through my writing.

CHORUS: Made a name!

YOUNG MASTER:

The nobility of the court,
In purple and vermilion
All were men of letters.
Lian li luo-luo-li-luo lian. . . .

[*Kneels to recite a spell to send off the gods.*]

I worshipfully send off the High
Perfected of the Three Realms.
Those of the Upper Realm return to the
heavenly halls.
Those of the Middle Realm return to the
central halls.
Those of the Lower Realm return to the
terrestrial headquarters.

I worshipfully send off the divinities, to return the gods to their shrines, return the
Buddhas to their temples, return the soldiers
and horsemen of the Five Camps to their
respective camps, and return Young Su back
to his prefecture. In my hands I hold a glow-
ing incense burner. Three cups of wine harmonize the ten thousand things. If you have
any other business, invite me again. If it is
nothing urgent, do not casually invite me.
Young Su fears that his worshipful send-off
has not been complete. Therefore, I beseech
the local tutelary deity to send off the gods
on my behalf again. You have been invited!
Mounting my horse and dismounting,
I come to lead the troops.

CHORUS: Come to lead the troops!

YOUNG MASTER:

    Urging people of the world to be as
        brothers,
    To be as man and wife.
    Guide each other,
    Be kind to one another,
    Get along together.

CHORUS: Get along together!

YOUNG MASTER:

    Today my disciples invited me
    To come and bless a vow.

CHORUS: Bless a vow!

YOUNG MASTER:

    Having blessed the vow
    I will protect my disciples.
    They will have big and small groups of
        fine offspring

CHORUS: Fine offspring!

YOUNG MASTER:

    Who shall climb the heights of
        scholarship
    And write excellent plays.
    Lian-li-luo. . . .

The Fall of the Goddess

The tensions between ancient mythology and modern science and technology are succinctly illustrated in Ling Chung's "The Fall of Moon Lady," which offers a goddess's perspective on the Apollo moon landing. Traditional lore claims that the moon is the home of the Jade Rabbit, whose image is visible on a full moon and shows the hare pounding a pestle, concocting elixirs; it is also the abode of Ch'ang-o, a woman who fled to the moon after acquiring some pills of a body-lightening elixir of immortality hoarded by her husband, the archer Yi. Four thousand years later, however, pursuers have caught up with her: mythology encounters the space age as the Moon Lady laments the next day's arrival of the astronauts of Apollo X. The poem is intriguing in that it is spoken from the perspective of the goddess, and it allows the reader to see what she sees and feel what she feels; earlier poems, such as the "Rhyme-Prose on the Goddess of the Lo," describe only the goddess's external appearance as an object of the narrator's desires.

The poetess first recalls the great age of T'ang poetry, the age of the poets Li Po (701–762) and Li Shang-yin (813?–858). But now celestial journeys that could only be imagined in earlier times have been realized, not by visionary shamans or poets but by the handlers of modern science. The shamans and Taoist masters of previous ages, their focus directed heavenward, sought to ascend to the stars; a realm of enchantment awaited them, and they left ordinary existence behind without glancing back. Now, however, the perspective shifts as a celestial being turns her gaze not toward the heavens but back toward the earth, and she finds there a realm disenchanted by the arrogance of technology. Science and technology, in the modern mythology of the West, are often viewed as soteriological curative agents; for the Moon Lady, however, the invading metallic sky gods of the space age bring only pollution and her inevitable fall toward midnight. Ch'ang-o is still very much alive in popular culture, however, and she is invoked during the Mid-Autumn festival, an all-night moon-viewing party held during the fall hunter's moon.

The poetess Ling Chung (born 1945) is the cotranslator, along with Kenneth Rexroth, of the anthology of women's poetry from which this verse is taken.

"The Fall of Moon Lady"
Before the landing of Apollo X

Girl in the moon, are you sorry
You stole the herb of immortality,
And night after night have to
Watch over the distant, emerald
Sea and the boundless jeweled sky?
—Li Shang-yin (813–858)

O stop, Jade Rabbit!
Stop chattering about the cloud-dwelling
    hills,
The dew-dyed reeds, Li Po's poetry and
    so on,
Stop dusting with your whiskers the dirt
    on my sleeves.
The dirt was spread from that globe,
It has confiscated my house,
And polluted the mirror of my mind.
I am homeless.

It's the tragedy of us gods
Capable of foreseeing the future.
Tomorrow, shining with metallic pride,
They will arrive to take over my home.
Tomorrow, I will hear from the trial of
    4000 years:
Life detention is my sentence.

Don't you see thousands of dead souls
Whirled in black fumes
Hastily coming to mourn over my fate?
As hastily as those long-ceased stars
That bent forward with their gleaming
    eyes
To stare at my ascension.

Tomorrow I will sink into darkness
Like a wing-broken china bird
Eternally
Falling toward midnight.

Contemporary Ch'an Practice: Ch'an Master Sheng-yen's *Faith in Mind*

Beginning in the late forties, official proscriptions against so-called feudal superstitions suspended religious activity on the mainland for several decades. On the island of Taiwan, however, where the rival Nationalist party relocated after 1949 and established a separate political sovereignty, traditional folkways and spiritual disciplines continued relatively undisturbed. One of the many religious practitioners who moved to the island is the Ch'an Buddhist teacher Master Sheng-yen (born 1931). Excerpts from his *Faith in Mind: A Guide to Ch'an Practice,* which offers insights into the actual practice of Ch'an Buddhism that are accessible to a modern Western audience, are presented here.

The book is structured as a commentary on the poem *Faith in Mind* attributed to Seng-ts'an (died 606), the Third Patriarch of Ch'an Buddhism. The expression "faith in mind" does not refer to a devotional or pietistic faith; it is the belief that the scattered mind that is caught up in the exigencies of day-to-day life is simultaneously the constant, unmoving mind called Buddha mind. The practice of Ch'an Buddhism is to realize this mind, which is often metaphorically suggested in female imagery as the Womb of Suchness *(Tathāgatagarbha),* a quality that is latent within all beings.

During lectures given at Ch'an retreats, Master Sheng-yen (who is addressed here by the honorific title of *Shih-fu,* or "master") provides his own line-by-line interpretation to make the seventh-century classical scriptures accessible to a lay audience; *Faith in Mind* is a written record of a series of such talks on the Dharma, or Buddhist teaching. These lectures serve as guides to the actual experience of hours-long meditation sessions held at retreats that may last for several days or several weeks. One of the techniques Master Sheng-yen employs to concentrate the attention of the practitioner is the *hua-t'ou,* an expression that means "source of the spoken word" or "before the spoken word." It often takes the form of a cryptic phrase or question that the practitioner then focuses on in meditation. Focusing on the *hua-t'ou* generates a sense of doubt; not doubt in the sense of suspicion but doubt as a strong desire to articulate an answer. The practitioner, however, is not allowed to give an answer until the sensation builds up into a "great ball of doubt"; once the meditator is in that state, something may serve as a catalyst to shatter that doubt.

Master Sheng-yen here asks, for example, "Who is standing in front of you?" or "What is this?" The *hua-t'ou* is often a line excerpted from a *kung-an* (Japanese *koan*) or from a Ch'an story. The question engenders in the practitioner a restructuring of ordinary ways of thinking that leads to new avenues of awareness and to an enhanced sensitivity to new possibilities of understanding. Another tool sometimes employed is to rap students on the shoulders with a yardstick-shaped "incense stick" to alleviate stiffness in the muscles and to keep the mind from wandering.

Much Western literature on Chinese Ch'an and Japanese Zen has emphasized the spiritual goals of "sudden enlightenment" and "nirvana" while glossing over the tedious hours of sitting meditation that, as Master Sheng-yen states, should be performed without attempting to attain any goals or enlightenment experience. There is no calculated "result" that can be obtained; to set up a goal and to distinguish between ignorance and enlightenment is to create artificial separations and barriers within the totality that is awakened Buddhahood. Master Sheng-yen sees the practice of Ch'an as a progression of the mind from scattered mind to one mind to no mind. The scattered mind can be calmed with sitting meditation that focuses on an awareness of one's own breathing; with greater practice, the mind can be unified in the experience of *samādhi,* a Sanskrit term that refers to an absorptive trancelike experience. With the help of paradoxical *hua-t'ou* or *kung-an* questions, however, one drops off ordinary thought and crosses the nonbarrier back to one's own original nature, to an experience that is neither scattered mind nor one mind but is something else again. That "something else again," which is knowable by experience but can only be suggested using ordinary speech, is indicated by the nonword "no-mind."

This experience takes place within the five aggregates, or *skandha*s, that make up a human being: the physical body, sensations, perceptions, volitional acts and thoughts *(karma),* and consciousness. These five aggregates are ordinarily considered the source of the suffering and unsatisfactoriness that keep one within the cycle of sorrowful existence known as *saṃsāra;* through proper Ch'an practice, however, these five themselves become the locus of a shift in perspective that is sometimes called nirvana. Hence, from an enlightened perspective, samsara and nirvana are not two separate things. As the character Monkey found out when he tried to somersault past the five mountain peaks (the five *skandhas*) that were actually the five fingers of the Buddha Amitābha, no matter where one goes, one is still in the palm of the Buddha's hand.

A native of the Shanghai region, Master Sheng-yen entered monkhood at the age of thirteen and left the mainland at twenty for Taiwan, where he spent six years in solitary retreat. He earned a doctorate at Risshō University in Tokyo in 1975. In addition to supervising several temples and Buddhist study institutes in Taiwan, in 1980 he also established the Institute of Chung-hwa Buddhist Culture in New York and has thus been responsible for transmitting Asian learning to an American environment. He has received transmission in both the Lin-chi and Ts'ao-tung traditions of Ch'an Buddhism. A sixty-seventh generation Dharma descendant of Bodhidharma, the First Patriarch of Ch'an Buddhism, Master Sheng-yen is also a fifty-seventh generation descendant of Lin-chi (Master I-hsüan) and a fiftieth generation descendant of Tung-shan (of the Ts'ao-tung tradition of Ch'an).

"Embarking on the Practice"

The Supreme Way is not difficult
If only you do not pick and choose.
Neither love nor hate,
And you will clearly understand.
Be off by a hair,
And you are as far apart as heaven from
      earth.

The sole purpose of a Ch'an retreat is to practice. You should keep your attention entirely on practice, without trying to attain any results. Since many of you have travelled far, or have worked hard to set aside the time, you have a great deal invested in this retreat. It is natural that you want to gain something. But once you enter the retreat, you must put aside any specific hopes.

Practicing with a goal in mind is like trying to catch a feather with a fan. The more you go after it, the more it eludes you. But if you sneak up on it slowly, you can grab it. The aim of practice is to train your patience and forbearance, to train your mind to become calm and stable. Any attachment or seeking will prevent your mind from settling down.

Today someone told me that the more he worked on the *hua-t'ou* the more tense he felt. It was as though his mind had become knotted up. His problem is that he wants to see quick results. Pursuing the *hua-t'ou* intensely with a desire to get enlightened is like tying yourself up and then poking yourself with a knife. The more you drive yourself the more tense you will feel. The same principle applies to the body. If you react to pain by tensing the body, the pain will only get worse. If any part of your body feels painful, you should try to relax it. Any involuntary movement of the body while sitting is also due to tension. Thus it is important to constantly maintain a state of relaxation.

Related to this are the problems that may develop from fixing your attention on a particular part of the body. For instance, some people try to make their breath flow smoothly. But in trying to control the breath, it becomes abnormal.

Don't pay attention to any phenomenon that occurs to the body; if you are concerned with it, problems will arise. It is the same with the mind. You will be unable to practice unless you disregard everything that happens to you mentally. If you feel distressed or pained in any way, just ignore it. Let it go and return wholeheartedly to the method. Place your mind directly on the method itself; concern yourself with nothing else.

The Supreme Way in the first line of the poem refers to the stage of Buddhahood. The wisdom of the Buddha is not difficult to perceive; it can be attained in the instant between two thoughts. The reason for this is that it has never been separate from us. It is always present. In fact, we all desire to realize this Supreme Way. If so, why are we unable to attain it?

The second line explains what prevents us. It is because we are always trying to escape our vexations. Precisely because we want to acquire the Buddha's insight and merits, we are unable to perceive Buddha nature.

Another reason why we cannot see our Buddha nature is that we are burdened with ideas. We make distinctions between *samsara* and *nirvana,* sentient beings and buddha, vexations and enlightenment. These ideas obstruct our perception of Buddha nature.

To paraphrase lines three and four: As soon as you discard your likes and dislikes, the Way will immediately appear before you. Here, Seng-Ts'an has something in common with Tao-Hsin, the Fourth Patriarch, and Hui-Neng, the Sixth Patriarch. The latter two frequently said that when you stop discriminating between good and evil, you will immediately perceive your original face. In other words, you will understand the Supreme Way.

When sitting, some of you are distracted with pain, or are trying to fight off drowsiness. At night, maybe you are angry at someone who is keeping you awake with his snoring. But instead of letting it annoy you, just observe the snoring. Soon the snores may become hypnotic and repetitive, actually pleasant sounding. If you start counting the snores, before you know it you will be asleep.

On the other hand, becoming attached to a certain pleasurable experience in meditation can also be an obstruction. One student I had would rock her body during sitting meditation. She felt that she had no control over the shaking; it just happened spontaneously. Actually, this was not caused by any physical tension, but by a subconscious motive. The rocking was comfortable to her. You cannot practice effectively if you give in to such things. By examining them, you will be able to control the mind.

Holding on to various likes and dislikes keeps you apart from the Way. Discarding them will bring you in accord with the Way. But if there is the slightest misconception about this, the distance between you and the Way will be as great as that between heaven and earth. Don't misinterpret this and think that since you are not supposed to attach to likes and dislikes, you should therefore not cultivate the Way. With this attitude it is useless to come on a Ch'an retreat.

When you first set out to practice you will definitely have a goal in mind. You may be frustrated with your present condition and aim either to change yourself or to improve your circumstances. Certainly there is something you hope to achieve by practicing. You cannot just practice aimlessly. So practice itself implies some intention or desire. To fulfill your original intentions, you must constantly keep your mind on the method of practice. But as you focus on the method you should not be thinking of what you want to accomplish, what level you want to reach, or what problems you want to get rid of. Instead, your mind should be exclusively applied to the method itself, free from all motives.

There is a saying that is useful for practitioners: "Put down the myriad thoughts. Take up the practice." The myriad thoughts are scattered, random, extraneous concerns. The practice is your method of cultivation. When your mind wanders to extraneous concerns, put them down as soon as they appear. But should you treat the method in the same way as a wandering thought—putting it down as soon as it appears? No. From moment to moment, put down extraneous thoughts and return your mind to the method of practice.

One time I asked a student, "Are you having many extraneous thoughts?" He replied, "Not too many." I said, "I'll bet I know one of them. You're thinking of your girl friend all the time, aren't you?" He retorted, "How can you say that?" After the retreat he said, "Originally, I wasn't thinking of my girl friend at all. But after Shih-fu mentioned her I couldn't stop thinking of her." I told him that he hadn't seen through his problem yet. He may have thought that his mind was not on his girl friend, but his concern was still there.

Perhaps you try to put down extraneous concerns but find that you just can't. Every time you put one down, it comes back again. This upsets you. You keep telling yourself, "Put it down. Put it down." Actually it doesn't matter if you can't put it down. If you eventually get to the point where you say to yourself, "It doesn't matter if I can't put it down," then you will be putting it down. You should not fear failure. Neither should you embrace it. You may conclude that the retreat is just not going well for you—your body is uncomfortable, your mind is in tumult. You are unable to control yourself. You haven't made the proper preparations. Why not forget this one and leave tomorrow? Maybe try again the next time. Don't succumb to this defeatist attitude. A Chinese proverb says: "A hundred birds in a tree are not worth one bird in the palm." If you let go of that one bird to go after the hundred you will end up with nothing. Even though you feel unprepared and doomed to failure, being here still presents a wonderful opportunity to practice.

"Overcoming Like and Dislike"

If you want it to appear,
Be neither for or against.
For and against opposing each other—
This is the mind's disease.

If you want the Buddha Way to manifest before your eyes, it is a mistake to harbor any preferences or aversions. This includes anything you hope to acquire, keep, discard, or avoid. When sitting seems to be going particularly well, the idea may pop into your mind that you are about to be enlightened. You begin to wait for this enlightenment experience. With this expectation, the mind has already abandoned its single-mindedness and has become confused and scattered. You will not be able to maintain your previous state of concentration.

On a prior retreat, one student was progressing so well that there were notable changes in his mental state. At that point he became frightened. He thought, "I'm happy with the way I am now. I don't really want any drastic changes. What if my friends don't recognize me?" He did not sit as well for the rest of the retreat.

This contradictory mentality often afflicts the practitioner. He wants to enter the door but at the same time is really afraid of entering. You come to a retreat with the desire to transform yourself. Indeed, practice can make you more mature, calm, and stable. It will certainly not change you into something less human, or ghost-like. Since ancient times there have been numerous practitioners who have gotten deeply enlightened and remained human, the only difference being that afterward they were more stable and filled with wisdom. There is no reason to fear changing too much.

Such a contradictory state of mind is common among ordinary people. When I left home as a young boy I was very excited about becoming a monk. But on the other hand, I had never been to a monastery and had some apprehension. I just did not know what would happen there. Many people who believe in heaven have similar fears about what it will be like after death.

These contradictions point to inherent weaknesses in our personality, of which we are usually unaware. It is only in the context of practice that these weaknesses are exposed. Once we discover and understand our weaknesses, we can prevent them from further obstructing our practice.

Though "for" and "against" are opposites, they are also very much related. If there is something that you like, there must be something else that you dislike. And if you cannot get what you like, you will change your mind and dislike it. To be caught in this conflict between like and dislike is a serious disease of

the mind. It is a barrier to practice. Practice is a process by which we recognize and treat the disease in our minds. When the disease completely disappears, the ultimate Way is revealed.

Without recognizing the mysterious principle
It is useless to practice quietude.

If you do not grasp the deep truth in the previous lines, no matter how hard you practice, your efforts will be futile. This is because there is a struggle within your mind. The previous thought is continually at war with the following thought. Under these circumstances, it is almost impossible to attain a peaceful state of mind.

Even if you do manage to overcome your scattered thoughts and reach a peaceful state, it would still be useless. You will be so happy to have entered this state that you will grasp it and not let it go. In the end, you have not achieved a concentrated mind but an attached mind. Nonetheless, a peaceful state of mind is at least better than one involved in a constant internal struggle. As long as you live alone you may be able to maintain it. But if you have to interact with people things may start bothering you. You may be disturbed by the noise of children, visits of friends or stress at work. Eventually, you will seek to avoid these things and meditate alone in a room.

Someone here has a habit of sometimes falling backwards while sitting. Today I cautioned her that if she does it hard enough, the shock may cause her to lose consciousness or even her ability to think rationally. She remarked, "That's not such a bad idea, after all. Now I have to struggle with all of the problems in my mind. If I get such a shock, my problems will simply disappear." I said, "That may be the case, but who will feed you and take care of you? Who will take care of your children?" A shock to your nervous system is not the same as enlightenment. Rather, it is a disease. Just because a person does not have any scattered thoughts does not mean that all his problems are resolved. If all you are interested in is a thoughtless state, just ask someone to hit you hard on the back of your head. There are too many people who cannot distinguish between true wisdom and a mere state of peacefulness. If you do not understand this distinction, even if you practice hard, at best you are being foolish.

You should not remain passively in peacefulness. Don't be afraid of difficulties. If your mind cannot settle down you should not feel any resentment. Cultivate non-aversion to the unpleasant and non-attachment to the pleasant. Taking a pleasurable state for enlightenment will get you into trouble. Enlightenment is not something we have to guard fiercely, not letting it go. If a pleasant state arises, don't get stuck on it, just continue to practice.

On a past retreat one person sat through four periods without stirring. Seeing that his condition was "too good," I struck him with the incense board. Thereupon he grabbed the board and hit me, saying, "I was in such a blissful state and now I have lost *samadhi*." Aside from the fact that practitioners should not have any attachments, it is not the purpose of Ch'an to remain in *samadhi*. It is not necessarily good for the mind to settle down quickly. Ch'an is a lively practice. It is not difficult to maintain a calm mind in a stationary situation. But in Ch'an one should be able to retain mental calmness even in a mobile state.

> The Way is perfect like great space,
> Without lack, without excess.
> Because of grasping and rejecting,
> You cannot attain it.

Great space does not refer to a nothingness, but rather to a totality. Though it includes everything, there is no individual existence. There is only the total, universal existence. Even before attaining the Way, practitioners should train themselves in the proper attitudes of one who is already enlightened. That is, they should discard the mentality of liking and disliking. So long as you practice diligently, that is the totality. After all, what you dislike and what you like are not separate from one another.

There was a landowner who hired many helping hands to work his fields. They were very good workers, but they had large appetites. On the one hand, he was pleased with their work and, on the other, he was annoyed that they ate so much. In the owner's mind this was a grave defect. To him it would be ideal if they would just do their job and not have to eat. Thus there is no need to rejoice when you think you have gotten what you like—it is exactly the thing you dislike, and vice versa.

For example, a couple may spend a lot of time and energy courting each other. Eventually they are married and are very happy together. But along with the happiness there are also some restrictions. They feel stuck in the daily routine and lack the freedom to do whatever they want. They reflect that there is a certain merit to remaining single. But at this point, it is already too late.

When we think we have gotten something, we have not really gotten it and when we think we have lost something, we have not really lost it. This is because in the reality of totality, there is no gain and no loss. There is nothing outside of your mind. It is because you choose and reject that you are not free. It is for this reason that you have an excess or a lack. You have an excess of what you want to be rid of, and a lack of what you want to acquire. It is only when there is no grasping or rejecting that there will be neither excess nor lack.

"Letting Go of Attachments"

> Do not pursue conditioned existence;
> Do not abide in acceptance of emptiness.

People can be attached either to existence, the outer world, or emptiness, the inner void. Most of us are probably attached to existence, clinging to our thoughts, our body, the environment around us. On the other hand, someone attached to emptiness may think: "Since there is nothing after death, it is the simplest solution for everything. After I die, I won't have to worry about anything anymore." Another emptiness attitude may be: "Since the world is illusory, then nothing matters and I can stay detached from everything." Those who are attached to emptiness may have a devil-may-care attitude. They may refuse to take anything in life seriously. Or they may even be susceptible to committing suicide.

Attaching to either existence or to emptiness are improper attitudes. I have spoken of the dangers of attaching to existence—grasping what you like and rejecting what you dislike. But to say that there is nothing to grasp and nothing to reject is also incorrect—this would be attaching to emptiness. A person may be meditating with a blank mind, minus all thoughts and concerns. While this may seem to be approaching enlightenment, it is actually quite different. In the enlightened state, the previous thought did not arise, the future thought will not arise, and the present thought does not arise. But someone in the blank state is just sitting there not thinking about or doing anything. In fact, he is not practicing. Indeed he does have a thought, which is: the previous thought arose, but it does not matter. A future thought may arise but, again, it does not matter. As to the present thought, let it be. This person may think that he has no attachment to his thoughts. But actually this is far from a true state of enlightenment. This kind of state is called "stubborn emptiness," as opposed to true emptiness.

If you practice to a point where you feel very tranquil, stable, and comfortable, that would be a peaceful state of mind. The best you can attain in this peaceful condition is a high *samadhi* state in the formless realm called the "emptiness *samadhi*." But if you become attached to such a state you would never see your self-nature. This would be considered an "outer path" practice.

> In oneness and equality,
> Confusion vanishes of itself.

Seeing that all is one means making no distinction between sage and sentient being, or between subject and object. This is another way of describing the totality of space. When you experience everything as equal, all distinctions will naturally disappear. While remembering not to abide either in existence or emptiness, you should also know that existence and emptiness are not separate.

Yet is everything really the same? Once I said that the Buddha sees all sentient beings as the same, and is aware of every single thought in the universe. Someone raised the point that if the Buddha's mind was constantly being bombarded with such a tremendous influx of thoughts, it would not be a very comfortable state. This would mean that the Buddha's mind is like a garbage can and the thoughts of all sentient beings are being dumped into it. It would be a heavy burden on the Buddha.

If you take a snapshot with a high-quality camera, everything in front of the lens will be imprinted on the film in minute detail. You can see the tip of each blade of grass and the outline of every leaf. Yet the camera does not think: "How annoying! All this junk is trying to get my attention." No. In one shot, it takes in everything without making distinctions among the objects—whether they are good or bad, long or short, green or yellow. But just because the camera does not make distinctions does not mean that the images on the film will appear confused or in the wrong order. On the contrary, everything is there clearly, and in place.

The Buddha's mind is like this. Having an equal mind means that there is no conception of relativity between things. Everything is absolute in the sense that there is no separation between you and others, between past and future. Because you see everything as equal, you would not choose one thing over another. Yet as soon as there are no longer any differences, it is as if existence simply disappears. For example, of everybody were male, the label "men" would no longer apply, since its only purpose is to distinguish them from women. Everyone being the same, there would be no need for names. If you take an equal attitude towards every-thing, all differences will disappear, along with existence itself.

Once I handed the incense board to a student and asked him, "What is this?" He grabbed the board and shook it a few times. He did that because there was no name for it. We may call it an incense board but this is only our mind making distinctions. Why must we call it "incense board"?

During a retreat, I stood in front of a certain person. I asked him, "Who is standing in front of you?" He replied, "An egg." I was very pleased to be an egg.

When the retreat was over, I asked him, "Why is Shih-fu an egg?" He answered, "When Shih-fu asked me the question I did not have any thought whatsoever in my mind. Since I had to give an answer, I just said something—and the word "egg" spontaneously came out of my mouth. Later I thought: 'That isn't quite right. How can Shih-fu be an egg? But I said it and it's said.' "

When he said "an egg," it was the correct answer. In fact, whatever he said at that moment would have been correct because he did not have any thought in his mind. He was in an absolute state, not making any distinctions. But once he began to entertain doubts, he lost the answer.

Perhaps in this retreat I will also stand in front of you and ask, "Who is standing in front of you?" Then, recalling the story I have just told, you may try to give a similar answer and call Shih-fu a horse. However, this would not be correct if you have the idea of giving a good answer. This is the mind of distinction. It is not the mind that treats everything as equal.

> Stop activity and return to stillness,
> And that stillness will be even more active.

Originally your mind may be in a relatively stable state. But when you realize that your mind is not completely unmoving, you may try to make it even calmer. However, the effort to still your mind will cause it to become more active. The mind that makes no distinctions is unmoving; there are no ups and downs. If you try to eliminate the ups and downs it would be like observing a pan of water. There are gentle ripples on its surface. But you want the surface to be completely still, so you blow on the water to flatten it out. This creates more ripples. Then you press the water with your hands to stop it from moving. The outcome is even more agitation. If you were to leave the water alone, the ripples would eventually subside and the surface would be still. Common sense tells us that we cannot force the water to become calm. When it comes to practice, however, it is difficult for us to apply the same principle.

When practicing, it is sufficient to just keep your mind on the method. It is unnecessary to reflect upon how well you are doing, or to compare whether you are in a better state now than you were half an hour ago. During the evening talk, I may ask you, "How are you doing today?" At this time you are allowed to express your feelings. But when you are practicing you should definitely not investigate your mental state and judge your practice.

Someone said to me, "Shih-fu, I feel very ashamed. I come to retreat time and again and yet I never make any progress." I said, "The very fact that you are still coming to retreat and practicing is proof that you are making progress."

Practice with an equal mind and don't distinguish between good and bad. Do not compare your condition before and after the retreat, or judge whether the method you are using is right or wrong. If you find you cannot use the method, you may change it, but first understand why you cannot use the method. You should not let curiosity dictate your practice, playing with one method today and another tomorrow, or switching methods from one sitting to the next. You should see that there are no real differences between the various methods. Hold on to one method and go into it as deeply as possible.

This is like your love relationships. When you love someone, you should persist in that relationship and not continually change partners. Likewise, keep to one method and do not keep changing your conception of practice. To change frequently will give you only trouble.

"Unifying the Mind"

> Only stagnating in duality,
> How can you recognize oneness?
> If you fail to penetrate oneness,
> Both places lose their function.

Whenever you make distinctions, your mind is in opposition. Opposition implies a duality. How is this relevant to practice? A practitioner usually wants to attain enlightenment or Buddhahood. But this creates a duality of subject and object. The person who is seeking to attain is separate from the attainment, the object of his search. In seeking to become one with Buddha, he separates himself from it. This is a state of opposition.

Or, perhaps the practitioner knows very well that he has never been separate from Buddha. But since he has not yet experienced this unity, he seeks the Buddha within himself. Yet even seeking the Buddha within himself creates opposition between his searching mind and the Buddha within. This way, oneness can never be attained.

If that is true, is it correct to practice without seeking anything at all? Every day we chant the Four Great Vows. The fourth is: I vow to attain Supreme Buddhahood. What is the purpose of changing this vow if aspiring to attain Buddhahood sets up an opposition? On the other hand, if we do not define our goal, is practice possible?

If you really believe there is no separation, then it is possible to practice without opposition. You must have faith in the fundamental unity to truly begin practicing. However, most people remain in duality. They may speak of one God, but they see themselves as separate from God. But in Ch'an, at the very beginning of your practice, you must have faith in non-duality. It is the same unity in the kung-an: "The myriad dharmas return to one. To what does the One return?" In other words, if all existence comes from one God, where does God come from?

The emphasis of Faith in Mind is on practice. Many of you are practicing counting the breath. The goal of this method is to reach a unified, or single-minded state. After you get to the point where there are no thoughts other than counting, eventually the counting just naturally stops. The numbers disappear, the breath disappears, and the idea of counting the breath is gone. The only thing left is a sense of existence. Using a Ch'an method such as the hua-t'ou may have a similar result in the beginning stages. At a certain point, the hua-t'ou may disappear, or you

simply cannot use it anymore. But this does not always mean that you have reached a single-minded state. You may still have the thought of trying to use the hua-t'ou. Only when the thought of practicing is gone will your mind be in a peaceful state of oneness.

A person who has experienced oneness is different from an ordinary person. His faith is stronger than one who can at best intellectually understand what it means to have no distinctions in one's mind. To personally experience it is quite another thing.

In Taoism there is the saying that the one gives rise to two, and the two give rise to the multiplicity of things. We should not think that the Third Patriarch is confusing Taoism with Buddhism. It is just that he employs Taoist terminology to express the teachings of Buddhism. The highest path of Taoism is not the same as that of Faith in Mind, for Ch'an transcends oneness. But we must get to the state of oneness before we can go beyond it.

The practice of Ch'an should progress in this sequence: scattered mind, simple mind, one mind, no mind. First we gather our scattered thoughts into a more concentrated, or simple, state of mind. From this concentrated state we can enter the mind of unity. Finally, we leap from the unified mind to the state of no mind. This final process can be accomplished more quickly using the Ch'an methods of hua-t'ou or kung-an.

To go from one mind to no mind does not mean that anything is lost; rather, it means that you are free of the single-minded state. Someone who dwells in one mind would either be attached to samadhi, or else would feel identified with a certain deity. It is only after you are freed from this unity and enter no mind that you return to your own nature, also called "wu," or Ch'an.

Even though this progression in the practice takes place, while you are actually practicing you should not think to yourself: "I am striving to concentrate my mind. I want to get to the state of one mind, to the state of no mind." If you have such ideas of seeking, you will be in trouble. Just concern yourself with your method;

persist with your method to the very end. This in itself is close to a state of unity. If you don't let go, eventually you will reach a point where the method disappears and you will experience one mind.

Once a meditator in his sixties said to me, "Shih-fu, I am very old. I may not have many years left. I really would like to get enlightened as soon as possible. If I don't get enlightened before I die, I will have wasted my life." I said, "Precisely because you are so old you shouldn't have any hopes of getting enlightened. Just practice." The man asked, "How can you tell me to practice and not show me how to get enlightened?" I replied, "If you have the idea of enlightenment, that is already your downfall; you cannot make much progress. If you do nothing but practice, at least you will approach the state of enlightenment. Even if you never get enlightened, the effort is never wasted."

Banish existence and you fall into existence;
Follow emptiness and you turn your back
on it.

In the Sung dynasty there was a famous prime minister by the name of Chang Shang-Yin who was opposed to Buddhism. He wrote many essays refuting Buddhism, and he would spend every evening pondering over how he could improve the essay he was then working on. His wife, observing his obsessive involvement and struggle with his writing, asked him, "What are you doing?" He said, "Buddhism is really hateful. I'm trying to prove there is no Buddha." His wife remarked, "How strange! If you say there is no Buddha, why bother to refute the Buddha? It is as if you are throwing punches into empty space."

This comment turned his mind around. He reflected: There may be something to Buddha after all. So he started studying Buddhism and became a well-known, accomplished lay practitioner of Ch'an. In fact, Chang Shang-Yin and Ch'an master Ta-Hui Tsung-Kao had the same master, Yuan-Wu K'o-Ch'in.

Thus if you try to destroy something, you are still bound up by it. For instance, suppose you try to clear a blocked pipe by pushing another object into it. Whatever was originally in the pipe is pushed out, but the new object is now blocking the pipe. When you try to use existence to get rid of existence, you will always end up with existence.

When you throw something away, it is gone. But does it cease to exist? In local terms, yes. In the broader picture, however, that is not the case. On this earth, no matter how hard you try to throw anything away, it will still stay somewhere on the earth.

There is a Chinese novel called *Monkey*. The hero is a "supermonkey" who is so powerful that he can travel a distance of 180,000 miles in one somersault. In the story, he was journeying to the Western Paradise of Amitabha Buddha. On the way, he came upon five tall mountain peaks. He figured that it would take one leap to get to the other side. First he took a rest, urinating at that spot. Then he somersaulted over the mountains. After he landed, he noticed a funny smell. He thought, "Some shameless monkey must have taken a leak here." Actually, he had never gotten to the other side of the mountains. He had just somersaulted back to the original spot.

The five mountains in the story symbolize the five *skandhas* within which sentient beings are trapped. All of your actions will boomerang back to you and you will have to take the consequences. If you throw anything away, it will be you who has to clean it up. You may think that you can avoid responsibility by passing it on to another person. In the short term, it may work. But ultimately, you have to deal with it yourself, and in addition, you have caused trouble to others.

Therefore you should not try to get rid of your vexations. Rather, you should be willing to accept them. Once someone said, "Shih-fu, my karmic obstructions are too great. Please recite mantras to remove them from me." I replied, "And what will happen to these karmic obstructions when I remove them from you? Should they become Shih-fu's?" If you have difficulties you should not consider them problems. If you are obsessed with these difficulties and try to eliminate them, you are only getting yourself into greater trouble.

Those who have just begun to practice experience many problems with their bodies and minds. They are constantly saying, "I have to overcome all these problems." But in trying to eliminate their problems, they struggle. This is what is meant by "Banish existence and you fall into existence."

The second line, "Follow emptiness and you turn your back on it," refers to practitioners who have experienced certain breakthroughs, and are approaching the state of emptiness. They may think, "I have eliminated all vexations. I no longer have any ignorance or attachment." But staying at this level would be considered "outer path" practice. The best one could reach is the emptiness *samadhi,* the highest level of the formless realm.

I have known many people who were extremely diligent and took their practice very seriously in the beginning, but gave up too soon. It is just as if when one side senses it is losing the battle, suddenly all resistance is gone and they are defeated very quickly. As long as everything is going well, they continue normally; but as soon as something goes wrong, everything simply collapses. So it is with certain practitioners who have been working hard and then suddenly stop completely. They feel that practice is basically useless. They think it is a great deception, because they have put a lot of energy into overcoming their problems, and have not eliminated them at all. In fact, their efforts have only increased their mental vexations, and have created physical ones as well.

Because of this, many people consider serious or energetic practice demonic. They think it is not normal to devote oneself so completely to practice. Such criticism is usually unjustified. However, it is true that a practitioner who does not know what he is doing may get into deep trouble, especially without proper guidance. He may not be in a demonic state, but very likely his practice cannot last long.

It is good to have a diligent and objective attitude towards practice. But to be attached to the idea of overcoming your problems will only lead to further trouble.

Buddhism Comes to America

American writers have been influenced by Buddhist thought since at least the time of Henry David Thoreau (1817–1862), who was once credited with one of the first translations from a Buddhist scripture to appear in an American publication. This was a passage, rendered from a French translation from the *Lotus Sutra,* which appeared in an 1844 volume of *The Dial,* a journal edited by Ralph Waldo Emerson (1803–1882). The translation is now known actually to have been the work of Elizabeth Palmer Peabody (1804–1894), an intellectual and social critic active in educational reform, the abolitionist movement, and rights for native North American cultures.

American interest in Buddhism, then, is not new to the twentieth century, but it was probably not until the publication of Jack Kerouac's (1922–1969) *The Dharma Bums* that the Buddhist term "Dharma" became a household word. Originally from a Catholic Franco-American community in Lowell, Massachusetts, Kerouac became stereotyped as the official spokesperson for the so-called beat generation of the late fifties, a generation associated with the romantic bohemianism of poetry readings, jazz improvisation, a life on the road, and the ingestion of mind-altering substances. Detractors of this life-style perceived it as a threat to the proprietary strictures and conventions of the type of sedentary suburban existence spreading across America in the fifties and sixties. This stereotype may loosely describe some aspects of Kerouac's life-style, but it is irrelevant to his vision as a writer and poet. The detractors probably did not realize that for Kerouac the word "beat" was associated not only with jazz beats and rhythms but with the French word *béat,* (pronounced "bay-aht"), whose etymological roots produced the English word "beatitude." To be *béat* means to be in awe, as before a hierophany of the sacred.

That Kerouac was in awe of the whole world is suggested in his *The Dharma Bums* (1958), a book dedicated to the T'ang poet Han-shan, who was himself in awe of Cold Mountain. Kerouac was well read in Buddhist literature in translation, which had been widely available since the publication in 1932 of Dwight Goddard's *A Buddhist Bible,* an anthology of early translations of Buddhist scriptures. *The Dharma Bums* may be interpreted at one level as a hitchhiker's guide to American life in the late fifties, but it also intimates strong parallels with such Japanese literary classics as Matsuo Bashō's (1644–1694) *Narrow Road to the Interior,* an inner journey to the center of the self expressed as an external pilgrimage through the sacred geography of Japan. A layperson, Bashō traveled in the guise of an errant Buddhist monk; he had the ability to evoke a sense of the universal and eternal in his singular descriptions of nature, of ordinary objects, and of ordinary people, whom he suspected were bodhisattvas in disguise.

Kerouac was deeply influenced by Bashō and wrote poetry in his style, and his prose descriptions of snapshots of American life in *The Dharma Bums* and other works evoke Bashō's sense of the eternal. Hoboes on trains and bums on skid row were truly *béat,* bodhisattvas and saints whose experience of the world was direct and unmediated by organized religion; for Kerouac, these were the true "Dharma Bums." They were homeless wanderers whose life-styles resembled those of the wandering monks of Siddhārtha Gautama, who left the householder's life to become forest dwellers in search of higher truths and a direct perception of reality. Kerouac described himself as a wandering monk traveling the huge triangular expanse between New York, San Francisco, and Mexico City, turning the "wheel of the Dharma" (the eightfold path was from ancient times iconographically depicted as an eight-spoked wheel), so that he might accumulate enough spiritual merit to be reborn in a Buddhist paradise. In his daily practice he reads the *Diamond Sutra,* echoing the direct spiritual realization of Hui-neng, the Sixth Patriarch, who upon hearing the text for the first time was inspired to turn his life in a new direction.

Although ostensibly a novel, *The Dharma Bums* is largely autobiographical, and the characters of Ray Smith, Henry Morley, Japhy Ryder, and Alvah Goldbook parallel in real life the figures of Jack Kerouac, his friend John Montgomery, and the poets Gary Snyder and Allen Ginsberg, respectively. While Kerouac's perspective is informed by concepts absorbed from Asian thought, he nevertheless articulates his own larger vision of the universe through an almost cinematically visual description of his immediate physical surroundings in America, whether they be mountains in the Sierras, the furnishings of Japhy Ryder's small shack, or the kitchens and bathrooms of Alvah Goldbook's cottage in Berkeley.

The Dharma Bums is dedicated to Han-shan, and the third chapter from the book excerpted here describes how Kerouac first encountered the writings of Han-shan in Japhy Ryder's shack, a place described almost as a small Zen monastic retreat transplanted to a spot near the University of California campus. Kerouac wants to see in Japhy an elderly, venerable Zen scholar, although Japhy could not have been much older than thirty at the time; Kerouac frames his own character, Ray, as an inquiring student. The chapter is virtually entirely dialogue, a conversation that creates no plot or action other than to initiate Ray (and hence the reader) into the imagery of Han-shan's mountain; the narrative thus takes the form of a teacher-pupil dialogue more characteristic of Buddhist scriptures and Chinese philosophical texts than of American novels of the late fifties.

Japhy's and Ray's interests in Han-shan are not purely academic: in the midst of a conversation on the finer points of translation they decide to emulate the Chinese poet and go climbing in the nearby Sierras, and in effect translate Han-shan's experience on Cold Mountain into the geography of the High Sierras of California. Kerouac, speaking through the character of Ray, suggests other more philosophical ways of looking at mountains in his conversation with Rol Sturlason, who sees in the rock gardens of Japan a metaphor for the nature of the universe. But Kerouac, characteristically more interested in human beings than boulders, is more appreciative of Japhy's compassion than of the dialectics of emptiness and form.

The Dharma Bums developed an almost cult following in the sixties, a tribute to Kerouac's ability to interpret an Asian cosmology in the American idiom. Some of his other works also reveal the influence of Asian thought: he wrote haiku poetry (evocative word images of only a few lines) after the style of the Japanese poet Bashō, who was a practitioner of Zen Buddhism; his verse "The Last Hotel" is a modern-day interpretation of the notion of the womb of the Tathāgata, or Buddha nature. He wrote a life of the Buddha and even composed a Buddhist scripture of his own, *The Scripture of the Golden Eternity* (1960).

Selection from *The Dharma Bums,* by Jack Kerouac

In Berkeley I was living with Alvah Goldbook in his little rose-covered cottage in the backyard of a bigger house on Milvia Street. The old rotten porch slanted forward to the ground, among vines, with a nice old rocking chair that I sat in every morning to read my Diamond Sutra. The yard was full of tomato plants about to ripen, and mint, mint, everything smelling of mint, and one fine old tree that I loved to sit under and meditate on those cool perfect starry California October nights unmatched anywhere in the world. We had a perfect little kitchen with a gas stove, but no icebox, but no matter. We also had a perfect little bathroom with a tub and hot water, and one main room, covered with pillows and floor mats of straw and mattresses to sleep on, and books, books, hundreds of books everything from Catullus to Pound to Blyth to albums of Bach and Beethoven (and even one swinging Ella Fitzgerald album with Clark Terry very interesting on trumpet) and a good three-speed Webcor phonograph that played loud enough to blast the roof off: and the roof nothing but plywood, the walls too, through which one night in one of our Zen Lunatic drunks I put my fist in glee and Coughlin saw me and put his head through about three inches.

About a mile from there, way down Milvia and then upslope toward the campus of the University of California, behind another big old house on a quiet street (Hillegass), Japhy lived in his own shack which was infinitely smaller than ours, about twelve by twelve, with nothing in it but typical Japhy appurtenances that showed his belief in the simple monastic life—no chairs at all, not even one sentimental rocking chair, but just straw mats. In the corner was his famous rucksack with cleaned-up pots and pans all fitting into one another in a compact unit and all tied and put away inside a knotted-up blue bandana. Then his Japanese wooden pata shoes, which he never used, and a pair of black inside-pata socks to pad around softly in over his pretty straw mats, just room for your four toes on one side and your big toe on the other. He had a slew of orange crates all filled with beautiful scholarly books, some of them in Oriental languages, all the great sutras, comments on sutras, the complete works of D. T. Suzuki and a fine quadruple-volume edition of Japanese haikus. He also had an immense collection of valuable general poetry. In fact if a thief should have broken in there the only things of real value were the books. Japhy's clothes were all old hand-me-downs bought secondhand with a bemused and happy expression in Goodwill and Salvation Army stores: wool socks darned, colored undershirts, jeans, workshirts, moccasin shoes, and a few turtleneck sweaters that he wore one on top the other in the cold mountain nights of the High Sierras in California and the High Cascades of Washington and Oregon on the long incredible jaunts that sometimes lasted weeks and weeks with just a few pounds of dried food in his pack. A few orange crates made his table, on which, one late sunny afternoon as I arrived, was steaming a peaceful cup of tea at his side as he bent his serious head to the Chinese signs of the poet Han Shan. Coughlin had given me the address and I came there, seeing first Japhy's bicycle on the lawn in front of the big house out front (where his landlady lived) then the few odd boulders and rocks and funny little trees he'd brought back from mountain jaunts to set out in his own "Japanese tea garden" or "tea-house garden," as there was a convenient pine tree soughing over his little domicile.

A peacefuller scene I never saw than when, in that rather nippy late red afternoon, I simply opened his little door and looked in and saw him at the end of the little shack, sitting cross-legged on a Paisley pillow on a straw mat, with his spectacles on, making him look old and scholarly and wise, with book on lap and the little tin teapot and porcelain cup steaming at his side. He looked up very peacefully, saw who it was, said, "Ray, come in," and bent his eyes again to the script.

"What you doing?"

"Translating Han Shan's great poem called 'Cold Mountain' written a thousand years ago some of it scribbled on the sides of cliffs hundreds of miles away from any other living beings."

"Wow."

"When you come into this house though you've got to take your shoes off, see those straw mats, you can ruin 'em with shoes." So I took my softsoled blue cloth shoes off and laid them dutifully by the door and he threw me a pillow and I sat crosslegged along the little wooden board wall and he offered me a cup of hot tea. "Did you ever read the Book of Tea?" said he.

"No, what's that?"

"It's a scholarly treatise on how to make tea utilizing all the knowledge of two thousand years about tea-brewing. Some of the descriptions of the effect of the first sip of tea, and the second, and the third, are really wild and ecstatic."

"Those guys got high on nothing, hey?"

"Sip your tea and you'll see; this is good green tea." It was good and I immediately felt calm and warm. "Want me to read you parts of this Han Shan poem? Want me to tell you about Han Shan?"

"Yeah."

"Han Shan you see was a Chinese scholar who got sick of the big city and the world and took off to hide in the mountains."

"Say, that sounds like you."

"In those days you could really do that. He stayed in caves not far from a Buddhist monastery in the T'ang Hsing district of T'ien Tai and his only human friend was the funny Zen Lunatic Shih-te who had a job sweeping out the monastery with a straw broom. Shih-te was a poet too but he never wrote much down. Every now and then Han Shan would come down from Cold Mountain in his bark clothing and come into the warm kitchen and wait for food, but none of the monks would ever feed him because he didn't want to join the order and answer the meditation bell three times a day. You see why in some of his utterances, like—listen and I'll look here and read from the Chinese," and I bent over his

shoulder and watched him read from big wild crowtracks of Chinese signs: "Climbing up Cold Mountain path, Cold Mountain path goes on and on, long gorge choked with scree and boulders, wide creek and mist-blurred grass, moss is slippery though there's been no rain, pine sings but there's no wind, who can leap the world's ties and sit with me among white clouds?"

"Wow."

"Course that's my own translation into English, you see there are five signs for each line and I have to put in Western prepositions and articles and such."

"Why don't you just translate it as it is, five signs, five words? What's those first five signs?"

"Sign for climbing, sign for up, sign for cold, sign for mountain, sign for path."

"Well then, translate it 'Climbing up Cold Mountain path.' "

"Yeah, but what do you do with the sign for long, sign for gorge, sign for choke, sign for avalanche, sign for boulders?"

"Where's that?"

"That's the third line, would have to read 'Long gorge choke avalanche boulders.' "

"Well that's even better!"

"Well yeah, I thought of that, but I have to have this pass the approval of Chinese scholars here at the university and have it clear in English."

"Boy what a great thing this is," I said looking around at the little shack, "and you sitting here so very quietly at this very quiet hour studying all alone with your glasses. . . ."

"Ray what you got to do is go climb a mountain with me soon. How would you like to climb Matterhorn?"

"Great! Where's that?"

"Up in the High Sierras. We can go there with Henry Morley in his car and bring our packs and take off from the lake. I could carry all the food and stuff we need in my rucksack and you could borrow Alvah's small knapsack and carry extra socks and shoes and stuff."

"What's these signs mean?"

"These signs mean that Han Shan came down from the mountain after many years roaming around up there, to see his folks in town, says, 'Till recently I stayed at Cold Mountain, et cetera, yesterday I called on friends and family, more than half had gone to the Yellow Springs,' that means death, the Yellow Springs, 'now morning I face my lone shadow, I can't study with both eyes full of tears.' "

"That's like you too, Japhy, studying with eyes full of tears."

"My eyes aren't full of tears!"

"Aren't they going to be after a long long time?"

"They certainly will, Ray . . . and look here, 'In the mountains it's cold, it's always been cold not just this year,' see, he's real high, maybe twelve thousand or thirteen thousand feet or more, way up there, and says, 'Jagged scarps always snowed in, woods in the dark ravines spitting mist, grass is still sprouting at the end of June, leaves begin to fall in early August, and here am I high as a junkey—' "

"As a junkey!"

"That's my own translation, he actually says here am I as high as the sensualist in the city below, but I made it modern and high translation."

"Great." I wondered why Han Shan was Japhy's hero.

"Because," said he, "he was a poet, a mountain man, a Buddhist dedicated to the principle of meditation on the essence of all things, a vegetarian too by the way though I haven't got on that kick from figuring maybe in this modern world to be a vegetarian is to split hairs a little since all sentient beings eat what they can. And he was a man of solitude who could take off by himself and live purely and true to himself."

"That sounds like you too."

"And like you too, Ray, I haven't forgotten what you told me about how you made it in the woods meditating in North Carolina and all." Japhy was very sad, subdued, I'd never seen him so quiet, melancholy, thoughtful his voice was as tender as a mother's, he seemed to be talking from far away to a poor yearning creature (me) who needed to hear his message he wasn't putting anything on he was in a bit of a trance.

"Have you been meditating today?"

"Yeah I meditate first thing in the morning before breakfast and I always meditate a long time in the afternoon unless I'm interrupted."

"Who interrupts you?"

"Oh, people. Coughlin sometimes, and Alvah came yesterday, and Rol Sturlason, and I got this girl comes over to play yabyum."

"Yabyum? What's that?"

"Don't you know about yabyum, Smith? I'll tell you later." He seemed to be too sad to talk about yabyum, which I found out about a couple of nights later. We talked a while longer about Han Shan and poems on cliffs and as I was going away his friend Rol Sturlason, a tall blond goodlooking kid, came in to discuss his coming trip to Japan with him. This Rol Sturlason was interested in the famous Ryoanji rock garden of Shokokuji monastery in Kyoto, which is nothing but old boulders placed in such a way, supposedly mystically aesthetic, as to cause thousands of tourists and monks every year to journey there to stare at the boulders in the sand and thereby gain peace of mind. I have never met such weird yet serious and earnest people. I never saw Rol Sturlason again, he went to Japan soon after, but I can't forget what he said about the boulders, to my question, "Well who placed them in that certain way that's so great?"

"Nobody knows, some monk, or monks, long ago. But there is a definite mysterious form in the arrangement of the rocks. It's only through form that we can realize emptiness." He showed me the picture of the boulders in well-raked sand, looking like islands in the sea, looking as though they had eyes (declivities) and surrounded by a neatly screened and architectural monastery patio. Then he showed me a diagram of the stone arrangement with the projection in silhouette and showed me the geometrical logics and all, and mentioned the phrases "lonely individuality" and the rocks as "bumps pushing into space," all meaning some kind of koan business I wasn't as much interested in as in him and especially in good kind Japhy who brewed more tea on his noisy gasoline primus and gave us added cups with almost a silent Oriental bow. It was quite different from the night of the poetry reading.

Chronology of Chinese Dynasties

Hsia (Xia)	Protohistorical
Shang	ca. 1200–1059 B.C.E.
Chou (Zhou)	
Western Chou	1059–771 B.C.E.
Eastern Chou	771–ca. 249 B.C.E.
Spring and Autumn	722–468 B.C.E.
Warring States	403–221 B.C.E.
Ch'in (Qin)	221–207 B.C.E.
Han	
Former Han	206 B.C.E.–8 C.E.
Hsin (Xin) interregnum	9–25 C.E.
Latter Han	25–220 C.E.
Six Dynasties period	220–589
Sui	581–618
T'ang (Tang)	618–907
Five Dynasties	907–960
Sung (Song)	960–1279
Yüan (Yuan)	1279–1368
Ming	1368–1644

Ch'ing (Qing)	1644–1911

Modern era

Republican era (People's Republic of China)	1911–1949
(Republic of China on Taiwan)	1911–present
People's Republic (People's Republic of China)	1949–present

Additional Sources

The sources given here are intended to direct students to the most recent writings available on subjects represented in the anthology, although some works before 1991 are listed when particularly relevant. The Bibliography lists complete citations. For notes and complete references for the readings of the anthology, readers should consult the original works. I have not personally had access to all the books and articles listed here but am convinced they will be of use to students. Chinese names are listed surname first, as in the Bibliography, but without a comma separating first and last names.

General reference works and bibliographies. The *Encyclopedia of Religion* contains overviews of the history of Chinese religion as well as articles on more specific topics; bibliographies follow each entry. Students interested in a general background in Chinese history may consider the two recent surveys of Chinese history in Huang 1989 and Schirokauer 1991 and also consult the *Encyclopedia of Asian History*. Bibliographies and source guides for many major Asian texts are listed in de Bary and Embree 1989 and de Bary and Bloom 1990. Longer essays on specific works of Asian literature are included in Miller 1993, which is a teaching guide for Asian humanities. Entries on authors and literary works are listed by Chinese pronunciation in Nienhauser 1986, but for those unfamiliar with Chinese, a subject index in English provides access to important authors, works, and literary terms. This work contains extensive bibliographies following each entry, and its essays on traditional Chinese literature are valuable surveys of those fields. Many essays relevant to the readings included in this anthology are compiled in Hawkes 1989. For translations of primary sources of Chinese intellectual history and religion, see de Bary, Chan, and Watson 1960; of philosophy and religion, Chan 1963b; of Taoism, Kohn 1993; and of social history and religion, Ebrey 1981, which is also available in more recent editions.

Some primary texts in Chinese religion are compiled in Thompson 1973. Sources for Chinese religion written before 1991 are listed in the bibliographies by Thompson 1993 and 1985, A. Cohen 1991, and also in Ching 1993. For bibliographies of Taoism, see especially Seidel 1989–1990 and also Pas 1988; an essay on Taoist literature is included in Nienhauser 1986. Wu Yao-yü 1991 is a historical introduction to Taoism. For translations and analyses of Taoist texts, see the works by Kohn, particularly Kohn 1993, which is an anthology of translations, thematically arranged, with extensive bibliographic references. Popular Taoist legends are recounted in Ho and O'Brien 1990. Sources for many Confucian texts are provided in de Bary and Bloom 1990 and de Bary and Embree 1989. For Buddhist literature, see my subsequent discussion. Many journals on Asian studies include articles on Chinese religions, but the *Journal of Chinese Religions* is devoted to that subject.

Historical overviews of Chinese religion. For historical overviews of Chinese religion, see Ching 1993, Jochim 1986, Overmyer 1986, Thompson 1979, Eder 1973, as well as relevant articles in the *Encyclopedia of Religion.*

Shang and Chou dynasties. For historical studies of the Shang and Chou periods, see Powers 1992, Allan 1991, Shaughnessy 1991, K. C. Chang 1988, Hsu and Lindruff 1988, and Li Xueqin 1986. Watson 1962 is a general survey of pre-Han literature; Ching 1993 lists translations of most major pre-Han texts.

A standard version of the *Book of Changes* is Wilhelm 1967, but students should note that his translations of lines from the original text are indented in large type; the prose commentaries, however, are compiled and written by Wilhelm himself from various later works and are not part of the original text. For the original text only, see Legge 1963; for a modern translation, see Wu Jing-Nuan 1991. Kerson Huang's "I Ching 2000," a computer software program for divination by the *Book of Changes,* is available from Cheng & Tsui. Later forms of divination are discussed in R. Smith 1991 and K. Smith et al. 1990. The 1993 (vol. 8) special issue of the French-English bilingual journal *Cahiers d'Extrême-Asie* is devoted to Chinese divination.

For a complete translation of the *Book of History,* see Legge 1985b; ritual bronzes are the topic of Whitfield 1993. The *Book of Odes* is translated in Legge 1985c in its entirety, and selected poems are included in Watson 1984; see also the essay on the *Book of Songs* in Miller 1993. The *Tso chuan* is translated in Legge 1985d; for the most recent rendition of extensive selections, see Watson 1989. No English translations of the *Rites of Chou* exist; for later forms of dream divination recounted in that text, see Thompson 1988. Legge 1964 is a complete translation of the *Book of Rites;* a modern commentary on the chapter "Centrality and Equilibrium" is presented in Tu Weiming 1989.

For sources on Chou philosophers, see de Bary and Embree 1989, de Bary and Bloom 1990, and Ching 1993. Mencius's ethics are discussed in Ivanhoe 1990; for a complete translation of the works of Hsün Tzu, consult Knoblock 1988, 1990, and 1994. Hansen 1992 is a philosophical commentary on Taoist thought. For Chuang Tzu, see the essay on Chuang Tzu in Miller 1993; cartoons of the *Chuang Tzu* in Tsai 1992 are useful for transparencies.

The Chu culture of the *Songs of the South* is described in Lawton 1991; for earlier translations and commentaries on the *Songs* see Hawkes 1985 and Waley 1955. Modern observances of the midsummer Dragon Boat Festival that commemorates Ch'ü Yüan, the purported author of the *Songs,* are related in Stepanchuk and Wong 1991, which is intended for a general audience.

Han and Wei dynasties. Translations and interpretations of the thought of Wang Fu are the subject of Kinney 1990, which also translates his essay on dream interpretation and contains an older translation of his essay on spirit mediums, with complete references. See also Kinney 1991, as well as Pearson 1989. On recluses and hermits in early China, see Vervoorn 1990 and essays on the poetry of retreat in Miller 1993; encounters with modern-day hermits are recounted in Porter 1993. For a review of the latter work, see Munford 1993.

For Pan Chao's works, as well as those of other women, see "Women's Literature" in Nienhauser 1986; the most complete work on Pan Chao is still Swann 1932. General concepts of the goddess are discussed in Li Wai-yee 1993; Cahill 1993 is a historical study of a particular goddess, the Queen Mother of the West. An anthology of readings about women in East Asia is collected in Shimer 1982; for a transcultural anthology of sources on women's spirituality, consult Young 1993.

Six dynasties period. Those wanting a clear general introduction to the concepts of early Indian Buddhism may consult Rahula 1974. For somewhat dated but nonetheless useful general introductions to the history of Buddhism in China, see Ch'en 1964 and 1973; for more recent studies, consult relevant entries in the *Encyclopedia of Religion.* Prebish 1993 is a more recent reference work of Buddhist terms for the generalist; recent essays on Asian Buddhist spirituality are included in Yoshinori 1993. For more detailed studies, consult the monumental history of early Chinese Buddhism in Tsukamoto 1985; see also Buswell 1990, Donner and Stevenson 1993, Gregory 1991, King 1991, and Wright 1990, as well as the survey of Buddhist literature in Nienhauser 1986. On Pure Land in China, see Shih Heng-ching 1992 and Tanaka 1990. A philosophical introduction to the *Heart Sutra* according to Indian and Tibetan commentaries is presented in Lopez 1987.

For studies of women and gender in Buddhism in China and other Asian countries, see Cabezón 1992 and Gross 1992. Lives of Chinese Buddhist nuns in medieval times are recounted in K. Tsai 1994.

Watson 1993a is the most recent translation of the *Lotus Sutra;* a Chinese commentary on that text is translated in Kim 1990. Later Chinese views of Kuan-yin as a female deity are described in C. Yü 1990; her article on pilgrimages to sites sacred to Kuan-yin is included in Naquin and Yü 1992.

Schipper 1993, Robinet 1993, Wile 1992, and Wong 1992 describe Taoist concepts of the body and meditation. For concepts of the body relevant to Chinese medicine and acupuncture, see Wu Jing-Nuan 1993.

Sui and T'ang dynasties. Essays on religion in T'ang and Sung China are compiled in Ebrey and Gregory 1993. For a general history of Ch'an Buddhism, see Dumoulin 1988, but for more detailed studies, see Chien 1992, Faure 1991 and 1993, and Shih Heng-ching 1992. The 1992 issue of the *Cahiers d'Extrême-Asie* is devoted to articles on Ch'an Buddhism. Watson 1993b is the most recent translation of the works of I-hsüan, or Ch'an master Lin-chi.

For a complete translation of the works of Han-shan, consult Henricks 1990; one third of Han-shan's poems are translated in Watson 1992; selected verses are translated in Snyder 1990. Biographies of Han-shan and Po Chü-i are included in Nienhauser 1986.

For T'ang Confucians, see Barrett 1992 and the biography of Han Yü in Nienhauser 1986, which provides extensive bibliographies of his writings. Han Yü's sense of spirituality is discussed in Nienhauser 1991.

On women in the T'ang, see Kirkland 1991 and Schafer 1973; Taoist initiation rites for T'ang princesses are discussed in Benn 1991. A translation of the Japanese Noh drama *Yōhiki,* which is based on the story of Yang Kuei-fei, is included in Keene 1970.

Sung and Yüan dynasties. On modern ideas of the Great Ultimate, or *t'ai-chi,* reflected in the art of shadow boxing, see Delza 1985. For Confucianism in the Sung, see Ebrey 1991a and 1991b; for recent works on Chu Hsi, see Gardner 1990 and Tillman 1992. Chu Hsi's religious life is discussed in Chan 1987.

On the Taoist tradition of Perfect Truth or Complete Perfection, consult Tsui 1991.

Travel essays on the modern-day hermits of the Chung-nan (Zhongnan) region of northern China, where the founder of the Complete Perfection tradition lived as a recluse in the Sung dynasty, are related in Porter 1993. Taoist women are the subject of Cleary 1989, which is intended for a nonscholarly general audience.

For a history of Chinese drama, see Mackerras 1983 and the essay on drama in Nienhauser 1986; for Yüan drama, consult C. Shih 1976.

Ming dynasty. A complete translation of Wang Yang-ming's "Inquiry on the Great Learning" is included in Chan 1963a; for Wang's ethics, see Ivanhoe 1990. Biographies of Kao Ch'i and Hsü Wei are included in Nienhauser 1986 and also Goodrich and Fang 1976; the latter also contains biographies of Shen Chou and Mo Shih-lung.

For a complete translation of *Monkey,* see A. Yu 1977–1983; Waley 1958 is an abridged translation of the Chinese novel, and Kherdian 1992 is an animated but shorter retelling. For a concise analysis of the text, see Nienhauser 1986, s.v. *"Hsi-yu chi"* and also the essay in Miller 1993. A later novel that is styled as a supplement to *Monkey* is Lin and Schulz 1978; see Nienhauser 1986, s.v. *"Hsi-yu pu."* *Monkey* was the inspiration for Kingston's 1989 novel.

Ch'ing dynasty. Zeitlin 1993 is a recent study of Pu Songling (P'u Sung-ling); Pu's biography and writings are also discussed in Nienhauser 1986, s.v. *"Liao-chai chih-i."* His tales are retold in Van Over 1972. Recent translations of Chinese folktales are compiled in Chin, Center, and Ross 1989.

On Chinese law, consult Bodde and Morris 1967 and J. Cohen, Edwards, and Chen 1980. Ch'ing beliefs in sorcery are described in Kuhn 1990. Detective stories by a legendary Sung dynasty judge are translated in Chin, Center, and Ross 1992; for T'ang dynasty ghost stories, consult A. Cohen 1982. For an extensive study of Yüan Mei, see Waley 1970 and also Nienhauser 1986, s.v. "Yüan Mei."

A complete version of *The Story of the Stone* by Cao Xueqin is translated in the five-volume series begun by David Hawkes and completed by John Minford. Other translations are listed in Nienhauser 1986, s.v. *"Hung-lou meng,"* which relates a brief synopsis of the story; see also the relevant article in Miller 1993. For the religious and cultural significance of gardens such as Prospect Garden, the locus of much of the action in *The Story of the Stone,* see the introduction to Ji Cheng 1988 by Maggie Keswick; the religious context of miniature gardens is related in Stein 1990.

Modern era. Sources on modern fiction are provided in the bibliography in Lau, Hsia, and Lee 1981; for essays on the modern short story, see Huters 1990; for recent translations of additional short stories, consult Duke 1991. A critique of modern women writers is presented in Duke 1989; contemporary women's autobiographies are translated in Li Yu-ning 1992.

For studies on Confucianism in the modern world, see de Bary 1991a and 1991b, Rozman 1991, and Tu Weiming, Hjemanek, and Wachman 1992.

The fate of religion in modern China is described in Luo 1991, which relates the perspective of the Chinese government; MacInnes 1990 and Pas 1989 are observations by Western scholars. On the revival of traditional religions on the mainland, see Seymour and Wehrli (1994). Modern recluses and hermits are described in Porter 1993.

The god of theater is the subject of the works of Dean and van der Loon, as well as

Schipper 1966 and 1977, and Seaman 1978. Recent studies of Chinese mythology are Bonnefoy 1993 and Ke 1993; modern observances of the midautumn moon-viewing festival are described in Stepanchuk and Wong 1991.

Saso 1992 recounts recent studies of Buddhism on the mainland. An autobiographical account of a Buddhist master is translated in Chen-hua 1992; the writings of Master Sheng-yen are contemporary guides to Ch'an theory and practice. Fields 1992 and Tweed 1992 narrate the history of Buddhism in America; the former represents an insider's perspective; the latter is more academic in tone. On Elizabeth Palmer Peabody, see the brief article at Piez 1993.

Kerouac's understanding of Buddhism is recalled in Ginsberg 1990. Many of Kerouac's writings are as yet unpublished; his retelling of the life of the Buddha, *Wake Up*, has been published in installments in *Tricycle: The Buddhist Review* only since 1993.

Video Sources

Video, film, videodisk, and slide sources on China relevant to the study of Chinese religion are listed alphabetically by title. Distribution sources and other information are given when possible, but prices and availability are subject to change. For updated information on video sources (as well as computer software and data bases), consult the *Asian Studies Newsletter,* Association for Asian Studies, Inc., 1 Lane Hall, University of Michigan, Ann Arbor, Michigan 48109-1290.

Major suppliers in America for books, software, and videos on China are Cheng & Tsui Company, 25 West Street, Boston, Massachusetts, 02111; China Books & Periodicals, Inc., 2929 24th Street, San Francisco, California 94110 (telephone: 415-282-2994; fax: 415-282-0994); and Nan Hai Arts Center, 510 Broadway, Suite 300, Millbrae, California, 94030. A major mail-order distributor of international and domestic videos for sale and rent is Facets Video, 1517 West Fullerton Avenue, Chicago, Illinois, 60614, which carries a number of Chinese films.

China's Cosmopolitan Age: The Tang. 1993. 60 minutes. Produced by C. W. Shih of George Washington University. Explores the culture, government, art, and literature of the T'ang dynasty; presents the Buddhist center at Wu-t'ai Mountain and the Buddhist art of the Tun-huang caves and Lung-men grottoes. Companion text available. Contact the Annenberg/CPB Collection, Dept. CA94, P.O. Box 2345, S. Burlington, Vermont, 05407-2345.

Choice for a Chinese Woman: Enlightenment in a Buddhist Convent. 35 minutes. 1993. Description of the experiences of a young woman from rural China who leaves home to join a Buddhist nunnery. The film explores religious practices within the convent and considers the religious attitudes of a post-Mao society that has been officially encouraged to discount spiritual beliefs. Available from Films for the Humanities & Sciences, P.O. Box 2053, Princeton, New Jersey, 08543-2053.

The Cultural Revolution on Video. 60 minutes. Produced by Beijing Television Station. Black and white, in Chinese only. This documentary, by the Ninth National Congress of the Chinese Communist party of April 1969, took place but a few years after the development of the cult of Mao described by Jung Chang in the reading from *Wild Swans.* Contact the Center for Pacific Asia Studies, Stockholm University, S-10691, Stockholm, Sweden.

The Dragon Boat Festival. 30 minutes. Depicts the observance of the Dragon Boat Festival in a village in Fukien province. The festival commemorates the life and death of Ch'ü Yüan, who is traditionally credited with the *Songs of the South.* Available from the University of Washington Press, P.O. Box 50096, Seattle, Washington, 98145-5096.

A Dream of Red Mansions. 12 videotapes. Television series of the novel *The Story of the Stone.* This version is in Chinese, with no English subtitles, but subtitled versions have been aired on American public television stations and may be available from other sources. Available without subtitles from China Books & Periodicals.

The First Emperor of China. In videodisk format with bilingual Chinese and English commentaries, the *First Emperor* illustrates the excavations of the tomb of the first emperor of the Ch'in dynasty and contains a still-frame library of 5,000 slides. Available through Cheng & Tsui.

The God of Theater. Videos of the ritual performances of the god of theater and of other ritual dramas of southern China are in production and will be available from Kenneth Dean, Centre for East Asian Studies, McGill University, 3434 McTavish Street, Montreal, Quebec, Canada, H3A 1X9.

Heart of the Dragon. 1984. 12 cassettes, 57 minutes each. A twelve-part series on life in China in the eighties. Tape 4, *Believing,* is a concise introduction to traditional Confucian, Taoist, Buddhist, and popular religious practices in modern China, contrasted with the views of the believers of Maoist political ideology. Contains short segments on the cult of Mao. See also the chapter "Believing: Heaven, Earth, and Marx" in Clayre 1984, the companion text to this series. Tape 8, *Marrying,* describes modern rituals of matrimony and notions of marriage; tape 9, *Understanding,* illustrates Chinese notions of the body in relation to the larger cosmos. Available from Ambrose Video Publishing, Suite 2245, 1290 Avenue of the Americas, New York, New York, 10104.

Homage to Heaven, Homage to Earth. A slide series of 150 images of the Chinese collections at the Royal Ontario Museum in Toronto. Contact the Far Eastern Department, Royal Ontario Museum, 100 Queen's Park, Toronto, Ontario, Canada, M5S 2C6.

Kuan-yin Pilgrimage. 1988. 55 minutes. A documentary of pilgrimages to sites associated with the Buddhist deity Kuan-yin, produced and written by Chün-fang Yü. For related textual sources, see the producer's article "P'u-t'o Shan: Pilgrimage and the Creation of the Chinese Potalaka" in Naquin and Yü 1992, and see also C. Yü 1990. Available from the Department of Religion, Rutgers University, New Brunswick, New Jersey, 08903.

Lectures on Chinese Culture: 100 Video Series. 1993. A collection of one hundred half-hour illustrated lectures by Chinese scholars on the art, history, religion, philosophy, mythology, and folklore of China, produced by Peking University in conjunction with the Nan Hai Arts Center of Millbrae, California. Lectures are produced in Chinese, but the Arts Center is preparing English subtitles for segments requested by American viewers. Titles relevant to the study of Chinese religion are *Mount T'ai and Chinese Culture, Architecture of Mount T'ai, Peking Opera and K'un-ch'ü Opera, The Book of Odes, The Story of the*

Stone, Characterization in the Story of the Stone, Strange Tales of Make-Do Studio and *Characterization in the Strange Tales of Make-Do Studio, Chinese Religion and the Landscape, Confucius, The Brilliant Emperor of T'ang and Yang Kuei-fei, Arts of Ancient Chinese Alchemy, The Han Tombs of Ma-wang-tui, Ancient Chinese Bronzes, China's Buddhist Temples, China's Buddhist Images, Stone Grottoes of Yün-kang, Buddhist Tales from Cave Paintings, The Chinese New Year's Festival, The Dragon Boat Festival,* and *The Midautumn Festival.* (Titles are translated by the editor and are not necessarily those that will be prepared by Nan Hai.) Available from Nan Hai Arts Center, 510 Broadway, Suite 300, Millbrae, California, 94030.

Marriage of Swine Demon. 1990. 95 minutes. Video production of a puppet performance of the marriage of Pigsy in the novel *Monkey.* In Chinese, with no English subtitles. Available from China Books & Periodicals.

Monkey King Conquers the White-Boned Demon. 1990. 75 minutes. Video production of a puppet show of one chapter from the novel *Monkey.* In Chinese, with no English subtitles. Available from China Books & Periodicals.

Monkey King Looks West. 42 minutes. The novel *Monkey* was adapted into the repertoire of Peking opera, and various video recordings of operatic performances of *Monkey,* in Chinese only, are available at Chinese and Asian video rental agencies in major metropolitan areas. *Monkey King Looks West,* however, describes the lives of three Peking opera performers who have emigrated to America and try to maintain their artform in a new environment. From Filmakers Library, 124 East 40th Street, New York, New York, 10016.

The Mystery of Chi. This is one segment of the television series *Healing and the Mind* by Bill Moyers. *Ch'i,* the "flowing vital force" once described by Mencius, is explored in this documentary of modern Chinese medical and healing arts, which illustrates Chinese notions of the interactions of body and mind. Available from many media distributors.

New Year Sacrifice (Chu fu). 1956. Approximately 100 minutes. A motion picture, famous for its cinematography, adapted from Lu Hsün's short story *The New Year Sacrifice.* Directed by Sang Hu. The film is interpreted through the political ideology of the late fifties, but the essential plot is faithful to Lu Hsün's tale. Available in video format from major suppliers.

The Pacific Century: An Introduction to Modern Asia. [1992]. Ten videotapes, 57 minutes each. Color. Produced by the Pacific Basin Institute in cooperation with KCTS-9 Seattle and NHK Japan. Two segments from this series pertain to readings here. Video 4, *Writers and Revolutionaries,* an account of Chinese and Japanese social critics, devotes much time to the writings of Lu Hsün and his historical milieu. Video 7, *Big Business and the Ghost of Confucius,* explores the expression of traditional values in the development of the modern economies of Asia. Transcripts, accompanying texts, and study guides are available from the Annenberg/CPB Collection. For information, contact the Annenberg/CPB Collection, Dept. CA94, P.O. Box 2345, S. Burlington, Vermont, 05407-2345. For a review of the entire series, see Ozawa 1993.

Pilgrimage to the West. 12 videotapes. Twenty-five-part television series of the novel *Monkey.* This series is in Chinese, with no English subtitles, although versions with English subtitles have aired on American public television. Available from China Books & Periodicals.

Powers of Ten. Volume 1 of *The Films of Charles & Ray Eames.* 1989. 21 minutes. Produced by Eames Demetrios and Shelley Mills. This award-winning video is an unintentional visual commentary on the passage from *The Holy Teaching of Vimalakīrti* that describes the inconceivable liberation that is accessible to someone who can place the galaxies of the universe into a single pore of skin. *Powers of Ten,* which is an exploration of the concept of the infinity of the large and the small, suggests this inconceivable liberation by focusing on one pore; the image moves ten times farther out into space every ten seconds, until the viewer reaches the far edges of the universe; the focus then returns to earth, entering the pore and magnifying its component parts tenfold every ten seconds, until the viewer reaches the inner nucleus of a carbon atom. The limitlessness of space evokes an appreciation of what might be meant by the Buddhist term *śūnyatā,* the immeasurable infinity of the universe in all directions. The video also introduces the works of the artists Charles and Ray Eames. Available from Pyramid Film and Video, 2801 Colorado Avenue, Santa Monica, California, 90404.

Princess Yang Kwei Fei. 1955. 91 minutes. Color. Directed by Kenji Mizoguchi. Japanese cinematic rendition of the love story described in Po Chü-i's "Song of Unending Sorrow." Available in film format from New Yorker Films, 16 West 61st Street, New York, New York, 10023. For a video version, contact Cheng & Tsui.

The Silk Road. [1990]. Twelve videotapes, 55 minutes each. The series was produced by NHK Japan over a period of ten years; the narration is in English, with music by Kitaro. Each segment of this adventure-travel series contains materials relevant to Central Asian and Chinese history, geography, and culture, but *The Art Gallery in the Desert* is of particular interest to the study of religion, for it explores the caves of Central Asia that house some of the earliest known examples of Buddhist art in China. *Art Gallery* illustrates the confluence of Indian, Central Asian, and Chinese art styles. *The Silk Road* series, released in the United States by Central Park Media Corporation, is widely available through many media distributors.

Taoism. 25 minutes. Produced by Elda Hartley. Introduction to the fundamental ideas of Lao Tzu's *Tao-te ching,* which are then described in the context of Chinese landscape painting, architecture, and social customs. The narration is by John Blofeld. Available from the Hartley Film Foundation, Cat Rock Road, Cos Cob, Connecticut, 06807.

Taoism: A Question of Balance—China. 1978. 52 minutes. Part 11 of the *Long Search* series on religion produced by BBC TV in association with Time-Life. The title is somewhat misleading, for this is actually a documentary of Taiwanese popular folk practices such as funeral rites and local village festivals. Sometimes the term "Taoism" is used to describe popular folk practices, and that is how the term is understood here. Available through Ambrose Video Publishing, Suite 2245, 1290 Avenue of the Americas, New York, New York, 10104.

Bibliography

Allan, Sarah. 1991. *The Shape of the Turtle: Myth, Art, and Cosmos in Early China.* Albany: State University of New York Press.

Barret, Timothy Hugh. 1992. *Li Ao: Buddhist, Taoist, or Neo-Confucian?* New York: Oxford University Press.

Benn, Charles D. 1991. *The Cavern-Mystery Transmission: A Taoist Ordination Rite of A.D. 711.* Honolulu: University of Hawaii Press.

Birch, Cyril, ed. 1965. *Anthology of Chinese Literature.* New York: Grove Press.

Bodde, Derk, and Clarence Morris. 1967. *Law in Imperial China, Exemplified by 190 Ch'ing Dynasty Cases.* Cambridge: Harvard University Press.

Bonnefoy, Yves, ed. 1993. *Asian Mythologies.* Chicago: University of Chicago Press.

Brokaw, Cynthia. 1991. *The Ledgers of Merit and Demerit: Social Change and Moral Order in Late Imperial China.* Princeton: Princeton University Press.

Buswell, Robert E., Jr., ed. 1990. *Chinese Buddhist Apocrypha.* Honolulu: University of Hawaii Press.

Cabezón, José Ignacio, ed. 1992. *Buddhism, Sexuality, and Gender.* Albany: State University of New York Press.

Cahill, Suzanne E. 1993. *Transcendence and Divine Passion: The Queen Mother of the West in Medieval China.* Stanford: Stanford University Press.

Cao Xueqin. 1980. *The Story of the Stone.* Vol. 3, *The Warning Voice.* Translated by David Hawkes. Harmondsworth, Middlesex: Penguin Books.

Cao Xueqin. 1986. *The Story of the Stone.* Vol. 5, *The Dreamer Wakes.* Translated by John Minford. Harmondsworth, Middlesex: Penguin Books.

Chan, Wing-tsit. 1987. *Chu Hsi: Life and Thought.* Hong Kong: Chinese University Press.

———, trans. 1963a. *Instructions for Practical Living and Other Neo-Confucian Writings by Wang-yang Ming.* New York: Columbia University Press.

———, trans. 1963b. *A Source Book in Chinese Philosophy.* Princeton: Princeton University Press.

———, trans. 1963c. *The Way of Lao Tzu (Tao-te ching).* New York: Macmillan.

———, trans. 1986. *Neo-Confucian Terms Explained (The Pei-hsi tzu-i).* New York: Columbia University Press.

Chang, Jung. 1991. *Wild Swans: Three Daughters of China.* New York: Simon & Schuster.

Chang, Kwang-chih. 1988. *Art, Myth, and Ritual: The Path to Political Authority in Ancient China.* Cambridge: Harvard University Press.

Chaves, Jonathan, trans. 1986. *The Columbia Book of Later Chinese Poetry: Yüan, Ming, and Ch'ing Dynasties (1279–1911).* New York: Columbia University Press.

Ch'en, Kenneth. 1964. *Buddhism in China: A Historical Survey.* Princeton: Princeton University Press.

———. 1973. *The Chinese Transformation of Buddhism.* Princeton: Princeton University Press.

Chen-hua. 1992. *In Search of the Dharma: Memoirs of a Modern Chinese Buddhist Pilgrim.* Albany: State University of New York Press.

Chien, Bhikshu Cheng. 1992. *Sun-Face Buddha: The Teachings of Ma-tsu and the Hung-chou School of Ch'an.* Berkeley: Asian Humanities Press.

Chin, Yin-lien C., Yetta S. Center, and Mildred Ross. 1989. *Traditional Chinese Folktales.* Armonk, N.Y.: M. E. Sharpe.

———. 1992. *"The Stone Lion" and Other Chinese Detective Stories: The Wisdom of Lord Bau.* Armonk, N.Y.: M. E. Sharpe.

Ching, Julia. 1993. *Chinese Religions.* Maryknoll, N.Y.: Orbis Books.

———, trans. 1972. *The Philosophical Letters of Wang Yang-ming*. Canberra: Australian National University Press; and Columbia: University of South Carolina Press.

Clayre, Alasdair. 1984. *The Heart of the Dragon*. Boston: Houghton Mifflin.

Cleary, Thomas, trans. 1989. *Immortal Sisters: Secrets of Taoist Women*. Boston: Shambhala Publications.

Cohen, Alvin P., trans. 1982. *Tales of Vengeful Souls: A Sixth Century Collection of Chinese Avenging Ghost Stories*. Variétés sinologiques, new series, no. 68. Paris: Ricci Institute for Chinese Studies.

———, trans. 1991. *Publications on Religions in China, 1981–1989*. Asian Studies Program Occasional Papers Series, no. 15. Amherst: University of Massachusetts at Amherst.

Cohen, Jerome, Randle Edwards, and Fu-mei Chang Chen, eds. 1980. *Essays on China's Legal Tradition*. Princeton: Princeton University Press.

Conze, Edward. 1959. *Buddhist Scriptures*. Harmondsworth, Middlesex: Penguin Books.

Dean, Kenneth. 1993. *Taoist Ritual and Popular Cults of Southeast China*. Princeton: Princeton University Press.

———. 1994. Comic inversion and cosmic renewal: the god of theater in the ritual traditions of Putian. Proceedings of the International Conference on Chinese Culture and Popular Beliefs, May 1993. Taipei.

Dean, Kenneth, and Zheng Zhenman. 1993. Group initiation and exorcistic dance in the Xinghua region. *Min-su ch'u-i* 85:105–95.

de Bary, Wm. Theodore. 1991a. *Learning for One's Self: Essays on the Individual in Neo-Confucian Thought*. New York: Columbia University Press.

———. 1991b. *The Trouble with Confucianism*. Cambridge: Harvard University Press.

de Bary, Wm. Theodore, and Irene Bloom, eds. 1990. *Approaches to the Asian Classics*. New York: Columbia University Press.

de Bary, Wm. Theodore, Wing-tsit Chan, and Burton Watson, comps. 1960. *Sources of Chinese Tradition*. 2 vols. New York: Columbia University Press.

de Bary, Wm. Theodore, and Ainslee Embree, eds. 1989. *A Guide to Oriental Classics*. 3d ed. New York: Columbia University Press.

Delza, Sophia. 1985. *T'ai Chi Ch'uan (Wu Style) Body and Mind in Harmony: The Integration of Meaning and Method*. Rev. ed. Albany: State University of New York Press.

Donner, Neal, and Daniel B. Stevenson, trans. 1993. *The Great Calming and Contemplation*. Honolulu: University of Hawaii Press.

Duke, Michael S., ed. 1989. *Modern Chinese Women Writers: Critical Appraisals*. Armonk, N.Y.: M. E. Sharpe.

———, ed. 1991. *Short Stories and Novellas from the People's Republic, Taiwan, and Hong Kong*. Armonk, N.Y.: M. E. Sharpe.

Dumoulin, Heinrich. 1988. *Zen Buddhism: A History*. Vol. 1, *India and China*. New York: Macmillan.

Ebrey, Patricia Buckley. 1991a. *Chu Hsi's Family Rituals*. Princeton: Princeton University Press.

———. 1991b. *Confucianism and Family Rituals in Imperial China: A Social History of Writing about Rituals*. Princeton: Princeton University Press.

———, ed. 1981. *Chinese Civilization and Society: A Sourcebook*. New York: Free Press.

Ebrey, Patricia Buckley, and Peter N. Gregory, eds. 1993. *Religion and Society in T'ang and Sung China*. Honolulu: University of Hawaii Press.

Eder, Matthias. 1973. *Chinese Religion*. Tokyo: Society for Asian Folklore.

Encyclopedia of Asian History. 1988. Edited by Ainslee T. Embree. 4 vols. New York: Charles Scribner's Sons.

Encyclopedia of Religion. 1987. Edited by Mircea Eliade. 16 vols. New York: Macmillan.

Faure, Bernard. 1991. *The Rhetoric of Immediacy: A Cultural Critique of Chan/Zen Buddhism*. Princeton: Princeton University Press.

———. 1993. *Chan Insights and Oversights: An Epistemological Critique of the Chan Tradition*. Princeton: Princeton University Press.

Feuchtwang, Stephan. 1992. *The Imperial Metaphor: Popular Religion in China*. London: Routledge.

Fields, Rick. 1992. *How the Swans Came to the Lake: A Narrative History of Buddhism in America*. 3d ed., rev. and updated. Boston: Shambhala Publications.

Gardner, Daniel K. 1990. *Learning to Be a Sage: Selections from the* Conversations of Master Chu, *Arranged Topically*. Berkeley: University of California Press.

Ginsberg, Allen. 1990. "Kerouac's ethic." In *Un Homme grand: Jack Kerouac à la confluence des cultures/Un Homme grand: Jack Kerouac at the Crossroads of Many Cultures*, edited by Pierre

Anctil, Louis Dupont, Remi Ferland, and Eric Waddell. Ottawa: Carleton University Press.

Goddard, Dwight, ed. [1932] 1970. *A Buddhist Bible*. Boston: Beacon Press.

Goodrich, Carrington L., and Chaoying Fang, eds. 1976. *Dictionary of Ming Biography: 1368–1644*. 2 vols. New York: Columbia University Press.

Gregory, Peter N. 1991. *Tsung-mi and the Sinification of Buddhism*. Princeton: Princeton University Press.

Gross, Rita M. 1992. *Buddhism after Patriarchy: A Feminist History, Analysis, and Reconstruction of Buddhism*. Albany: State University of New York Press.

Hanson, Chad. 1992. *A Daoist Theory of Chinese Thought*. New York: Oxford University Press.

Hawkes, David. 1989. *Classical, Modern, and Humane: Essays in Chinese Literature*. Edited by John Minford and Siu-kit Wong. Hong Kong: Chinese University Press.

———, trans. 1973. *The Story of the Stone*. Vol. 1, *The Golden Days*. Harmondsworth, Middlesex: Penguin Books.

———, trans. 1977. *The Story of the Stone*. Vol. 2, *The Crab-flower Club*. Harmondsworth, Middlesex: Penguin Books.

———, trans. 1985. *The Songs of the South: An Ancient Chinese Anthology of Poems by Qu Yuan and Other Poets*. Harmondsworth, Middlesex: Penguin Books.

Henderson, John B. 1991. *Scripture, Canon, and Commentary: A Comparison of Confucian and Western Exegesis*. Princeton: Princeton University Press.

Henricks, Robert G. 1990. *The Poetry of Han-Shan: A Complete, Annotated Translation of* Cold Mountain. Albany: State University of New York Press.

Ho, Kwok Man, and Joanne O'Brien. 1990. *The Eight Immortals of Taoism: Legends and Fables of Popular Taoism*. New York: Penguin Books.

Hsiao ching. 1982. Edited by Juan Yüan. *Shih-san-ching chu-shu* edition. Beijing: Chung-hua shu-chü.

Hsu Cho-yun and Katheryn M. Linduff. 1988. *Western Chou Civilization*. New Haven: Yale University Press.

Huang, Ray. 1989. *China: A Macrohistory*. Armonk, N.Y.: M. E. Sharpe.

Huters, Theodore, ed. 1990. *Reading the Modern Chinese Short Story*. Armonk, N.Y.: M. E. Sharpe.

Ivanhoe, Philip J. 1990. *Ethics in the Confucian Tradition: The Thought of Mencius and Wang Yangming*. Atlanta: Scholars Press.

Ji Cheng. 1988. *The Craft of Gardens*. Translated by Alison Hardie. New Haven: Yale University Press.

Jochim, Christian. 1986. *Chinese Religions: A Cultural Perspective*. Englewood Cliffs, N.J.: Prentice-Hall.

Katō, Bunnō, Yoshirō Tamura, and Kōjirō Miyasaka, trans. 1975. *The Threefold Lotus Sutra*. Tokyo: Kosei Publishing.

Ke, Yuan. 1993. *Dragons and Dynasties: An Introduction to Chinese Mythology*. New York: Viking Penguin.

Keene, Donald. 1970. *Twenty Plays of the Nō Theatre*. New York: Columbia University Press.

Kerouac, Jack. [1958] 1986. *The Dharma Bums*. New York: Viking Penguin.

———. 1960. *The Scripture of the Golden Eternity*. N.p.

———. 1993. *Wake Up*. Published serially in *Tricycle: The Buddhist Review* 2, no. 4 (Summer)–.

Kherdian, David. 1992. *Monkey: A Journey to the West*. Boston: Shambhala Publications.

Kim, Young-ho. 1990. *Tao-sheng's Commentary on the Lotus Sutra: A Study and Translation*. Albany: State University of New York Press.

King, Sallie B. 1991. *Buddha Nature*. Albany: State University of New York Press.

Kingston, Maxine Hong. 1989. *Tripmaster Monkey: His Fake Book*. New York: Alfred A. Knopf.

Kinney, Anne Behnke. 1990. *The Art of the Han Essay: Wang Fu's* Ch'ien-fu lun. Tempe: Arizona State University Press.

———. 1991. Predestination and prognostication in the *Ch'ien-fu Lun*. *Journal of Chinese Religions* 19 (Fall):27–45.

Kirkland, Russell. 1991. Huang Ling-wei: A Taoist priestess in T'ang China. *Journal of Chinese Religions* 19 (Fall):47–73.

Knoblock, John, trans. 1988, 1990, 1994. *Xunzi: A Translation and Study of the Complete Works*. 3 vols. Stanford: Stanford University Press.

Kohn, Livia. 1991. *Taoist Mystical Philosophy: The Scripture of Western Ascension*. Albany: State University of New York Press.

———. 1992. *Early Chinese Mysticism: Philosophy and Soteriology in the Taoist Tradition*. Princeton: Princeton University Press.

———. 1993. *The Taoist Experience: An Anthology*. Albany: State University of New York Press.

Kuhn, Philip A. 1990. *Soulstealers: The Chinese Sorcery Scare of 1768.* Cambridge: Harvard University Press.

Lau, S. M., C. T. Hsia, and Leo Ou-fan Lee, eds. 1981. *Modern Chinese Stories and Novellas: 1919–1949.* New York: Columbia University Press.

Lawton, Thomas, ed. 1991. *New Perspectives on Chu Culture during the Eastern Zhou Period.* Princeton: Princeton University Press.

Legge, James, trans. [1899] 1963. *The I Ching.* 2d ed. New York: Dover Publications.

———, trans. [1885] 1964. *The Sacred Books of the East.* Vols. 27–28, *The Li Ki.* Edited by F. Max Müller. Delhi: Motilal Banarsidass.

———, trans. [1893–1895]. *The Chinese Classics.* 2d ed., rev. Reprint. 5 vols. Taipei: Southern Materials Center.
1985a. Vol. 1, *Confucian Analects, The Great Learning, The Doctrine of the Mean.* Vol. 2, *The Works of Mencius.*
1985b. Vol. 3, *The Shoo King, or the Book of Historical Documents.*
1985c. Vol. 4, *The She King, or The Book of Poetry.*
1985d. Vol. 5, *The Ch'un Tsew with The Tso Chuen.*

Leung, Man-Kam. 1991. The study of religious Taoism in the People's Republic of China (1949–1990): A bibliographic survey. *Journal of Chinese Religions* 19 (Fall):113–26.

Li, Wai-yee. 1993. *Enchantment and Disenchantment: Love and Illusion in Chinese Literature.* Princeton: Princeton University Press.

Li Xueqin. 1986. *Eastern Zhou and Qin Civilizations.* New Haven: Yale University Press.

Li Yu-ning, ed. 1992. *Chinese Women through Chinese Eyes.* Armonk, N.Y.: M. E. Sharpe.

Lin, Shuen-fu, and L. Schulz, trans. 1978. *The Tower of Myriad Mirrors: A Supplement to the Journey to the West.* Berkeley: Asian Humanities Press.

Liu Jung-en. 1972. *Six Yüan Plays.* Harmondsworth, Middlesex: Penguin Books.

Lopez, Donald S. 1987. *The Heart Sūtra Explained: Indian and Tibetan Commentaries.* Albany: State University of New York Press.

Lu Xun. 1980. *Lu Xun: Selected Works.* Translated by Yang Xianyi and Gladys Yang. Vol. 1. 2d ed. Beijing: Foreign Languages Press.

Lü-shih ch'un-ch'iu. 1979. *Ssu-pu ts'ung-k'an cheng-pien* edition. Taipei: Commercial Press.

Luo Zhufeng. 1991. *Religion under Socialism in China.* Translated by Donald E. MacInnes and Zheng Xi'an. Armonk, N.Y.: M. E. Sharpe, 1991.

MacInnes, Donald E. 1990. *Religion in China Today: Policy and Practice.* Maryknoll, N.Y.: Orbis Books.

Mackerras, Colin. 1983. *Chinese Theater: From Its Origins to the Present Day.* Honolulu: University of Hawaii Press.

Mao Tse-tung. 1965. *Selected Works of Mao Tse-tung.* Beijing: Foreign Languages Press.

Meyer, Jeffrey F. 1991. *The Dragons of Tiananmen: Beijing as a Sacred City.* Columbia: University of South Carolina Press.

Miller, Barbara Stoler, ed. 1993. *Masterworks of Asian Literature in Comparative Perspective: A Guide for Teaching.* Armonk, N.Y.: M. E. Sharpe.

Minford, John, trans. 1982. *The Story of the Stone.* Vol. 4, *The Debt of Tears.* Bloomington: Indiana University Press.

Munakata, Kiyohiko. 1991. *Sacred Mountains in Chinese Art.* Urbana: University of Illinois Press.

Munford, Theresa. 1993. Review of *Road to Heaven: Encounters with Chinese Hermits,* by Bill Porter. *Far Eastern Economic Review* (7 October):39.

Naquin, Susan, and Chün-fang Yü, eds. 1992. *Pilgrims and Sacred Sites in China.* Berkeley: University of California Press.

Nienhauser, William H., Jr. 1991. Han Yü, Liu Tsung-yüan and boundaries of literati piety. *Journal of Chinese Religions* 19 (Fall):75–104.

———, ed. 1986. *The Indiana Companion to Traditional Chinese Literature.* Bloomington: Indiana University Press.

Nylan, Michael. 1993. *The Canon of Supreme Mystery by Yang Hsiung.* Albany: State University of New York.

Overmyer, Daniel L. 1986. *Religions of China: The World as a Living System.* San Francisco: Harper & Row.

Ozawa, Terutomo. 1993. Review of *The Pacific Century: An Introduction to Modern Asia,* produced by the Pacific Basin Institute. *Journal of Asian Studies* 52, no. 2 (May):512–21.

Paludan, Ann. 1991. *The Chinese Spirit Road: The Classical Tradition of Stone Tomb Statuary.* New Haven: Yale University Press.

Pas, Julian F. 1988. *A Select Bibliography on Taoism.* Stony Brook, N.Y.: Institute for Advanced Studies of World Religions.

———, ed. 1989. *The Turning of the Tide: Religion in China Today.* Hong Kong: Oxford University Press.

Pearson, Margaret. 1989. *Wang Fu and the Comments of a Recluse.* Tempe: Arizona State University.

Piez, Wendell. 1993. Anonymous was a woman—again. *Tricycle: The Buddhist Review* 3, no. 1 (Fall):10–11.

Po, Sung-nien, and David Johnson. 1992. *Domesticated Deities and Auspicious Emblems: The Iconography of Everyday Life in Village China.* Publications of the Chinese Popular Culture Project 2. Berkeley: IEAS Publications.

Porter, Bill. 1993. *Road to Heaven: Encounters with Chinese Hermits.* San Francisco: Mercury House.

Powers, Martin J. 1992. *Art and Political Expression in Early China.* New Haven: Yale University Press.

Prebish, Charles S. 1993. *Historical Dictionary of Buddhism.* Metuchen, N.J.: Scarecrow Press.

Pu Songling. 1989. *Strange Tales from Make-Do Studio.* Translated by Denis C. Mair and Victor H. Mair. Beijing: Foreign Languages Press.

Rahula, Walpola. 1974. *What the Buddha Taught.* 2d ed., rev. and enl. New York: Grove Press.

Rexroth, Kenneth, and Ling Chung. 1972. *Women Poets of China.* New York: New Directions.

Robinet, Isabelle. [1979] 1993. *Taoist Meditation: The Mao-shan Tradition of Great Purity.* Translated by Julian F. Pas and Norman J. Girardot. Albany: State University of New York Press.

Roth, Harold David. 1992. *The Textual History of the* Huai-nan Tzu. Ann Arbor, Mich.: Association for Asian Studies.

Rozman, Gilbert, ed. 1991. *The East Asian Region: Confucian Heritage and Its Modern Adaptation.* Princeton: Princeton University Press.

Saso, Michael. 1990. *Blue Dragon, White Tiger: Taoist Rites of Passage.* Honolulu: University of Hawaii Press.

———, trans. 1992. *Buddhist Studies in the People's Republic of China: 1990–1991.* Honolulu: University of Hawaii Press.

Schafer, Edward H. 1973. *The Divine Woman: Dragon Ladies and Rain Maidens in Tang Literature.* Berkeley: University of California Press.

Schipper, Kristofer M. 1966. The divine jester: Some remarks on the gods of the Chinese marionette theater. *Bulletin of the Institute of History and Philology, Academia Sinica* 21 (Spring):81–94.

———. 1977. Neighborhood cult associations in traditional Tainan. In *The City in Late Imperial China,* edited by G. William Skinner, 651–76. Stanford: Stanford University Press.

———. 1993. *The Taoist Body.* Berkeley: University of California Press.

Schirokauer, Conrad. 1991. *A Brief History of Chinese Civilization.* San Diego: Harcourt Brace Jovanovich.

Seaman, Gary, 1978. *Temple Organization in a Chinese Town.* Taipei: Orient Cultural Service.

Seidel, Anna. 1989–1990. Chronicle of Taoist studies in the West: 1950–1990. *Cahiers d'Extrême-Asie* 5:223–347.

Seymour, James, and Eugen Wehrli, eds. 1994. *The Revival of Traditional Religions.* Vol. 26, no. 3 of *Chinese Sociology and Anthropology: A Journal of Translations.*

Shaughnessy, Edward L. 1991. *Sources of Western Zhou History: Inscribed Bronze Vessels.* Berkeley: University of California Press.

Sheng-yen, Master. 1982. *Getting the Buddha Mind: On the Practice of Ch'an Retreat.* New York: Dharma Drum Publications.

———. 1987a. *Faith in Mind: A Guide to Ch'an Practice.* New York: Dharma Drum Publications.

———. 1987b. *The Poetry of Enlightenment: Poems by Ancient Ch'an Masters.* New York: Dharma Drum Publications.

———. 1988. *Ox-Herding at Morgan's Bay.* New York: Dharma Drum Publications.

———. 1990a. *The Infinite Mirror.* New York: Dharma Drum Publications.

———. 1990b. *The Sword of Wisdom: Lectures on* The Song of Enlightenment. New York: Dharma Drum Publications.

———. Forthcoming. *Complete Enlightenment.* New York: Dharma Drum Publications.

———. Forthcoming. *Zen Wisdom: Knowing and Doing.* New York: Dharma Drum Publications.

Shih, Chung-wen. 1976. *The Golden Age of Chinese Drama: Yüan Tsa-chü.* Princeton: Princeton University Press.

Shih, Heng-ching. 1992. *The Syncretism of Ch'an and Pure Land Buddhism.* New York: P. Lang.

Shimer, Dorothy Blair, ed. 1982. *Rice Bowl Women: Writings by and about the Women of China and Japan.* New York: New American Library.

Smith, Kidder, Peter J. Bol, Joseph A. Adler, and Don J. Wyatt. 1990. *Sung Dynasty Uses of the I Ching.* Princeton: Princeton University Press.

Smith, Richard J. 1991. *Fortune-tellers and Philoso-*

phers: Divination in Traditional Chinese Society. Boulder, Colo.: Westview Press.

Snyder, Gary. [1969] 1990. *Riprap and Cold Mountain Poems*. San Francisco: North Point Press.

Sommer, Deborah A. 1993. Ch'iu Chün's (1421–1495) *On the Conduct of Sacrificial Offerings*. Ph.D. diss., Columbia University, New York.

Stein, Rolf. A. 1990. *The World in Miniature: Container Gardens and Dwellings in Far Eastern Religious Thought*. Stanford: Stanford University Press.

Stepanchuk, Carol, and Charles Wong. 1991. *Mooncakes and Hungry Ghosts: Festivals of China*. San Francisco: China Books and Periodicals.

Su Xiaokang and Wang Luxiang. 1991. *Deathsong of the River: A Reader's Guide to the Chinese TV Series He Shang*. Ithaca: Cornell University East Asia Program.

Swann, Nancy Lee. [1932]. 1968. *Pan Chao: Foremost Woman Scholar of China*. New York: Russell & Russell.

Tanaka, Kenneth K. 1990. *The Dawn of Chinese Pure Land Buddhist Doctrine: Ching-ying Hui-yüan's Commentary on the* Visualization Sutra. Albany: State University of New York Press.

Taylor, Rodney L. 1990. *The Religious Dimensions of Confucianism*. Albany: State University of New York Press.

Thompson, Laurence G. 1973. *The Chinese Way in Religion*. Belmont, Calif.: Wadsworth Publishing.

———. 1979. *Chinese Religion: An Introduction*. 3d ed. Belmont, Calif.: Wadsworth Publishing.

———. 1985. *Chinese Religion in Western Languages: A Comprehensive and Classified Bibliography of Publications in English, French, and German through 1980*. Ann Arbor, Mich.: Association for Asian Studies.

———. 1988. Dream divination and Chinese popular religion. *Journal of Chinese Religions* 16:73–82.

———, comp. 1993. *Chinese Religion: Publications in Western Languages, 1981 through 1990*. Edited by Gary Seaman. Ann Arbor, Mich.: Association for Asian Studies.

Thurman, Robert A. F. 1976. *The Holy Teaching of Vimalakīrti*. University Park: Pennsylvania State University Press.

Tillman, Hoyt Cleveland. 1992. *Confucian Discourse and Chu Hsi's Ascendancy*. Honolulu: University of Hawaii Press.

Tsai Chih Chung. 1992. *Zhuangzi Speaks: The Music of Nature*. Translated by Brian Bruya. Princeton: Princeton University Press.

Tsai, Kathryn Ann. 1994. *Lives of the Nuns: Biographies of Chinese Buddhist Nuns from the Fourth to the Sixth Centuries*. Honolulu: University of Hawaii Press.

Tsui, Bartholomew P. M. 1991. *Taoist Tradition and Change: The Story of the Complete Perfection Sect in Hong Kong*. Hong Kong: Christian Study Centre on Chinese Religion and Culture.

Tsukamoto Zenryu. 1985. *A History of Chinese Buddhism from its Introduction to the Death of Hui-yüan*. Translated by Leon Hurvitz. Tokyo: Kodansha International.

Tu Weiming. 1989. *Centrality and Commonality: An Essay on Confucian Religiousness*. Albany: State University of New York Press.

Tu Weiming, Milan G. Hjemanek, and Alan Wachman, eds. 1992. *The Confucian World Observed: A Contemporary Discussion of Confucian Humanism in East Asia*. Honolulu: University of Hawaii Press.

Tweed, Thomas A. 1992. *The American Encounter with Buddhism, 1844–1912: Victorian Culture and the Limits of Dissent*. Bloomington: Indiana University Press.

van der Loon, Piet. 1977. Les origines rituelles du théâtre chinois. *Journal asiatique* 265:141–68.

———. 1992. *The Classical Theater and Art Song of South Fukien: A Study of Three Ming Anthologies*. Taipei: SMC Publishing.

Van Over, Raymond. 1972. *A Treasury of Chinese Literature*. New York: Fawcett Premier.

Vervoorn, Aat. 1990. *Men of the Cliffs and Caves: The Development of the Chinese Eremitic Tradition to the End of the Han Dynasty*. Hong Kong: Chinese University Press.

Waley, Arthur. 1955. *The Nine Songs: A Study of Shamanism in Ancient China*. London: G. Allen and Unwin.

———. [1957] 1970. *Yuan Mei: Eighteenth Century Chinese Poet*. Stanford: Stanford University Press.

Watson, Burton. 1962. *Early Chinese Literature*. New York: Columbia University Press.

———, trans. 1963a. *Hsün Tzu: Basic Writings*. New York: Columbia University Press.

———, trans. 1963b. *Mo Tzu: Basic Writings*. New York: Columbia University Press.

———, trans. 1964. *Chuang Tzu: Basic Writings*. New York: Columbia University Press.

———, trans. 1984. *The Columbia Book of Chinese Poetry from Early Times to the Thirteenth Century*. New York: Columbia University Press.

————, trans. 1989. *The Tso chuan: Selections from China's Oldest Narrative History*. New York: Columbia University Press.

————, trans. 1992. *Cold Mountain: 101 Chinese Poems*. 2d ed., rev. Boston: Shambhala Publications.

————, trans. 1993a. *The Lotus Sutra*. New York: Columbia University Press.

————, trans. 1993b. *The Zen Teachings of Master Lin-chi*. Boston: Shambhala Publications.

Whitfield, Roderick. 1993. *The Problem of Meaning in Early Chinese Ritual Bronzes*. Colloquies on Art and Archeology in Asia, no. 15. London: University of London.

Wile, Douglas. 1992. *Art of the Bedchamber: The Chinese Sexual Yoga Classics Including Women's Solo Meditation Texts*. Albany: State University of New York Press.

Wilhelm, Richard, trans. [1950] 1967. *The I Ching or Book of Changes*. 3d ed. Princeton: Princeton University Press.

Wong, Eva, trans. 1990. *Seven Taoist Masters: A Folk Novel of China*. Boston: Shambhala Publications.

————, trans. 1992. *Cultivating Stillness: A Taoist Manual for Transforming Body and Mind*. Boston: Shambhala Publications.

Wright, Arthur F. 1990. *Studies in Chinese Buddhism*. Edited by Robert M. Somers. New Haven: Yale University Press.

Wu Ch'eng-en. [1943]. 1958. *Monkey*. Translated by Arthur Waley. New York: Grove Press, Inc.

Wu Hung. 1989. *The Wu Liang Shrine: The Ideology of Early Chinese Pictorial Art*. Stanford: Stanford University Press.

Wu Jing-Nuan. 1991. *Yi Jing*. Honolulu: University of Hawaii Press.

————. 1993. *Ling Shu: or The Spiritual Pivot*. Honolulu: University of Hawaii Press.

Wu Yao-yü. 1991. *The Taoist Tradition in Chinese Thought*. Ethnographics Press. Los Angeles: University of Southern California.

Yampolsky, Philip B., trans. 1967. *The Platform Sutra of the Sixth Patriarch*. New York: Columbia University Press.

Yoshinori Takeuchi, ed. 1993. *Buddhist Spirituality*. Vol. 1, *Indian, Southeast Asia, Tibetan, and Early Chinese*. Vol. 9 of *World Spirituality: An Encyclopedic History of the Religious Quest*. New York: Crossroad Publishing.

Young, Serinity, ed. 1993. *Sacred Texts by and about Women: A Universal Anthology*. New York: Crossroad Publishing.

Yu, Anthony, trans. 1977–1983. *The Journey to the West*. 4 vols. Chicago: University of Chicago Press.

Yü, Chün-fang. 1990. Feminine Images of Kuan-yin in post-T'ang China. *Journal of Chinese Religions* 18 (Fall):61–89.

Yu, David C. 1985. *Guide to Chinese Religion*. Boston: G. K. Hall.

Zeitlin, Judith T. 1993. *Historian of the Strange: Pu Songling and the Chinese Classical Tale*. Stanford University Press.

Glossary

Herein I describe important terms and people not otherwise identified in the introductions to the readings; some figures from popular lore or ancient history are not identifiable. Major figures are listed again primarily to provide a convenient reference for their dates and for alternate romanizations of their names. All dates before roughly the eighth century of the common era, and many thereafter, are subject to differing interpretations. The Wade-Giles system of romanization is followed whenever possible, unless the selection from the original text uses the pinyin system. To assist the reader, alternate spellings of a Chinese term are given in parentheses when the two romanization systems differ. Any term with an apostrophe belongs to the Wade-Giles system; any term with the letters *b, d, g, q, x,* or *z* follows the pinyin system.

Ānanda: One of the historical disciples of Siddhārtha Gautama; his name literally means "bliss."

Apsara: Flying divinities of Buddhist mythology.

Asura: Godlike titans of Indian mythology.

Arhat: In Buddhism, a "worthy one" who has attained spiritual perfection.

Bao-chai (Pao-ch'ai): Bao-yu's cousin, whom he is tricked into marrying.

Bao-qin (Pao-ch'in): A young woman who is Bao-yu's relative on his mother's side.

Bao-yu (Pao-yü): The main character of the novel *The Story of the Stone.* His name literally means "Precious Jade."

Baozhi (Pao-chih): A Ch'an master of the fifth or sixth century.

Bhikshu: A Buddhist monk.

Bhikshuṇī: A Buddhist nun.

Bodhi: Sanskrit term for enlightenment or awakening.

Bodhidharma (floruit ca. 520): First Patriarch of Ch'an Buddhism in China.

Bodhisattva: Sanskrit term that literally means "enlightened being," an expression that may refer to powerful divinities or even to human beings who have attained spiritual perfection.

Border Warden Ying: A figure from the *Tso chuan* noted for his filial piety.

Brahmā: One of the highest gods of Indian mythology.

Brahman: Someone of the Brahman class, the priestly class of ancient Indian society.

Chang T'ien-i (Zhang Tian'i; born 1906): Writer and social critic.

Chang Tsai (Zhang Zai; 1020–1077): Noted Sung dynasty philosopher of the classics.

Chen Tuan (Ch'en T'uan; died 989): Mountain recluse versed in alchemy.

Ch'en Ch'un (Chen Chun; 1159–1223): Sung philosopher of the classics.

Ch'en P'ing (Chen Ping; before 175 B.C.E.?): According to tradition, the creator of puppets.

Ch'eng (cheng): Quality of inner integrity or sincerity.

Ch'eng Hao (Cheng Hao; 1032–1085): Noted Sung dynasty philosopher of the classics; brother of Ch'eng I. Studied with Chou Tun-i.

Ch'eng I (Cheng Yi; 1033–1107): Noted Sung dynasty philosopher of the classics. Studied with Chou Tun-i.

Ch'i *(qi):* A vital force or vital energy that pervades the human body; in modern scientific terms it might be understood as neural pathways. A force that also pervades the entire universe. The concept has many different interpretations.

Chiao-fu (Jiaofu): A man named Cheng Chiao-fu who tried to flirt with two women by the Yangtze River; they promptly disappeared, and only then did he realize they were goddesses.

Ch'ien *(Qian):* The first of the sixty-four hexagrams of the *Book of Changes;* associated with creativity and heaven.

Ch'ien Lei (Qian Lei): Divinity of uncertain identity.

Ch'iu Ch'ang-ch'un (Qiu Changchun; 1148–1227): Student of Wang Che.

Chou Tun-i (Zhou Dunyi; 1017–1073): Philosopher noted for his concept of the Great Ultimate.

Chu Hsi (Zhu Xi; 1130–1200): Philosopher of the classics.

Chu Jung (Zhu Rong): Divinity associated with fire.

Ch'ü Yüan (Qu Yuan; 340?–278 B.C.E.): A virtuous official who drowned himself in protest of the world's corruption. Traditionally considered the author of the *Songs of the South (Ch'u Tz'u* or *Chu ci).*

Chuan Hsü (Zhuan Xu): Another name for Kao Yang, a divinity of the north, or a mythic ruler of antiquity.

Chuang Tzu (Zhuangzi; 369?–286? B.C.E.): Philosopher of the Chou period; known also as Chuang Chou (Zhuang Zhou).

Confucius (551–479 B.C.E.): Thinker of the Chou period whose sayings were collected by his students in the *Analects.*

Cousin Zhen (Chen): One of the principal patriarchs of Bao-yu's family.

Dharma: A Sanskrit Buddhist term that when capitalized means reality, truth, or the teaching of Buddhism; sometimes also called the Law, in the sense of natural law rather than legal instruments. When lowercased, it refers to individual phenomena.

Dhyāna: Sanskrit term for meditative or concentrative states.

Duke of Chou (Zhou): Brother of King Wu and regent to Wu's young successor, King Ch'eng. According to traditional dates, he was regent from 1115–1108 B.C.E.

Eight subdivisions of the year: The four seasons, the spring and fall equinoxes, and the winter and summer solstices.

Emperor Ku (Gu): Mythic ruler of high antiquity.

Emperor Yama: The ruler of the underworld of the dead.

Emperor Yi (correctly transliterated "Emperor I," but to avoid confusion in English, "Yi" is used in place of "I."): According to tradition, the last good emperor of the Shang; his son was Emperor Shou (also known as Emperor Chou), who was conquered by the succeeding Chou dynasty.

Emperor Yao: Mythic sage ruler of high antiquity. Abdicated his throne to a commoner who was to become Emperor Shun, and gave him his two daughters in marriage. These women were later considered goddesses of the Hsiang (Xiang) River.

Emperor Shun: Mythic sage ruler of high antiquity who succeeded to Emperor Yao.

Emperor Yü: See Great Yü.

Fei Lien (Fei Lian): Divinity of the wind.

Feng Lung (Feng Long): Celestial divinity associated with thunder and clouds.

Five Agents: Also called the Five Elements or Five Phases, the five elemental forces of the universe: water, earth, metal, fire, and wood.

Five Camps: Camps of spirit soldiers believed to protect all sides of a village.

Five Despots: Five hegemons of the seventh century B.C.E.

Five good fortunes: Also known as the five blessings of longevity, wealth, physical and mental health, cultivation of virtue, and a fitting end to one's life. See the "Great Norm" from the *Book of History*.

Fu Fei: Another name for the goddess or spirit of the Lo River.

Fu Yüeh (Fu Yue): A figure who appeared in a dream to the Shang king Wu-ting (reign 1339–1281 B.C.E.), who later appointed him as minister.

Gandharva: Celestial divinities of Indian mythology.

Garuda: Birdlike divinities of Indian mythology.

Great Gentleman Fu: Honorific epithet for Fu Hsüan-feng (Fu Xuanfeng; born 28 C.E.), who labored for other people on a farm. After he went fishing, he first placed the fish in an open basket under water to give them the opportunity to escape if they so desired.

Great Yü (Great Yu): Legendary figure of high antiquity who created a cosmos from chaos by structuring waterways to drain wetlands for human habitation. According to one legend, his father Kun (Gun) had dammed up waters and created chaos.

Han Chung (Han Zhong; third century B.C.E.): One of the spiritual adepts dispatched by the first emperor of the Ch'in dynasty in the third century B.C.E. to search for substances that would ensure immortality. Han never returned.

Han Yü (Han Yu; 768–824): Major literary figure of the T'ang dynasty.

Heavenly Officers: Perfected Taoist immortals now serving as celestial bureaucrats.

Herdboy: Mythic figure, now a star, who is banned to one end of the Milky Way for once dallying with the Weaving Girl, who is confined to the opposite end. They may meet once a year on the seventh day of the seventh lunar month.

High Perfected of the Three Realms: The highest Taoist deities.

Ho ts'ai-a: Exclamatory expression.

Hsiang, goddesses of (Xiang): Two female figures associated with the Hsiang River.

Hsiao Chiang-p'ing (Xiao Jiangping): Fictive man of great sexual energy.

Hsü Fei-ch'iung (Xu Feiqiong): A mythic woman of great beauty.

Hsü Wei (Xu Wei; 1521–1593): Ming painter and poet.

Hsüan Ming (Xuan Ming): Lesser divinity associated with the northern direction.

Hsüan Wu (Xuan Wu): Protector divinity associated with the northern direction. Iconographically depicted as part snake and part tortoise.

Hsüan Yüan (Xuan Yuan): A term for a star and for a mythic figure called the Yellow Ancestor.

Hsüan-tsang (Xuanzang; 600–644): Buddhist monk who traveled to India to acquire Buddhist scriptures; a noted translator. His life is fictionalized in the character of Tripitaka in the novel *Monkey,* also known as *The Journey to the West.*

Hsün Tzu (Xunzi; born ca. 312 B.C.E.?): Important philosopher of the Chou period.

Huang-ti: Mythic Yellow Emperor of high antiquity. Associated with the curative powers of medicine.

Huang T'ing-chien (Huang Tingjian; 1045–1105): Poet and calligrapher. P'an-pan was a courtesan.

I-hsüan (Yixuan; died 867): Name of the Ch'an teacher known as Master Lin-chi (Linji).

Iron horses: Horse-shaped chimes.

Īśvara: Another name for Brahma in Buddhist mythology.

Jambudvīpa: In Buddhist cosmology, this world inhabited by human beings.

Jia Rong (Chia Jung): Son of You-shi, the woman who is possessed, and Cousin Zhen, one of the patriarch's of Bao-yu's family.

Jia She (Chia She): Bao-yu's uncle.

Ju Shou (Ru Shou): Protector divinity associated with the western direction.

Kalpa: In Indian thought, a measure of incalculably large numbers of things.

Kang Youwei (K'ang Yu-wei; 1858–1927): Political and social reformist.

Kao Ch'i (Gao Qi; 1336–1374): Ming poet.

Kao Tzu (Gao Zi; ca. 420–ca. 350 B.C.E.): Rival of Mencius who posited that righteousness is something external, not internal, to human beings.

Kao Yang (Gao Yang): A lord regarded by many of the kingdoms of the third century B.C.E. as a high ancestor.

Kao-tsu: Founding ruler (reign 618–626) of the T'ang dynasty.

Kiṃnara: Centaurlike beings of Indian mythology.

King Wen: One of the virtuous founders of the Chou dynasty; according to traditional dates, ruled from 1169–1116 B.C.E.

King Wu: One of the virtuous founders of the Chou dynasty; according to traditional dates, ruled from 1122–1116 B.C.E., although modern scholars suggest dates of 1027–1025 or 1087–1085 B.C.E.

Ko Hung (Ge Hong; 283–343): Compiled the *Book of the Master Who Embraces Simplicity.*

Kośa Śāstra: One of the philosophical commentaries on Buddhist scriptures.

Koṭi: Sanskrit term for measuring incalculably large numbers.

Kou Mang (Gou Mang): Protector divinity associated with the eastern direction.

Kuan Fu-tzu: See Lord Kuan.

Kuan-yin (Guanyin): Buddhist divinity of compassion and mercy. Known in Sanskrit as Avalokiteśvara; in Japanese, as Kannon; and in Tibetan, as Chenrezi.

Kumārajīva (ca. 350–410): Famous translator who rendered Buddhist scriptures into Chinese.

Kun (Gun): See "Great Yü."

K'un (Kun): The second of the sixty-four hexagrams of the *Book of Changes.* Associated with receptivity and the earth.

Laṅkāvatāra Sūtra: The "Scripture of the Visit to Lanka," an account of the Buddha's teachings to the king of what is now Sri Lanka.

Lantern Festival: Festival of lights held fifteen days after the lunar New Year's Festival.

Lao Tzu (Laozi; floruit sixth century B.C.E.?): Purported author of the *Tao-te ching (Daodejing).*

Laozi: See Lao Tzu.

Li Hao-ku (Li Haogu; thirteenth century): Yüan dynasty playwright.

Li He (Li Ho; 791–817): Tragic poet. According to literary lore, a child prodigy; he died in his twenties.

Li Po (Li Bo; 701–762): Celebrated poet of the T'ang dynasty.

Li sao: Poetic lament attributed to Ch'ü Yüan.

Li Wan: Bao-yu's older widowed sister-in-law.

Licchavi: Name of the republic in which Vimalakīrti resides.

Liu Hsi: Figure from a popular play in the repertoire of Fukien opera.

Lokapāla: In Buddhist cosmology, one of the four guardian divinities of the four directions.

Lord Kuan (Lord Guan; 160–219): Honorific title of Kuan Yü (Guanyu), also known as Kuan Ti (Guandi), or Emperor Kuan, and Kuan Kung (Guangung), or Duke Kuan. Famous warrior who came to be revered as the god of war and justice. Noted for safely conducting the wife of Liu Pei (Liu Bei; 162–223), his comrade, through five guarded passes when Kuan Yü and the wife were taken prisoner together. When their captors allotted them only one sleeping room, Kuan Yü stood through the night with a lighted candle in his hand, proving his faithfulness to his friend Liu Pei.

Lord Pao (Lord Bao; died 1062): Honorific title for Pao Ch'eng (Bao Cheng), a famous judge who became the subject of a genre of detective stories.

Lu Hsün (Lu Xun; 1881–1936): Writer and social critic.

Lu Xun: See Lu Hsün.

Magnolia Maiden: Figure from a popular play in the repertoire of Fukien opera.

Mahākāśyapa: One of the historical disciples of Siddhārtha Gautama.

Mahāsattva: Sanskrit term that literally means "great being." Honorific epithet.

Maheśvara: Another name for Siva, who in Buddhist mythology rules over one of the heavens of Buddhist cosmology.

Mahoraga: Serpentine beings of Indian mythology.

Mañjuśrī: Buddhist archetype of the quality of wisdom.

Mao Tse-tung (Mao Zedong; 1893–1976): Founding figure of the People's Republic of China, which was established in 1949. Also known as Chairman Mao.

Māra: One of a group of tempting and seductive trickster figures of Buddhist mythology.

Mencius (371–289 B.C.E.?): Philosopher noted for his concepts of human nature.

Midautumn Festival: Moon-viewing festival held on the night of the fall hunter's moon; an opportune occasion for lovers' trysts, as women would not otherwise be permitted to be out of doors at night.

Ming-ti of Han: Emperor Ming (reign 57–75 C.E.) of the Latter Han dynasty.

Mo Shih-lung (Mo Shilong; 1539–1587): Ming poet and aesthetic theoretician.

Mount Diamond: Another name for Mount Great Iron Circle, one of the peaks around Sumeru.

Mu: Measure of land; one-sixth of an acre. Also written *mou*.

Mu Wang: King Mu, a Chou dynasty ruler who reigned from 947–928 or 998–968 B.C.E.

Nāga: A serpentine being of the waters in Indian mythology.

Nü-kua or **Nü Kua** (Nügua or Nü Gua): Also known as Nü Wa, a mythic divinity attributed with fashioning the world in a primordial time. She is human from the waist up; her lower body is a spiral snake form.

Nuo: A type of exorcism to dispel baneful influences.

Pan Chao (Ban Zhao; ca. 48–ca. 112): Han dynasty historian.

Paranirmitavaśavartin gods: Radiant divinities of Buddhist mythology.

P'i-p'a (pipa): A lute or mandolin.

P'ing-i (Pingyi): A rain god.

Po-ch'i (Boqi): Crown prince of the ninth century B.C.E. who respected his father's wish to disinherit him so that the son of a favorite concubine could become crown prince in his stead.

Po Chü-i (Bo Ju'i; 772–846): Poet of the T'ang dynasty.

Prajñāpāramitā: Perfection of wisdom. *Prajñā* means wisdom or insight; *pāramitā* means perfection, or literally, "to go beyond" to another shore.

Pratyekabuddha: In Buddhist thought, someone who attains enlightenment on his own, as opposed to a *śrāvaka*, or "hearer," someone who attains enlightenment only after hearing or learning of it from someone else.

Pu Songling (P'u Sung-ling; 1640–1715): Literati and collector of tales of the supernatural.

Rākshasa: A type of demon in Indian mythology.

Sahā world: In Buddhist cosmology, this world of sorrows.

Śakra: Another term for Indra, who in Buddhist mythology rules a heaven over the peaks of Sumeru.

Saṅgha: Sanskrit term for the Buddhist community of male and female laypersons and monastics. Also romanized as *saṁgha.*

Shang-ti (Shangdi): Lord on High.

Shao Hao: A mythic ruler of high antiquity.

Shen Chou (Shen Zhou; 1427–1509): Ming painter and poet.

Shen-sheng: Crown prince of the seventh century B.C.E. who was framed by his stepmother, his father's favorite consort, and possibly by his own father, and was wrongfully accused of patricide. Rather than protesting his innocence and potentially implicating his father, Shen-sheng hung himself in the family's ancestral temple. He thus came to be regarded as a paragon of filial piety. The stepmother consequently made her own son crown prince.

Shun: See Emperor Shun.

Siddhārtha Gautama (ca. 566–486 B.C.E.?): Religious adept who later became known as the "Buddha," the awakened or enlightened one.

Six dusts: The six senses of seeing, hearing, tasting, smelling, touching, and thinking, following an Indian conception of the body that considers the mind a sense organ.

Skandhas: Sanskrit term for the five "aggregates" that together form a human being: physical form or matter; elemental sensations; perceptions; volitional acts and attitudes, or karma; and consciousness.

Śrāvaka: A "hearer." Someone who attains enlightenment after hearing or learning of it from someone else.

Ssu (si): A type of sacrifice; usually a general term for any kind of sacrifice.

Stellar Gods of the Northern Dipper: Divinities associated with the stars of the Big Dipper.

Sun Pu-erh (Sun Bu'er; 1119–1183): Follower of Wang Che.

Śūnyatā: Empty, void, unlimited, infinite. A Sanskrit term that refers to the ultimate lack of a permanent, self-existent self-nature in all things, which suggests not nihilism but the ever-changing interdependence and interconnectedness of all things.

Sukhāvatī: Buddhist Sanskrit term for the "sweet land," "happy land," or "pure land" of the Buddha Amitabha, where the sincerely devoted may be reborn.

Sumeru: In Indian cosmology, a mountain that is at the center of the universe.

Sūtra: The discourses of the Buddha, which when committed to writing became scriptures.

Suzuki, D. T. (1870–1966): Buddhist scholar whose writings and translations made Buddhist texts available to the West.

Tan-chun (T'an-ch'un): Bao-yu's half-sister.

T'ang the Successful (Tang): Also known as T'ang the Completer or Ch'eng T'ang. Virtuous founder of the Shang dynasty.

T'ang of Yin: See T'ang the Successful.

Tathāgata: Sanskrit term that means "The One of Suchness" or "The One Who Thus Comes and Thus Goes." An epithet for a Buddha.

Te (de): Quality of inner integrity and strength; often translated as "virtue."

Third Maiden of Mount Hua: Figure from a popular play in the repertoire of Fukien opera.

Three abundances: Abundant harvests throughout the three growing seasons.

Three Realms: Heaven, earth, and the underworld. In Buddhist cosmology, the realm of desire, the realm of form, and the formless realm.

T'ien (tian): Heaven.

Tou Wen-ch'ing maiden: Figure from a Fukien version of the Yüan drama "Story of the Shoe Left Behind" *(Liu-hsieh chi).*

Tsang Shen (Zang Shen): Another name for Tseng Tzu (Zengzi; 505–ca. 436 B.C.E.), a pupil of Confucius. He was noted for saying that one's body is a gift from one's parents and should be cared for accordingly.

Ts'ao family (Cao): The surname of Pan Chao's husband's family.

Ts'ao Hsüeh-ch'in (Cao Xueqin; 1715–1763): Novelist and author of *The Story of the Stone,* which is also known as *The Dream of*

Red Mansions or *The Dream of the Red Chamber*.

Ts'ao Kuo-hua (Cao Guo-hua): Figure from a Fukien version of the Yüan drama "The Story of the Shoe Left Behind" *(Liu-hsieh chi)*.

Tso Ch'iu-ming (Zuo Qiuming; fifth century B.C.E.): Compiled the *Tso chuan* (Zuo-zhuan), a commentary on the *Spring and Autumn Annals*.

Upāsaka: A Buddhist layman.

Upāsikā: A Buddhist laywoman.

Upāya: Sanskrit term for the liberative techniques a skilled Buddhist adept uses to lead other beings to spiritual perfection; sometimes also translated as "skillful means" or "tactfulness."

Vaiśravaṇa: A heavenly king of Buddhist mythology who rules a kingdom to the north of the mountain Sumeru.

Vajrapāṇi: A bodhisattva who protects the followers of Buddhism; it is sometimes manifested in a wrathful aspect.

Wandering Girl: Goddess of the Han River.

Wang Che (Wang Zhe; 1112–1170): Known also as Wang Ch'ung-yang (Wang Chong-yang). Founding figure of the Ch'üan-chen (Quanzhen) tradition of Taoism.

Wang Ch'iao (Wang Qiao): Also called Master Wang, a mythic immortal who left the world on the back of a bird.

Wang Yang-ming (Wang Yangming; 1472–1529): Ming thinker and military strategist.

Wen Ch'ang (Wen Chang): A constellation.

Wen Wang: See King Wen.

Wu Ch'eng-en (Wu Cheng'en; ca. 1500–1582): Author of the novel *Monkey*, or *The Journey to the West*.

Wu Wang: See King Wen.

Wu-ti of Liang: Emperor Wu (reign 502–549) of the Liang dynasty. Purportedly met with Bodhidharma.

Xi-chun (Hsi-ch'un): Bao-yu's female cousin.

Xianglin's Wife (Hsianglin): Protagonist of "The New-Year Sacrifice."

Xiang-yun (Hsiang-yün): Distant cousin of Bao-yu.

Yaksha: In Indian mythology, a type of demon.

Yang: The complement of *yin;* one of the two fundamental cosmic forces of the universe. Yang is associated with the qualities of activity, maleness, light, dryness, and warmth.

Yen Hui (Yan Hui, 521–490 B.C.E.): Also known as Yen Yüan (Yan Yuan) or Yen Tzu (Yanzi). Confucius's favorite disciple.

Yang Kuei-fei (Yang Guifei; died 756): Imperial consort to the T'ang emperor Hsüan-tsung (reign 713–756), who was also known as the "Brilliant Emperor."

Yao: See Emperor Yao.

Ye Fa-shan (Yeh Fa-shan; floruit seventh century): Shaman who was in the service of the T'ang emperor Kao-tsung (reign 649–683).

Yen Tzu: See Yen Hui.

Yi-weng: Familiar nickname for Huang Yi-an.

Yin: Another term for the Shang dynasty.

Yin: A type of sacrificial offering that conveys the pure intent of the sacrificer.

Yin: The complement of *yang;* one of the two fundamental cosmic forces of the universe. Yin is associated with the qualities of passivity, femaleness, darkness, moisture, and cold.

You-shi (Yu-shih): Wife of Cousin Zhen, one of the principal patriarchs of Bao-yu's family.

Yüan Mei (Yuan Mei; 1716–1798): Writer and collector of tales of the supernatural.